The
BOOK of the
HAKUTAKU

a Bestiary of Japanese Monsters

written and illustrated
by
MATTHEW MEYER

Edited by Zack Davisson

ISBN: 978-0-9852184-5-4

www.matthewmeyer.net
www.yokai.com

This book is dedicated to all the yōkai lovers out there wherever you may be, and to the fans who helped make this book possible through crowdfunding.

A. Takeshita, A.J. Bohne, Aaron Dilliplane, Aaron W Thorne, Abdullah A. Al Shuaibi, Adam Hyde, Adam Preljevic, Adi Juarsa, Adrian Sherstobitoff, Ahmed Nasser, AKYN, Al Billings, Albert Lew, Albert Martinez Molto, Alberto Pérez-Bermejo , Aleksandra Kasman, Alessandro "NeatWolf" Salvati, Alessandro Marco Serpe, Alex Bussers, Alex Hamelin, Alex Neilson, Alex Norris, Alex Thornton-Clark, Alex Wainwright, Alex Young, Alexander Bordo, Alexander Gudenau, Alexander Hawson, Alexander Ransom, Alexandru Fagadar, Alexis Perret, Alistair Gilmour, Alistair Knight, Allen Robert Sorensen, Allen Varney, Alvaro Herranz Fuero, Alvin Rosa, Alyssa Curby, Amanda Kadatz, Amanda Maus, Amanda San Miguel, Amanda Shakibapour, Amber Galster, Ammon D Turner, Amorita Malagon, Amr Helmi, Amy Gray, Andreas Hamm, Andreas Meeks, Andrew Bleecker, Andrew Dickinson, Andrew Lacroce, Andrew Lohmann, Andrew Ly, Andrew Martin, Andrew Peregrine, Andrew Shue, Andrew Smallwood, Andrew South, Andrew Talarico, Andrey Alekseenko, Andy Swartz, Ang Puay Lin Celeste, Angelia D Pitman, Angelique Blansett, Angus Abranson, Anita Gray Saito, Anita Morris, Ann Voelkel, Anna Bannon, Anna-Lucia Stone, Anne-Louise Monn, Annika Samuelsson, Ansari Hélène , Anticia, Antti Hallamäki , Antti Luukkonen, April Gutierrez, Artur Guerra Ibañez, Ash Brown, Ashley Saporito, Ashli Tingle, Athena Claxton, Aurel Jahnke, Austin Austin, Austin Schwartz, Azlipah Razali, Baldrs Draumar, Barbara Adams, Barclay Hygaard, Barry Moore, Beatty-Sensei, Belinda Tomov, Ben Herron, Ben McFarland, Benita K, Benjamin A Daws, Benjamin Bell, Benjamin Fox, Benjamin Gaiser, Benjamin Taylor, Benoit Posluszny, Bet - Berg, Beth Harmony, Beth Jones, Bethany Cai, Blaine Ross, Bo L. Nyby, Bobby Cox, Brad Gabriel, Bradford Hsu, Bradford Pomeroy, Bradley Troup, Brandon Hall, Brandon Lawrence, Brandon Neal, Brandon Snyder, Brennan Rowe, Brent Millard, Bret Hall, Brett Augustine, Brett Illies, Brett McLean, Brian Clark, Brian Dysart, Brian Isserman, Brian King, Brian Monkelbaan, Brian Schultz, Brianne Bedard, Briday Vincent, Brideron Pierre-luc, Brigitte Colbert, Brook West, Bryan K Borgman, Bryan Vestey, Bryn Neuenschwander, Byron Olson, Cake Mu Bai, Callum Barnard, Calvin Jim, Camille Lucas, Campbell Ruddock, Cara Young, Careen N Ingle, Carl-Erik Kristian Engqvist, Carlos Fabri, Carlos García Ferrer (AFD), Carlos Rehaag, Carly Jerome, Casey Coste, Catalin Saitan, Cathy Green, Chad Locke, Chance Valentine, Chandler Byrne, Channon H Price, Charles Dee Mitchell, Charles Hons, Charles Kowalski, Charles Liao, Charles Perich, Chase Hopper, Chelsie E Hargrove, Cheryl Costella, Chinami Namba, Chris Basler, Chris Kelley, Chris Olsen, Chris Ploof, Chris Skuller, Chris Smith, Christel Gonzalez Canales, Christian Fitzi, Christina Hughes, Christopher D Meid, Christopher Garvey, Christopher Garvey, Christopher Glen Stritch, Christopher Lee McCown, Christy Barcellona, Chuck Wilson, Cindy Kennedy, Claire Rosser, Clifton Royston, Clifton Thompson, Clinton Rose, Clinton Rose, Cobrite Copies, Cody Melcher, Collette J Ellis, Corey Fulton, Corinna Seidel, Craig Hackl, Craig Hiscock, Craig S. Weinstein, Craig Smuda, Craig Tubb, Cullen Gilchrist, CW "Fuzzy" Lausten, D Cackowski, D Smartvlasak, Dai-Oni, Damian A, Damon-Eugene Rich, Dan Sellers, Dana Maley, Dane Patterson, Daniel Belov, Daniel Clark, Daniel Czarnecki, Daniel Greenspun, Daniel Hrynczenko, Daniel Ketzer, Daniel Lloyd, Daniel Moersdorf, Daniel Nissman, Daniel Roelker, Daniel Szymański, Daniel Wolterink, Darren Davis, Darren Eurwyn Lewis, Darren Tang, Darrin Griffin, Daryl Toh, Dave R, David Ameer Tavakoli, David Broyles, David Cano Escario, David Childs, David Epstein, David Heiligmann, David Hernández , David Hill, David Hochman, David Koo, David Kraus, David Millians, David Palau, David Penney, David Quinn, David Quist, David Robinson, David Rubenach, Dawn Oshima, Dean Rutter, Deborah Kleiner Ward, Deborah Spiesz, Demetry Rohlfing, Denis Maddalena, Derek Brazzell, Derek Connell, Derek Finn, Derek Yao, Deric Hughes, Diego Sanchez Ramirez, Dion Perez, Diyah Dwiastuti, Dominick Cancilla, Donald Bleeker, Donna Minar, Douglas Candano, Douglas Hamilton, Douglas Schutz, Duncan Auld, Dwight Bishop, Dylan Holland, Dylan Horley, Dylan Ostrander, Edbert Fernando Widjaja, Edgar Sanchez Castillo, Edmond Courtroul, Eduardo Gonzalo Gasparik, Edward Andrews, Edward Drummond, Edward Lynden-Bell, Edward MacGregor, Eileen Hutson, EL Winberry, Elaine Maulucci, Eli Scripps, Elizabeth Aoki, Elizabeth Legner, Ellen Jane Keenan, Elliot Hager Smith, Emily Simpson, Emma Rossi, Emmanuel Mahe, Eric Hamilton, Eric James, Eric Schulzetenberg, Eric Yamanuha, Erik & Anna Meyer, Erik Archambault, Erik Hillenbrink, Erik Norman Berglund, Erik Renberg, Erik Stein, Erin Dupuy, Erin Machniak, Erin Sayers, Erin Valenciano, Ethan James Dodd, Ethan Weiler, Ethan Wilke and Yoshimi Sawada, Eva M. Crespo, Evan Jones, F. Meilleur, Ferenc Dobay, Fermin Serena Hortas, Filip Källman , Filippa, Caro y Pier, Fiona Hampton, Flint Olsen, Frances Caddick, Frances McGregor, Francis R Muhawij, Frank Laycock, Frank Nissen, Franklin Crosby, Frederick Cheng, Fumihiro Ohchi, G A Oldfield, Gabriel Matuszczyk, Gallon Jocelyn, Gardner Monks, Garth Kidd, Gary Gaines, Gavin O'Reilly, Genevieve Amyot, Geoffrey Englebach, Geoffrey Heeren, Geoffrey Tunbridge, George Gaspar, George Ianus, George VanMeter, Gerald J Smith, Gerard Almeida Silva, German Sanchez, Gilles Poitras, Gillian Berman, Gim Cheong Lim, Glen Brixey, GMarkC, Gordhan Rajani, Gordon Garb, Grace L. Thooft, Grace Spengler, Grant M. Evans, Grant Voakes, Gregory Voss, Guillaume Desrosiers-Couture, Guillaume Ehny, Gusty737, Gwen Sato-Herrick, H Lynnea Johnson, Hailey Fredrikson, Hanna Wallner, Hannah Brown, Hannah Thoo, Hans Hagen, Harrison Steel, Hayes Edgeworth, Hendrik Faber, Henry Eshleman, Henry Jacobs, Henry Kaiser, Hieu Le, Hunter Harris, Huw James Prosky, I. Mennings, Ian A O'Neil, Ian Baker, Ian Borchardt, Ian M Lamberton, Ilsa Enomoto, Imran Inayat, Ines Kunzendorf, Ingmar Weltin, Isaac Ehrlich, Isaac Emery, Isabel Jauss, Isabella Cociloco-Kozzi, Ismeralda Chen, Israel J Flores, Itai Berman, Ivan Jan, Ivan O., Ivy Wui, Izzy Watts, Jack Chen, Jack D. Eudy, Jacob "Nott Scott" Wahlquist, Jacob Albritton, Jacob Derby, Jacob Elias, Jacob Rotschield, Jacqueline Skelton, James Binnion, James Carr, James Crowell, James Gibbons, James Miller, James Moore, James Preston, James Steinberg, Jameson Melbourne, Jamie Lee, Jamie R Lahowetz, Jamie Taylor, Jane Anders, Janelle Becker, Jankowski Steven Michael, Jared Levin, Jared Mortlock, Jasmine Braam, Jasmine Caesar-Walker, Jason Careaga, Jason Ezra, Jason Gush, Jason Warriner, Jason Willis, Jason Wong, Jayson Chen, Jeff J Cleary, Jeff Matsuya, Jeffrey Campbell, Jeffrey D Sherman, Jemal Hutson, Jen Huber, Jennie LaVaque, Jennifer Blaikie, Jennifer Hanselman, Jennifer Knutson, Jennifer Lovelady, Jennifer O'Brien, Jennifer Schlee, Jens Cramer, Jeremie Veisse, Jeremy Jacobs, Jeremy Noye, Jerry Goodnough, Jesse Hartman, Jesse Moore, Jesse N Hirschmann, Jessica Till, Jesús Asvalia Sánchez López, Jill Norton, Jill Vassilakos-Long, Jim Phillips, Jim Rittenhouse, Jim VanDeventer, Jim White, Jimmy Chang, Jimmy Ray "JR" Tyner 3rd, Jiří Vinklář, Joanna Wheeler, Joe Sargent, Joel Lee, Johannes Größel, John Baker, John Carberry, John Mead, John Rudd, John Schilder, John West, John William Bass, Johnny D Sutterfield, Johnson Taing, Jon Cherry, Jonathan Jacobs, Jonathan K Lee, Jonathan Lambert, Jonathan

Massey, Jonathan Royon, Jonathan Stephen Cromie, Jonathan Westmoreland, Jonathon Burgess, Jordy Meow, Jörg Bennert, Jorge Madrigal, Jørgen Holand , Jose L. Equiza, Josh "The Bruiser" Furr, Josh S Talley, Joshua Ayakatubby, Joshua Cheek, Joshua H. Elias, Joshua Villines, Joshua W. Pittman, Josie Doefer, Joyce Boss, Juan Oliveira Martinez, Judy Bonney, Julia Bae, Julian Chan, Julian Gluck, Julie Phillips, Julio Luna, Jussi Myllyluoma, Justin D Short, Justin Henry, Justin Max Jarvis, Justin McFerren, Justin Smith, MD, MPS, Kabe Jest Long, Kai Thomas, Kaitlin Thorsen, Kaito & Sora, Karen J. Hall, Kari Ronning, Karin Froschauer, Karl Schmidt, Karra Libunao, Kat Emralde, Kat Let, Kate Stock, Katelyn Rhoades, Katherine DiPierro, Katherine Schuttler, Kathryn Blue, Kathryn Christofersen, Kathryn Hemmann, Kathryn Molinelli-Ruberto, Kay James, Kay Markert, Kayla Charlonne, Keir Liddle, Keith James Andreano, Kellen Casem, Kelly Lowrey, Kelsea Klassen, Kendra Stansak, Kenneth Kelth Jr., Kenneth Torgerson, Kenneth Walz, Kenny Beecher, Kenny Clem, Kent, Kent Taylor, Keri Palmetto, Kerry Drew, Kevin Bella, Kévin Fuster , Kevin Hildreth, Kevin Keller, Kevin McDonald, Kevin Peters, Kevin Searle, Kevin Winter, Kim Zimmer, Kimberly Campbell, Kimberly Sleszynski, Kimseng Ky, Kinson Wong, Kira Graham, Kirsten M. Rasmussen, Kirsty March, Kirstyn Humniski, Kit Baker, Konstantin Kalichava, Kou Takai, Kristen Beno, Kristian "Rompcat" Jaech, Kristin Bonafide, Kristoffer Brandberg, Kurt Rivera, Kyle Coltrin, Kyle Franklin, Kyle McLauchlan, Kyle smith, l Wong, Lachlan Bakker, Lana Riordan, Lara Guidon, Lara Zwerling, Larry Lynch-Freshner, Larry Nation Jr, Lars Van Angelo, Lauren Kimble, Lauren McConnell, Lauren Schmidt, Lauren Sugrue, Laurence Shapiro, Laurie Edwards, Lawrence Barnard, Lawrence Curtis Fothe, Lazaro Roberts, Lee Shan Keng Lester, Lee Smith, lefirenet, Len Makalapua Ahgeak, Lena Melton, Lenore Wagner, Leonard Glenroy Lie, Leonard Hourvitz, Leslie Bernard, Leslie Goldman, Li Chih Tsung, Lily E. Charbonneau, Linda A. Bruno, Lindsey Wilson, Linnea Nilsson, Lisa Disterheft, Lisa Kaiffer, Lisa Krepper, Lisarte Barbosa, Lois Blood Bennett, Lord Bob, Lorenzo D'Antonio, Louis Bournival, Luis Alvarez, Luis E. Gomez, Luisa Carnevale Baraglia, Lukas Stobie, Luke Martin, Luke Robertson, Lyle Gogh, Lynne Whitehorn, Madelaine McSorley, Maggie Birmelin, Maggie Young, Manuel Jesús Morillo Jiménez , Man-Yee Mok, Marc Cardwell, Marc Rütz , Marc Tischhauser, Marcel Bonner, Marco Gonzalez, Maria Holland, Marie Terskikh, Mark Bradley, Mark Dwight, Mark Vardy, Mark Wilmot, Markus Forsman, Markus Hermelingmeier, Markus Reubelt, Markus Stadler, Markus Ullrich, Markus Veijalainen, Martha Johnston, Martin Dick, Martin Larsson, Marvin Ziesenies, Mary J Lloyd, Mary L'Etoile , Masahiko Teranishi, Mason Guzman, Matt Cockburn, Matthew Dive, Matthew Karabache, Matthew Morgan, Matthew Pemble, Matthew Ruehlen, Matthew S McCroskey, Matthew Wellens, Matthew Wojciechowski, Mauro Ghibaudo, Max Kaehn, Max Norris, Meg Kingston, Megan Tolentino, Megumi Hull, Melanie Hook, Melinda A Lowery, Melody-Ann Jones Kaufmann, Melvin Ryan Thompson, Merja Jokinen, Mia Beresford, Michael Blanchard, Michael Brewer, Michael Dzanko, Michael Dzanko, Michael Foertsch, Michael Janney, Michael Krzak, Michael Lee, Michael Meltzer, Michael Pearl, Michael R McGough, Michael Simpson Jr., Michael Smith, Michael Surbrook, Michael Woo, Michael Zappe, Michael Zeller, Micheil Rust, Michelle Goldsmith, Miguel Angel Barranco Tirado, Mikael Grankvist, Mike Barnfield, Mike Buckley, Mike Urano, Milo Peppers, Minoru Taniguchi, Mirei Magik, Misia Clive, Mitchell Engen, Moy Bardera Illescas, N. Takashi Osborn, Nadine Czaika, Nan Braun, Natalia Toronchuk, Natalie Hasell, Nataline Viray-Fung, Natasha Chisdes, Nathan Cody Mazza, Neal Solmeyer, Neil R King, Neville Isles, Nicholas C. Herold, Nicholas Wilson, Nick Hand, Nick Tibbetts, Nicole James, Nicole Kegler, Nik Halton, Nikolas M Paseman, Nina Thøgersen , Noah Crawford, Noah Hall, Norbert Preining, Noriko & Hiroto Ichihashi, Odessa Knight, Oliver Halor, Olivier Lejade, Otter, P Tracy, Pablo Pérez Gómez , Patrick Donoghue, Patrick Magisson, Patrick Swasey, Patrick Tan, Patty Kirsch, Paul "oyukiɪ3ɪɪ" Reynolds, Paul Beck, Paul Butler, Paul Dale, Paul Gorman, Paul Granich, Paul Hachmann, Paul J Hodgeson, Paul Jarman, Paul Long, Paul Richardson, Paul Thomas Smith, Paul Thorgrimson, Paul Weller, Paula & Kenton Meyer, Paula Okeefe, Paula Schlax, Pedro Alfaro, Pedro Ziviani, Penchour, Peter L Brown, Peter Mazzeo, Peter Prince, Peter Rodgers, Petr Drahokoupil, Petter Wäss , Philip Montgomery, Philippe Niederkorn, Phillip J Thomas, Phillip Oyer, Pitchayapol Chunhachatchavalkul, Piya Wannachaiwong, Poh Wee Han, Prathep Narula, Priya Monrad, Py Hahn, R. B., R.M. Williams II, Rachael A Hixon, Rafael Delphino dos Santos, Raina DeVries, Rajbir Dhalla, Ralph Lachmann, Randall Nichols, Raymond Kloss, Raymond Lee Barnes, Reasha Lafromboise, Rebecca Collis, Rebecca Wigandt, Rei W. Rothberg, Rene van der Horst, Rex Strowbridge, Richard Draper, Richard Freeman, Richard Harrison, Richard Loh, Richard Valdes, Rita Barrueto, Rob Falconi, Rob Jaspersohn, Robert Cudinski, Robert F Smith, Robert Farley, Robert Harrison, Robert J Duncan, Robert Klatt, Robert Mayers, Robert Wolfe, Roberto Sanchez, Robin Horton, Romikus, Rommy M Driks, Ronny Hess, Rose Pohlman, Rosemary Chalmers, Ross Snyder Jr, Rudi Dornemann, Rusty Waldrup, Ryan Scott, Salman Khan, Sam Loefler, Sam West, Samantha Gross-Galindo, Samantha O., Sara Cox, Sara Johnson, Sarah Howes, Sashell George, Satchel Clay Fenenga Parker, Saverio Mori, Scanner Luce, Scott Drechsler, Scott Evans, Scott Harrison, Scott Richardson, Scott Waites, Sean Eustis, Sean Heath, Sean Holland, Sean Leow, Sean Pelkey, Sean Williams, Sebastian Levenson, Sebastian Ortlieb, Seth Sollenberger, Shabir S, Shane Young, Sharon Bussey-Reschka, Shaun Gilroy, Shaun Thomas, Shauny Nicole Daquin, Shawn Rios, Shean Mohammed, Sheila Mazur, Sian Nelson, Simon M N Nielsen, Simon Mackenzie, Simon Stroud, Simon Wares, Sky Iouan, Snehal Patel, Son Dang, Sophie Crockett, Spencer Fothergill, Spencer Wile, Stacey Anne Cole, Stefanie Boscarino, Stefanie Kreutzer, Stenman in Sweden, Stephanie Rosario, Stephanie Spong, Stephanie Turner, Stephen Chiu, Stephen Hazlewood, Stephen Shiu, Steve Argyle, Steve Blease, Steve Chubaty, Steven Grey, Steven Long, Steven Lord, Steven Moy, Steven Rosenstein, Stewart Falconer, Stingrae Spacey, Stuart Frowen, Stuart Lloyd, Susan Adami, Susan Bailey, Susan Mair, Susanne Schörner , Tabi 'Greyson' Lim Pey Wen, Talal Salah Alyouha, Tamara Slaten, Tapu Kokoro, Tatiana Alejandra de Castro Pérez and Ehedei Guzmán Quesada, Tawnly Pranger, Teng Ming Kiat William, Terence, Tetsuya Ishibashi, Thad Doria, That Snow Moon, The Kyuggles, The Wyler Family, Theresa Verity, TheSequelReturns, Thomas Binder, Thomas Chan, Thomas J. Wood, Thomas Nicosia, Tiberius Hefflin, Tieg Zaharia, Tim Cooke, Tim Ellis, Tim Suter, Timolution, Timothy Elrod, Timothy Gerritsen, Timothy Szczesuil, Tina Mammoser, Tobias Koske, Todd, Todd Ikemoto, Tom Tyler, Tommaso Scotti, ToneDeaf, Tony Contento, Tony Hoang, Tony McDowell, Tony Zastrow, Tove Bjerg, Tracy Fretwell, Trent Brown, Tricia Owens, Tristan Giese, Trystan Vel, Tyler Mason, Uri Bivens, V Shadow, Valdimir Shotton, Vanessa Van de Voorde, Vaughan Monnes, Veronica Beaudion, Victor W Allen, Victoria Pullen, Vida Cruz, Vincent MEYER, W. David Lewis, Wade Pittman, Walter Delgado, Walter R Swindell, Wanda Aasen, War Bunny Artz, Wee Heavy L Walter-Stern, Wicak Hidayat, Wikars Marcus, Willem Stolk, William Alsobrook, William Bishop, William Janss, William Northey, William P, Wilmer Imperial, Winson Quan, Winston Kou, Wouter Storme, Xenia Novi, Yohane Größel, Z Wood, Zachary Grayer, Zachary Tyler, Zack Bates, Zack Griffith, Zack Ringler, ZeroXDun, Zola Cass

CONTENTS

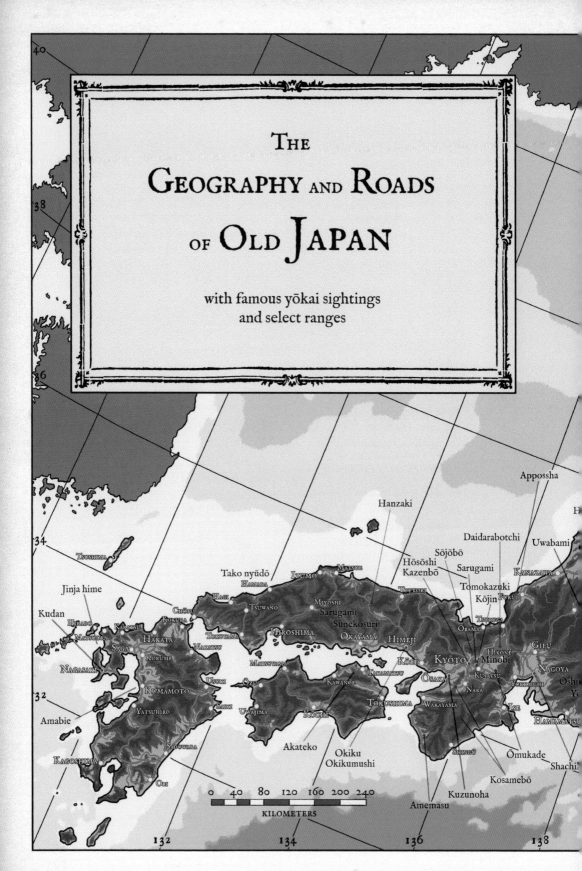

The
GEOGRAPHY AND ROADS
OF OLD JAPAN

with famous yōkai sightings
and select ranges

40

38

36

34

Appossha

Hanzaki

Daidarabotchi   Uwabami

Sōjōbō
Hōsōshi   Sarugami
Kazenbō

Tsushima

Tako nyūdō   Izumo   Matsue
Hamada
Tomokazuki
Jinja hime
Hagi   Tsuwano   Miyoshi   Tottori   Kōjin
Chōfu
Kudan   Kokura   Sarugami   Tsuruga   Fukui
Hirabo   Karatsu   Sunekosuri   Obama
Matsura   Tokuyama   Hiroshima
Saga   Hakata   Nakatsu   Okayama   Himeji   Hikone
Kurume   Matsuyama   Kōbe   Kyōto   Minobi
Usuki   Kawanoe   Takamatsu   Ōsaka   Kusatsu
Nagasaki   Ōzu   Nara   Yokkaichi
Kumamoto   Saiki   Tokushima   Wakayama
Yatsushiro   Uwajima   Kōchi   Ise
Amabie   Hamamatsu

Kasanazawa

Gifu

Nagoya
Oshi
Yo

32

Akateko
Okiku
Okikumushi   Shingū   Ōmukade

Kagoshima   Sadowara   Kuzunoha   Shachi
Kosamebō
Obi   Amemasu

0   40   80   120   160   200   240

KILOMETERS

132   134   136   138

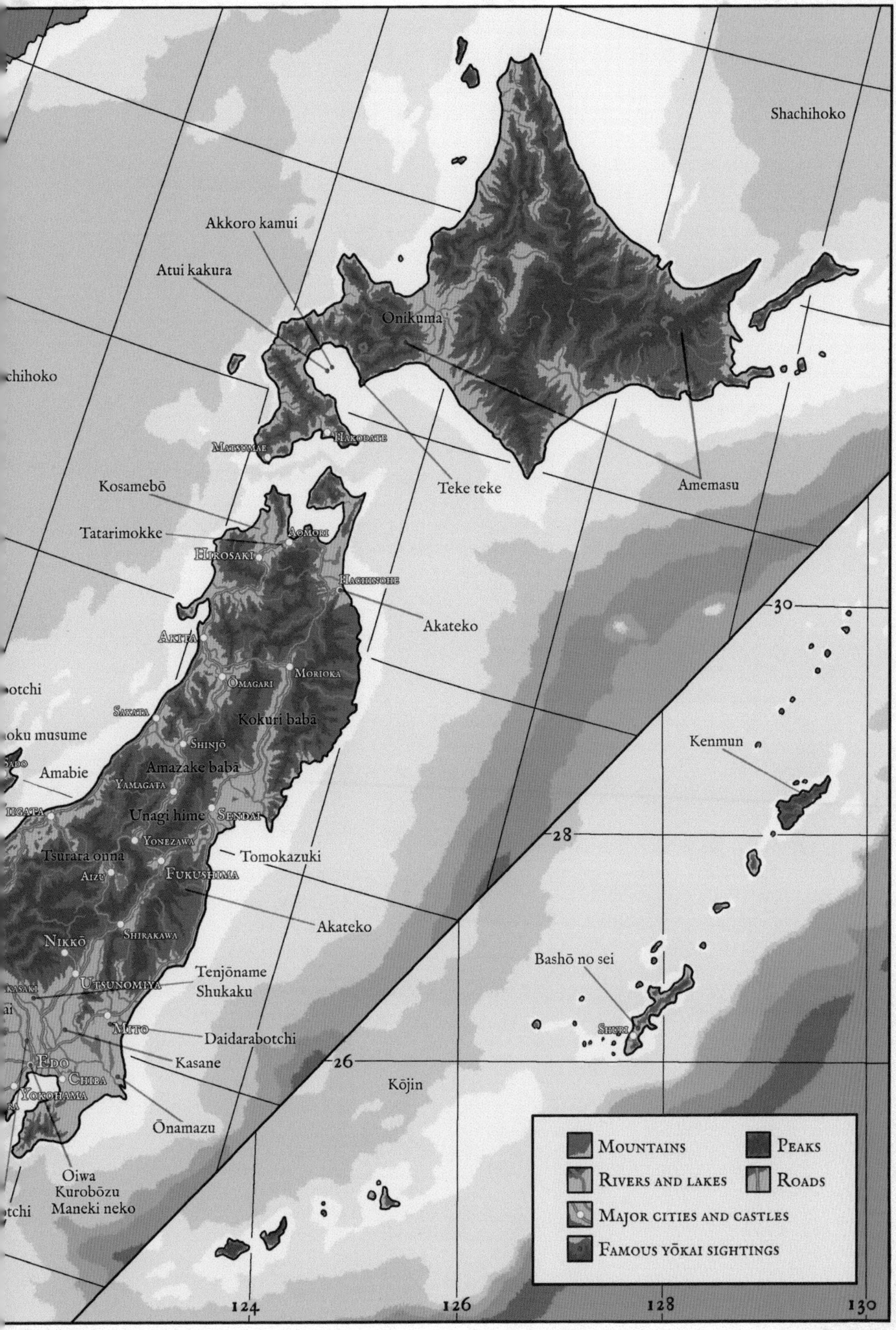
Shachihoko
Akkoro kamui
Atui kakura
Onikuma
chihoko
Matsumae
Hakodate
Teke teke
Amemasu
Kosamebō
Tatarimokke
Aomori
Hirosaki
Hachinohe
Akateko
30
Akita
Morioka
Omagari
otchi
Sakata
Kokuri babā
oku musume
Shinjō
Kenmun
Sado
Amabie
Amazake babā
Yamagata
Niigata
Unagi hime
Sendai
28
Yonezawa
Tsurara onna
Tomokazuki
Aizu
Fukushima
Akateko
Shirakawa
Nikkō
Bashō no sei
Tenjōname
Shukaku
Utsunomiya
Shuri
Mito
Daidarabotchi
Kasane
26
Edo
Chiba
Kōjin
Yokohama
Ōnamazu
Oiwa
Kurobōzu
Maneki neko
tchi
Mountains
Peaks
Rivers and lakes
Roads
Major cities and castles
Famous yōkai sightings
124
126
128
130

Language Notes

Japanese is one of the most difficult languages for native English speakers to learn. This is due to its difficult conjugations, three writing systems, and various levels of "polite" speech. Fortunately, the one area where Japanese is not difficult is pronunciation—with only five vowel sounds and no diphthongs, Japanese words are relatively easy to pronounce.

However, even transliterated Japanese can be confusing. Some letter combinations are pronounced differently than they would be in English. To further complicate things, there are numerous methods of transliteration, each following different standards. The result can be various spellings of the same word.

To minimize confusion, here is a brief guide on how to pronounce the Japanese words in this book.

Syllables

Japanese is written with a syllabary, not an alphabet. Most syllables are made up of vowel-consonant pairs, with an exception being the letter n. The five Japanese vowel sounds are a, i, u, e, o. These are pronounced like the sounds in father, feet, food, feather, and foe. Each vowel receives a full syllable. They do not aspirate with neighboring vowels. For example, the name jinja hime has five separate syllables (ji/n/ja/hi/me), not four (jin/ja/hi/me). The name amabie has four syllables (a/ma/bi/e), not three (a/ma/bie).

Macrons

It is common to find double vowels like aa, uu, ee, oo, ou. These pairs are usually indicated by macrons: ā, ū, ē, ō. Some vowel combinations, like aa, look awkward written with Latin characters. Other combinations like ee and oo might be mistakenly read using English pronunciation. For example, Sōjōbō is easier to read than Soujoubou. Ōmukade is easier to read than oomukade. Macrons are pronounced with two syllables: so/o/jo/o/bo/o and not so/jo/bo. o/o/mu/ka/de and not oo/mu/ka/de.

Compound Words

Japanese is written primarily with kanji, hiragana, and katana. Most words are only a few characters in length. Because of this, Japanese does not need to use spaces or hyphens to differentiate between words. This is not a problem when reading in Japanese. However, transliterating the same words into Latin characters can lead to long strings of letters that are difficult to parse.

Names like himamushinyuudou, hizounokasamushi, and shumokumusume can be quite difficult to read. In this book, spaces have been inserted into some yōkai names at natural breaks to make them more legible. Broken apart this way, names like himamushi nyūdō, hizo no kasamushi, and shumoku musume are comparatively easy to read.

The macrons and spaces used in this book are aesthetic and meant to make reading the Japanese words easier. Yōkai encountered outside of this book may be written differently.

Introduction

Collecting Yōkai

Yōkai have been collected and categorized for thousands of years. An ancient legend tells of an encyclopedia called The Book of the Hakutaku, which was given to the emperor by a magical beast. This book contained information about all the spirits, gods, and demons in the universe. It was lost long ago, but parts of it were copied down. People have been collecting information about the spirit world in supernatural encyclopedias ever since. Nowhere was this tradition of collecting yōkai more passionate and widespread than in Japan.

While yōkai are antique, the majority of them were not invented until the 16th century and onwards. In ancient times, yōkai were imagined as invisible, malevolent forces lacking physical form. The most popular legends involved oni (demons) and onyrō (vengeful ghosts). This changed during the Muromachi Period with the arrival of a series of picture scrolls depicting the night parade of one hundred demons. In this long procession, grotesque and comical monsters cavort and dance from sunset to sunrise. The earliest picture scrolls did not include names or stories to accompany the creatures. Some of them were recognizable as ghosts from popular Heian Period classics. Others were household objects with comical human-like features—a type of yōkai known as tsukumogami. These depictions of hordes of strange monsters laid the foundation for a massive yōkai boom in the coming centuries.

During the Edo Period, artists copied the picture scrolls, adding new yōkai to the parade. They gave names and invented stories for the creatures. The flourishing economy and new technologies allowed for the mass production of illustrated books. Demand for cheap reading material was high. Artists like Toriyama Sekien collected yōkai from around the country and bundled them into illustrated, multi-volume encyclopedias. As demand for yōkai grew, artists looked back into Japanese literature and history for inspiration. They copied monsters from ancient Chinese classics, reinterpreting them through a Japanese lens. They even invented new yōkai based on puns and reflecting contemporary societal issues.

When the Edo Period ended, Japan began to modernize rapidly. Belief in yōkai quickly faded away as scientific discoveries began to explain away the mysteries of the past. However, the appeal of yōkai remained strong. Folklorists like Inoe Enryō and Yanagita Kunio collected folk tales and superstitions from around the country. The cartoonist Mizuki Shigeru further helped save yōkai from disappearing by bringing them to pop culture and reintroducing them to the post-war world. Like those before him, he collected his yōkai in illustrated encyclopedias, and tried to document as much of Japan's folklore as he could.

Today, the appeal of yōkai remains strong. Universities preserve and present yōkai in vast searchable folklore databases—a sort of online Book of the Hakutaku. Thanks to the internet, yōkai have become accessible to people all over the world. And the ancient tradition of collecting them continues today in the form of collectible card games, video games, television, movies—and of course books like this one.

Origins in Foreign Folklore

Yōkai are often understood as Japanese monsters. However, not all yōkai are necessarily Japanese. The word can refer to mysterious spirits and phenomena from anywhere in the world. Foreign monsters like Dracula and Frankenstein's creature are often included under the yōkai umbrella. Many yōkai which are traditionally viewed as Japanese actually originate in other cultures. Even some of the most quintessential and famous yōkai—like kitsune, kappa, and oni—have roots in earlier sources from China and India.

Bits and pieces of foreign cultures have gradually trickled into Japan and been absorbed into Japanese culture. This has been happening for thousands of years, through both direct and indirect exchange. Trade and diplomatic missions to China exposed Japan to the gods, traditions, and superstitions of the Asian continent. The ancient Japanese borrowed much from China, including folk religions and mysticism. Practices like onmyōdō (yin-yang magic), astrology, medicine, and methods for appeasing evil spirits were strongly influenced by Chinese philosophy.

The introduction of Buddhism to Japan brought Indian cosmology and philosophy with it, filtered through a Chinese lens. Indian mythology had little trouble being accepted and disseminated throughout Japan. Local Shinto gods and spirits were interpreted as manifestations of the Buddhas and Hindu gods.

Even without direct exchange of stories, it is possible for folklore to travel across the world. Trade between China and the Near East along the Silk Road have also had an indirect effect on Japanese folklore. As Indian ideas traveled through Central Asia on their way to China, they were influenced by the countries that they passed through, picking up influences from Western and Islamic cultures. For example, the wind bag carried by the Japanese god Fūjin is believed to have originated as the cloak of Boreas, the ancient Greek god of the north wind. Alexander the Great's conquests brought Greek culture and art styles to Central Asia. They fused with Buddhism, and eventually made their way to China, Korea, and then Japan. The effects of this exchange are quite visible in the art history of these countries, but they can also be found in the folklore.

Many of the yōkai in this book have roots in foreign cultures. Centuries of exchange of stories and gods has had a profound effect on the development of Japanese folklore. Over time they evolved and were reinterpreted over and over again, taking on unique identities. They are both foreign-born and authentically Japanese.

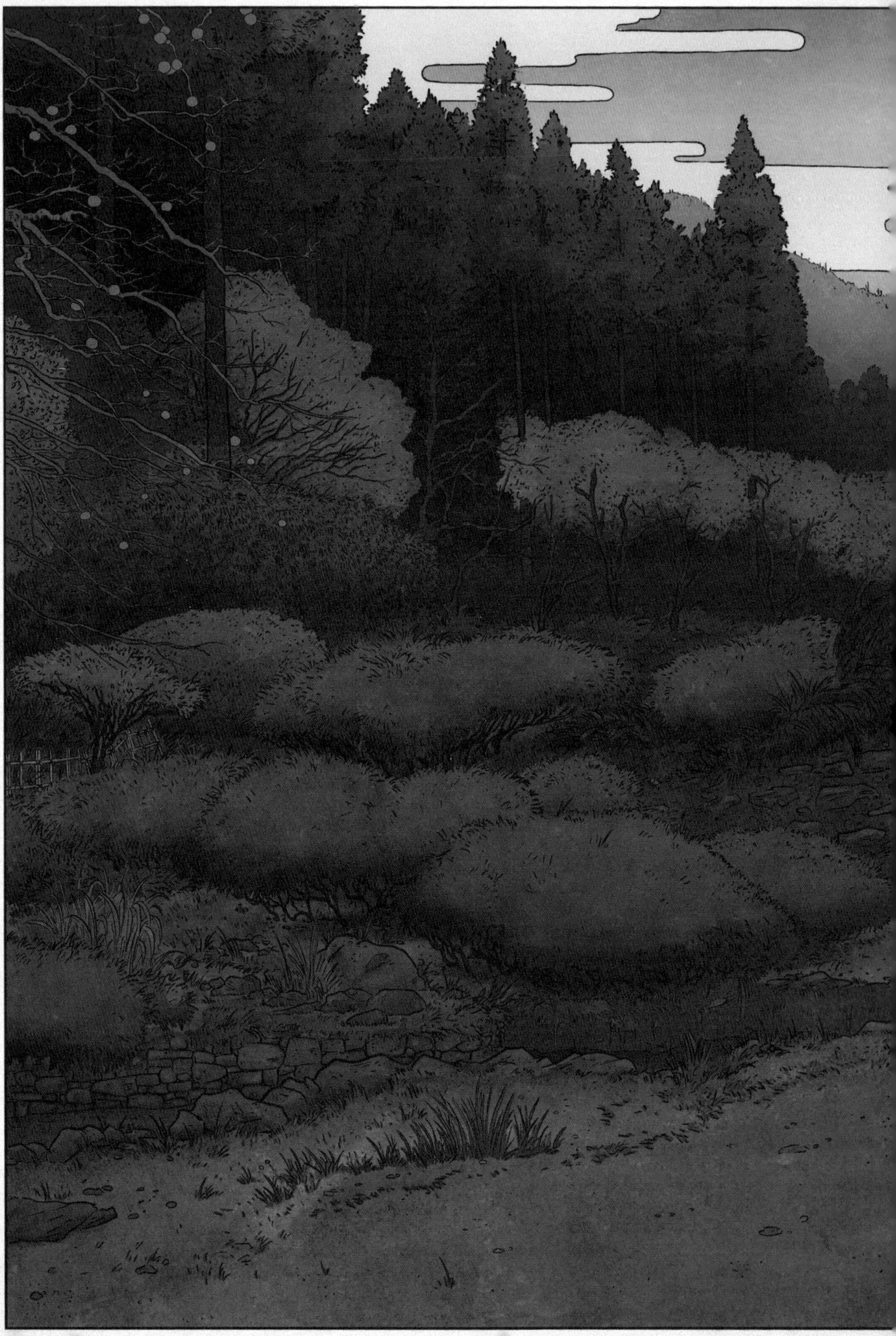

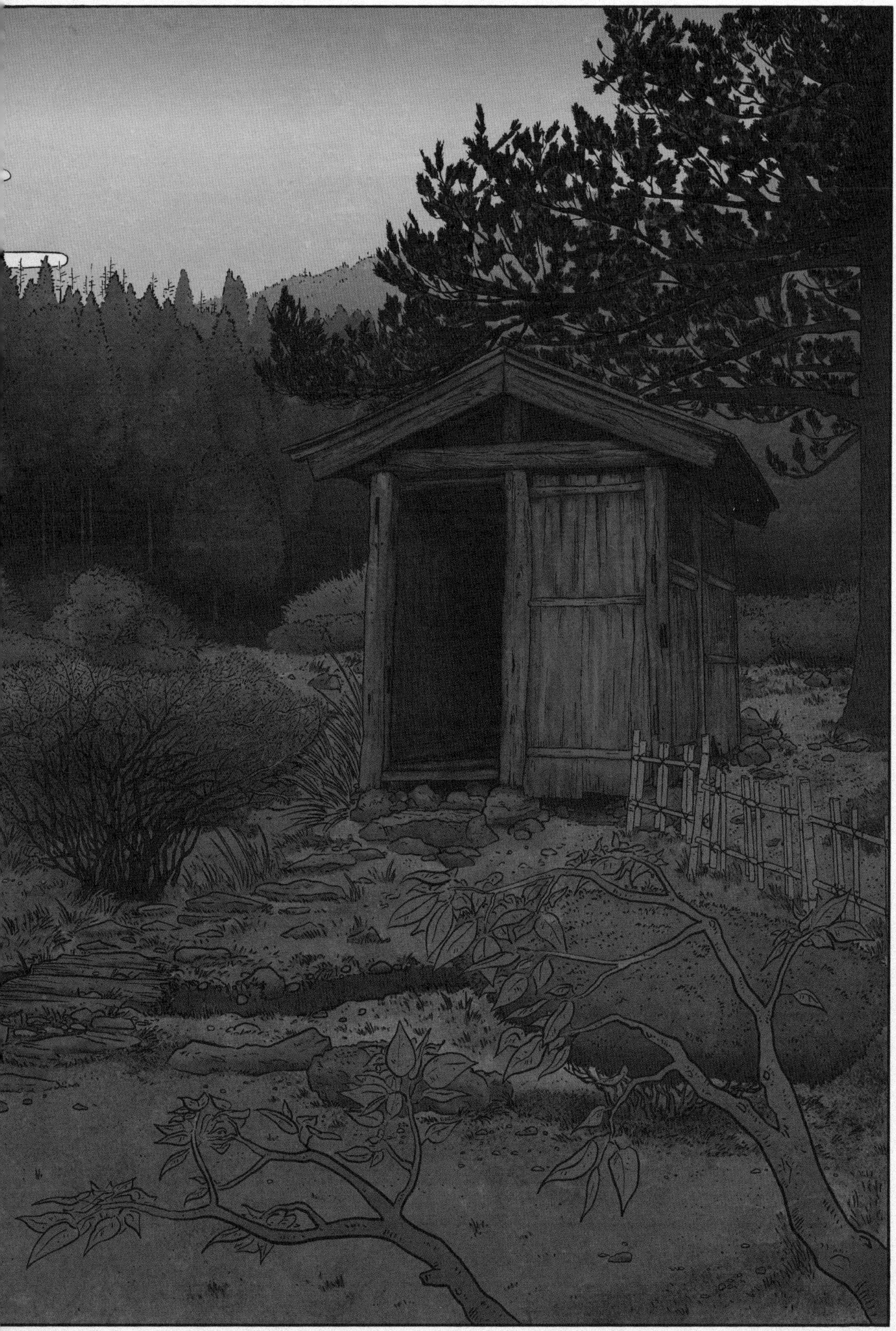

Hakutaku 白澤

Translation: white marsh; based on the Chinese name for the same creature
Alternate names: kutabe
Habitat: remote, holy mountains
Diet: unknown; likely herbivorous

Appearance: Hakutaku are wise chimerical beasts that resemble white oxen. They have nine eyes—three on their head, and three on each of their broad sides. They have a pair of horns above each set of eyes. Hakutaku live in remote mountains. They speak human languages and are knowledgeable about all things. They are extremely rare, only manifesting during the reign of a wise and virtuous leader. A hakutaku's appearance is considered to be an extremely good omen.

Interactions: Because of the incredible knowledge that hakutaku possess, paintings of them were popular in Japan during the Edo period. Hakutaku images and icons were kept as good luck charms and as wards against evil spirits, disease, and other yōkai. Because hakutaku know all, it was believed they repelled evil things.

Origin: The hakutaku, like many other holy beasts, originally comes from Chinese legends. In China, it is known as the bai ze.

Legends: Long ago, a hakutaku taught the Chinese emperor Huangdi (c. 2698–2598 BCE) the names of the various kinds of yōkai and monsters in the world. The emperor was performing an imperial tour of all his lands. In the east near the sea, he climbed a mountain, and there he encountered a hakutaku. The two spoke about a great number of things. The hakutaku told the emperor that in all of creation there were 11,520 different kinds of yōkai. The emperor recorded everything the hakutaku had said, which was preserved in a volume known as the *Hakutaku zu* (The Book of the Hakutaku). This encyclopedia recorded the names of every kind of yōkai along with what kind of evils they perform, the disasters they bring, as well as how to deal with them. Unfortunately, the *Hakutaku zu* was lost long, long ago. No surviving copies exist. However, fragments of it were copied into other texts, so bits and pieces of the hakutaku's wisdom remain.

While the hakutaku is most commonly associated with China, Japanese stories also exist. A legend from the end of the Edo Period describes a hakutaku encounter in Toyama Prefecture. It occurred on Tateyama, one of the tallest and holiest mountains in Japan. The hakutaku, called a kutabe in this legend, warned people that a deadly plague would soon sweep through the lands. The kutabe instructed them that anyone who painted its image and hung it in their home would be protected from sickness and harm. Since then, the hakutaku has been revered and even worshiped as a protective spirit of medicine.

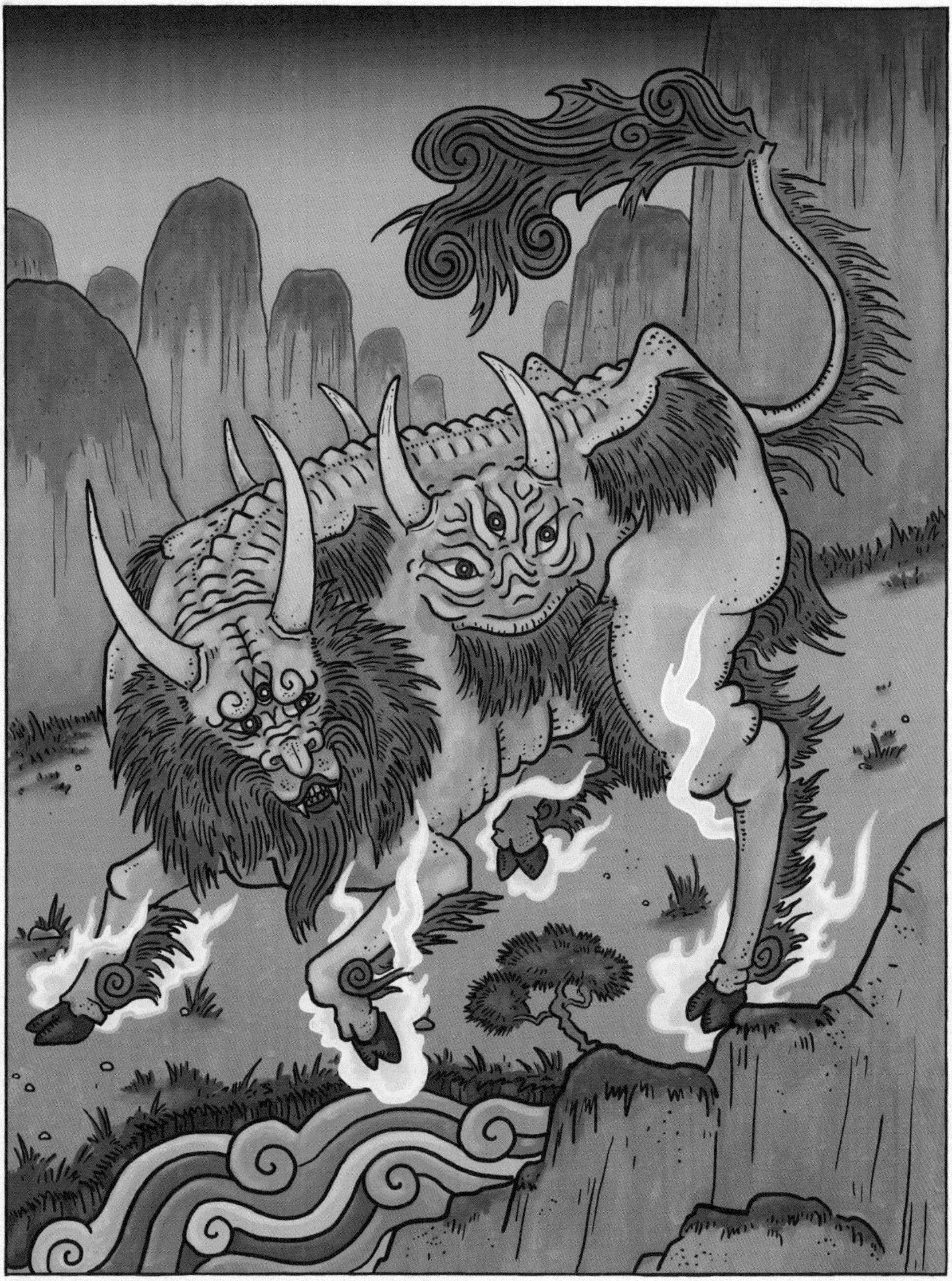

KUDAN 件

TRANSLATION: none; written with characters that mean "human" and "cow"
HABITAT: farms, particularly in Kyūshū and western Japan
DIET: never survives long enough to feed on anything but its mother's milk

APPEARANCE: Kudan are prophetic creatures that take the form of cows with human faces. Very rarely, they also take the reverse appearance: a cow's face on a human body. They are born from cows and can speak human languages. The birth of a kudan is believed to be an omen of some significant historical event.

BEHAVIOR: Kudan are born with the ability to speak. Just after birth, a kudan will deliver one or more prophecies. The content of their prophecies varies. Sometimes kudan speak of great harvests or terrible famines. Sometimes they foretell plagues, droughts, or other disasters. Sometimes they predict terrible wars. Whatever it is, the prophecy of a kudan never fails to come true. Tragically, a kudan always dies soon after speaking its prophecy.

ORIGIN: Kudan are a relatively recent yōkai, having entered the public consciousness near the end of the Edo Period. This was an era of great social and political upheaval. The fall of the shōgunate and the restoration of imperial authority, combined with the rapid changes brought about by the opening of trade with the West caused widespread uncertainly and turmoil throughout Japan. During this time, stories of kudan being born were published in newspapers across the country.

Among the events predicted by kudan are the Russo-Japanese War and the Pacific War. Because of their uncanny ability to see the future, the word of a kudan was viewed as absolute truth. During the Edo period, newspapers looking to add emphasis to a story would include the words *kudan no gotoshi*, or, "just as if a kudan had said it" to their articles. This phrase is still used today as a way of assuring readers of the veracity of a story.

Because of their reputation for honesty, images of kudan were used as talismans for good luck, prosperity, and protection from sickness and disaster. Newspapers advised their readers to hang the printed images of kudan in their houses for protection and good fortune. Kudan were such popular yōkai that their taxidermized remains were often carted around in traveling sideshows. These objects were made of stillborn deformed calves, or of different animal parts stitched together to create a chimera-like stuffed animal. Audiences could pay a small fee to peek at these specimens and receive some of their good luck. A few of these preserved kudan survive in museums today.

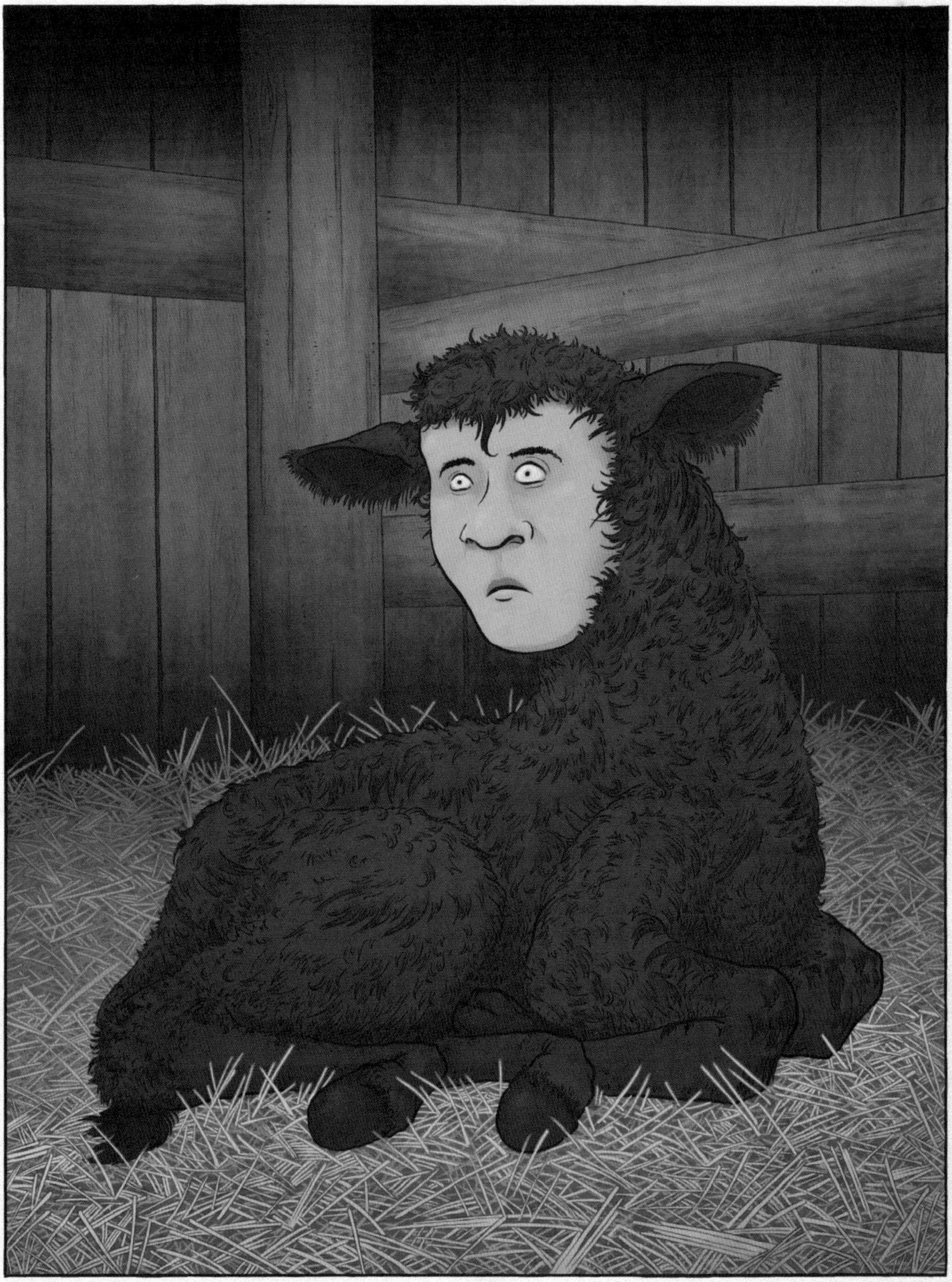

Kotobuki 寿

TRANSLATION: congratulations, long life
ALTERNATE NAMES: jū
HABITAT: unknown; supposedly lives in India
DIET: unknown; likely herbivorous

APPEARANCE: The kotobuki is an auspicious chimerical beast whose body is made up of parts from the twelve animals of the Chinese zodiac. It has the head of a rat, the ears of a hare, the horns of an ox, the comb of a rooster, the beard of a sheep, the mane of a horse, the neck of a dragon, the back of a boar, the shoulders and belly of a tiger, the front legs of a monkey, the rear legs of a dog, and the tail of a snake. A number of alternate versions exist as well, swapping the body parts for different zodiacal animals.

ORIGIN: The kotobuki first appeared in the Edo Period. Woodblock prints of it were popular gifts. Little explanation about the creature was included in these prints, other than that it was said to come from India and could understand human speech. Merely possessing an image of the kotobuki was believed to protect a person from sickness and disease and bring good fortune to their home.

Good luck charms featuring the various animals of the zodiac were popular in the Edo Period, especially during the New Year season. While it is traditional to give presents and display artwork with the new year's zodiac sign on it, an image with all twelve zodiac signs was even luckier. Even without any explanation, people recognized the twelve zodiac animals hidden in this beast. Furthermore, the word kotobuki connotes celebration and congratulations. This made the kotobuki instantly identifiable as a powerful and auspicious creature.

Shō Chiku Bai

While the twelve animals of the zodiac are instantly recognizable as lucky images, it isn't only animals which have that symbolism. Plants are used in the same way too. During the winter, the three most common auspicious plants are pine (*shō*), bamboo (*chiku*), and plum (*bai*). They are known as *saikan no sanyū* (the three friends of midwinter) due to the fact that they remain healthy even in the cold of winter. This makes them perfect for New Year decorations. Botanical displays called *kadomatsu* which decorate the front doors of shops and houses are made of these three plants. The shō chiku bai motif has been used since the Heian Period in clothing, paintings, greeting cards, product packaging and just about every other form of art that exists. These plants, like the kotobuki, are recognizable as symbols of prosperity and congratulations.

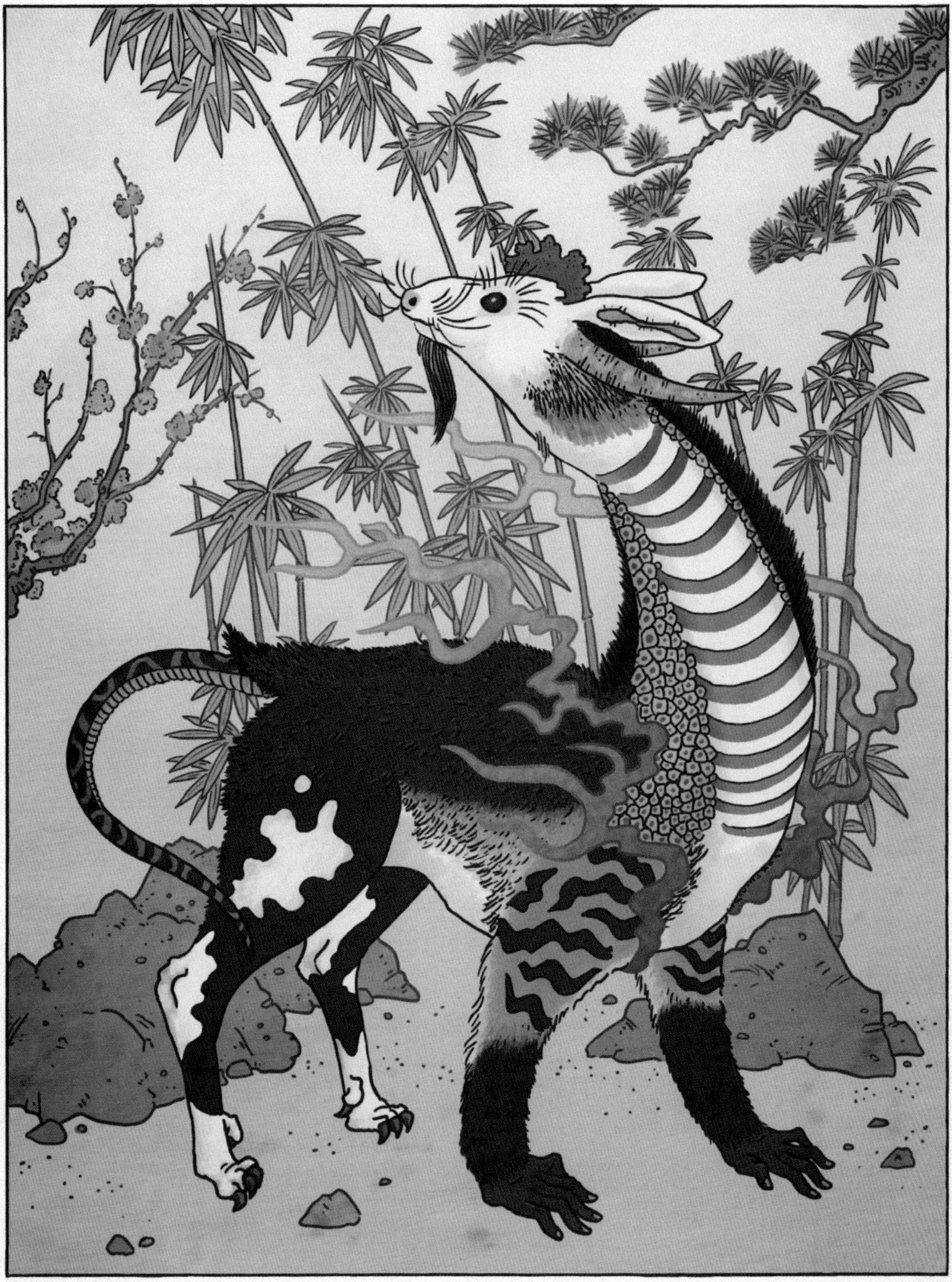

Myōbu 命婦

TRANSLATION: noble lady; one of the titles for ladies of the imperial court
ALTERNATE NAMES: byakko (white fox)
HABITAT: shrines and places sacred to Inari
DIET: mainly carnivorous, but they also enjoy tofu, sekihan, and inarizushi

APPEARANCE: Myōbu are celestial kitsune (fox spirits) with white fur and full, fluffy tails reminiscent of ripe grain. They are holy creatures and bring happiness and blessings to those around them.

INTERACTIONS: Myōbu statues are most often found at Inari shrines, taking the place of the koma inu which adorn most other shrines. These foxes act as both guardians and symbols of good luck. People leave offerings of sake, *sekihan* (red rice and red beans), *inarizushi*, and fried tofu for the fox spirits at these shrines. These foods are all said to be favorites of kitsune.

ORIGIN: Foxes have been considered holy animals in Japan since before recorded history began. The farmers of ancient Japan revered foxes, which preyed on crop-destroying mice and rats. Foxes have long been associated with Inari, the god of the harvest. Inari is said to use foxes as servants and messengers. The foxes who serve Inari are the holy, white-furred myōbu—in contrast with red-furred kitsune, who are the wicked trickster foxes found in folklore.

Myōbu statues often carry sacred objects in their mouths, such as the round jewel carried by koma inu in other shrines. In addition, myōbu frequently carry spiral-shaped keys, sheaves of grain, and scrolls. Each of these has special significance in Inari worship. The round jewel represents the soul of Inari and is a symbol of a grain storehouse. The spiral key is an archaic design for keys used with traditional farm warehouses. It represents the desire to unlock the storehouse; i.e. the soul of Inari. The sheaves of grain represent the five grains (wheat, rice, beans, awa millet, and kibi millet) which are important in East Asian traditions. Finally, the scroll represents knowledge and wisdom.

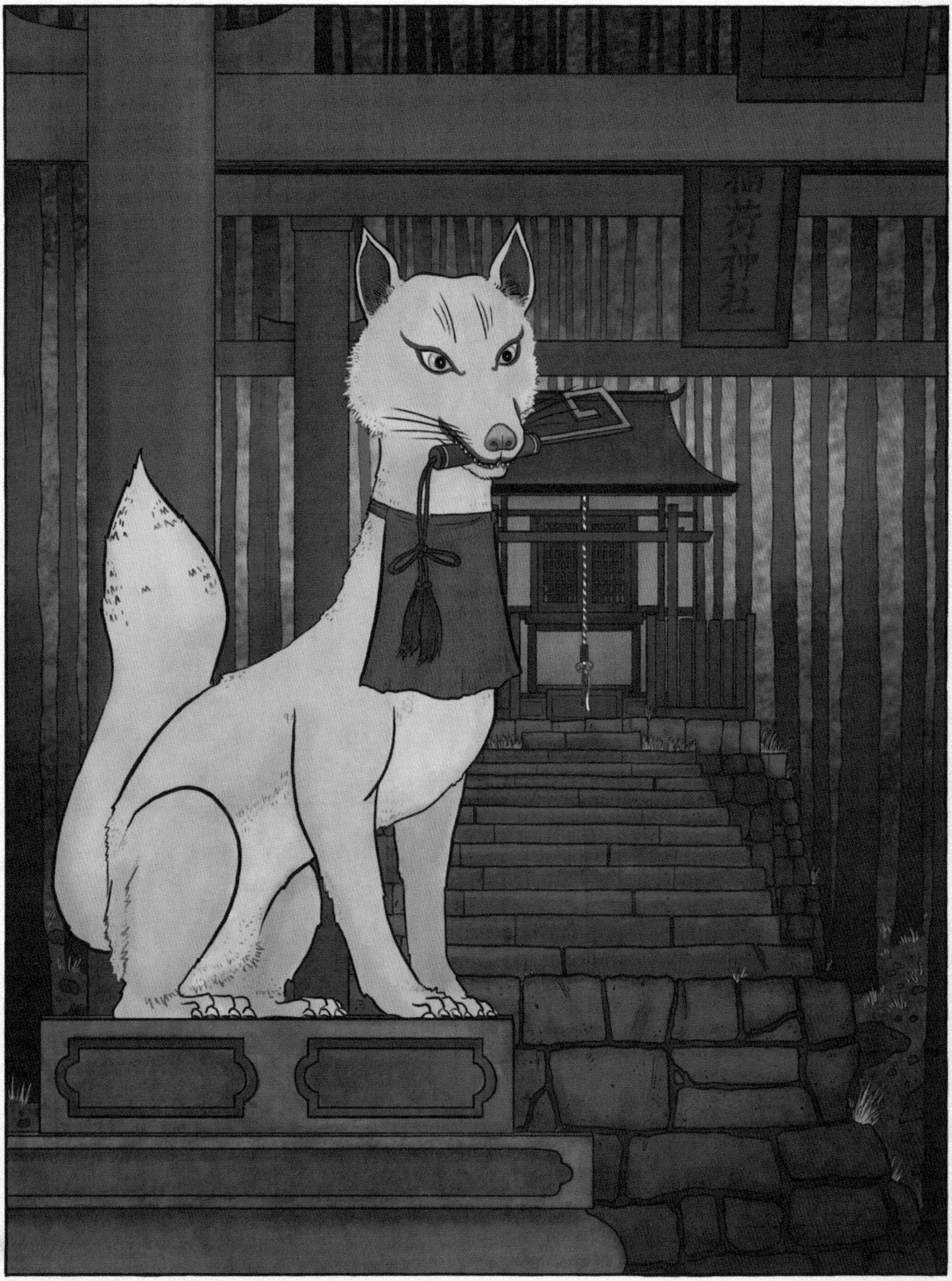

NIGAWARAI 苦笑

TRANSLATION: bitter smile
HABITAT: human-inhabited areas
DIET: cynicism and ill-will

APPEARANCE: Nigawarai are large, ugly yōkai with horns and green-tinged, hairy bodies. They wear dirty rags. Their hairy mouths are twisted into what looks like a forced smile. Their hands end in sharp, poisonous claws which can paralyze small animals.

BEHAVIOR: Nigawarai are created out of the negative feelings of human beings—particularly ill-humor and forced, feigned amusement. As their name suggests, they are related to the uncomfortable smiles that people make when trying to hide feelings of discomfort. They cause ill-will, disgust, and encourage arguments among those around them. They both feed off and spread these negative feelings.

INTERACTIONS: The poison from a nigawarai's claws can be used in cooking, which makes food terribly bitter. However, it also has the ability to cure stomach pain. This makes nigawarai a useful yōkai for medicinal purposes.

ORIGIN: The earliest references to nigawarai go back to the Muromachi period where they appear in long picture scroll paintings depicting the night parade of one hundred demons. The monsters in these scrolls appeared with no descriptions, so the artist's original intentions for this yōkai are unknown. Over the centuries, nigawarai was copied over and over onto other yōkai scrolls. Later artists invented its name and came up with its description. Through the work of numerous artists over many years, nigawarai gradually evolved the traits that it is known for today.

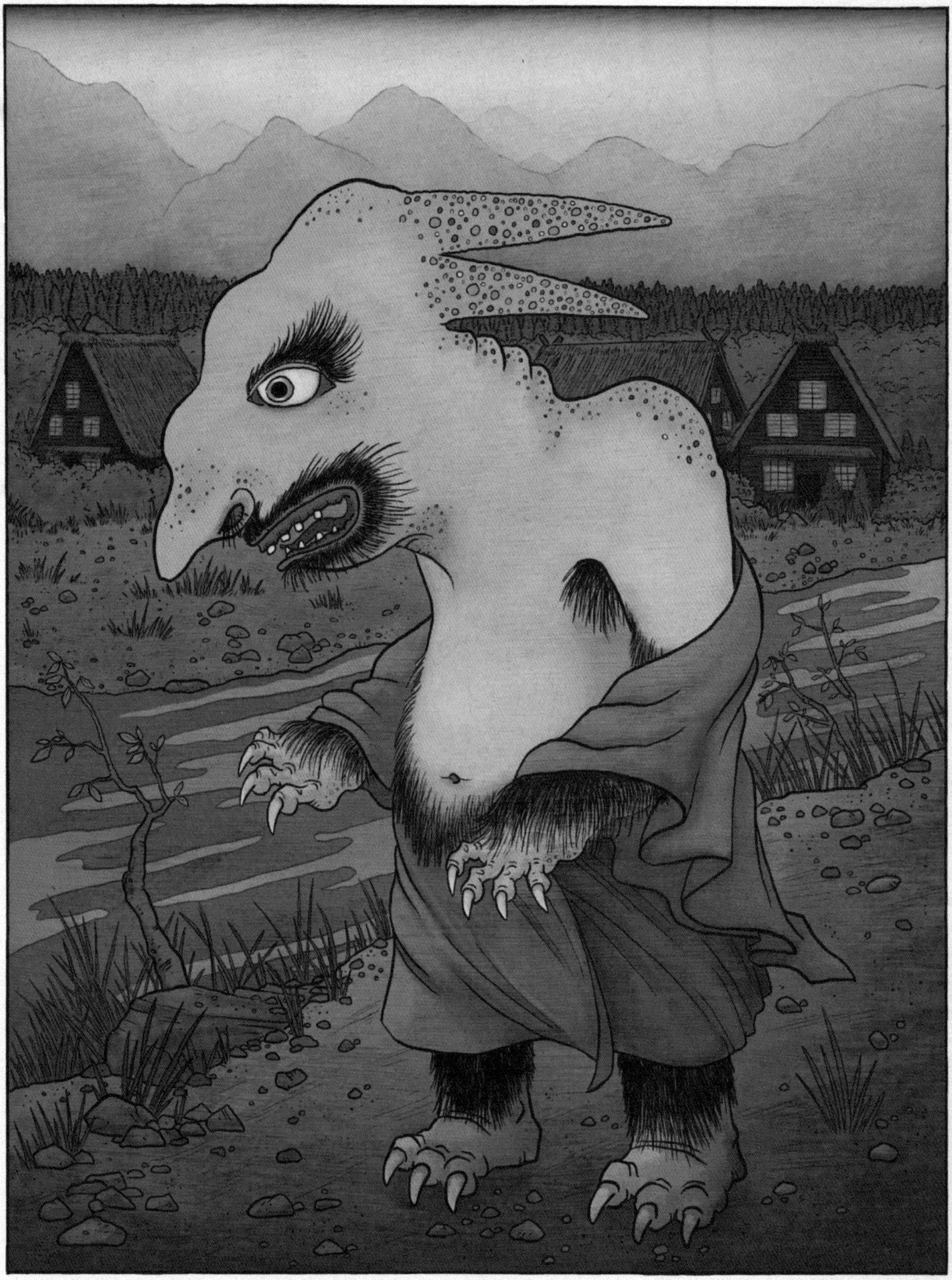

Dōnotsura 胴面

TRANSLATION: torso face
ALTERNATE NAMES: akahadaka
HABITAT: unknown
DIET: as a human

APPEARANCE: Dōnotsura's body appears much like that of a human's, except that it is missing everything from the neck up. Its extremely large facial features are prominently displayed on its torso, as its name implies.

ORIGIN: Dōnotsura appears on yōkai picture scrolls, but only in name and image. Like many yōkai originating in picture scrolls, no stories or descriptions from folklore exist to explain what it does or where it comes from. However, its most likely origin is from a play on words. There is an expression in Japanese—*dono tsura sagete*—which is used to scold a person who is inappropriately unashamed when they should be too embarrassed to show their face. The figurative meaning of this idiom is to lower a mask over one's face (as in, "How dare you come here wearing that face!"). Dōnotsura seems to be a stricter interpretation of this idiom; its face has been literally lowered down to his torso.

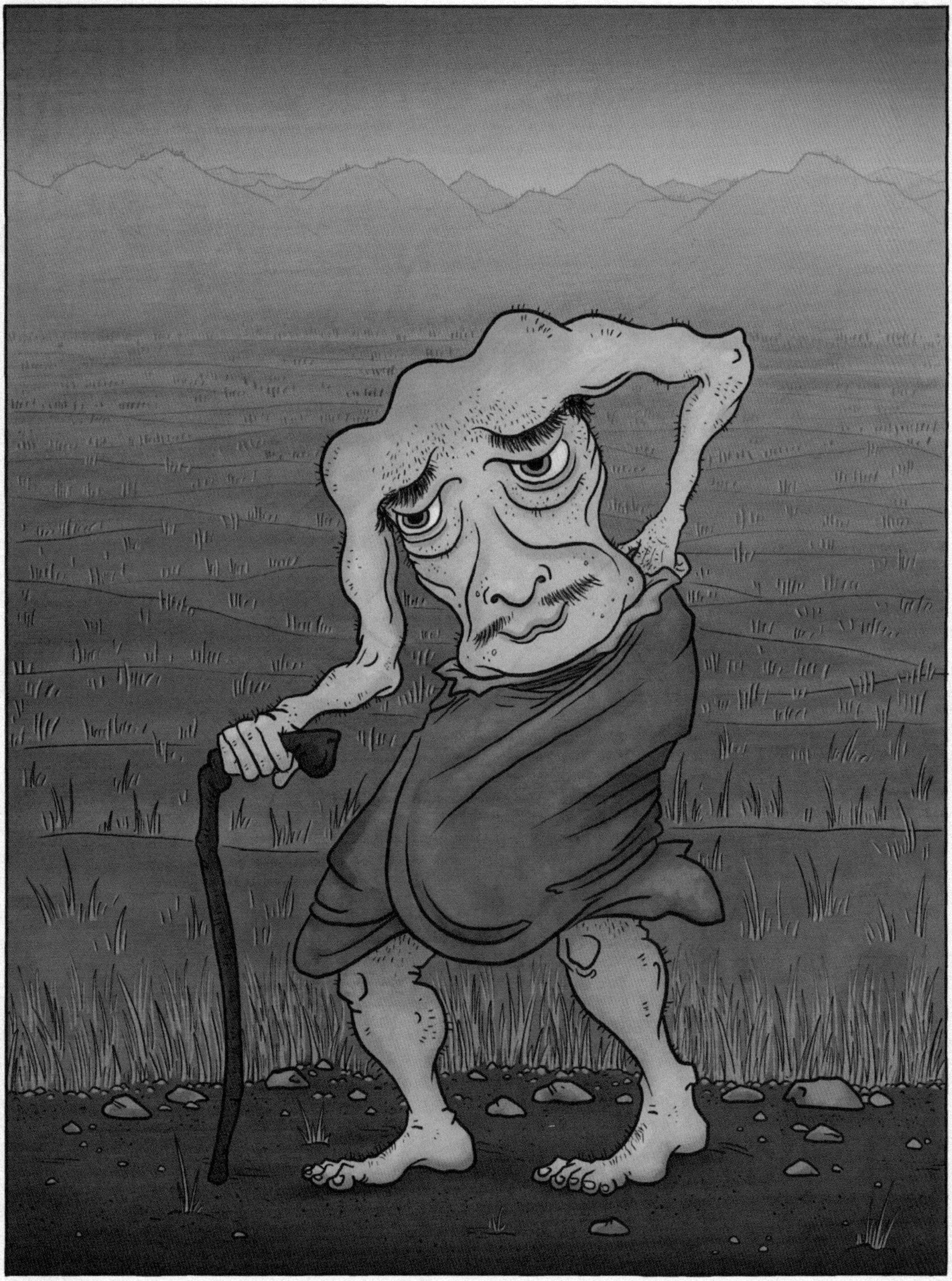

SHUMOKU MUSUME 撞木娘

TRANSLATION: hammer girl
HABITAT: mountain passes and lonely roads
DIET: unknown

APPEARANCE: Shumoku musume looks like a human girl with one exception: she has a bald head with long eyestalks protruding from the sides of her head, causing her to resembling a hammerhead shark or a slug. Her eyestalks end in enormous, round eyeballs. She wears a furisode kimono—a style worn by young, unmarried women.

ORIGIN: Shumoku musume is not a major yōkai yet her image is fairly well known. This is because she was included in *obake karuta*, a yōkai-themed version of a popular children's card matching game. Although no story accompanies her in obake karuta, her card says that she jumps out to scare travelers in the Usui Pass separating Gunma and Nagano Prefectures.

The word *shumoku* refers to the wooden hammers used to ring temple bells. It is the same word that gives hammerhead sharks their Japanese name: *shumokuzame*. It is possible that shumoku musume is actually the tsukumogami of a bell hammer, but it is not clear. Her name may be a reference to the shape of her head and nothing else.

SPOOKY CARD GAMES

Karuta is a playing card game which was invented in the 16th century. It is a competitive game between two or more players, with one more person acting as a reader. The cards are laid out on the floor with their images facing up. The reader recites a proverb, while each player searches for the corresponding card and tries to take it before the other players can. Whoever collects the most cards wins.

During the Edo period, a variation of karuta known as obake karuta became popular. Each obake karuta card has a picture of a yōkai and a single hiragana character on its front. Rather than proverbs, the reader gives clues which describe the yōkai and correspond to the hiragana character on the image. Obake karuta was especially popular among children because of its subject matter and as a tool for teaching reading.

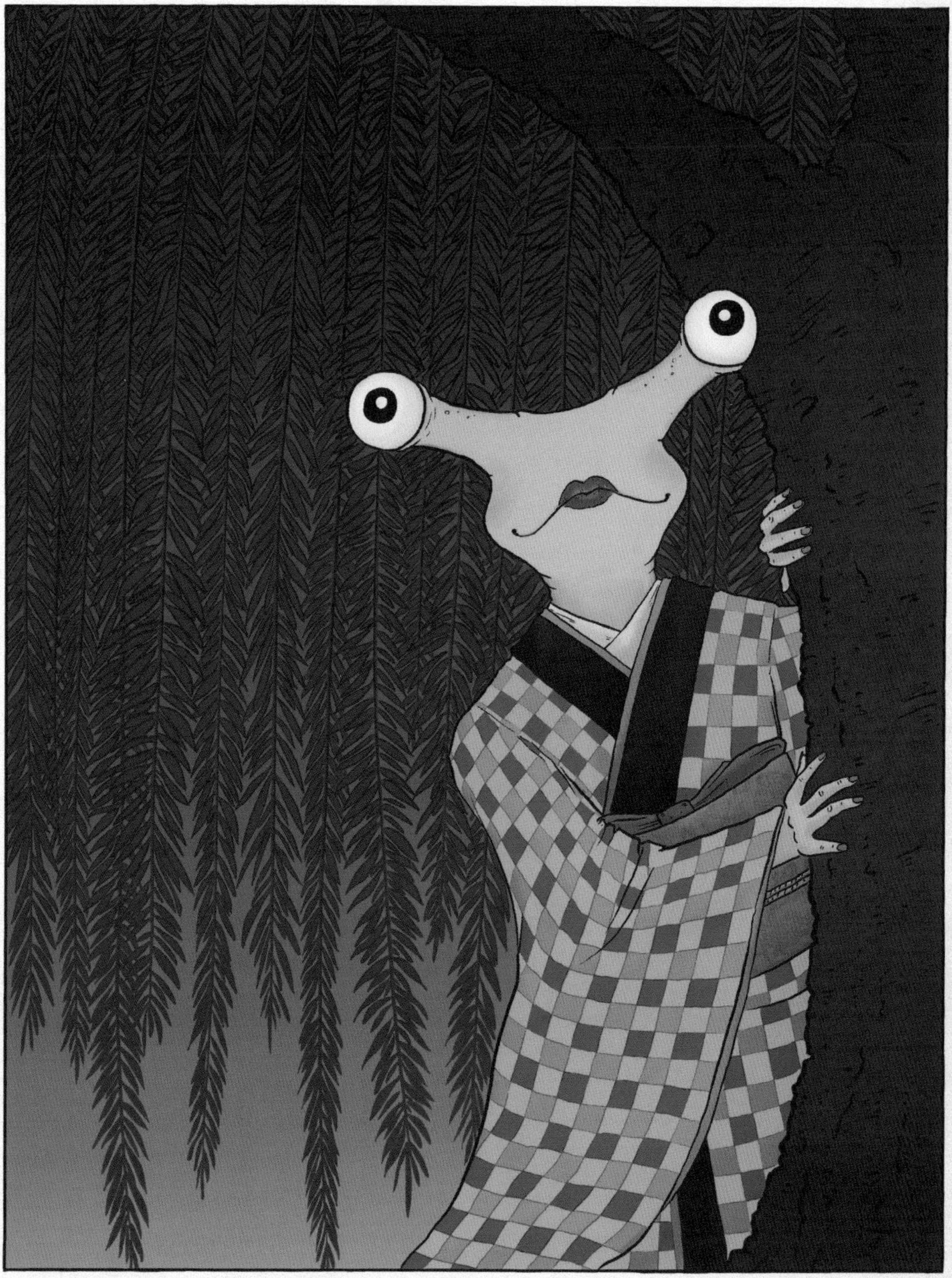

KANAZUCHIBŌ 金槌坊

TRANSLATION: hammer monk
ALTERNATE NAMES: daichi uchi (earth striker), ōari (giant ant), yari kechō

APPEARANCE: Kanazuchibō is an odd-looking yōkai which has been depicted in several different ways by different artists. It usually has long flowing hair, big buggy eyes, and a beak-like mouth. Sometimes it appears bird-like, while other times it is a grotesque, misshapen goblin-like creature. It holds a large mallet over its head, ready to strike another yōkai.

ORIGIN: A mallet-wielding yōkai appears in many of the earliest yōkai picture scrolls with no name or description. Various names like kanazuchibō and daichiuchi were invented during the Edo period.

No description of kanazuchibō's behavior was ever recorded. Many yōkai scholars have made guesses at its true nature. It may be a spirit of cowardice. Its posture and its hammer evoke the proverbs "to strike a stone bridge before crossing" (i.e. to be excessively careful before doing anything) and "like a hammer in the water" (i.e. to stare at the ground and watch your steps; walking like a hammer in a river, with its heavier head sinking below the surface, and its lighter wooden handle floating above it). Perhaps this is a yōkai which haunts cowards. Or perhaps it turns people into cowards when it haunts them.

Toriyama Sekien included a version of kanazuchibō in his book Hyakki tsurezure bukuro. He re-imagined it as a tsukumogami born from a *keyari*—a hairy spear used as decoration and in parades. He dubbed this yōkai it yari kechō, or "spear hair chief."

OKKA 大化

TRANSLATION: a baby-talk corruption of *obake* (monster)
ALTERNATE NAMES: akaheru, chikarakoko, gamanoke (frog spirit); countless others

APPEARANCE: Okka is a small, bulbous yōkai. It is a round, bright red creature with big eyes, two clawed feet, and a diminutive tail. There are many variations of this yōkai, separated by minor differences in color, number of appendages, facial features, and hair.

ORIGIN: Okka appears in many old yōkai picture scrolls. Since it was originally unnamed, countless names have been invented to describe this yōkai. The word okka is a baby-talk variation of obake, a generic term ghosts and monsters. There is an established pattern of monsters being named in baby-talk; waira, otoroshi, gagoze, and uwan are all thought to be baby-talk variations of local words for scary things.

Based on its appearance, some scholars have suggested that okka may be a frog spirit. It has also been suggested that okka may be a tsukumogami, as it appears alongside other tsukumogami in paintings. Though it was never given a name or an explanation, okka remains a common sight in yōkai picture scrolls. It is frequently the target of kanazuchibō's hammer. However, this may be no more than a coincidence. Painters frequently copied yōkai straight from earlier scrolls, and without any description there is no way of knowing if the original painting of okka was placed with kanazuchibō for a specific reason or only because they looked amusing together.

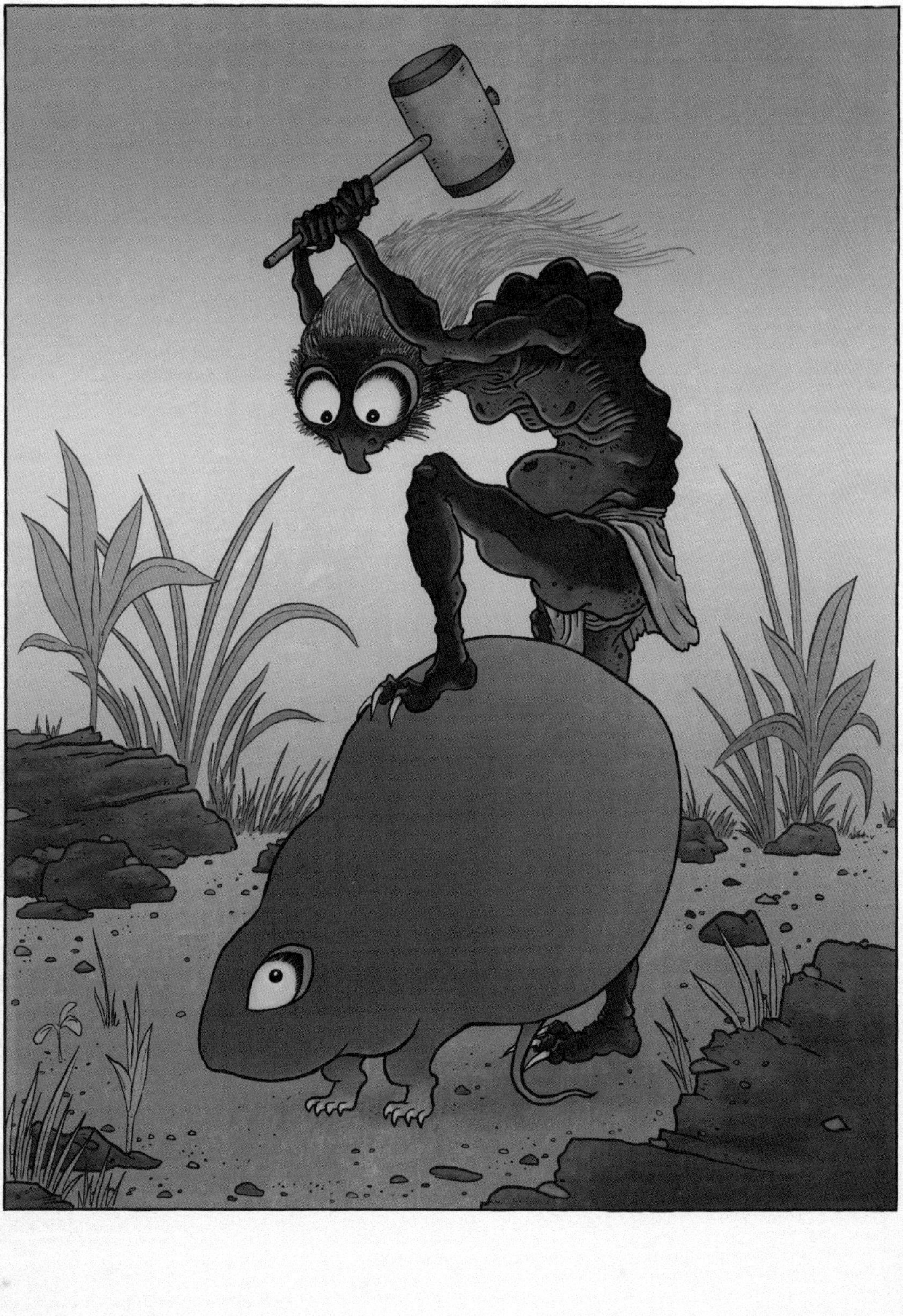

Sunekosuri 脛擦り

TRANSLATION: shin rubber
ALTERNATE NAMES: sunekkorogashi, sunekkorobashi, sunekajiri
HABITAT: human-inhabited areas
DIET: omnivorous

APPEARANCE: Sunekosuri are small, mischievous spirits from Okayama Prefecture. They appear on rainy nights in streets and alleys where people travel. They are most often described as dog-like in appearance, though they are occasionally said to resemble cats.

INTERACTIONS: Sunekosuri run up behind people who are walking on dark, rainy nights. They rub against their shins, weave in and out of their legs, nuzzle against the knees, and otherwise make it difficult to walk. Although their nuzzling is often aggressive enough to make a person stumble or even fall, sunekosuri do not intentionally harm humans.

A few local variations of this yōkai are slightly more dangerous. Sunekkorogashi and sunekkorobashi both mean "shin toppler." Sunekajiri means "shin biter." Although not malevolent like other kinds of yōkai, these spirits are blamed for the occasional tumble, and ensuing bruises or bloody noses.

ORIGIN: Sunekosuri is a relatively modern yōkai. It did not appear in writing until Satō Seimei's 1935 yōkai encyclopedia *Genkō zenkoku yōkai jiten*, although it is impossible to tell how far back oral traditions go. Despite its newness, it has appeared a number of times in manga and film. Due to its cute depictions and pet-like nature it has become a well-known and well-loved yōkai.

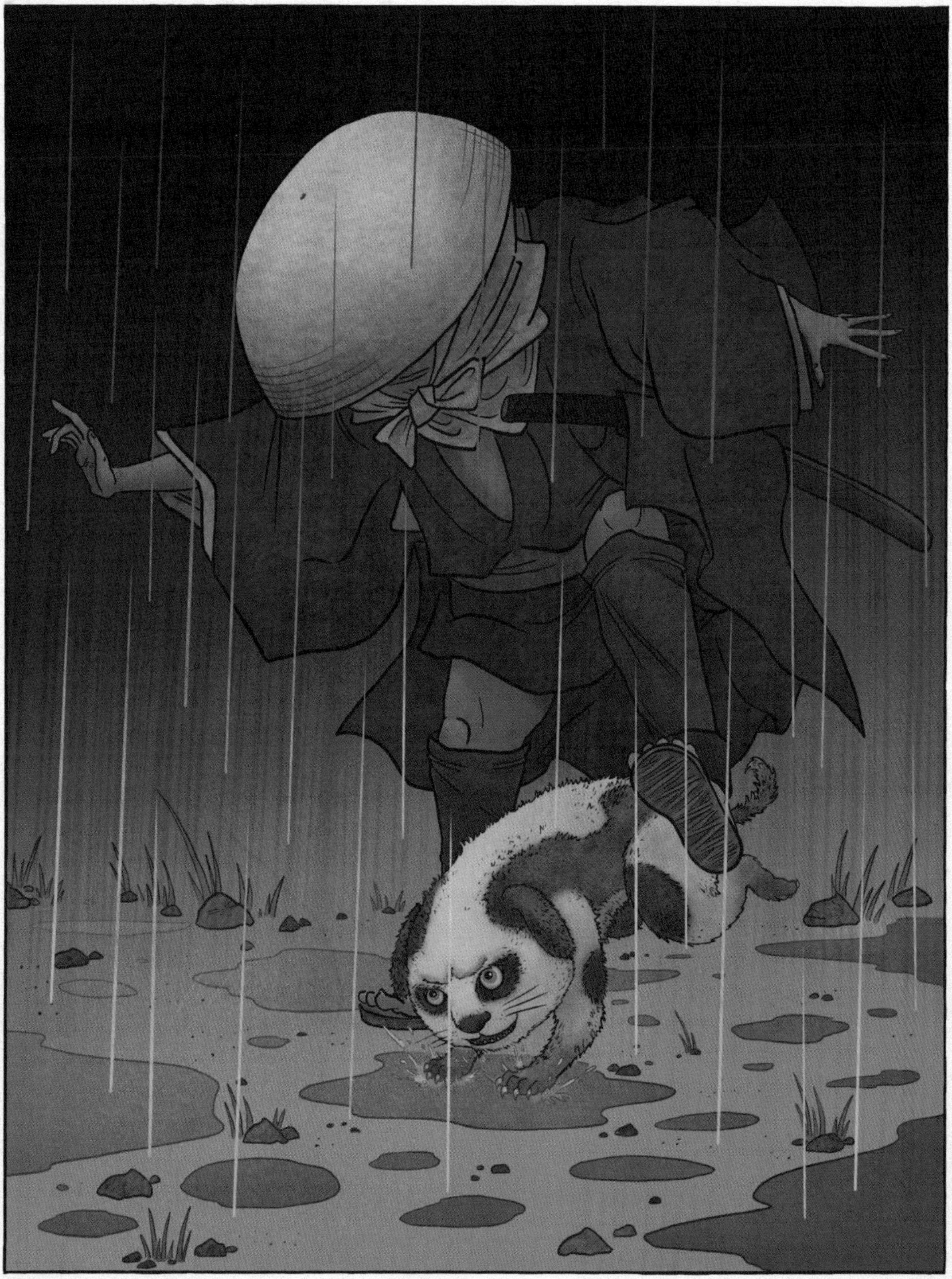

Kosamebō 小雨坊

TRANSLATION: light rain monk
HABITAT: mountain roads
DIET: as a human; likely follows a monk's diet

APPEARANCE: Kosamebō are yōkai which look like Buddhist monks. They loiter about empty mountain roads at night. As their name implies, they only appear during nights when light rain is falling.

INTERACTIONS: Kosamebō accost travelers and beg for alms like spare change, spare food, or bits of millet to eat. Though frightening, disturbing, and perhaps a bit annoying, they do not pose any serious danger to humans.

ORIGIN: Kosamebō is described by Toriyama Sekien in his yōkai encyclopedia *Konjaku hyakki shūi*. Sekien describes them as appearing on the roads going through Mount Omine and Mount Katsuragi, two holy mountains in Nara Prefecture with popular pilgrimage trails. They are also part of the local folklore of the Tsugaru region of Aomori Prefecture.

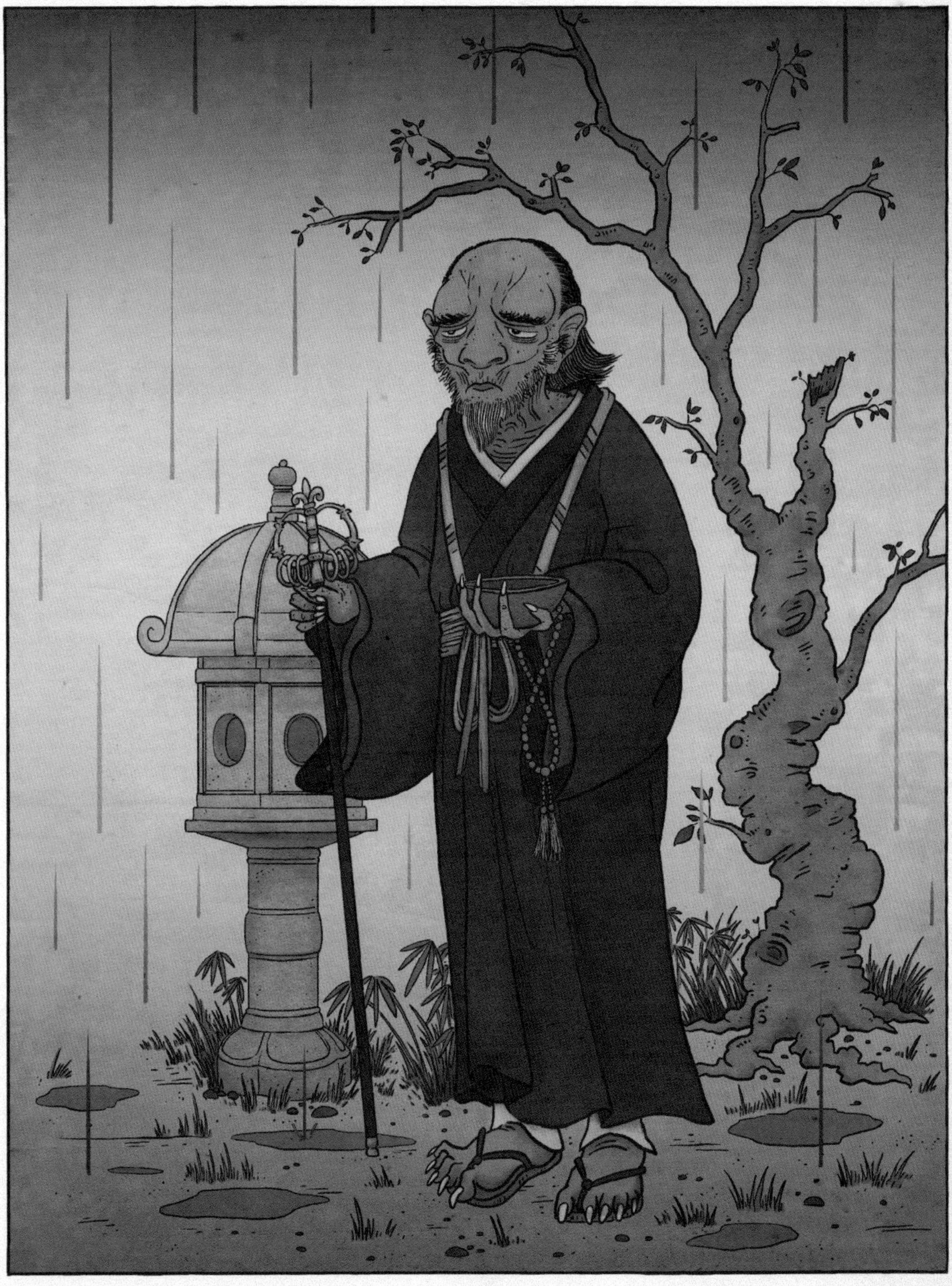

MINOBI 蓑火

TRANSLATION: raincoat fire
ALTERNATE NAMES: minomushibi, minoboshi; varies widely from place to place
HABITAT: wet rural areas

APPEARANCE: Minobi are phenomena that appear on rainy days in rural areas, particularly during the rainy season. Often, they appear near bodies of water such as rivers or lakes like Lake Biwa in Shiga Prefecture. Minobi begin as a number of tiny fireballs which glow like fireflies. They float about in the air and gather in large numbers.

INTERACTIONS: Minobi get their name from a tendency to gather around people wearing *mino* (traditional straw raincoats). They stick to raincoats and begin to burn. When someone attempts to brush off or swat out the fire, instead of going out, the minobi multiplies. The fire grows larger and larger until eventually the person is forced to strip off the raincoat and leave it on the road.

ORIGIN: Minobi are found all over Japan, although often by different names and blamed on different culprits. Sometimes this phenomenon is thought to be caused by natural gas escaping from the ground (as it is with other mysterious fireballs like onibi and kitsunebi). Most often it is said to be the work of mischievous kitsune, itachi, or tanuki. Because they appear more frequently during the rainy season, sometimes minobi are believed to be fireflies or other insects such as the *minomushi* (bagworm moth).

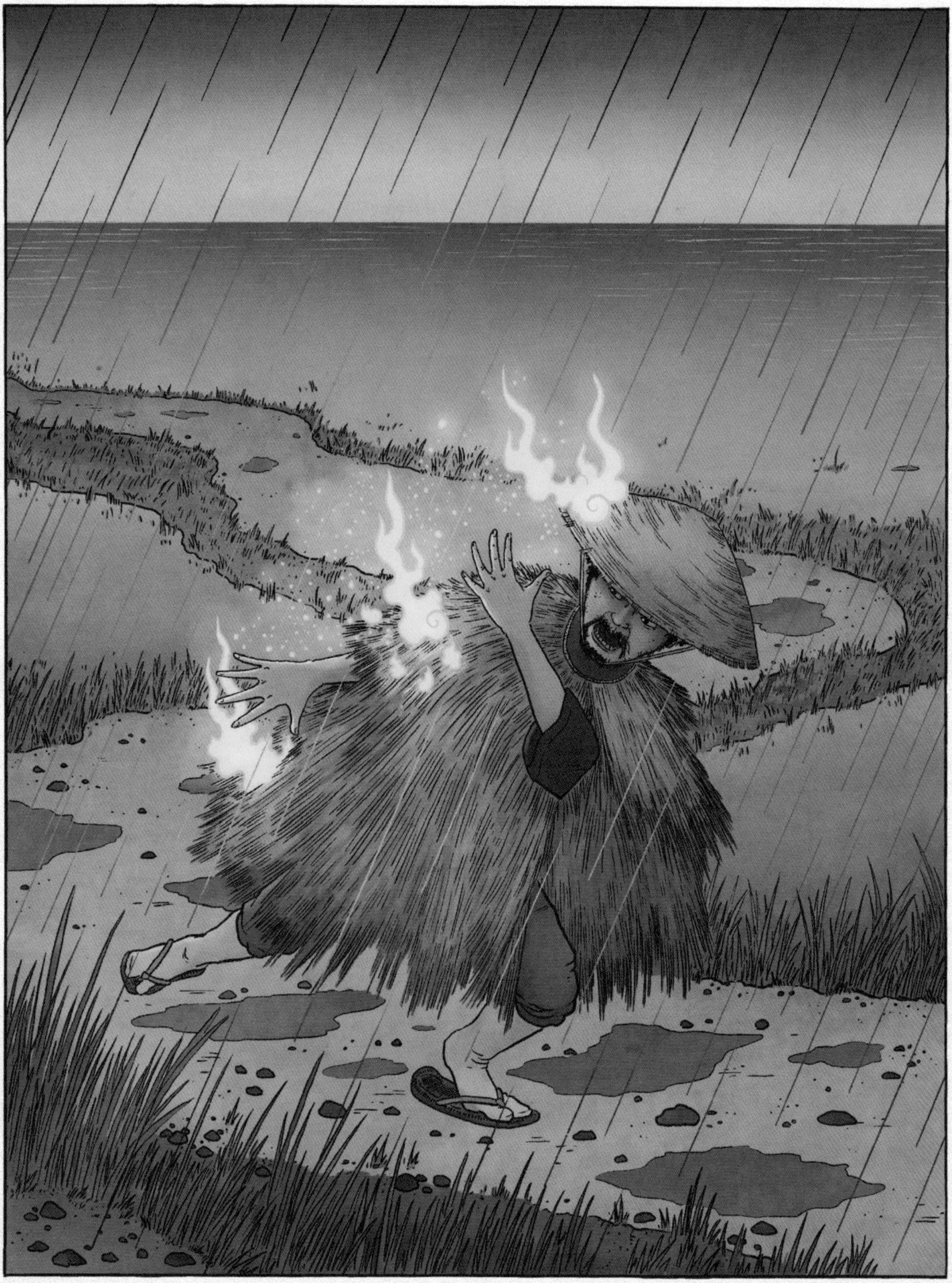

USHIROGAMI 後神

TRANSLATION: the spirit behind you
HABITAT: haunts cowardly people
DIET: thrives on its victims' fear

APPEARANCE: Ushirogami look like ghosts with long black hair, white kimono, and no feet. They have long, twisting bodies which allow them to leap high into the air. A large, single eyeball is located on the top of their heads.

INTERACTIONS: Ushirogami's favorite tactic is to scare people by leaping out and appearing right behind them. This is how they get their name. They tug on the hairs on the back of a person's neck and then vanish when that person turns around to see what touched them. Other pranks that ushirogami enjoy include placing icy cold hands or breathing hot breath onto the necks of their victims. Sometimes they call up strong gusts of wind to blow umbrellas away.

Ushirogami particularly like going after cowardly young women walking alone at night. They sneak up behind the women and untie their hair, causing it to fall all over the place. Or they run their hands through the women's hair and mess it around, tangling it up.

ORIGIN: Ushirogami are thought to be a kind of *okubyōgami*—spirits that causes cowardice, or that specifically target cowardly people. Their name comes from the words *ushiro* (behind) and *kami* (spirit). However, there is a hidden pun in their name: kami can also mean hair, so ushirogami can also mean the hairs on the back of your neck.

The phrase *ushirogami wo hikikaeru* ("to have the hairs on the back of your neck pulled") means to do something with painful reluctance. It describes a person who must do something that they really don't want to do. As they search for some way out of their task, they turn around and look behind them as if the hairs in the back of their head were being pulled on.

The pun is that the ushirogami (spirit) is pulling on your ushirogami (hair), causing you to become cowardly and not want to do something. Thus, ushirogami could be described as both external entities which cause fear and as the internal personification of your own cowardice or reluctance.

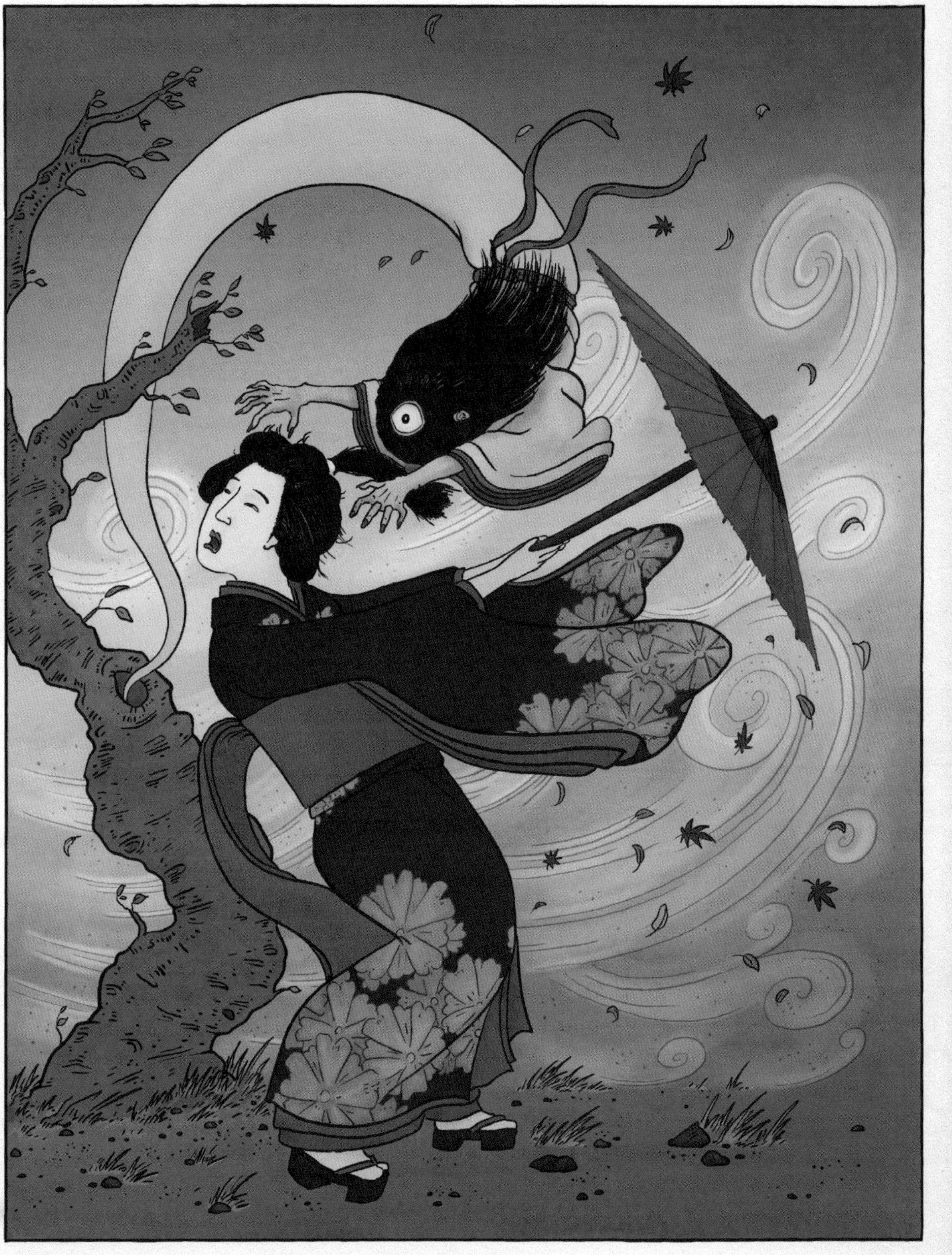

KAZENBŌ 火前坊

TRANSLATION: monk before the fire
HABITAT: Toribeyama, a mountain in Kyōto
DIET: none; it is fueled only by its attachment to this world

APPEARANCE: Kazenbō are ghostly apparitions which resemble burnt monks wreathed in flames. They appear on Toribeyama, a mountain in Kyoto which has been used as a burial site since the Heian Period.

BEHAVIOR: Kazenbō occasionally appear before travelers on Toribeyama. They don't do anything harmful and their fires are not hot, but their horrific appearance is disturbing. They materialize, suffer and writhe in flames which never completely consume them, and disappear.

ORIGIN: During the Heian Period, Toribeyama was an important burial ground and cremation site, especially for the city's nobility. In times of major epidemics, the bodies of those who died from disease were cremated there. The smoke rising from the mountain from all the bodies being burned was said to be unending.

Towards the end of the 10th century, a number of monks decided to offer themselves up in ritual sacrifice by fire. They believed that in doing so, they would rid themselves of their worldly attachments along with their bodies, and thus achieve enlightenment. The ceremony was open to the public. A large number of people came to witness. The event proceeded as planned; the monks sacrificed their bodies in the fire. However, a number of these monks did not actually pass on to nirvana. Instead, their souls remained on earth, bound to where they died. They must not have been able to truly give up their attachments to the material world. Ever since, their doomed ghosts have haunted Toribeyama, appearing as ghostly beggar-monks wreathed in the fires of ignorance and sin.

BUDDHISM AND YŌKAI

In Buddhism, the root sin from which all others are born is attachment. Specifically, attachment to the impermanent, material world. This covers things like wealth and power, but also the perception that our bodies are not separate from our consciousness. Thus, attachment to our physical selves and even our lives is a kind of ignorance. Our attachments serve as an impediment to reaching enlightenment. A person who is able to completely detach his or herself from this ignorance would no longer be reincarnated after death but would achieve nirvana—a state of freedom from suffering and rebirth.

A person who is unable to relieve his or herself from attachment is doomed to be reborn over and over again eternally. When that attachment is particularly strong, a person might be reincarnated not as a human, but as a ghost or a demon. A great deal of yōkai are born this way—former humans, now doomed to suffer as wretched monsters until their souls can be redeemed.

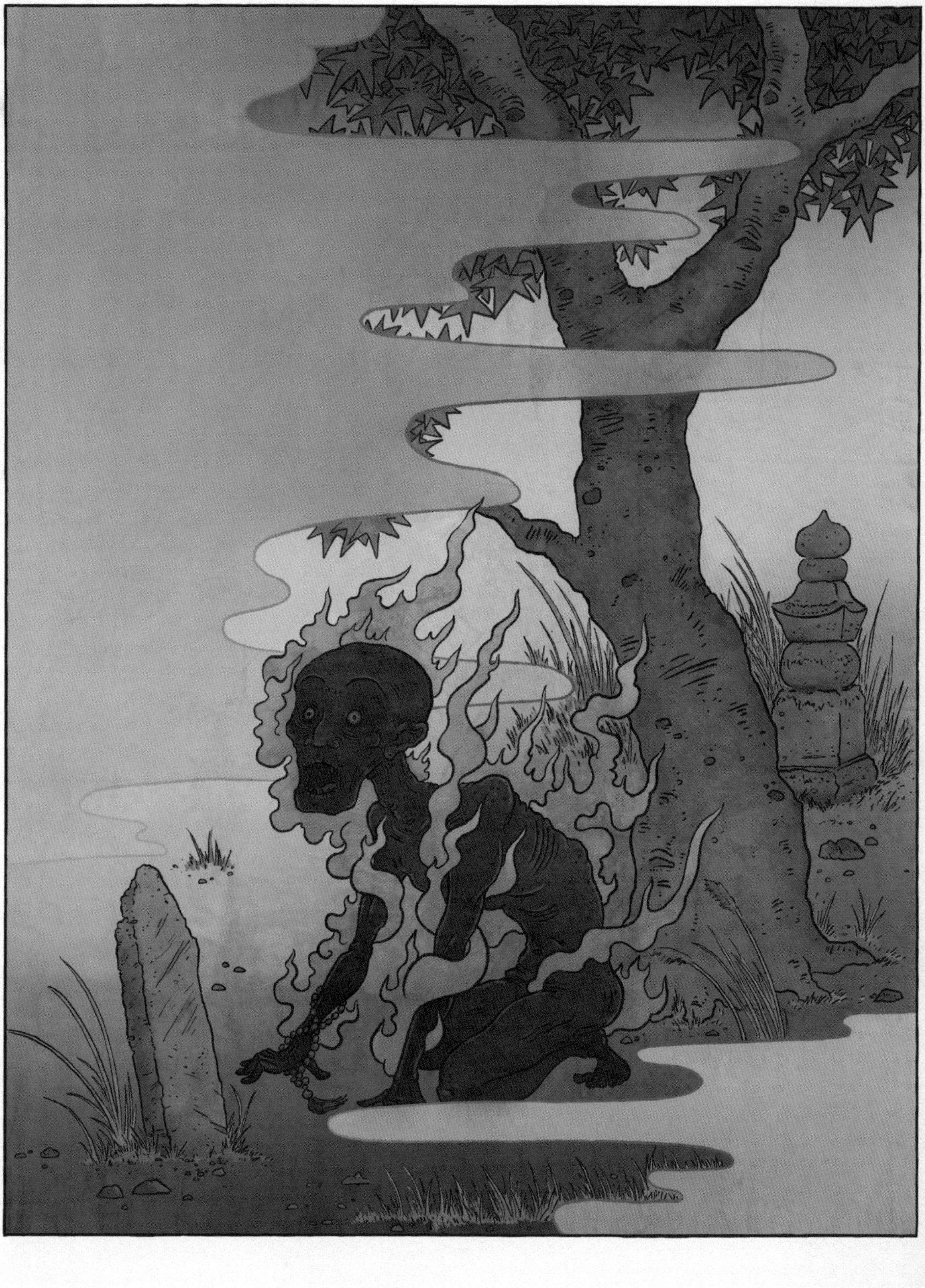

YONAKI BABĀ 夜泣き婆

TRANSLATION: night-weeping hag
ALTERNATE NAMES: nakibabā
HABITAT: human-inhabited areas; loiters outside of homes and temples
DIET: feeds off of others' sadness

APPEARANCE: Yonaki babā look like old women with scraggly, unkempt hair and plain robes. They haunt families which have been recently struck by tragedy.

BEHAVIOR: Yonaki babā remain outside of the houses of the bereaved and weep loudly through the night. They are attracted by the sadness of those within. Although they appear to be sharing in the sadness, it is said that they in fact weep out of scorn, mocking those who truly grieve.

INTERACTIONS: A yonaki babā's weeping is contagious. Those who hear it cannot help but weep as well. Yonaki babā often return to the same house over and over for many nights. Families which are repeatedly visited by yonaki babā invariably fall to ruin.

ORIGIN: Because yonaki babā appearances are often precursors to the ruin of an entire family, it has been suggested that yonaki babā may belong to a class of spirits called *yakubyōgami*—kami of bad luck and misfortune. These spirits inflict sickness and suffering wherever they go. Before modern medicine, plagues and natural disasters were thought to be the works of yakubyōgami.

Conversely, it has been suggested a yonaki babā's arrival may be a divine warning that disaster is near. Rather than bringing disease and ruin herself, a yonaki babā may be a kind of divine herald with the duty of warning humans that misfortune, sickness, and death are on the way.

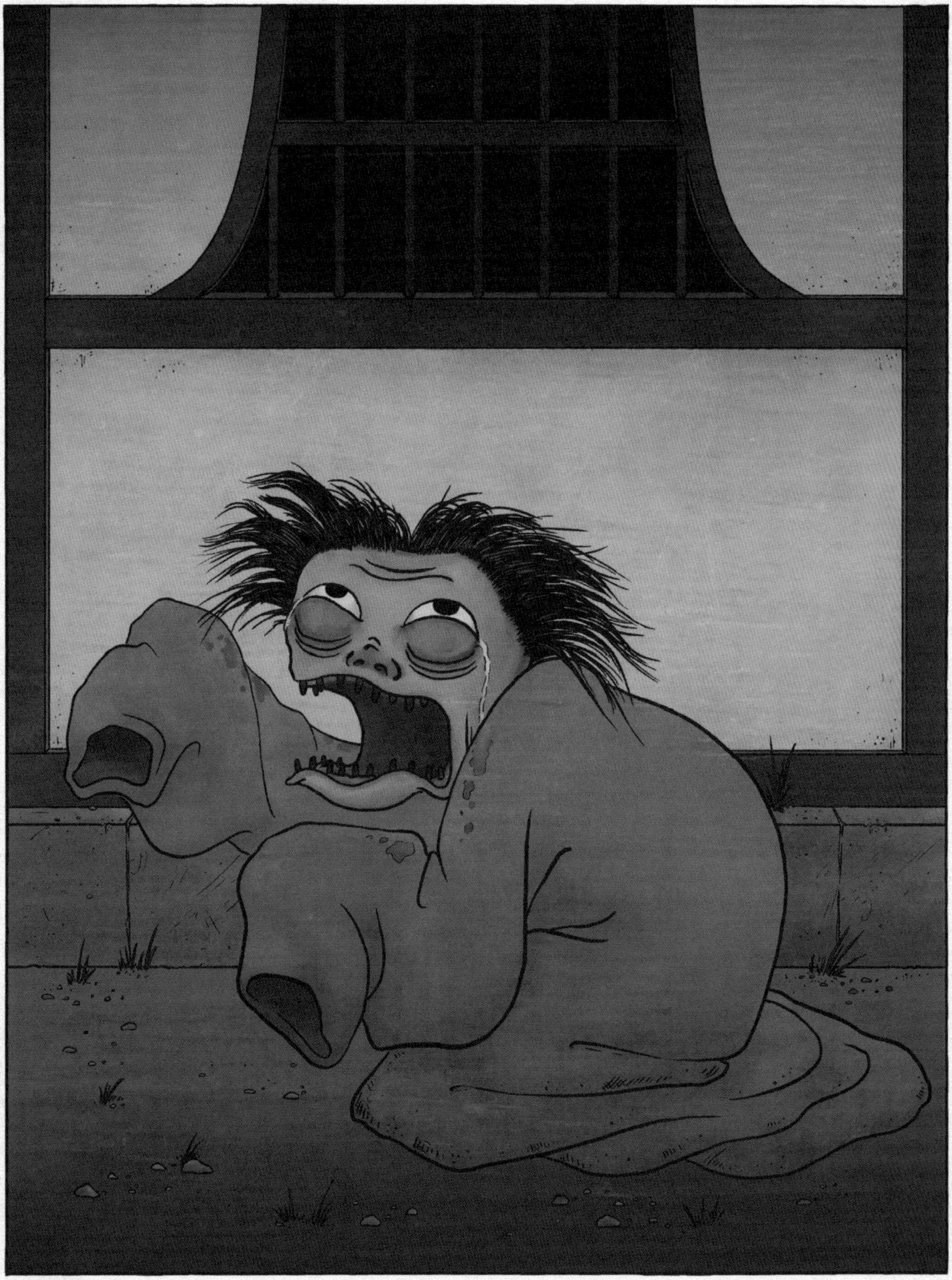

Amazake babā 甘酒婆

Translation: amazake hag
Alternate names: amazake banbā
Habitat: dark, snowy streets; particularly in northern urban areas
Diet: amazake and sake

APPEARANCE: Amazake babā are yōkai from northeastern Japan which appear like haggardly old women. They are practically indistinguishable from ordinary old women, which makes them difficult to recognize as yōkai—until it is too late.

INTERACTIONS: Amazake babā appear on snowy winter nights, traveling from house to house. They knock on doors and call out, "Might you have any *amazake* (a sweet, low alcohol content form of sake)?" Those who answer, whether yes or no, fall terribly ill. According to superstition, it is possible to keep amazake babā from your house by hanging a cedar branch over the door.

A variation of amazake babā from Yamanashi prefecture is called amazake banbā. They travel from house to house trying to sell sake and amazake. The consequences of replying to one are the same as with an amazake babā, but the way to keep them at bay is slightly different. They will leave you alone and go on to the next house if you hang a sign at the front door that says, "We do not like sake or amazake."

ORIGIN: Long ago amazake babā was considered to be a spirit of disease—specifically smallpox. During smallpox outbreaks, there were large increases in amazake babā sightings in major urban centers across Japan, not just in the northeast. Rumors of old women roaming the streets at night selling sake and spreading sickness were rampant in large cities such as Edo, Kyōto, Ōsaka, and Nagoya. Fear of smallpox was a major concern in urban centers and contributed to the popularity of amazake babā rumors.

Since the eradication of smallpox, amazake babā has been downgraded from a spirit of smallpox to a spirit of the common cold. Statues of amazake babā can be found in large cities. Parents visit these statues to leave offerings of sake and amazake in hopes that their children will not become sick.

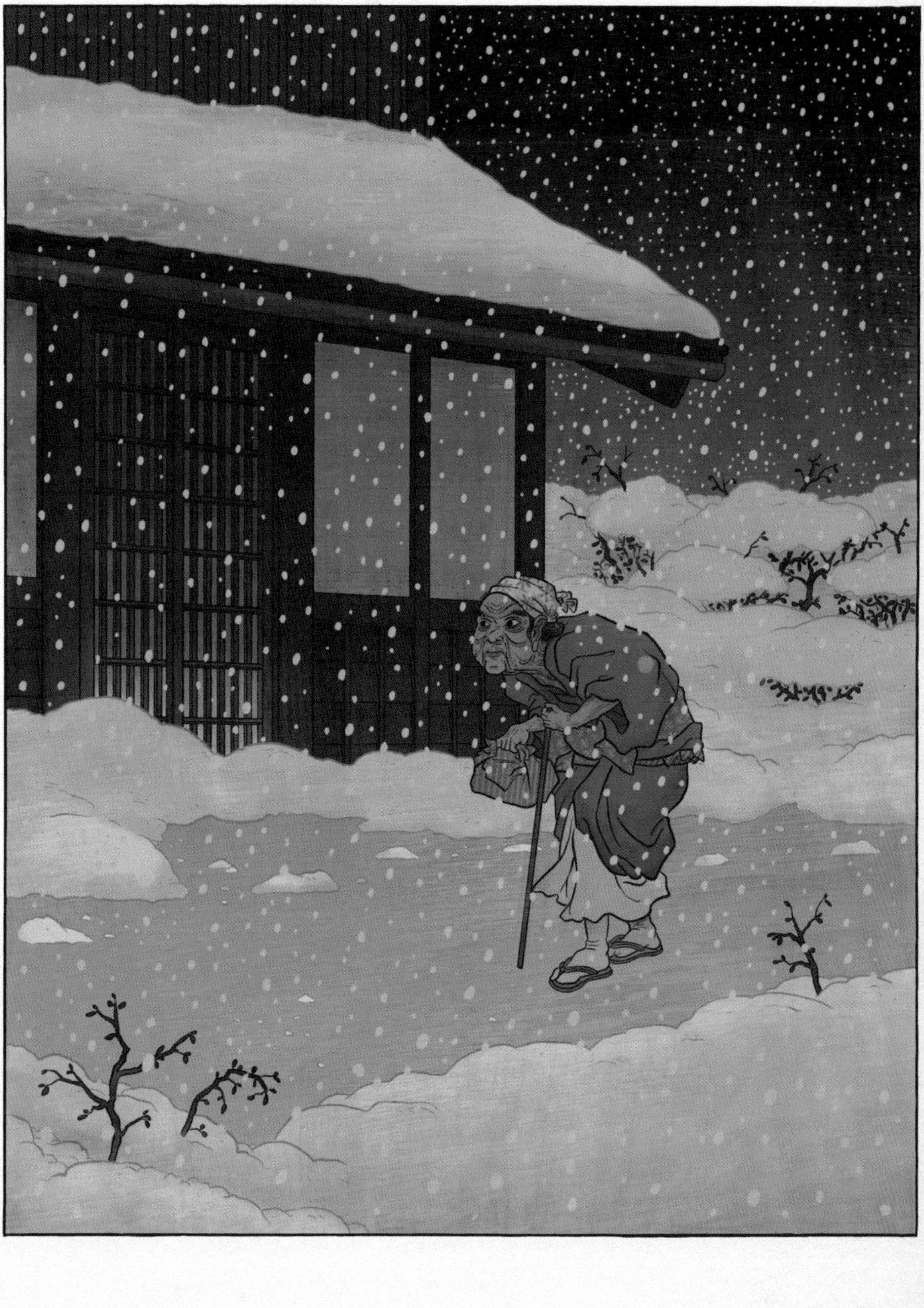

Tsurara onna 氷柱女

TRANSLATION: icicle woman
ALTERNATE NAMES: tsurara nyōbō, shigama nyōbō, suga nyōbō, kanekōri nyōbō
HABITAT: snowy areas; only seen during winter
DIET: loneliness; can also eat ordinary food

APPEARANCE: Tsurara onna are born from the loneliness of single men during the winter. They appear as exceptionally beautiful human women. When the winter snows melt and icicles can no longer be seen hanging from roofs, tsurara onna disappear along with the cold weather.

INTERACTIONS: Despite their icy origins, tsurara onna are warm and loving spirits. They often fall in love with and even marry humans—however these marriages always end in tragedy. The beautiful bride vanishes when the spring comes, leaving her lover confused and heartbroken.

Because they look and behave like human women, it is difficult to identify a tsurara onna. One telltale sign is an unwillingness to enter a bath. Stories tell of women who refuse to take a bath despite their husbands' constant pressuring. Eventually, they relent and enter the bath. After that, these wives are never seen again; all that remains are a few shards of ice floating in the tub.

LEGENDS: Long ago in Echigo Province, a young man gazed out his window on a snowy winter night. As he wistfully admired the scene, he wished that he could find a wife as beautiful as the icicles hanging from his roof. Suddenly, there was a knock at his door. A woman's voice called out, as beautiful and clear as ice: "Hello! I was traveling along this road, but the snow is too heavy, and I can journey no further. Might I stay for the night?" The woman's face was as beautiful as her voice. The young man welcomed her inside and worked hard to make sure her stay was as comfortable as possible.

Several months later, the woman was still staying at the house. She had forgotten about her journey altogether. The woman and the young man fell deeply in love and got married.

One morning the young bride went out shopping. She did not return. The young man waited for her night after night. He asked everyone he knew if they had seen his wife. Nobody had. He searched all around. There was no sign of her. Eventually the snows melted, the plum blossoms bloomed, and spring arrived. His heart was broken, but he forced himself to accept that his bride had left him. Later that year, he married a young woman from his village.

The following winter, the young man found himself looking out the window at the long icicles hanging from his roof. Suddenly, there was a knock at the door. His beautiful bride from the previous winter was standing outside of his house. He was shocked. "I searched for you every day! Why did you vanish without a word?" he cried.

The woman replied coldly, "We promised to love each other forever. You said that our bond was as long and as solid as the beautiful icicles hanging from your roof. Yet, you remarried so quickly!" She turned and left with a sad look on her face.

The young man's new wife appeared, asking what was going on. "It's nothing. Go back inside," he told her. He started after the woman.

Suddenly there was loud crash near the front of the house, followed by a shriek. The new wife ran to the door to see what had happened. There, lying in the front yard, was her husband. He was dead, pierced through the brain by an enormous icicle which had fallen from the roof.

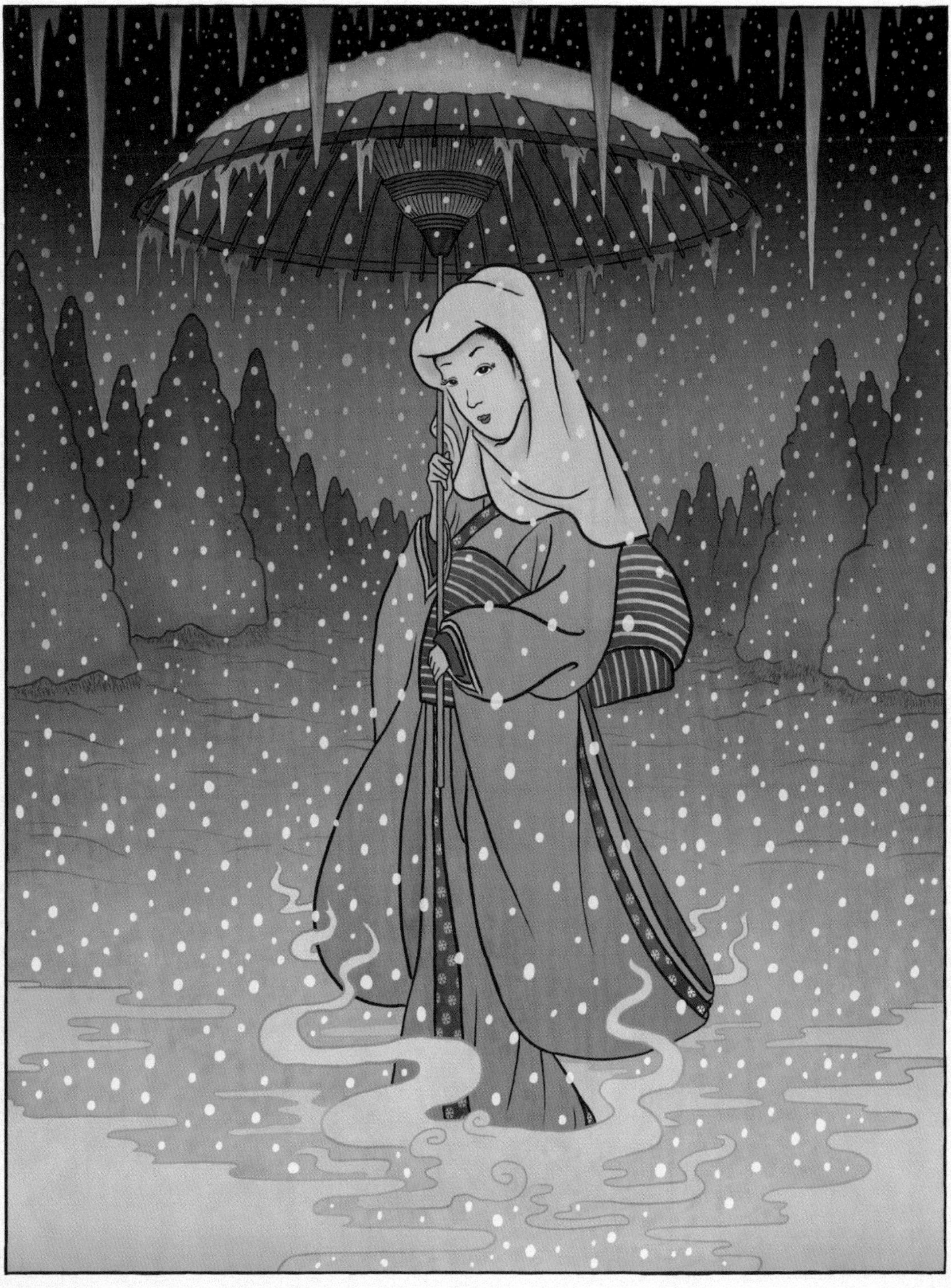

OSHIROI BABĀ 白粉婆

TRANSLATION: face powder hag
ALTERNATE NAMES: oshiroi bāsan
HABITAT: dark streets at night, particularly near snowy mountains
DIET: unknown

APPEARANCE: Oshiroi babā are ghastly old hags who appear near the end of the year in mountainous areas. They are accompanied by a telltale *jara jara* sound, as if someone were dragging a mirror while hobbling through the streets. Their backs are hideously twisted, bent like an old woman who has had a lifetime hard work. They carry a cane in one hand, a sake bottle in the other, and wear a broken straw hat. Their most defining feature is their wrinkly old face which is caked with thick, sloppy, white face powder.

INTERACTIONS: Oshiroi babā don't interact with humans often. For the most part, their looks alone are awful enough that anyone who sees them quickly runs away. They occasionally accost people, demanding makeup or trying to buy sake. In this way they resemble other old hag yōkai who wander the streets at night, such as amazake babā. However, unlike most other hags, oshiroi babā—while ugly and scary—are not dangerous.

ORIGIN: According to some local legends, oshiroi babā are a kind of yuki onna who descend from mountains into villages on snowy nights. Other legends say that they are more similar to yama uba, who occasionally demand makeup from travelers or appear at the bases of mountains to buy alcohol. According to Toriyama Sekien, oshiroi babā serve as the attendants of Shifun Senjō, the goddess of rouge and makeup.

WHITE FACES, BLACK TEETH

The artwork of the Edo Period is well known for its depictions of women wearing distinctive makeup. The palette of this time consisted of three basic colors: white, red, and black. The whiten the face, a lead-based pigment called *oshiroi* was applied thickly with a brush. The whiter the better. The lips, cheeks, and fingernails were colored red using a pigment made from safflowers. Upon getting married, women would blacken their teeth by swishing in their mouths a concoction made from vinegar and iron filings—a style called *ohaguro*. Upon giving birth to her first child, a woman would shave off her eyebrows, and would sometimes paint a new set of fake eyebrows high up on her forehead.

Yōkai are often depicted wearing excessive amounts of makeup. Picture scrolls show ogrish women applying thick white makeup and smiling with mouths full of black teeth. And there are yōkai—like oshiroi baba and ohaguro bettari—who are named for these makeup styles. It seems that even ghosts and spirits were not exempt from fashion trends.

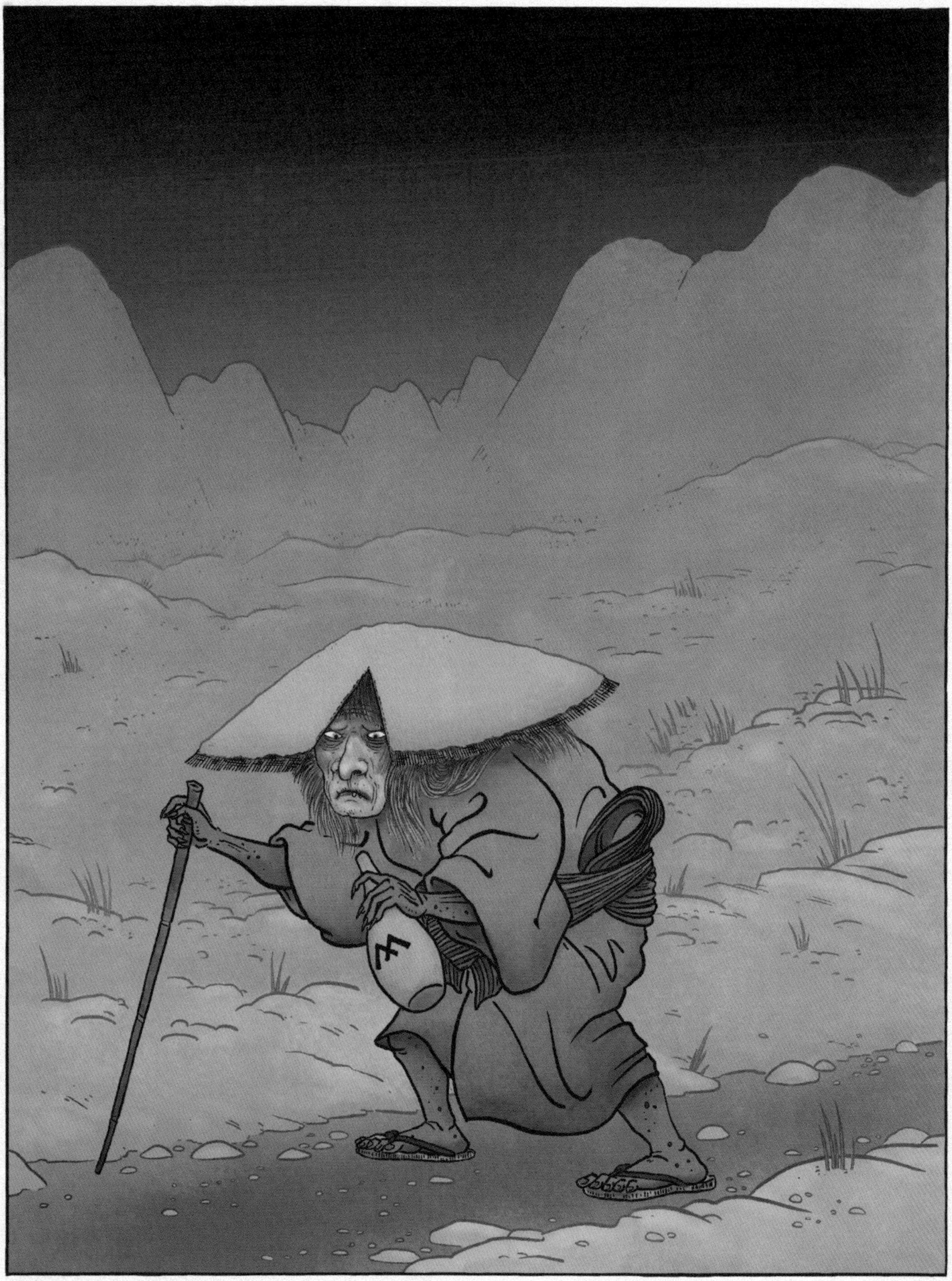

JAKOTSU BABĀ 蛇骨婆

TRANSLATION: snake bones hag
HABITAT: Bukan, a mythical country far to the west
DIET: as a human

APPEARANCE: Jakotsu babā is a scary old hag and a shaman with the power to control snakes. She is described as carrying a blue snake in her right hand and a red snake in her left.

BEHAVIOR: Very little is recorded about Jakotsu babā's history or life. Her behavior is the subject of speculation by storytellers. She supposedly lives near a place called "the snake mound." She scares those who wander too close to her home by attacking them with her snakes.

ORIGIN: It's not quite clear where this yōkai originally comes from. She was recorded in 1780 by Toriyama Sekien in his book *Konjaku hyakki shūi*. Because she carries two snakes, Sekien speculated that Jakotsu babā originally came from the mythical country of Bukan (also called Fukan; known as Wuxian in Chinese). The race of people who lived in Bukan were shamans, and they used snakes prominently in their divinations. Bukan is recorded in the *Sengaikyō* (Chinese: *Shan hai jing*), which Toriyama Sekien uses as his source for this record. It was supposedly located far to the west, past China on the Asian continent.

According to Sekien, long ago there was an important man in Bukan named Jagoemon who lived in a place known as "the snake mound." His wife was known as Jagobā (i.e. "Jago's wife"). Over time, her name was corrupted into Jakotsu babā. Jagoemon is not a famous historical or mythical figure, so Sekien's reference may have been invented for fun.

Prior to *Konjaku hyakki shūi*, the name jakotsu babā appears as a vulgar slang word for an old woman in various pulp fiction and kabuki plays of the 1760s and 1770s. Some scholars believe that Sekien may have taken a popular buzzword of his time, transformed it into a yōkai, and attached a simple backstory.

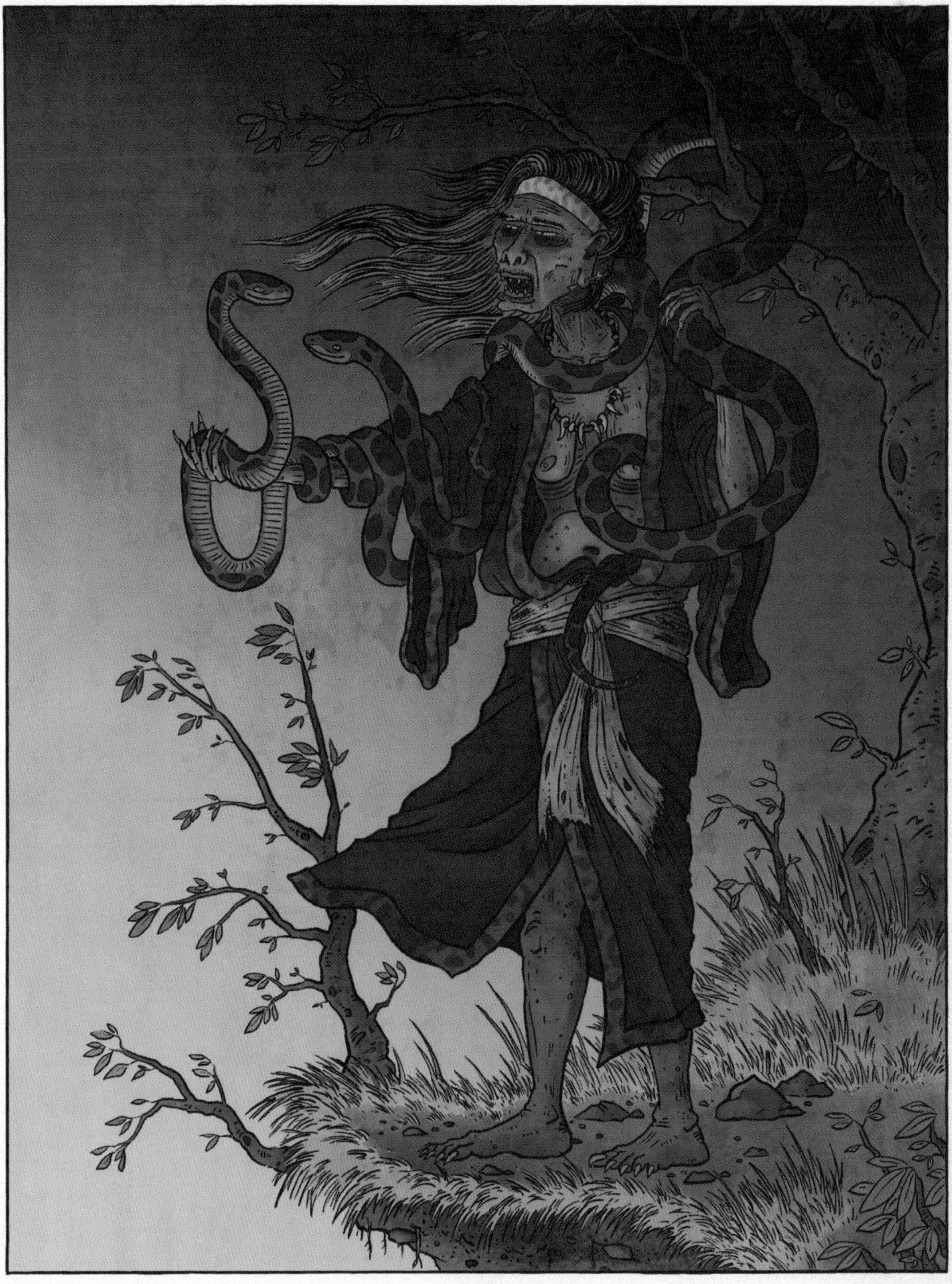

Uwabami 蟒蛇

TRANSLATION: giant snake, great serpent
ALTERNATE NAMES: orochi, daija
HABITAT: wilderness
DIET: carnivorous; gluttonous and very fond of alcohol

APPEARANCE: Uwabami are enormous serpents. Apart from their incredible size, they closely resemble ordinary snakes. They make their homes in the wilderness, far from civilization.

BEHAVIOR: Uwabami are capable of eating things that are much larger than their bodies, and in quantities that seem like more than they should be able to eat. They are also extremely fond of drinking and can consume huge quantities of sake. They can shape-shift into objects and creatures, including humans. Floods and rock slides are often blamed on evil uwabami.

ORIGIN: Snakes have been a part of folklore since prehistoric times. They are symbols of life, death, and eternal youth—the shedding and re-growing of their skin was viewed as a magical ability. Because they can slip into the tiniest cracks, penetrating deep, dark places inaccessible to humans, they were seen as tenacious and clever creatures.

The word *uwabami* is slang for a heavy drinker. The comes from the uwabami's legendary fondness for sake and its ability to drink more than a creature as large as it should be able to.

LEGENDS: Long ago, an uwabami lived in Ōnuma Lake of Shinano Province. Every year he would transform to a handsome young man and visit the mountains to see the cherry blossoms. One spring, he saw a beautiful young woman alone under the blossoms. She was Kuro hime, daughter of the powerful lord Takanashi Masamori. Kuro hime also spied the handsome man who was watching her and found him irresistible. They became acquainted and soon fell in love.

The uwabami traveled to Masamori's castle. He introduced himself as the great snake of Ōnuma Lake, guardian deity of the Shiga Highlands. He professed his love for Kuro hime and asked the lord for her hand in marriage. Masamori immediately refused. The uwabami did not give up and returned every day to ask for Kuro hime's hand. Finally, Masamori gave his conditions: "If you can keep up with me on horseback and complete seven laps around my castle, I will give you my daughter." The uwabami agreed.

Masamori devised a plan to kill the creature. He had his servants plant swords in the grass all around the castle. When the race began, Masamori spurred his horse into action. The uwabami could not outride the lord, so he transformed into a snake to keep pace. The swords planted around the castle pierced and tore his body. Masamori was an expert rider and knew where the swords were hidden so he easily avoided the traps. When they had completed seven laps, the uwabami's body was ragged. Rivers of blood flowed from his wounds, and he collapsed. Masamori's trap had worked.

When the uwabami awoke, he realized that he had been tricked. He returned to his lake and summoned a storm, the likes of which had never been seen. Ōnuma Lake swelled and overflowed, flooding everything around. Houses were knocked down, fields were flooded, villages were washed away. No humans or animals escaped annihilation. However, the mountains around Masamori's castle shielded it, and the castle stood firm.

Kuro hime watched from the safety of the castle. She was heartbroken when she saw the destruction. She traveled to Ōnuma Lake, where she threw herself into the water and drowned. When the uwabami learned what had happened, he banished the storm clouds and commanded the flood to recede. The lake shrank back to its original borders. Kuro hime was never seen again.

The uwabami is still worshiped today as the guardian deity of the Shiga Highlands. There is a small shrine called Daija Jinja located near Ōnuma Lake where the snake is enshrined. Every August, the villagers gather there to honor the uwabami and remember the story of Kuro hime.

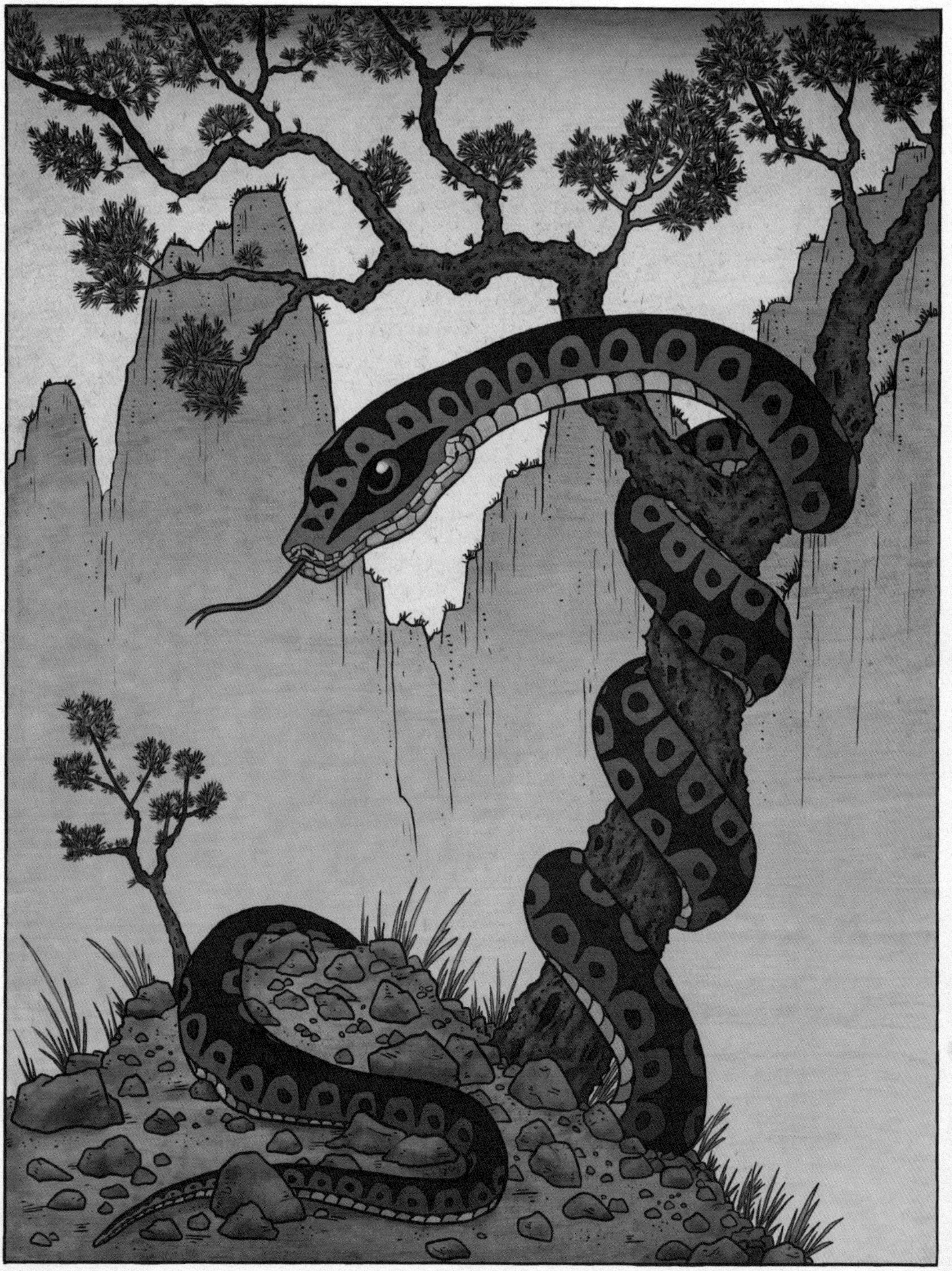

ŌMUKADE 大百足

TRANSLATION: giant centipede
ALTERNATE NAMES: mountains and caves; any dark and humid place big enough to hold it
HABITAT: large mountains and deep forests
DIET: carnivorous

APPEARANCE: Ōmukade are monstrous mukade (*Scolopendra subspinipes*)—centipedes with dark bodies and bright orange legs and heads. They are often depicted with dragon-like features. While ordinary mukade can grow up to 20 cm in length, the upper size limit on yōkai mukade is unknown.

BEHAVIOR: Like their smaller relatives, ōmukade are vicious and highly aggressive. The bite of a regular mukade is venomous and extremely painful, but rarely fatal. Ōmukade, on the other hand, are much more venomous and powerful. They have even been known to attack dragons.

An ōmukade's exoskeleton is so tough that it can't be pierced by weapons. They have one weakness—human saliva is toxic to them. A weapon coated in saliva is able to pierce through its armor and wound it.

INTERACTIONS: Ōmukade encounters are extremely rare. However, when they happen they pose a threat to all in the area. Throughout history, the responsibility of exterminating these monsters has fallen on the shoulders of brave warriors.

LEGENDS: There is a famous bridge in Shiga Prefecture known as *Seta no Karahashi*. Long ago, a great serpent appeared on the bridge and would not move. The villagers were too afraid to approach the serpent, and so they could not cross.

One day, the brave warrior Fujiwara no Hidesato came to the village and learned of the serpent on the bridge. He feared nothing so he crossed the bridge, trampling over the serpent's great body with his heavy feet. It slithered back into the lake. The bridge was clear again.

That night, a beautiful woman visited Hidesato. She introduced herself as the daughter of the dragon king of Like Biwa. The dragon king had sent her to Hidesato to ask for his help. Her family was being tormented by an ōmukade who lived on Mount Mikami. She believed that Hidesato was a brave warrior who had trampled her so fearlessly. Hidesato agreed to help the dragon king. He took up his sword and his bow and headed to the mountains.

Upon reaching Mount Mikami, Hidesato saw an enormous centipede coiled around its top. It was so long that its body wrapped around the mountain seven and a half times. He fired his arrows at it until only one arrow remained but he was unable to pierce the beast's armor. Hidesato coated the tip of the arrow in his saliva. He said a prayer to Hachiman, the god of warriors. This time his arrow struck true. He brought down the ōmukade.

The dragon king's daughter was so grateful to Hidesato that she rewarded him with marvelous gifts: a bag of rice which never became empty no matter how much rice was taken from it; a roll of silk which never ran out no matter how much was cut from it; a cooking pot which always produced the most delicious food without the need for fire; and a large temple bell, which Hidesato donated to Mii-dera. The grateful dragon king also taught Hidesato the secret to defeating Taira no Masakado, a rebel whom Hidesato had been ordered to defeat by the emperor.

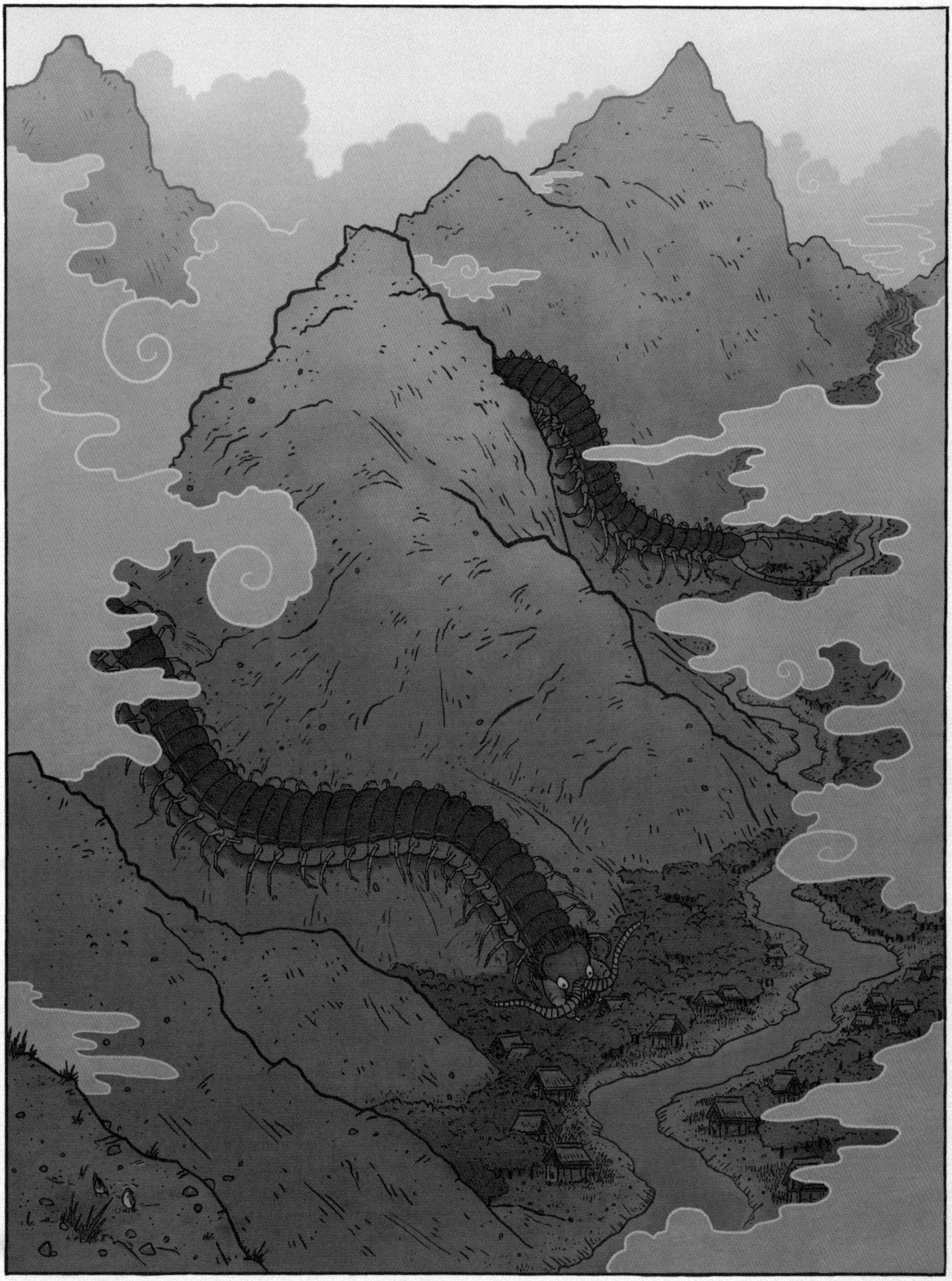

DAIDARABOTCHI 大太郎法師

TRANSLATION: giant; literally "Big Tarō the priest"
ALTERNATE NAMES: daidarabō, daidabō, daidara hōshi, daitarōbō, deidarabotchi, dairanbō, dendenhome, reirabotchi, ōki bochabocha; many others
HABITAT: mountains all over Japan
DIET: omnivorous

APPEARANCE: Daidarabotchi are colossal humanoids which resemble bald-headed priests. They have big rolling eyes, long, lolling tongues, and pitch-black skin. They share similarities with other giants like ōnyūdō and umi bōzu, but they are by far the largest giants found in yōkai folklore.

BEHAVIOR: Daidarabotchi are so large that their movements shape the world. They build mountains by piling up rocks and dirt. They pick up and move mountains to other places. When they walk, they leave lakes and valleys in their footprints. Many places across Japan are reported to have been made by daidarabotchi. Some are even named after them.

ORIGIN: Some of the oldest folk stories in Japan are legends of giants. Because of this, daidarabotchi have countless regional name variations. Most of them are local variations of the same theme: a giant priest. However, priest is often used as slang and doesn't necessarily refer to members of the clergy. Similarly, the name Tarō is such a common Japanese name that it is often used as a placeholder name and does not refer to an actual person. So, while daidarabotchi can be translated as "Big Tarō the priest," it is more of a figurative name than a literal one.

LEGENDS: Mount Fuji is said to have been made by a daidarabotchi. The giant scooped and dug up all the dirt in Kai Province (Yamanashi Prefecture) to make the mountain, and that is why the area around Mount Fuji is a large basin. When he ran out of dirt, he gathered more by digging in Omi Province (Shiga Prefecture). The area he dug there became Lake Biwa.

The towns of Daita in Setagaya, Tōkyō and Daitakubo in Saitama are named after daidarabotchi. Both places are said to have been formed by daidarabotchi long ago.

Daizahōshi Pond in Nagano Prefecture is another form of daidarabotchi and is believed to have been created by one. Senba Lake in Ibaraki Prefecture is also said to fill the footprint of a particularly large daidarabotchi.

The Takabocchi Plateau in Nagano's Yatsugatake quasi-national park is said to have been formed when a daidarabotchi lay down to rest his back for a bit.

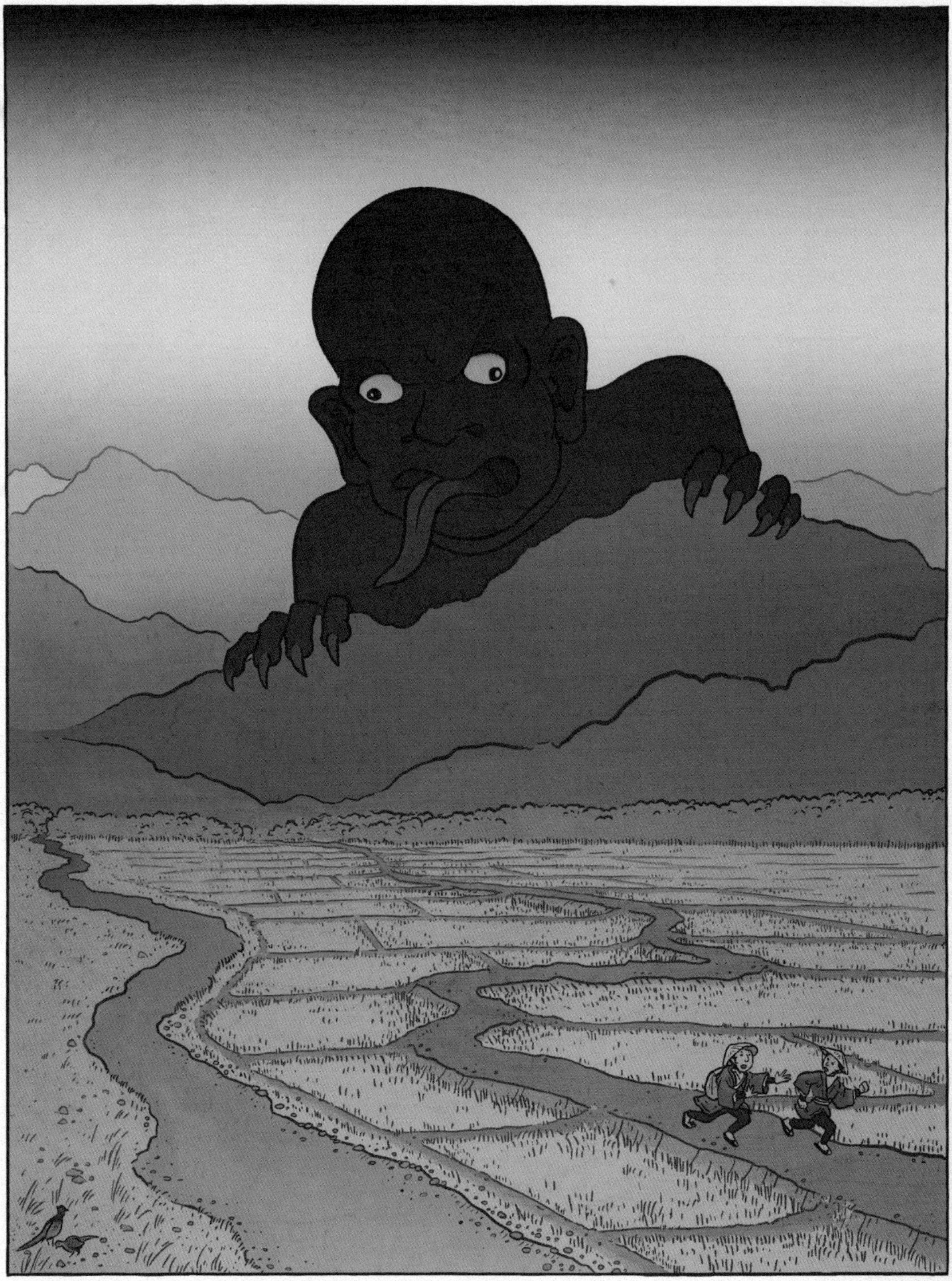

Onikuma 鬼熊

TRANSLATION: demon bear
HABITAT: mountains and forests
DIET: omnivorous

APPEARANCE: Onikuma are bears which have lived an extraordinarily long time and transformed into yōkai. Onikuma continue growing beyond even the largest ordinary bears. They walk on two legs and are big enough to pick up cows and horses. They can easily move boulders than ten men could not budge. They are so powerful that they can crush a monkey in the palm of their hand.

BEHAVIOR: Onikuma behavior is similar to ordinary bears. They live deep in the mountains, far away from humans. They are nocturnal. They hunt and scavenge and are able to eat just about anything. Onikuma rarely venture out of their habitats. However, like ordinary bears, onikuma will occasionally emerge from the forests and go into villages in search of food.

INTERACTIONS: Due to their reclusive nature, encounters between onikuma and humans are rare. When they do occur, they are often violent. Onikuma sometimes wander into human-inhabited areas in search of food, usually livestock. Onikuma are capable of grabbing livestock and carrying them back into the forest. When this happens, the villagers have no choice but to try to hunt and kill the onikuma.

Special tactics are required to hunt onikuma. First, hunters use strong timber to build a sturdy wooden structure resembling a square well casing. This is covered with wisteria vines and used to plug up the entrance of the onikuma's den. Sticks and brush are pushed through the narrow openings around the den plug. The onikuma instinctively pulls these things into the den and piles them up in back, like a nest. As more and more sticks are inserted, the den fills up until there is no more space. The onikuma then pushes its way out through the vine-covered plug. As it emerges, it is stabbed with long spears and shot with rifles.

One such onikuma hunt was recorded during the Kyōhō era (1716-1736). The hide taken from the beast was reported to be large enough to cover more than six tatami mats.

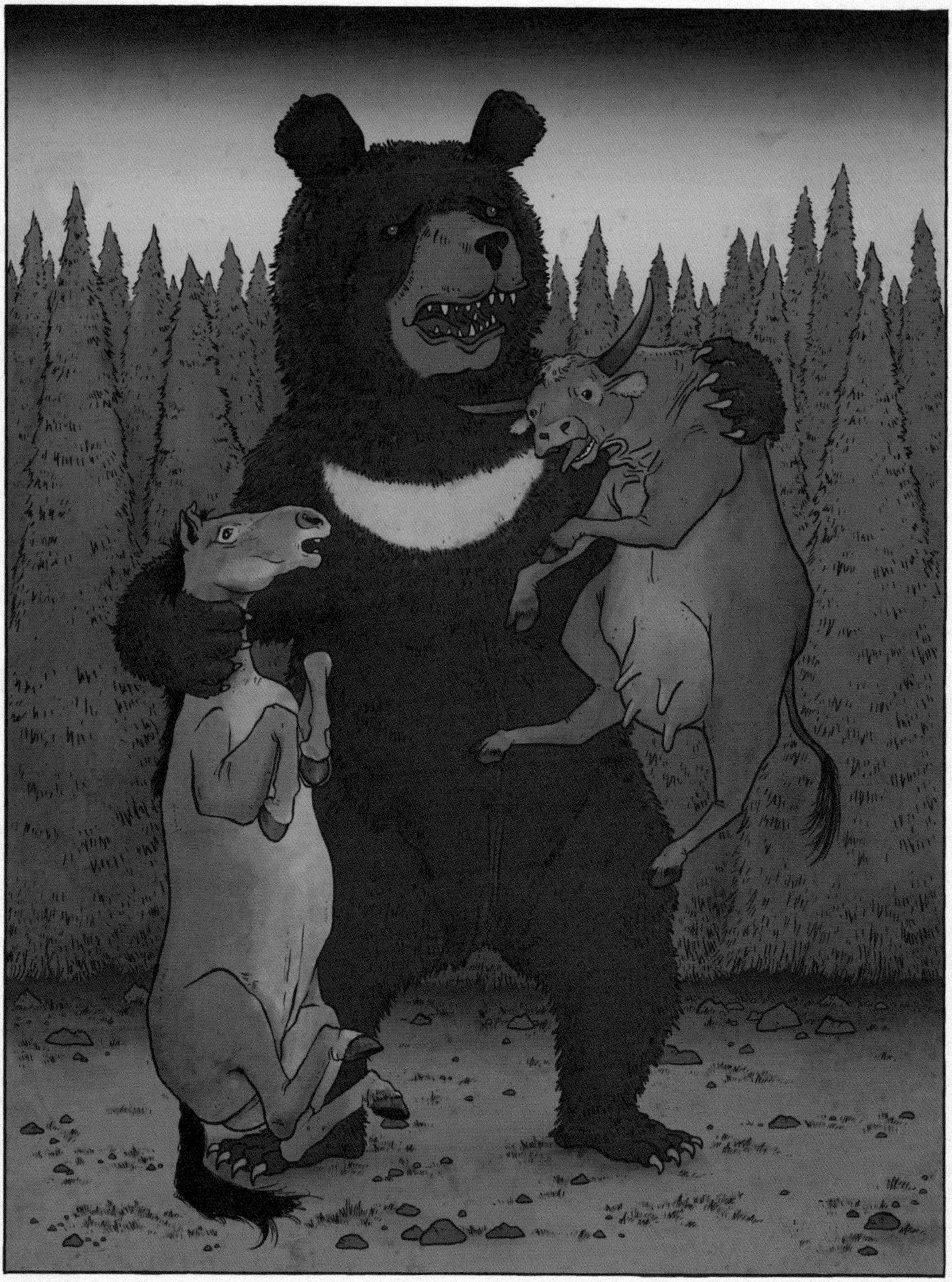

Hōkō 彭侯

TRANSLATION: based on the Chinese name for the same creature; literally "evergreen lord"
HABITAT: inside of trees
DIET: unknown; probably herbivorous

APPEARANCE: Hōkō are nature spirits which inhabit thousand-year old trees. They resemble black dogs with human-like faces and no tails.

BEHAVIOR: Being tree spirits, hōkō are said to resemble kodama or yamabiko. However, Toriyama Sekien goes out of his way to mention that despite the similar appearance hōkō are a separate yōkai.

INTERACTIONS: Most hōkō encounters are accidental. They usually involve an old woodcutter chopping into a camphor tree with an axe, and blood spurting out from the tree from the hōkō living inside. Nevertheless, there are a number of records of hōkō appearing in Japanese and Chinese chronicles. Hōkō are recorded as being edible; the ancient Chinese records that mention them include accounts of hōkō being stewed and eaten. Apparently, they taste sweet and sour, and are similar to dog meat.

ORIGIN: Hōkō is the Japanese pronunciation of this spirit's Chinese name: penghou. According to legend, its name was recorded in the yōkai encyclopedia *Hakutaku zu*. The last surviving copy of this book was lost thousands of years ago, so the true meaning of the name is difficult to decipher.

Because of gradual changes in the writing systems of China and Japan, the characters used to write hōkō do not translate perfectly into Japanese. Legends refer to the hōkō being found inside of camphor trees. However, the first characters in its name refers to a different kind of evergreen in Japanese: the sakaki (*Cleyera japonica*). This is an important, sacred tree in Shinto. The second character in its name was used as a title for feudal lords. It's not clear that these were the intended meanings in the original Chinese though.

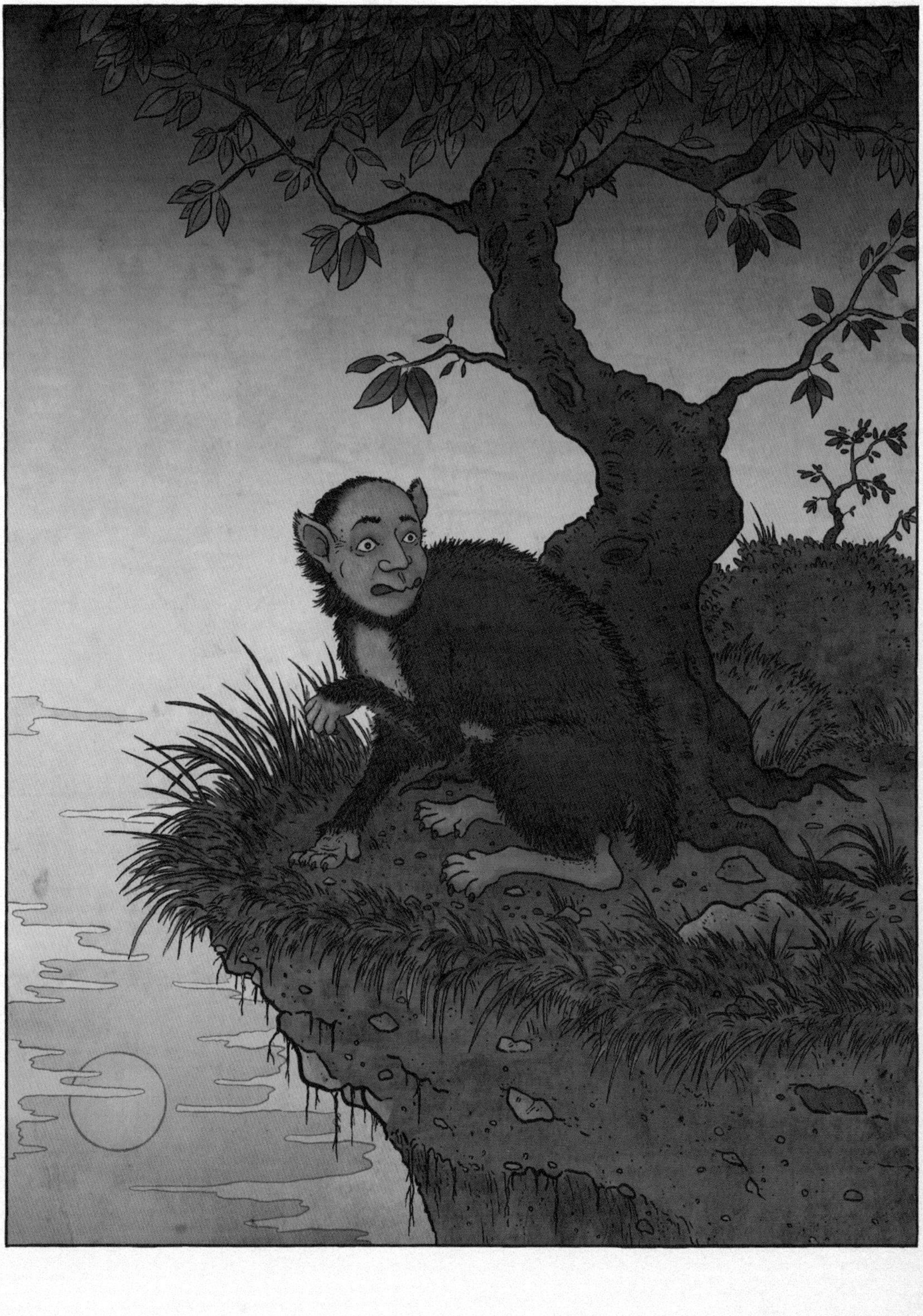

SARUGAMI 猿神

TRANSLATION: monkey god, monkey spirit
ALTERNATE NAMES: enjin
HABITAT: mountain forests far from human civilization

APPEARANCE: Monkeys are viewed as pests by farmers. They dig up crops, steal food from gardens, and sometimes even attack pets and small children. Sarugami are bigger, more vicious, and smarter versions of the monkeys which inhabit Japan. They can speak, and they sometimes even wear human clothes.

INTERACTIONS: When sarugami interact with humans it almost always ends in violence. Most legends involve sarugami kidnaping young women from a village. Heroes are then called upon to venture into the wilderness and slay the beasts.

ORIGIN: Sarugami are an example of fallen gods—spirits once revered as deities but who have since been forgotten and degenerated into yōkai. Monkeys were once worshiped as gods in parts of Japan. Hiyoshi Taisha at the southern part of Lake Biwa was an important center of monkey worship. Monkeys were messengers and servants of the sun because they become most active at sunrise and sunset. Monkey worship was popular among ancient farmers, who also awoke and retired with the sun. As people advanced beyond subsistence farming, monkey worship faded away. Eventually the monkey gods were forgotten.

Though the monkey cults vanished, sarugami worship somewhat continued throughout the middle ages in esoteric religions such as Kōshin. Monkeys were viewed as servants of mountain deities, acting as intermediaries between our world and the gods. The famous "see no evil, hear no evil, say no evil" monkeys (*mizaru*, *kikazaru*, and *iwazaru*) come from Kōshin and are a remnant of ancient sarugami worship.

LEGENDS: Long ago a giant monkey lived in the mountains of Mimasaka Province. Every year it would demand a sacrifice of a young woman from the villages around the mountain. A hunter happened to be staying at the house of the young woman who was chosen to be that year's sacrifice. The hunter took pity on the young woman. He offered to take her place as a sacrifice. The hunter and his dog were loaded into a large chest and taken up into the mountains by priests to be presented to the sarugami.

After some time, a giant monkey more than two meters tall emerged from the woods. It was accompanied by an entourage of over one hundred monkeys. The hunter and his dog leaped from the chest and attacked. Monkey after monkey was slain, until only the sarugami remained. The sarugami possessed one of the priests and spoke through him. It asked for forgiveness and promised never to demand another sacrifice if the hunter would spare its life. The hunter allowed to sarugami to run away. True to its word, the sarugami has never since asked for another sacrifice.

In Ōmi Province there lived an elderly farmer and his young daughter. The farmer toiled in his fields every day, while his daughter waited to be married off. But there were no suitors. One day, the farmer mumbled to himself, "If only there was someone who would marry my daughter and come work in my field... Even a monkey would be ok!"

Suddenly, a sarugami appeared nearby. It performed all the old man's farm work. Then it demanded the old man's daughter as payment. The old man refused. The sarugami grew angry at him for breaking his word. It kidnapped the man's daughter and ran deep into the mountains. It kept the daughter tied up in a sack in its den.

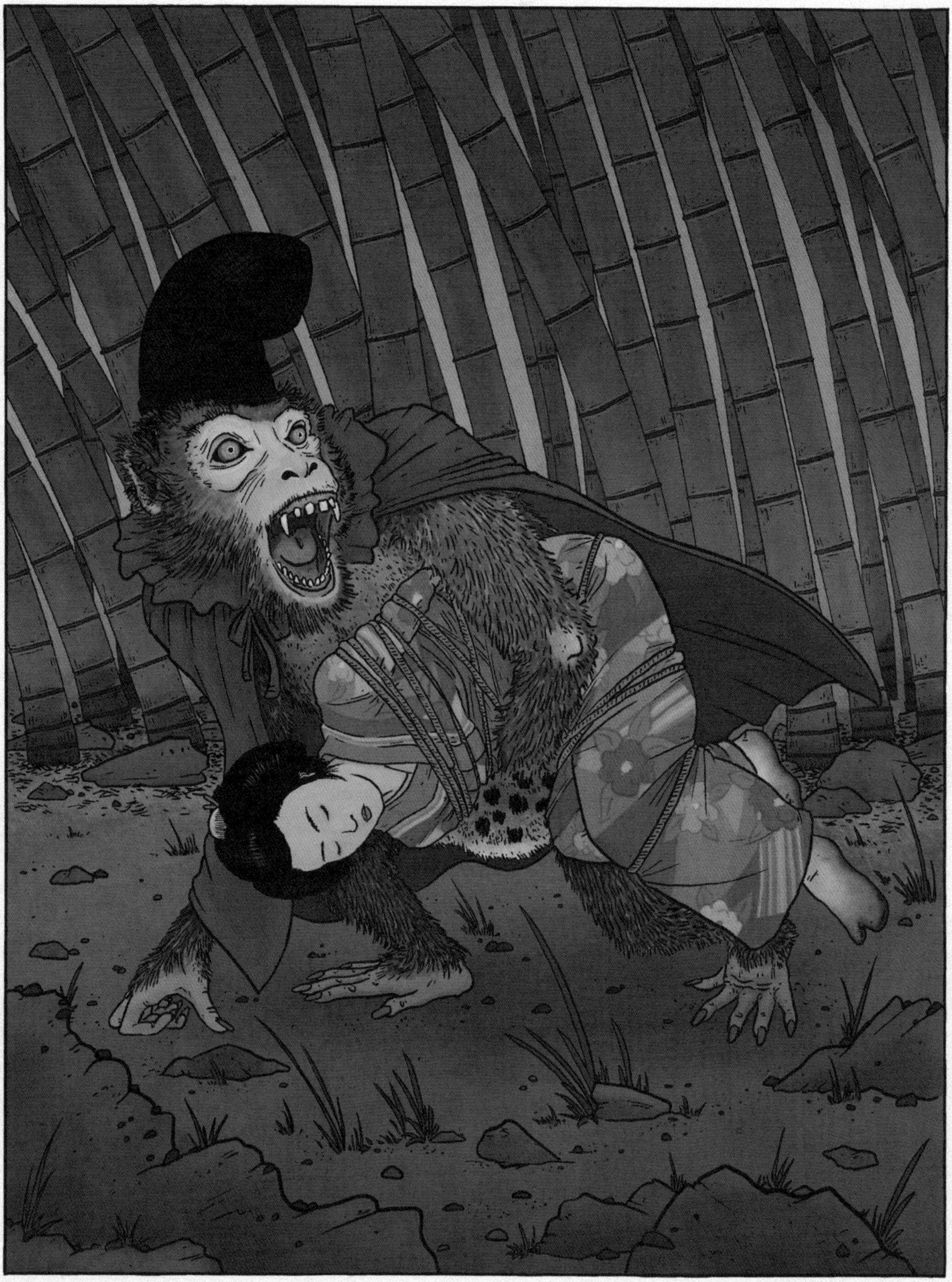

OBARIYON おばりよん

TRANSLATION: piggyback rider
ALTERNATE NAMES: bariyon, onbu obake, ubariyon, obosaritei
HABITAT: human-inhabited areas, near roads
DIET: unknown

APPEARANCE: Obariyon are child-sized monsters from Niigata prefecture which love riding on people's backs.

INTERACTIONS: Obariyon lurk in bushes and trees by the side of the road. When a traveler walks by an obariyon's hiding place, it leaps out onto their back and shouts, "obariyon!" If the traveler relents and carries the obariyon on his back, the monster becomes heavier and heavier with each footstep. In addition, this mischievous yōkai chews on the scalp of the person carrying it, further adding to their misery. To protect against an obariyon's head-chewing, some villages developed the custom of wearing metal bowls on their heads.

According to some tales, as the obariyon becomes heavier and heavier, it eventually crushes its victim under its weight. However, more commonly, when a person has dutifully carried the obariyon the whole way home, it turns out that the strange burden was actually a sack of money. The helpful bearer becomes incredibly rich.

ORIGIN: The name obariyon comes from a phrase in a local Niigata dialect requesting a piggyback ride. Differences in local dialects are reflected in the many different names for this spirit. Though it varies from place to place, it is always some form of a childish request to be carried piggyback.

Although the exact origins of this particular creature are unclear, folk tales about yōkai which demand to be carried or cared for are common across Japan. There is a recurring theme that those who persevere when dealing with children will prosper. Just as those who put up with the strange demands of the obariyon may find themselves blessed with a bag of gold, those who manage to deal with the demands of raising young children will eventually reap the rewards. In this way, obariyon may be a metaphor for child-rearing. While the demands of the obariyon seem selfish and burdensome, those who are willing to endure for the entire journey find that the hard work was worth it in the end.

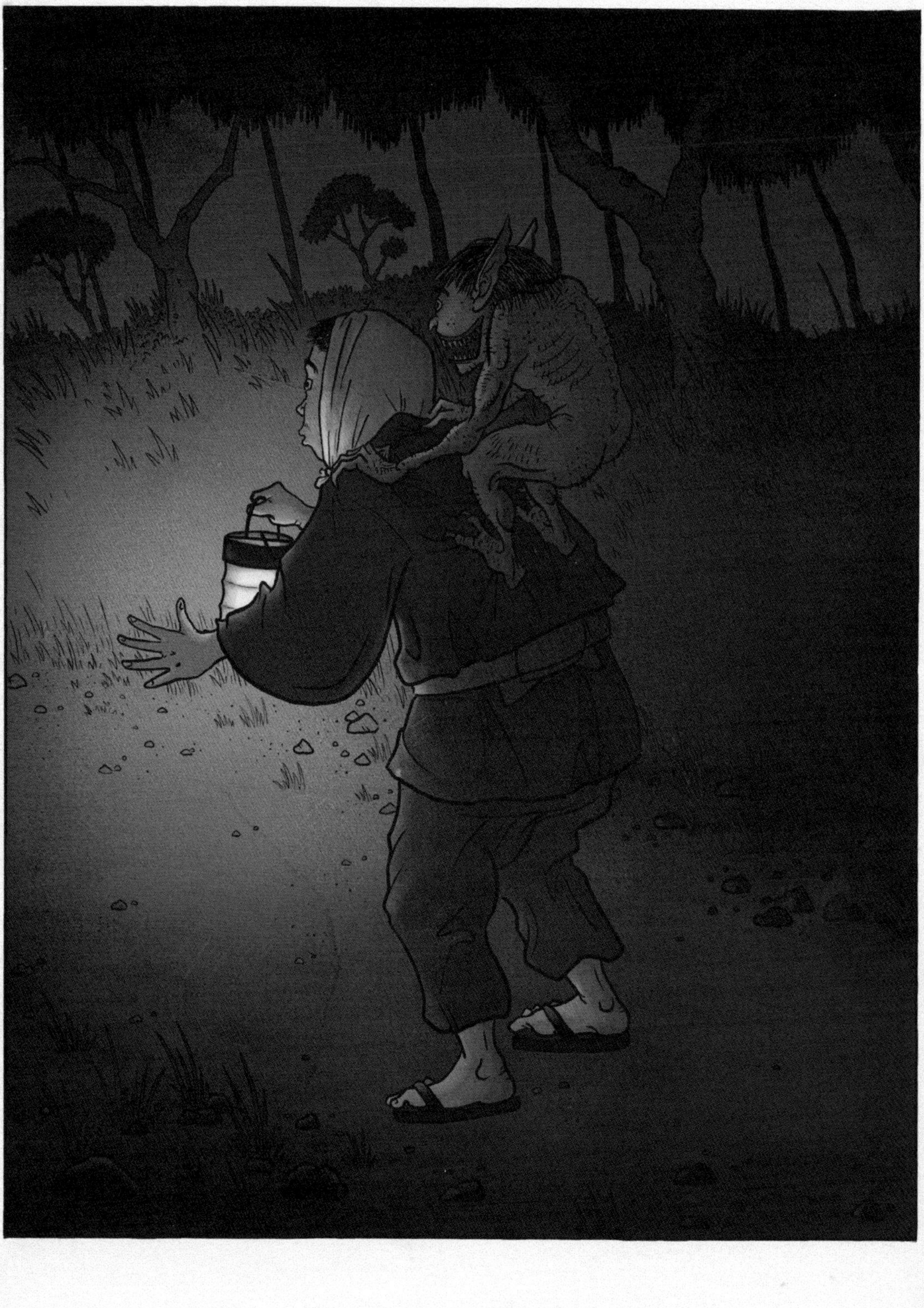

Kenmun 水蝹

TRANSLATION: water spirit
ALTERNATE NAMES: kenmon, kawatarō, yamawaro
HABITAT: the Amami islands
DIET: primarily fish and shellfish

APPEARANCE: Kenmun are hairy water and tree spirits from the Amami islands in southern Japan. They look like a cross between a kappa and a monkey. Kenmun closely resemble their Okinawan cousins, kijimunā. Their bodies are covered in dark red or black hair, and they have long, thin legs and arms. They are slightly larger in size than a human child. Their mouths are pointed, and on top of their heads is a saucer-like depression which holds a small amount of oil or water. Their bodies smell like yams. Their drool is rank.

BEHAVIOR: Kenmun live in banyan trees and spend their days in family groups playing in the mountains or near the water. They particularly enjoy sumo wrestling, at which they are highly skilled. As the seasons change, they migrate back and forth from the mountains to the sea.

Kenmun have a number of strange abilities. They are able to change shape and often disguise themselves as people, horses, or cows. They can change into plants and blend in with the surrounding vegetation, or even disappear entirely. Kenmun also create light. Their drool glows eerily, as do their fingertips. They can create fire from the tips of their fingers. Sometimes they use this fire to light the oil in their head-dishes. When phantom lights are seen in the mountains or on the shores of the Amami islands, locals attribute this to kenmun.

Kenmun hunt at night. They light up their fingertips to search for food in the dark. They primarily feed on fish and small shellfish. They also enjoy slugs, and they pull snails out of their shells and roll them up like rice balls. (It is possible to identify a banyan tree inhabited by a kenmun by the snail shells piled up among its roots.) They hate octopus and giant clams and will have nothing to do with them.

INTERACTIONS: Kenmun avoid inhabited areas and flee when large groups of people are nearby. They occasionally aid lone woodcutters and people gathering firewood by carrying heavy loads for them. They remember those who treat them kindly or do them favors. A fisherman who saves a kenmun from being attacked by an octopus is sure to earn its eternal gratitude. Some elderly islanders who have befriended kenmun are able to call them down from the mountains to show their grandchildren. They love competition, especially sumō wrestling. When their head-dish is filled, they have supernatural strength and cannot be beaten. However, kenmun like to mimic people. If a challenger stands on their head or bows low, the kemun will do so too, spilling their head-dish and draining their strength.

Kenmun enjoy pranks. They shapeshift into animals and try to scare humans. Or they offer false directions to make people helplessly lost. They have no shame about stealing food and utensils.

Kenmun occasionally do wicked things. They are sensitive to insults, particularly about their body odors. If a person talks about bad smells or farts while in the mountains, any kenmun who overhears it will take it personally. Kenmun can steal the souls of living humans, turning them catatonic. They then pull them into rivers or force them to eat snails. Their victims are later found unconscious beneath banyan trees. Even children can have had their souls stolen. Afterwards, they will behave like kenmun, living in banyan trees and leaping from tree to tree when villagers try to catch them. If a kenmun's banyan tree is cut, the kenmun will place a curse on the woodcutter. The victim's eyes will swell up and go blind. Eventually they will die.

Hanging a pig's foot bones or *Pittosporum tobira* branches from the eaves of rooves keeps kenmun away. Threatening to throw an octopus at one is enough to send them running. If an octopus is not available, they will run away from anything you throw as long as you pretend it's an octopus.

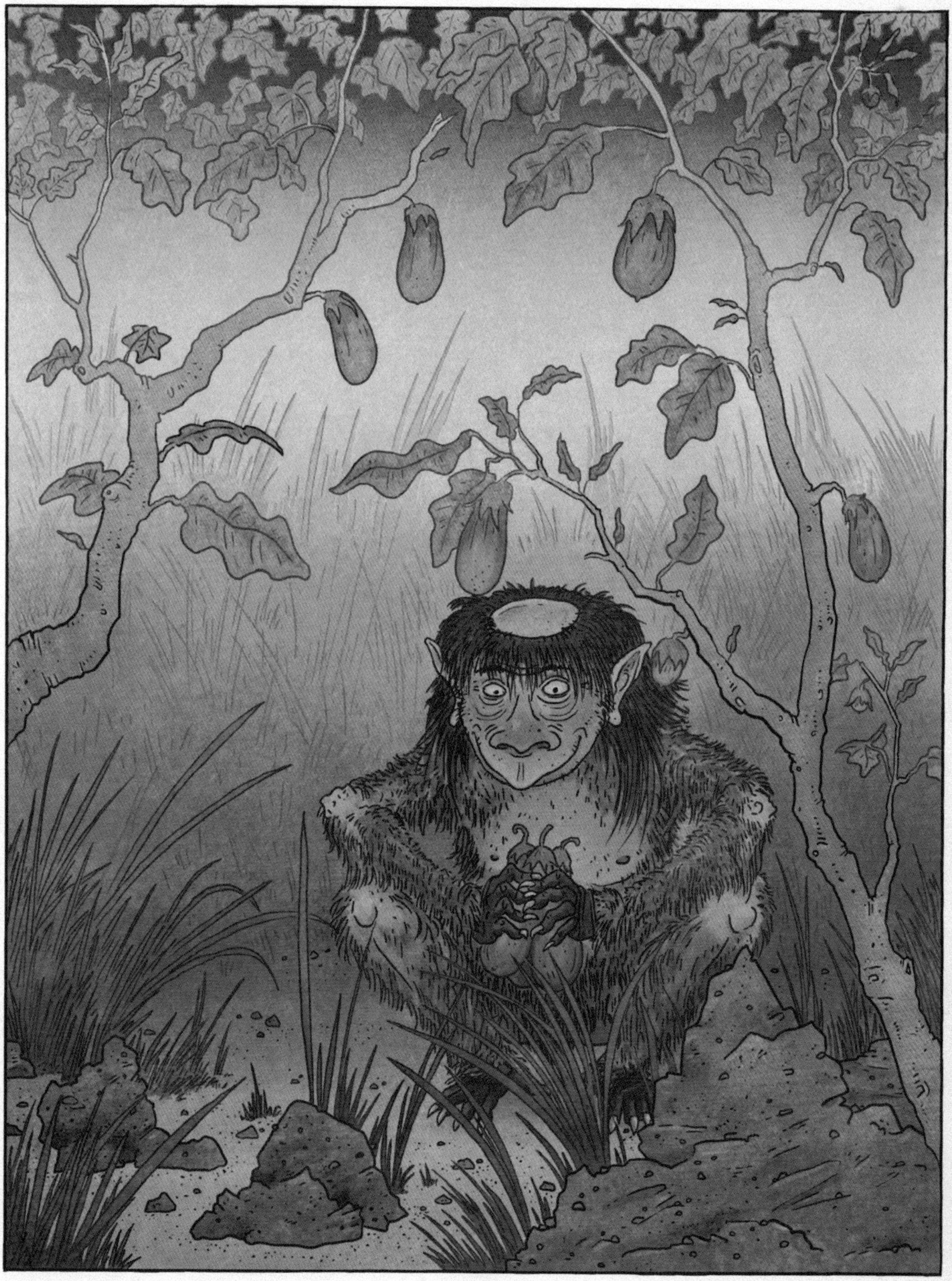

Bashō no sei 芭蕉精

TRANSLATION: banana tree spirit
HABITAT: the Ryūkyū archipelago

APPEARANCE: Bashō no sei are the spirits of the Japanese banana tree (*Musa basjoo*). Banana trees are native to the islands of Okinawa but are common in ornamental gardens across Asia. Bashō no sei usually appear as human faces amongst the broad, flat banana leaves. Stories about banana tree spirits are numerous across Japanese, Chinese, and Ryūkyūan folklore.

INTERACTIONS: Bashō no sei are not usually hostile or threatening towards people. They generally limit themselves to startling humans by suddenly appearing next to them. For example, in one story a bashō no sei takes the form of a young woman, appears next to a meditating monk, and asks him if even inanimate plants can attain Buddhahood.

Bashō no sei are not completely without danger. They sometimes assault and even impregnate humans. According to some superstitions, women should not to walk near banana trees past 6 pm. If they do, they will surely run into a yōkai among the broad leaves. Sometimes bashō no sei appear as monsters. Other times as handsome young men. Whatever the form, shortly after the woman will become pregnant. Her baby will be born with tusks or fangs like that of a demon. What's more, the following year and every year after that, the woman will give birth to more demon children. Whenever such creatures are born they must be killed by feeding them a poisonous drink made of powdered *kumazasa* (a type of bamboo grass). This is supposedly the reason why kumazasa is commonly found growing near houses in Okinawa.

ORIGIN: The Edo period herbalist Satō Chūryō recorded his observations about these spirits in an essay. According to him, Ryūkyū's banana orchards were so large that they contained rows of trees many miles long. If you walked past them at night, you were guaranteed to experience something strange. He observed that the spirits that come out of the banana trees did not cause direct harm to people other than spooking them. Nevertheless, they could be avoided if you carried a sword.

Chūryō theorized that banana trees weren't necessarily unique in having spirits. However, because their leaves are so large, and they were planted in such large numbers, it is particularly easy for humans to see these trees' spirits. He believed that was the reason for the large number of superstitions about banana trees in comparison with other plants.

LEGENDS: In Nagano Prefecture, a priest was sitting outside and reciting sutras when a beautiful young woman appeared and attempted to seduce him. The priest grew angry. He stabbed the woman with his sword and she ran away. The next morning, the priest found a bloody trail left by the woman he had stabbed. The trail lead to the temple's gardens, where a bashō tree was lying on the ground, cut in two. The priest then realized that the woman had been the spirit of the tree.

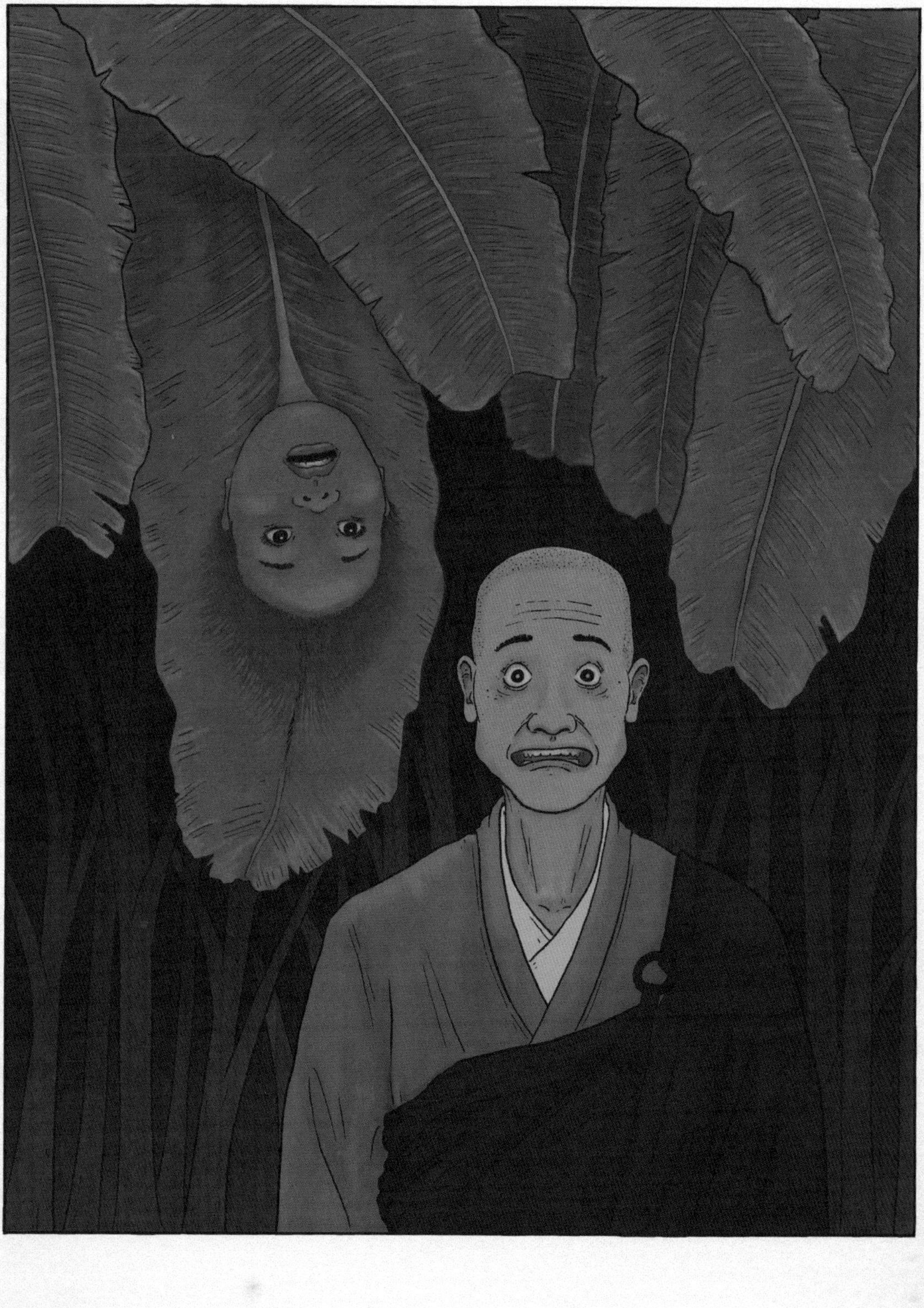

Ninmenju 人面樹

TRANSLATION: human face tree
ALTERNATE NAMES: jinmenju
HABITAT: mountain valleys

APPEARANCE: The ninmenju is a strange tree which bears flowers that look like human heads. These heads cannot speak, but they can smile and even laugh. In the autumn, they bear face-shaped fruit which tastes both sweet and sour.

INTERACTIONS: If a person laughs at the tree, the head-shaped flowers will laugh back at that person. If they laugh too strongly, the heads will wilt and fall off the trees.

ORIGIN: The ninmenju is an example of folklore that has traveled over great time and distance to become what it is.

Ninmenju first appears in Japan in the Edo Period encyclopedia *Wakan sansai zue*. This book documented animals, plants, and yōkai from both inside and outside of Japan. The description is paraphrased from the *Sansai zue* (Chinese: *Sancai tuhui*), an encyclopedia published in 1609. This book describes a tree bearing human-faced fruit which originated in the foreign land of Daishi (大食). Daishi comes from the Ming Chinese name for the Islamic world, which in turn comes from the Persian word for Muslims—*tāzī*. This was derived from the Tayy, an Arabic tribe which flourished under the Abbasid Caliphate.

There is a tree in Islamic folklore called the waq waq tree which is similar to the ninmenju. This tree was described as bearing fruit shaped like humans and animals. The fruit could speak, and even tell secrets about the future. Yet it would die a few days after being picked. These trees grew on the mythical island of Waq Waq in the land of Zanj, an area in Africa near present-day Zanzibar. Arab legends say that Alexander the Great spoke to a waq waq tree during his conquests, and it foretold his death.

The waq waq tree may in fact be the same tree which comes from Daishi and is referred to in *Wakan sansai zue*. Through trade along the Silk Road between the Islamic world and Ming China, it is possible that this Arabic myth made its way across the Asian continent and eventually became the model for the ninmenju.

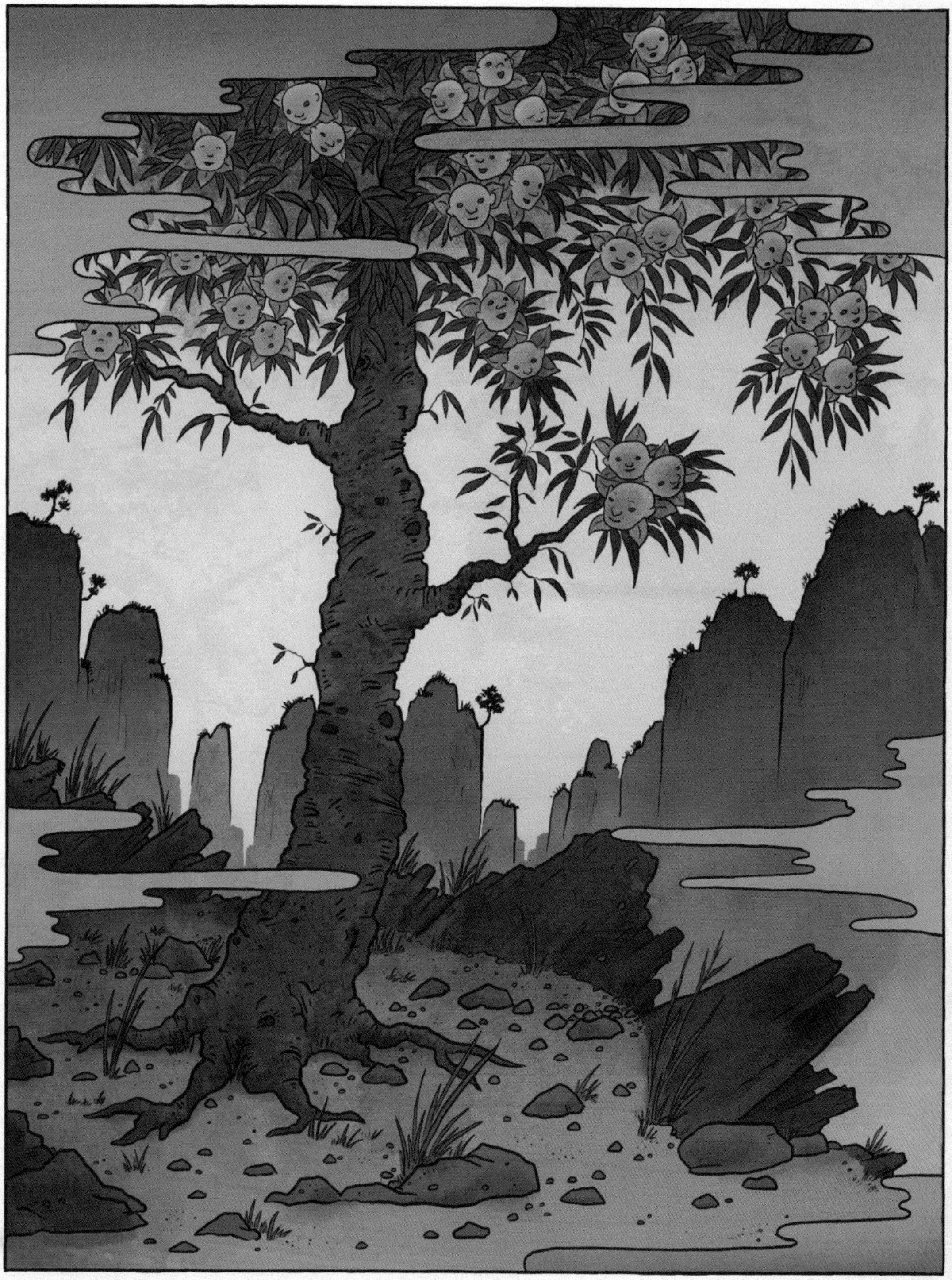

Akateko 赤手児

TRANSLATION: red child hand
HABITAT: Japanese honey locust (*Gleditsia japonica*) trees
DIET: none

APPEARANCE: The akateko appears as its name implies: as a red, disembodied hand belonging to a child. They can be found hanging in Japanese honey locust trees.

INTERACTIONS: An akateko drops down from its tree as people pass underneath it. Aside from giving its victims a nasty surprise and the general creepiness of a disembodied red child's hand, it is not known to cause harm.

Some people claim to have seen the figure of a furisode-wearing beautiful girl of 17 or 18 years standing underneath an akateko's tree. Those who witness her are immediately struck with a powerful fever. It is not clear what relationship this girl has to the akateko—if she is part of the same apparition or another spirit entirely.

ORIGIN: The origin of akateko is said to be a certain tree in front of an elementary school in the city of Hachinohe, Aomori Prefecture. However, there are local versions of this phenomenon in Fukushima and Kagawa Prefectures as well. In these prefectures, akateko sometimes work together with another yōkai called aka ashi. They grab at the feet of pedestrians, causing them to stumble and fall. It has been suggested that akateko and aka ashi are two forms of the same yōkai.

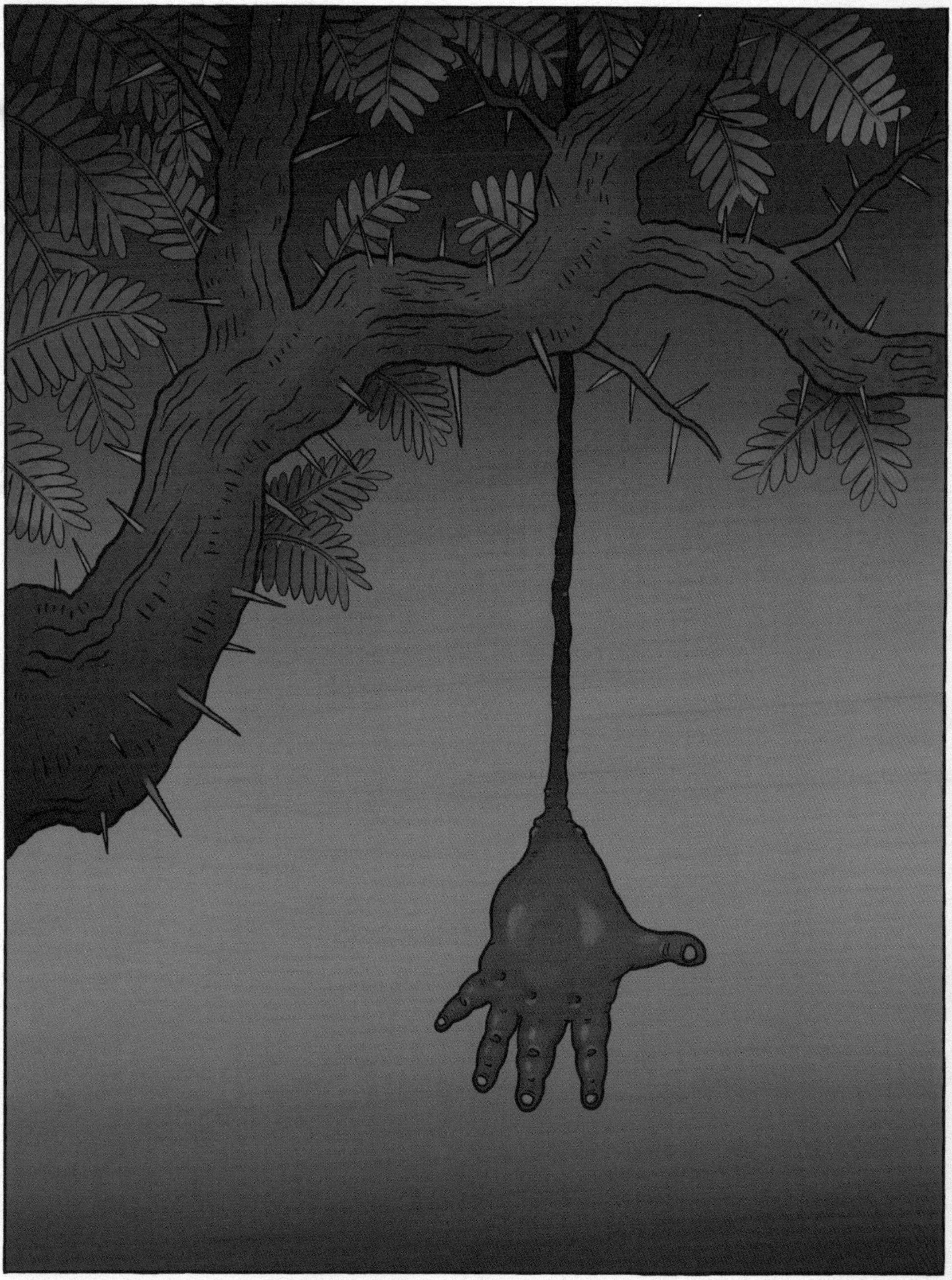

TEKE TEKE テケテケ

TRANSLATION: onomatopoeic; the sound of her walking on her hands
ALTERNATE NAMES: shaka shaka, pata pata, kata kata, koto koto, hijikake babā
HABITAT: urban areas, along roads
DIET: none; survives solely on its grudge

APPEARANCE: Teke teke are ghosts who appear in a number of urban legends. They are almost always women, though in a few versions of this urban legend they are male. Teke teke appear as someone cut in half at the waste, running about on their hands. This creates the distinctive *teke teke* sound from which they get their name.

INTERACTIONS: Teke teke chase their victims down dark roads. Despite having no legs, a teke teke can run fast enough to catch victims escaping in speeding cars. It can supposedly crawl at speeds of up to 150 km per hour. When a teke teke catches its victims, *something* terrible happens—although the legends are not always clear what. In some versions of the story, the teke teke carries a sickle. It slices its victims in half at the waist and steals their legs. Some say that she is searching for her lost legs. Others say that she is angry at humanity for not helping her when she was alive—she is simply out to slaughter as many people as she can.

ORIGIN: Every town has its own version of the teke teke urban legend. In some stories the teke teke was the victim of a tragic accident. In others it was suicide. In some stories magic charms can protect you from its wrath. In others, nothing can protect you; death is certain. Sometimes the teke teke's victims even become teke teke themselves. There are so many versions of the legend that it is impossible to know what the original story was, or where it began. However, a number of common threads point towards a woman from Hokkaidō named Kashima Reiko.

LEGENDS: In the years after World War II, Kashima Reiko, an office worker in Muroran, Hokkaidō, was assaulted and raped by American military personnel. That night, she leaped off a bridge onto the railroad tracks and was hit by an oncoming train. The impact was so forceful that her body was torn in half at the waist. The severe cold of the Hokkaidō night caused her blood vessels to contract and prevented her from bleeding out. Instead, she writhed in pain for several minutes. She crawled along the tracks all the way to the station where she was seen by an attendant. Instead of trying to help her, the station attendant covered her with a plastic tarp. She died a slow, agonizing death.

Shortly after hearing the legend, Kashima Reiko will appear and ask you a riddle. This will come either in a dream or in a mysterious phone call. The only way to escape death is to answer her questions exactly the right way. She will ask you: "Do you need your legs?" You must reply: "I need them right now." Then, she will ask you: "Who told you my story?" You must reply: "Kashima Reiko." (The kanji used for her name are specific: *ka* as in mask (仮面); *shi* as in death (死); *ma* as in demon (魔); *rei* as in ghost (霊); *ko* as in accident (事故). If you answer her riddles without mistakes, she may let you live.

If you fail to answer her questions accurately, three days later you will see the ghost of a woman with no lower half. The teke teke will try to catch you. When she does, she will tear you in half and steal your lower body.

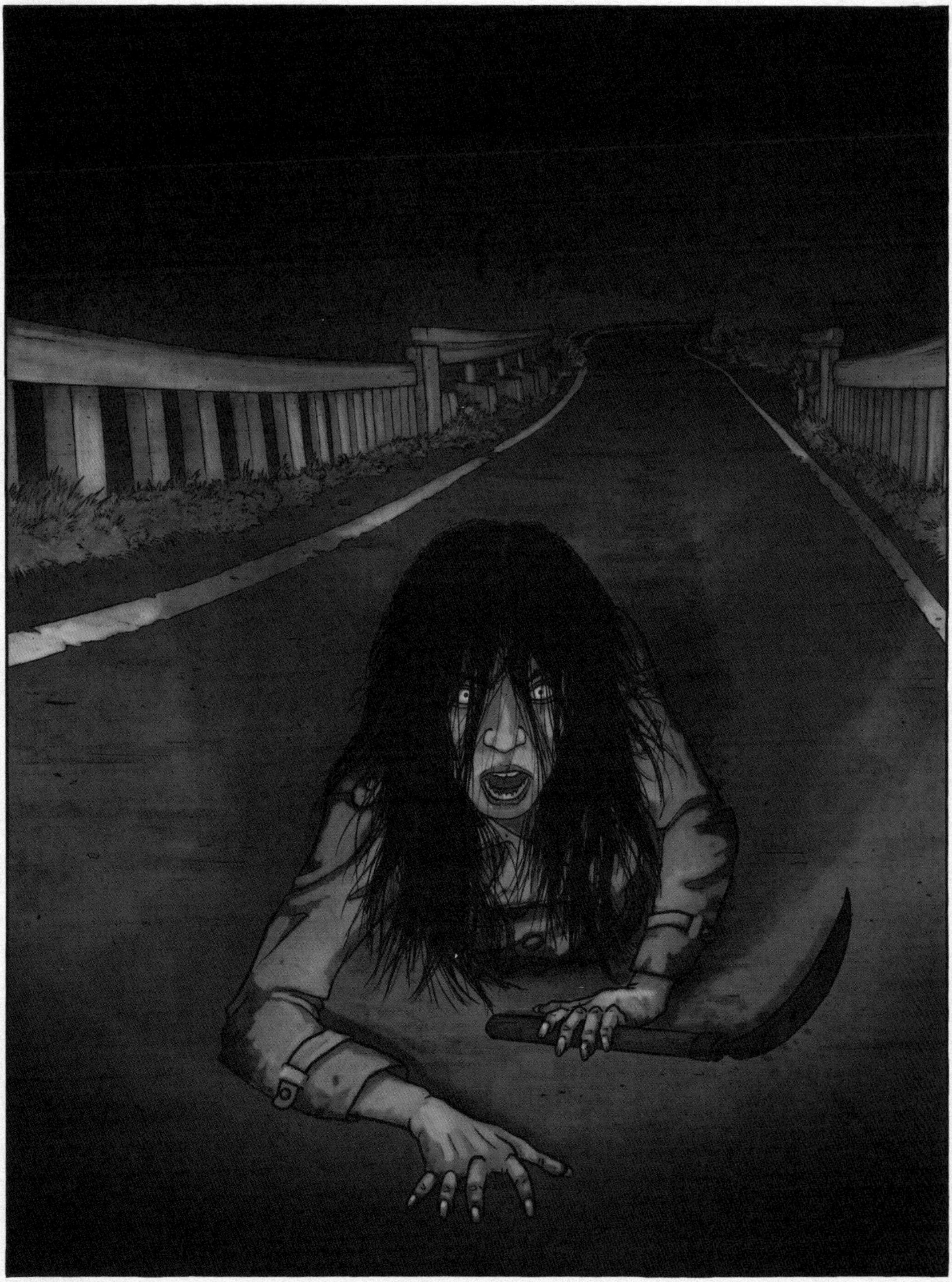

Hōsōshi 方相氏

TRANSLATION: minister of the four directions; the one who sees in all directions

APPEARANCE: A hōsōshi wears the mask of an oni and special robes (the particular outfit varies depending on which shrine the ritual is being performed at). It carries a spear in its right hand and a shield in its left. In ancient times, hōsōshi were official government ministers and priests in the imperial court. The name refers not only to the title, but to a demon god which priests would dress up as during yearly purification rituals. This god appears as a four-eyed oni who can see in all directions and punishes all evil.

BEHAVIOR: During the early Heian Period, the hōsōshi's duties included leading coffins during state funeral processions, officiating at burial ceremonies, and driving corpse-stealing yōkai away from burial mounds. By donning the mask and costume, the hōsōshi (priest) became the hōsōshi (god) and was able to scare away evil spirits. The hōsōshi's most famous duty was a purification ceremony called *tsuina*.

Tsuina was performed annually on Ōmisoka—the last day of the year. The ritual was done at shrines and government buildings (such as the imperial palace). In this ritual, the hōsōshi and his servant would run around the shrine courtyard (covering "the four directions"), chanting and warding the area against oni and other evil spirits. Meanwhile, a number of attending officials would shoot arrows around the hōsōshi from the shrine or palace buildings, symbolically defending the area against evil spirits. Other observers would play small hand drums with ritualistic cleansing significance.

ORIGIN: *Hōsō* was a concept related to divination, the four directions, and the magical barriers between the human world and the spirit world. It dealt with creating and maintaining these boundaries and barriers. This included things like planting trees or placing stones in the four corners of an area or utilizing existing features like rivers and roads to serve as natural boundaries. By maintaining these natural boundaries, the spiritual boundaries between the worlds could also be maintained. The ultimate goal was keeping the imperial family and other government officials safe from supernatural harm.

The concept originated in ancient Chinese folk religion, where it is called *fangxiang*. The *fangxiangshi* was an exorcist who wore a four eyed mask and a bear skin. Over time, Chinese folk religion mixed with Buddhism and Taoism, and then made its way to Japan. The Japanese hōsōshi's rituals and costume were derived from this syncretic folk belief.

Eventually the Japanese version evolved away from its Chinese roots. The hōsōshi came to be seen not as a god which keeps oni away, but as an oni itself. Rather than exorcising evil spirits, the hōsōshi became an evil spirit. It was the imperial officials who chased away and exorcised the hōsōshi. This may have been due to changing perceptions during the Heian Period about the concept of ritual purity. The hōsōshi, associated with funerals and dead bodies, came to be viewed as unclean. It was inappropriate for such a creature to be on the same side as the imperial household, so it became the target of the ritual instead of the officiator.

While the governmental position of hōsōshi no longer exists today, some shrines still perform annual tsuina rituals involving the hōsōshi. The celebration of Setsubun, in which beans are thrown at people wearing oni masks, is also derived from this ancient ritual.

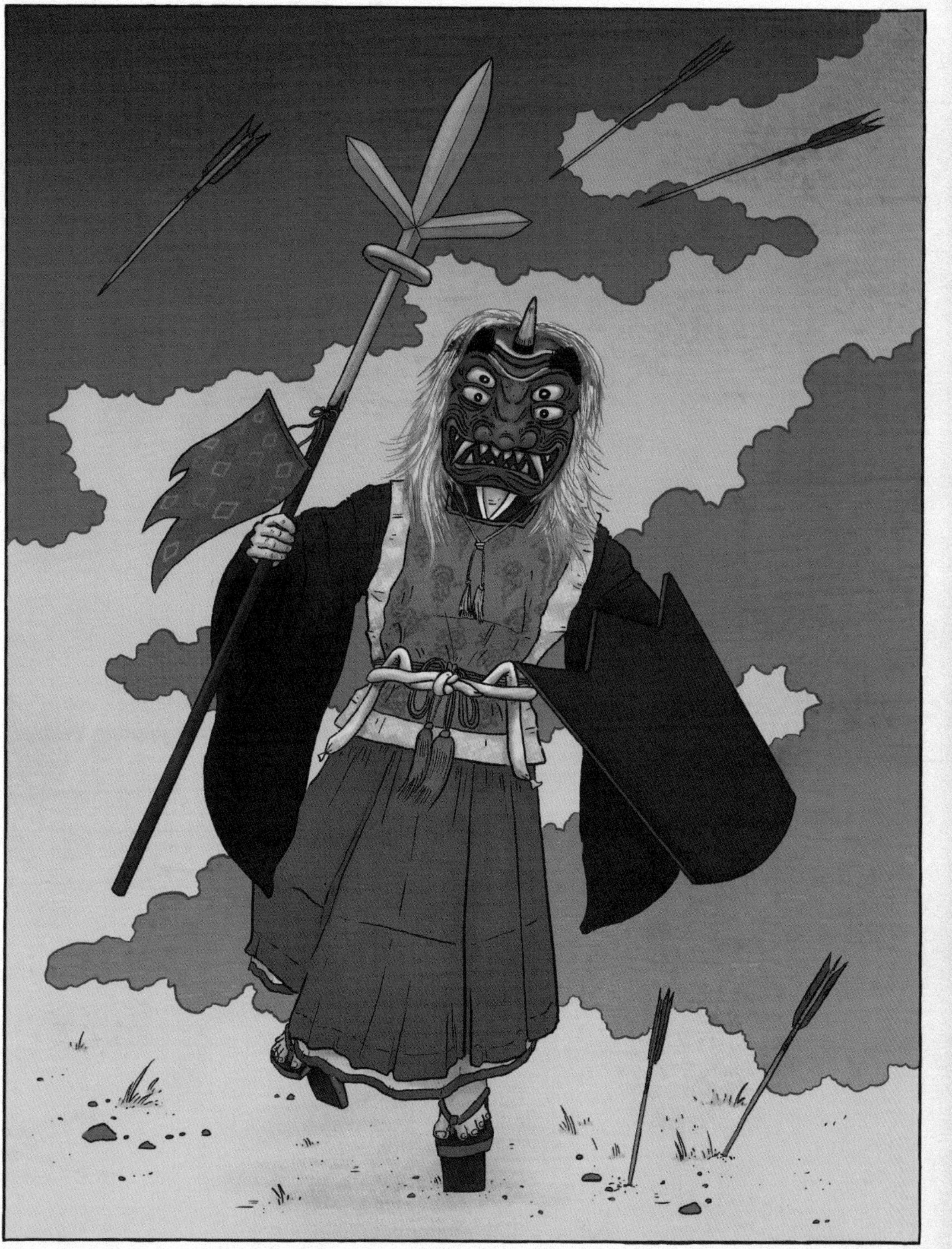

SHŌKI 鍾馗

TRANSLATION: none; this is the Japanese pronunciation of his Chinese name

APPEARANCE: Shōki (known in Chinese as Zhong Kui) is a legendary hero and deity from ancient China. He is ugly, with a large hulking body, a long flowing beard, and fearsome piercing eyes. He is usually shown carrying a sword and wearing a court official's cap. Due to his ability to vanquish, exorcise, and even control oni and other spirits, Shōki is known as "the demon queller." He is so feared by oni that his image alone scares them away. The demons he defeats sometimes become his servants. It is said that he commands 80,000 demons.

ORIGIN: Shōki originated in ancient China during the 700s. His story reached Japan by the late Heian Period, and his popularity reached its height during the Edo Period. Paintings and statues of him are still used as good luck charms. Shōki's image appears on flags, folding screens, and hanging scrolls. Small statues of him can sometimes be seen on the roofs of older houses in Kyōto. Shōki is strongly associated with Boys' Day, a holiday in May. He is revered as a god of protection from demons and sickness (particularly smallpox, which was believed to be spread by evil spirits). He is also a god of scholarship.

LEGENDS: Shōki lived in Shanxi Province in China during the Tang dynasty. His life's goal was to become a physician in the court of Emperor Xuanzong. Shōki was a smart and diligent student. He trained hard and passed all the exams to become a physician. He placed first out of all the applicants and should have easily received the position. However, Shōki was tremendously ugly. When the emperor saw his face, he immediately rejected Shōki's application even though he was the most qualified for the job.

Shōki was devastated. His dreams shattered, he committed suicide on the steps of the imperial palace. The emperor was moved by Shōki's dedication. He regretted denying the application of such a talented and brilliant man because of his looks. The emperor decreed that Shōki receive a state burial of the highest rank—an honor usually reserved for royalty. He then posthumously awarded Shōki the title "Doctor of Zhongnanshan."

Years later, the emperor became gravely ill. Delirious with fever, he dreamed that he saw two oni. The larger one was wearing the clothing of a court official. It grabbed the smaller oni, killed it, and ate it. Then, it turned to the emperor and introduced itself as Shōki. He vowed to protect the emperor from evil. When the emperor woke up, his fever was gone.

Xuanzong commissioned the court painter to make a painting of Shōki based on his dream. Shōki became a popular deity across China (and later, Japan). He was revered as a god of scholarship for his great devotion to his studies, and as a protector against disease and evil spirits.

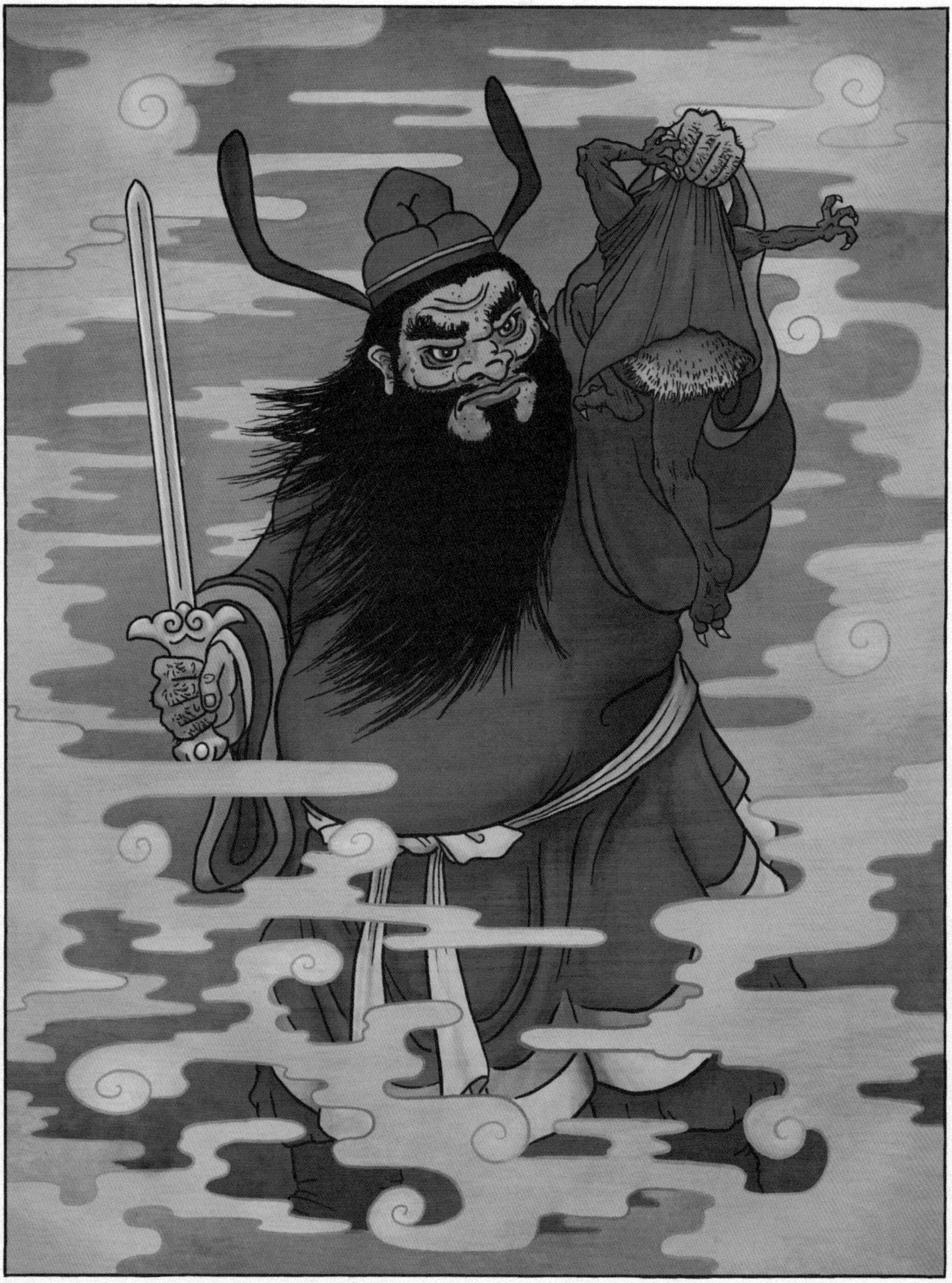

Sōjōbō 僧正坊

TRANSLATION: high priest
ALTERNATE NAMES: Kurama tengu, Kurama sōjōbō
HABITAT: Mount Kurama

APPEARANCE: Sōjōbō is the name of a great tengu who lives on Mount Kurama in the northern part of Kyōto. His home is in Sōjōgatani, a valley located deep within the interior of the mountain. Sōjōbō has long, white hair, an incredibly long nose, and possesses the strength of one thousand tengu. Sōjōbō is first in rank among tengu and is often referred to as their king. As the king of the tengu, Sōjōbō possesses a knowledge of magic, military tactics, and swordsmanship unsurpassed by any other.

ORIGIN: Sōjōbō is known through his connection to Kurama Temple, an isolated temple which practices a unique branch of esoteric Buddhism. Kurama Temple has long had a connection with both the ascetic mountain religions called yamabushi as well as the tengu which these religions revere. Because Sōjōbō resides there, Mount Kurama is also considered to be the mountain most important to tengu. According to Kurama Temple, Sōjōbō is either one rank below Maō-son— part of the holy trinity which is central to the Kurama faith—or is in fact an incarnation of Mao-son himself.

LEGENDS: Although his name is well known, not much is written about Sōjōbō. The most famous legend is that he trained a young boy named Ushiwakamaru. Ushiwakamaru wished to learn from him and traveled deep into Sōjōgatani to undergo a long and arduous training. This was a dangerous quest. Tengu are fierce and unpredictable, and Sōjōbō was rumored to eat children who wandered too deep into the forest. However, Sōjōbō was impressed with the young boy's bravery and agreed to train him.

Ushiwakamaru grew up to become Minamoto Yoshitsune, who lived from 1159-1189 CE. As one of the main heroes in *The Tale of the Heike*, Yoshitsune is still revered as one of Japan's most celebrated warriors. His unmatched swordsmanship is credited to the training he received from Sōjōbō, the tengu of Mount Kurama.

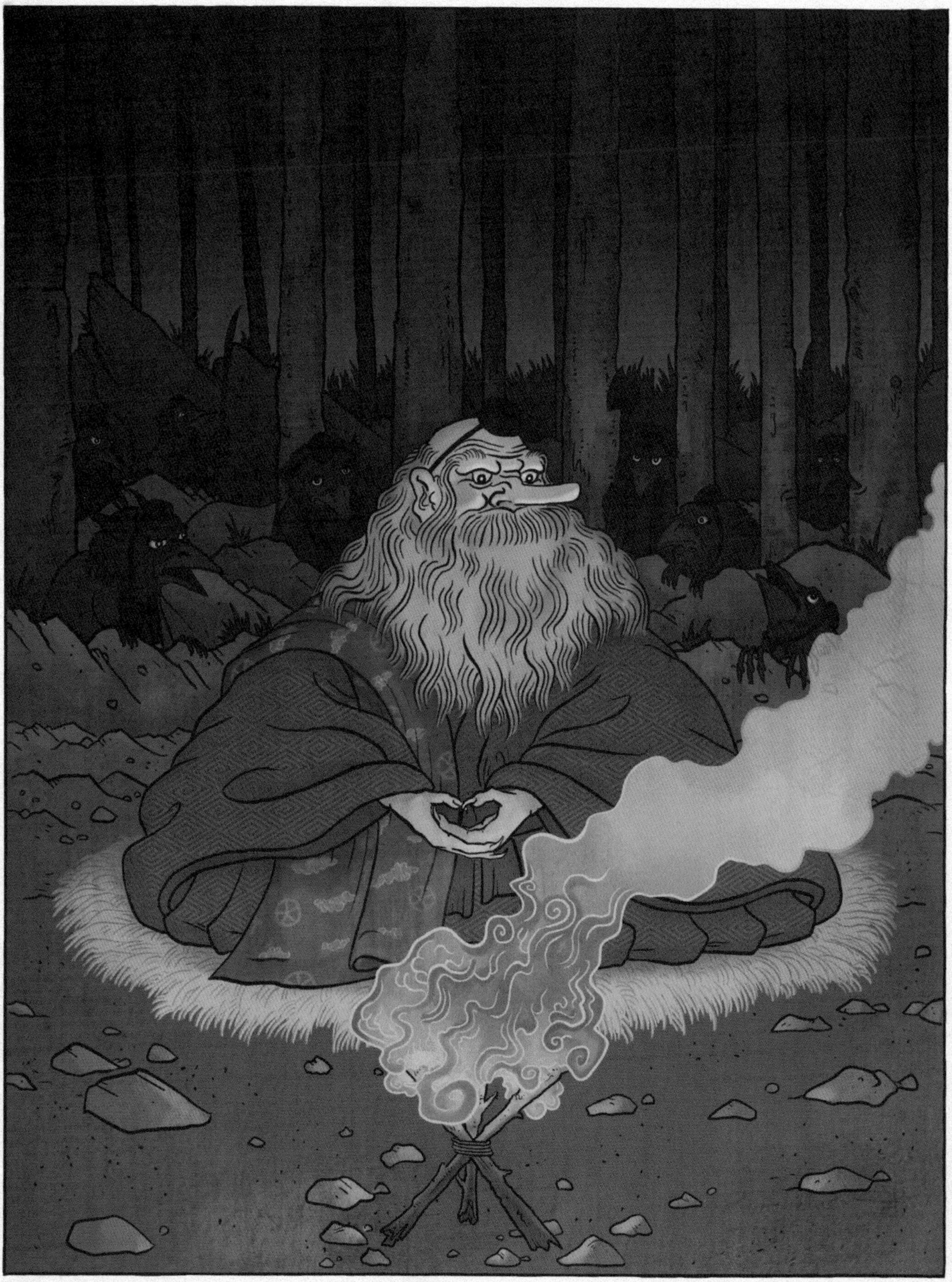

SHOKUIN 燭陰

TRANSLATION: torch shadow
ALTERNATE NAMES: Shokuryū (torch dragon)
HABITAT: Mount Shō, near the Arctic Ocean
DIET: none; he does not need to eat, drink, or breathe

APPEARANCE: Shokuin is a mighty god with the face of a human and the body of a red dragon. His serpentine body is said to be 1000 *ri* long (a ri is an ancient unit of distance which varies quite a bit from age to age and place to place). This is an immeasurable distance, meaning that he is impossibly large. He lives at the foot of Mount Shō, near the northern sea. His eyes glow like beams from a lighthouse and his breath is so strong that it changes the seasons.

BEHAVIOR: When Shokuin opens his eyes, daylight falls upon the earth. When he closes them, it becomes night. When he inhales it becomes summer. When he exhales it becomes winter. Shokuin does not need to eat, drink, or breathe to survive. But when he chooses to breathe it causes huge gusts of wind.

ORIGIN: Shokuin originally comes from China. Shokuin is the Japanese pronunciation of the characters that make up his name. In China he is known as Zhuyin or Zhulong. Many yōkai were lifted straight from Chinese by Japanese authors—some of them more or less word for word, others undergoing considerable transformation and reinterpretation depending on how much liberty the authors decided to take. Toriyama Sekien's description of Shokuin doesn't undergo too much of a change from his source. He copied the *Sengaikyō* (Chinese: *Shan hai jing*), an encyclopedia of fantastical Chinese mythological creatures. However, Shokuin appears in a number of other Chinese books. Many stories contain contradictory statements about precisely where he lives and other details about him. It isn't clear exactly where his home of Mount Shō is located. Toriyama Sekien describes it as being near the Arctic Ocean.

Due to his size and the effects that his blinking and breathing has on the day/night and seasonal cycles, Shokuin may have been an ancient Chinese fire or solar deity. He might even have been a personification of the sun. It has also been suggested that Shokuin may have been the aurora borealis. An ancient Chinese name for the northern lights was "red spirit," and the location of Shokuin far to the north further supports this theory. To the ancient Chinese, the aurora may have looked like a giant red dragon thousands of kilometers long writhing across the northern sky.

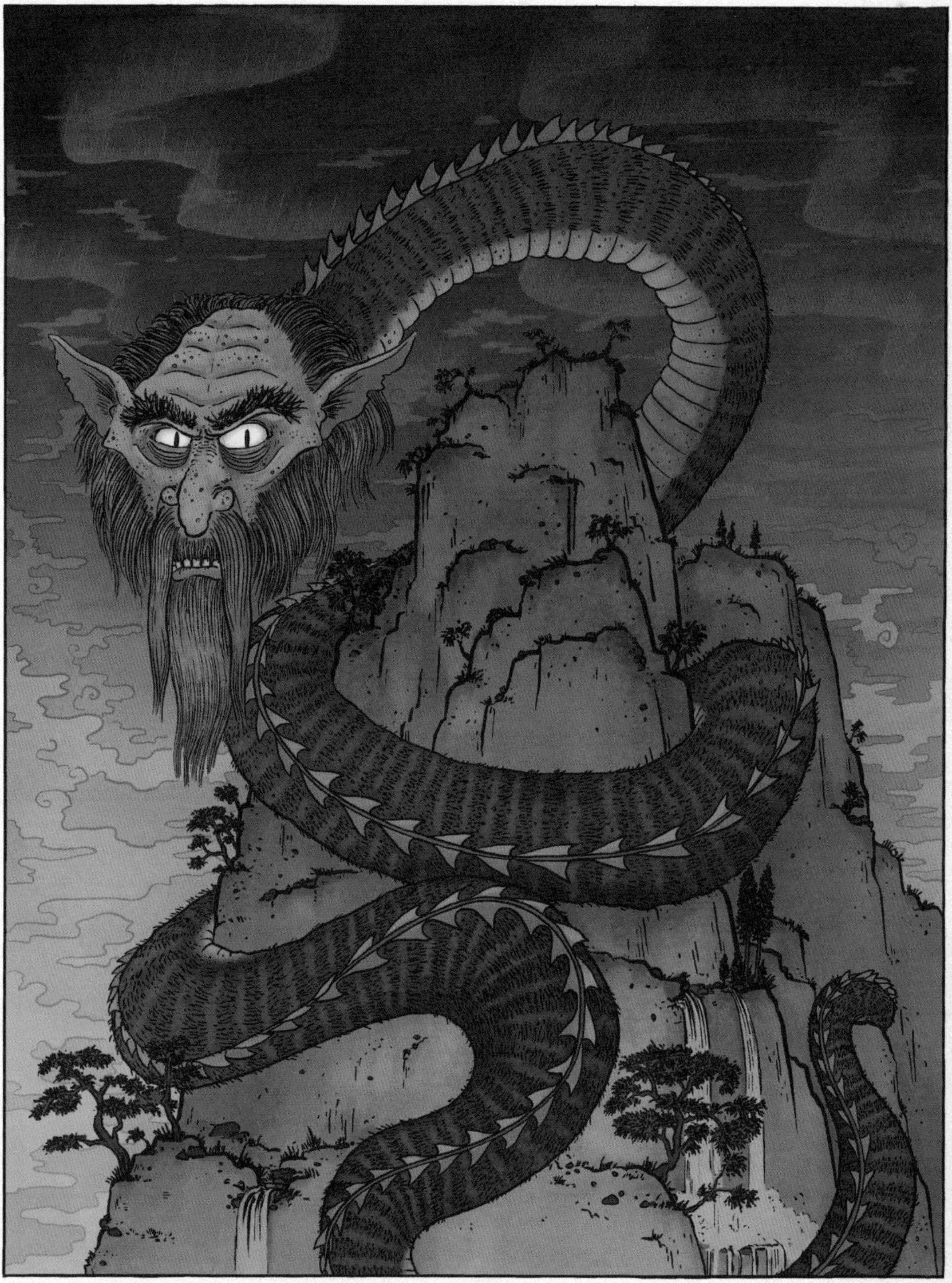

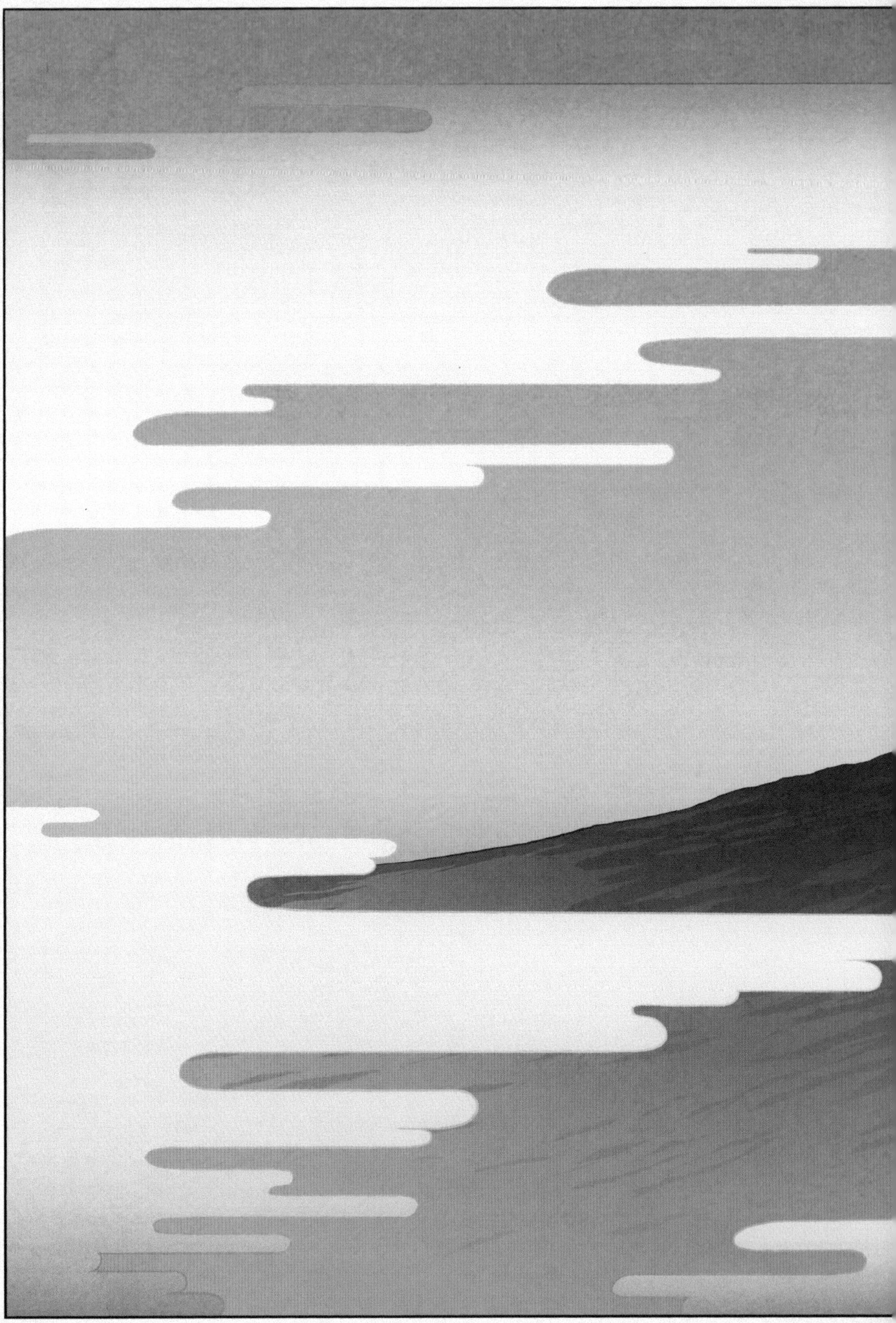

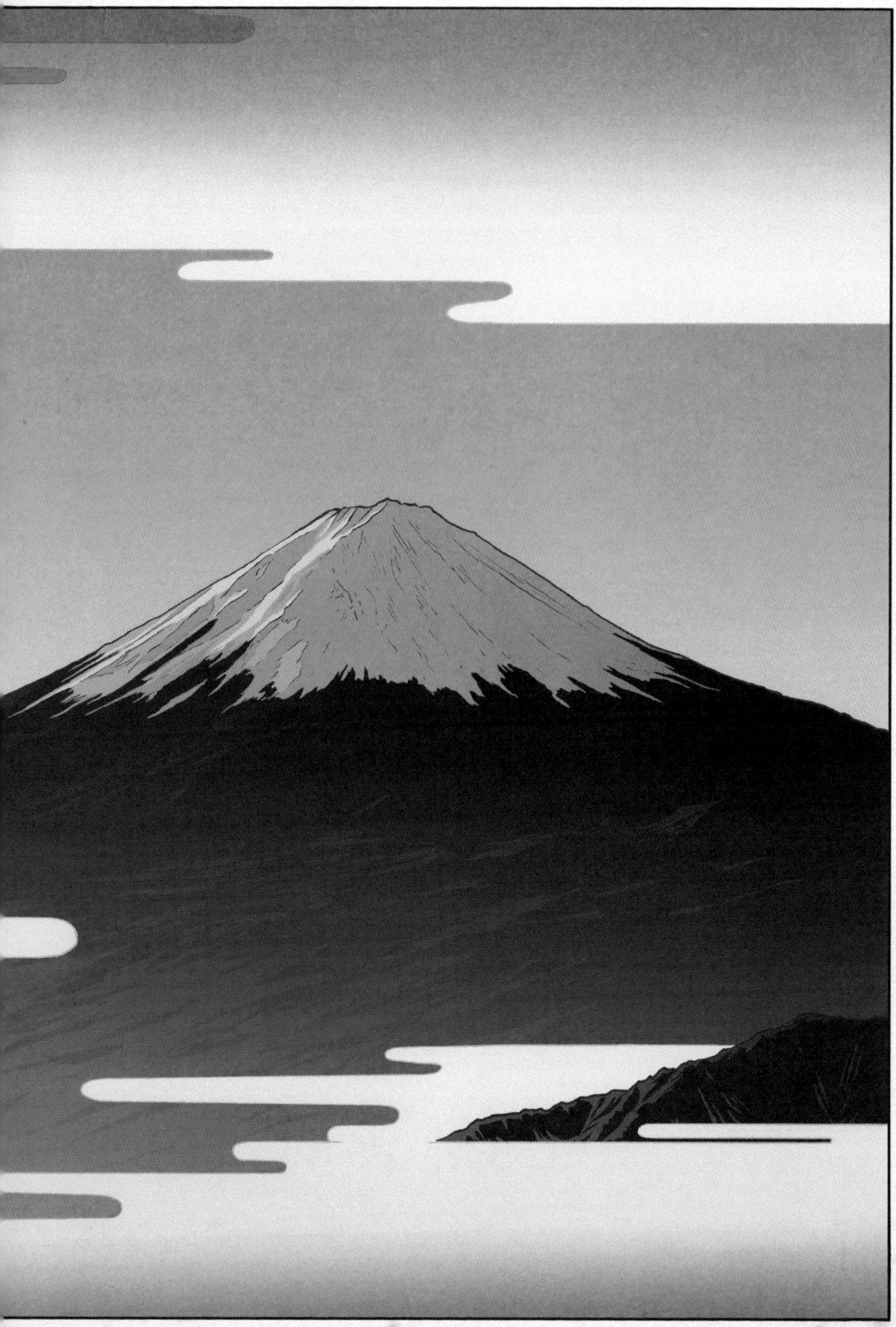

SEIRYŪ 青竜

TRANSLATION: azure dragon; Qinlong
ALTERNATE NAMES: Shōryū, Seiryō, Sōryū, Chinron
HABITAT: the eastern sky

APPEARANCE: Seiryū is a large blue-green dragon with a long tongue. Its home is in the eastern sky. It spans seven of the twenty-eight Chinese constellations, taking up one quarter of the night sky. The constellations which make up the horn and neck of the dragon are located in Virgo. The constellation which makes up the chest of the dragon is located in Libra. The constellations which make up its heart, belly, and tail are located in Scorpius. The final constellation makes up its dung and is located in Sagittarius.

INTERACTIONS: Seiryū is one of the shijin, or Four Symbols. These are important mythological figures in Taoism. Seiryū is the guardian of the east. The dragon is associated with the Chinese element of wood, the season of spring, the planet Jupiter, and the colors blue and green. It represents the virtue of benevolence and symbolizes creativity. Seiryū controls the rain. It is enshrined in Kyōto at Kiyomizu Temple, in the eastern part of the city.

THE FOUR HOLY BEASTS

Seiryū, Suzaku, Byakko, and Genbu make up a grouping of gods known as the *shijin*: The Four Holy Beasts. They are known by a number of different names, such as the Four Benevolent Animals and The Four Symbols. They were brought to Japan from China in the 7th century CE. They are strongly associated with Taoism, feng shui, the seasons, astrology, the five-element theory, and other forms of Chinese mysticism. The ancient capitals of Fujiwara-kyō, Heijo-kyō, and Heian-kyō were built in correspondence to these beliefs, with each of the quadrants of the city dedicated to one of the Four Symbols. Excavations of ancient burial mounds in Nara have revealed paintings of the shijin decorating the four directions on tomb walls.

After the Heian Period, the influence of astrology gradually waned. Worship of the Four Holy Beasts was supplanted by worship of the Four Heavenly Kings of Buddhism. However, their use as symbols continues.

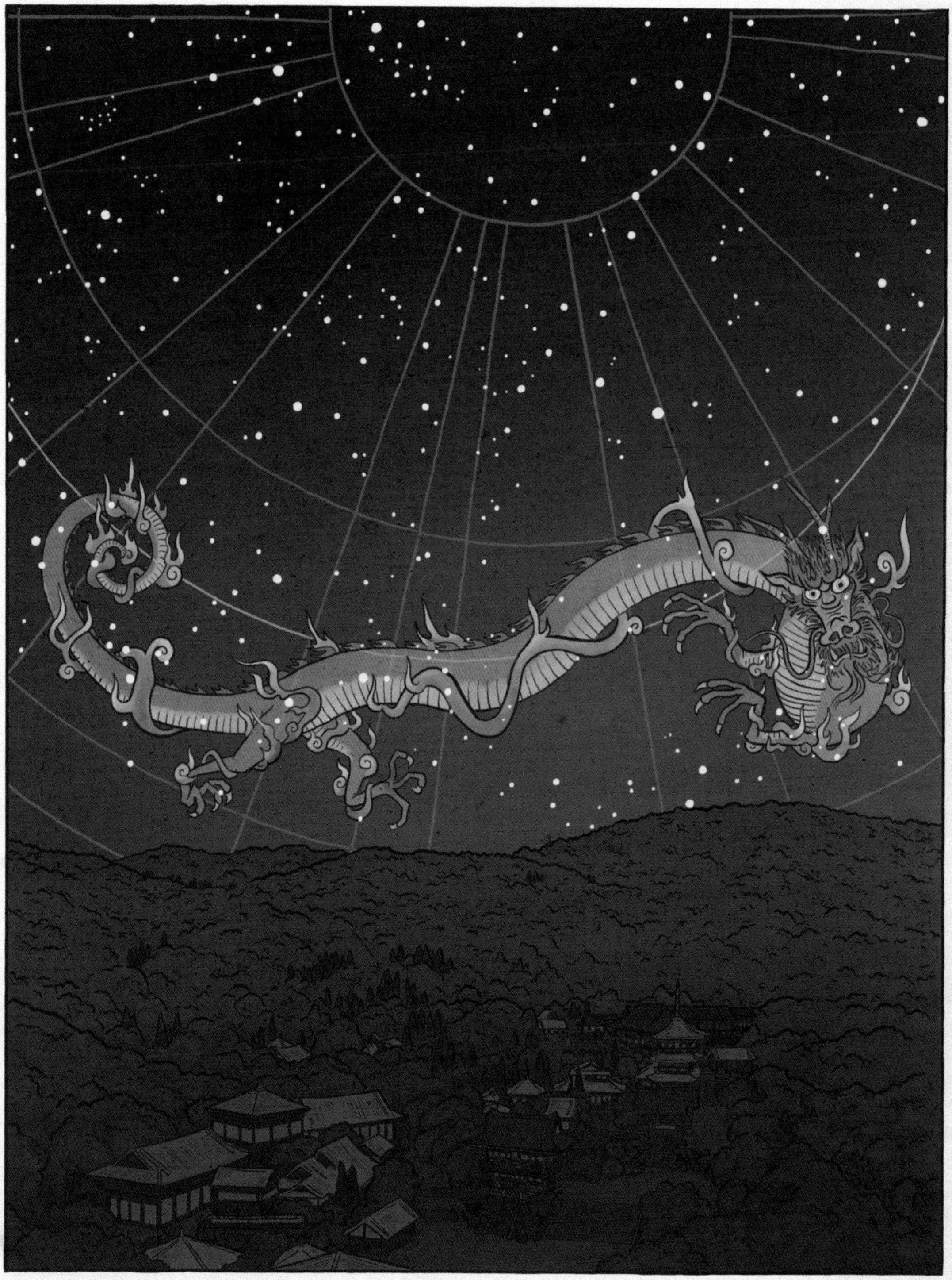

Suzaku 朱雀

TRANSLATION: vermilion bird; Zhuque
ALTERNATE NAMES: Sujaku, Shujaku, Chūchue
HABITAT: the southern sky

APPEARANCE: Suzaku is a large, scarlet, phoenix-like bird. Its home is in the southern sky. Suzaku spans seven of the twenty-eight Chinese constellations, taking up one quarter of the entire sky. The constellation which makes up the left wing of the bird is located in Gemini. The constellation which makes up his head feathers or comb is located in Cancer. The constellations which make up its head, beak, and body are located in Hydra. The constellation which makes up its right wing is located in Hydra and Crater. The constellation which makes up its tail feathers is located in Corvus.

INTERACTIONS: Suzaku is one of the shijin—the guardian of the south. It is associated with the Chinese element of fire, the season of summer, the planet Mars, and the color red. It represents the virtue of propriety. Suzaku controls heat and flame. The ancient capitals of Fujiwara-kyō, Heijo-kyō, and Heian-kyō were each guarded on the south by a large gate called Suzakumon. Beyond Suzakumon was a wide avenue called Suzaku Boulevard, which served as the main north-south road. In Kyōto, this road ran from the Imperial Palace to the gate at the southern limits of the city, Rashōmon. Today, though the gates are long gone, Suzaku Boulevard (now called Senbon Avenue) remains an important road in the city.

ORIGIN: Because they look similar, Suzaku is often confused with hōō, the Chinese phoenix. The attributes and symbolism of one are mixed or swapped with each other. Though it has been suggested that they may share a common origin—perhaps going back to the mythical bird Garuda in Indian mythology—there is no strong evidence linking these creatures.

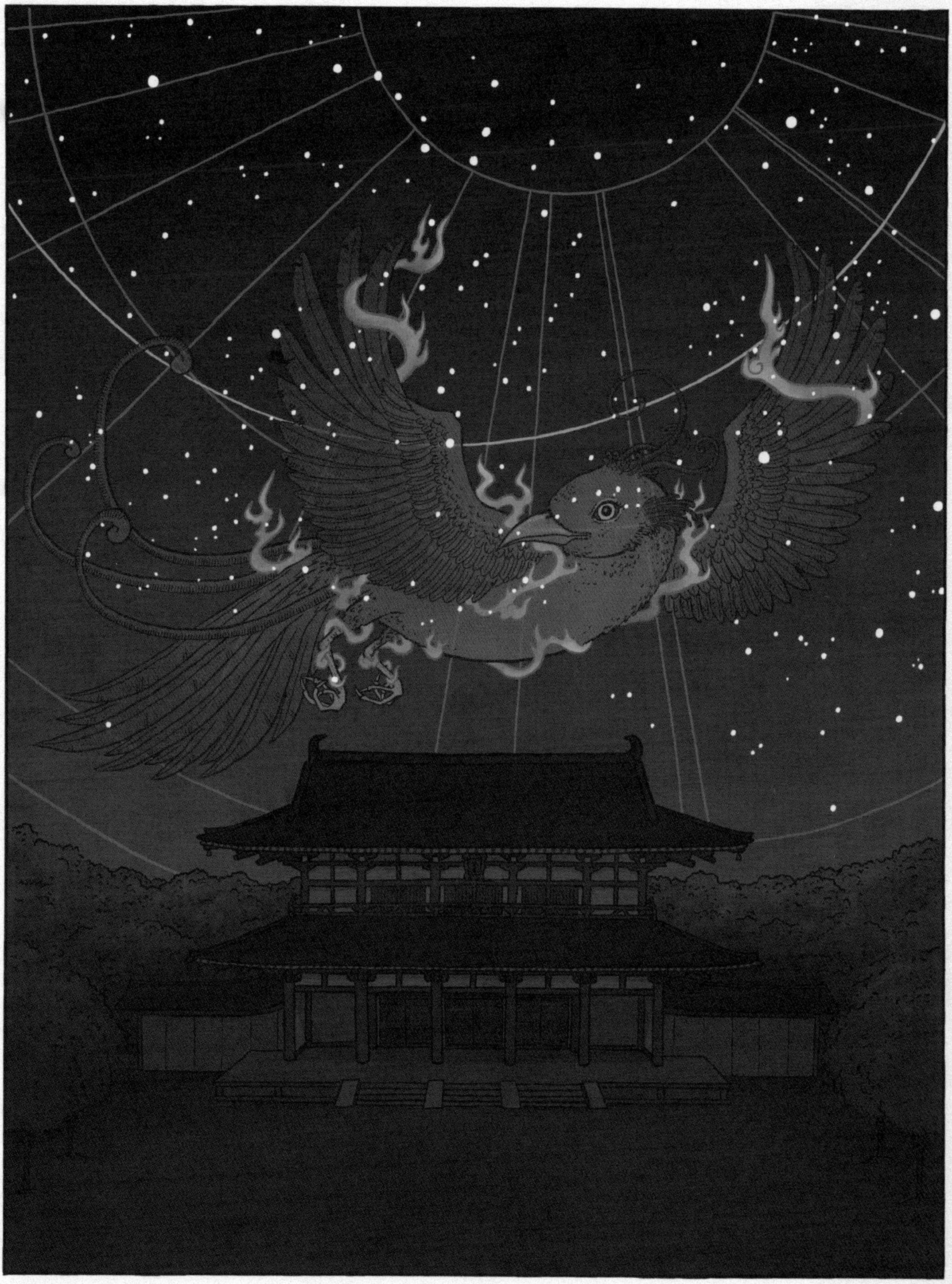

BYAKKO 白虎

TRANSLATION: white tiger; Baihu
ALTERNATE NAMES: Baifū
HABITAT: the western sky

APPEARANCE: Byakko is a celestial white tiger. Its home is in the western sky. It spans seven of the twenty-eight Chinese constellations, taking up one quarter of the entire sky. The constellation which makes up the rear of the tiger is located in Andromeda and Pisces. The constellations which make up the middle of the tiger are located in Ares and Taurus. The constellations which makes up its front legs and head are located in Orion.

INTERACTIONS: Byakko is one of the shijin—the guardian of the west. It is associated with the Chinese element of metal, the season of autumn, the planet Venus, and the color white. It represents the virtue of righteousness. Byakko controls the wind.

THE FIFTH ELEMENT

The Four Symbols are guardians of the four cardinal directions, as well as four of the five elements. However, there is a fifth holy beast who acts as the commander of the other four, as well as the symbol of the fifth Chinese element: earth. This creature is Ōryu (or Kōryu), the yellow dragon of the center. Ōryu is associated with the color yellow, the changing of the seasons, and the planet Saturn. It is located in the center of the cosmos. It represents the authority of the Emperor over all. It is known as Huanglong in Chinese and is viewed as an incarnation of the mythical emperor of China Huangdi. It is sometimes depicted not as a dragon, but as a kirin. While the yellow dragon is an important figure in China, it is far less so in Japan.

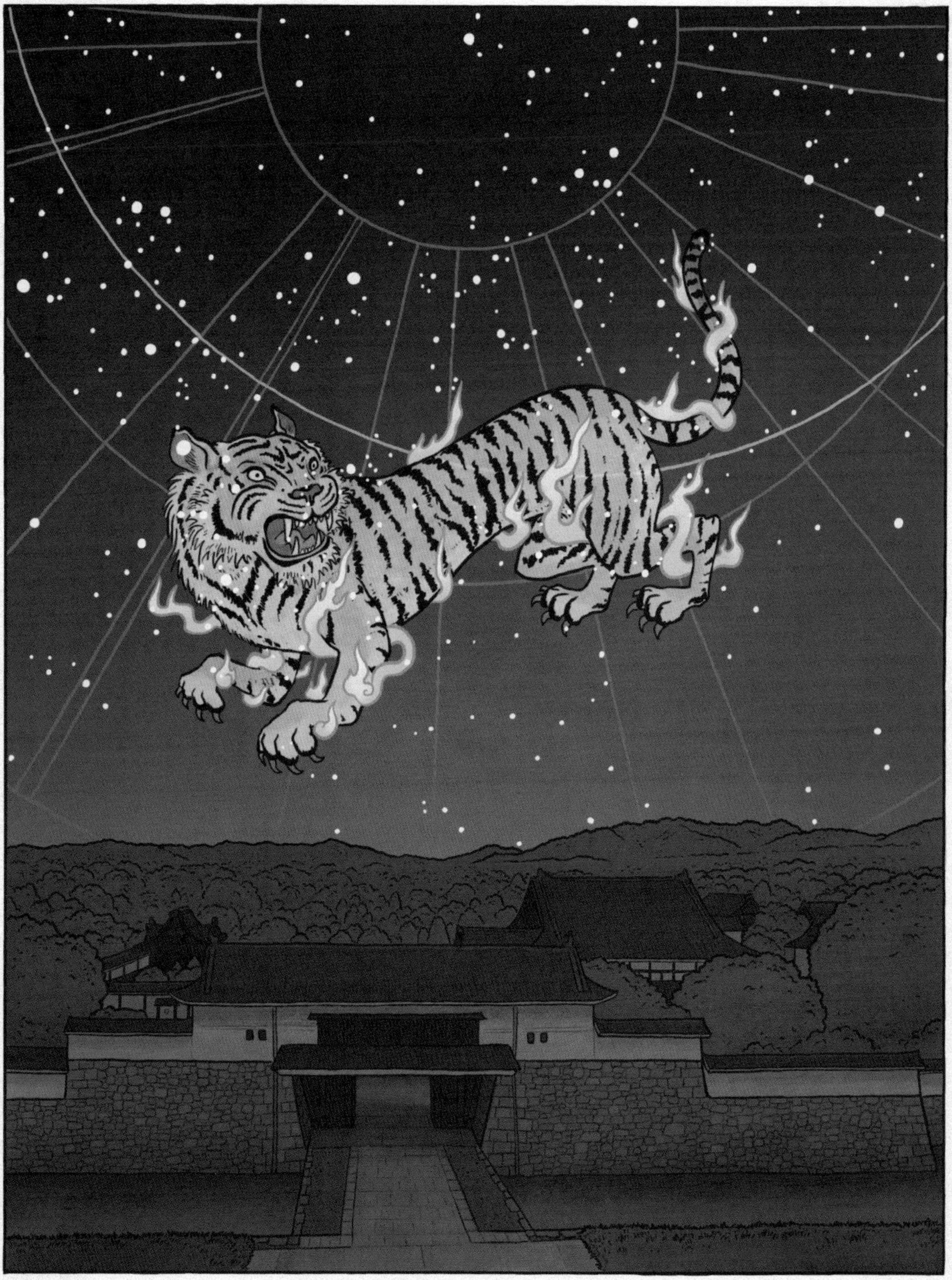

GENBU 玄武

TRANSLATION: dark warrior; Xuanwu
ALTERNATE NAMES: Genten jōtei (dark emperor of the heavens), Showan'ū
HABITAT: the northern sky

APPEARANCE: Genbu is a large tortoise or turtle combined with a snake. Sometimes it is represented as two separate creatures: a snake wrapped around a tortoise. Sometimes it is represented as a single creature: a tortoise-snake chimera. Its home is in the northern sky. It spans seven of the twenty-eight Chinese constellations, taking up one quarter of the entire sky. The constellation which makes up the snake's neck is located in Sagittarius. The constellations which makes up the tortoise's shell are located in Capricornus, Aquarius, and Pegasus. The constellations which make up the snake's tail are located in Pegasus and Andromeda.

INTERACTIONS: Genbu is one of the shijin—the guardian of the north. It is associated with the Chinese element of water, the season of winter, the planet Mercury, and the color black. It represents the virtue of knowledge. It controls the cold. Genbu is enshrined in the Genbu Shrine, north of Kyōto's Imperial Palace.

ORIGIN: Genbu is named differently than the other shijin. Rather than directly describing a color and animal (i.e. Black Tortoise), its name is written as *gen*, meaning dark, occult, or mysterious, and *bu*, meaning warrior. The word tortoise is not used because it was a slur in China. The euphemistic name was used instead.

Genbu's name comes from Chinese mythology, where it is synonymous with the Taoist god Xuanwu (the Chinese pronunciation of Genbu). Xuanwu was a prince who lived in prehistoric northern China. He resided in the mountains, far from civilization, where he studied Taoism as an ascetic. Xuanwu learned that to achieve full divinity he would have to purge both his mind and body of impurities. Though his mind had become enlightened, he still had to eat earthly food. Sin remained in his stomach and intestines. So, he cut them out and washed them in a river to purify them. When he did this, his stomach turned into a large demon tortoise and his intestines into a demon snake. The demons began to terrorize the countryside. Xuanwu subdued them, yet instead of destroying them he allowed them to atone for their sins by serving him as his generals. These two generals which became Xuanwu's—and Genbu's—symbol.

Genbu is associated with yin—the energy of darkness and shadow. In ancient China, it was worshipped as a god of the moon in addition to being the god of the north. Because the shell of a tortoise is like a suit of armor, Genbu is also viewed as a warrior deity. The tortoise shell is a symbol of heaven and earth, with the flat part of the lower shell representing the world and the dome of the upper shell representing the heavens. Tortoise shells were a popular tool in divination. Genbu too was thought to have soothsaying powers, as well as the ability to travel between the lands of the living and the dead. The tortoise is a symbol of longevity and immortality, while the snake is a symbol of reproduction and multiplication. Long ago it was believed that all tortoises were female and had to mate with snakes to reproduce. The intertwining of the two was a symbol not only of long life and fertility, but also of the balance of yin and yang.

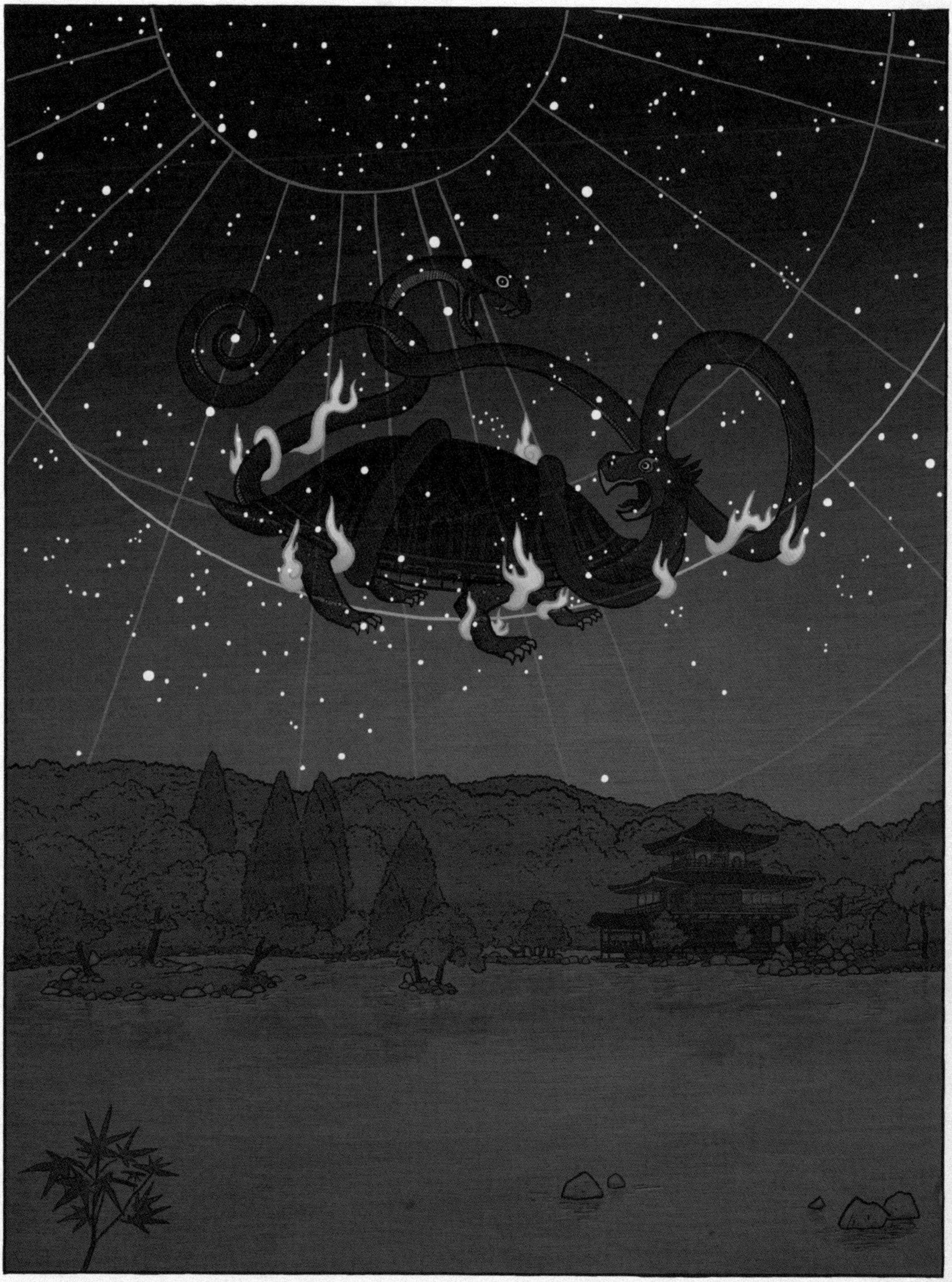

GYOKUTO 玉兎

TRANSLATION: jade rabbit
ALTERNATE NAMES: tsuki no usagi, getto (moon rabbit)
HABITAT: the moon
DIET: herbivorous; presumably with a fondness for mochi

APPEARANCE: The dark spots visible on the full moon are said to resemble a rabbit who lives in the moon.

BEHAVIOR: In Japan, the rabbit in the moon holds a wooden mallet which it uses to pound mochi (rice cakes) in a mortar. The mallet and mortar as also visible as dark spots on the moon. In China, the rabbit is believed not to be creating mochi, but is instead mixing the medicine of eternal youth.

ORIGIN: The myth of the rabbit in the moon is ancient. The earliest written version comes from the Jātaka tales, a 4th century BCE collection of Buddhist legends written in Sanskrit. The legend was brought along with Buddhism from India to China, where it blended with local folklore. It came to Japan from China in the 7th century CE, where it was again adapted and adjusted to fit local folklore.

The Japanese word for pounding mochi in a mortar like the rabbit is doing is *mochitsuki* (餅搗き). The word for the full moon is also *mochitsuki* (望月). The two are homophones.

LEGENDS: The Japanese version of the Sanskrit tale appears in *Konjaku monogatarishū*.

A fox, a monkey, and a rabbit were traveling in the mountains when they came across a shabby-looking old man lying along the road. The old man had collapsed from exhaustion while trying to cross the mountains.

The three animals felt compassion for the old man and tried to save him. The monkey gathered fruit and nuts from the trees, the fox gathered fish from the river, and they fed the old man. As hard as he tried, the rabbit, however, could not gather anything of value to give to the old man. Lamenting his uselessness, the rabbit asked the fox and monkey for help in building a fire. When the fire was built, the rabbit leaped into the flames so that his own body could be cooked and eaten by the old man.

When the old man saw the rabbit's act of compassion, he revealed his true form as Taishakuten, one of the lords of Heaven. Taishakuten lifted up the rabbit and placed it the moon. In that way, all future generations could be inspired by the rabbit's compassionate act. The reason it is sometimes difficult to see the rabbit in the moon is because of the smoke which still billows from the rabbit's body, obscuring his form.

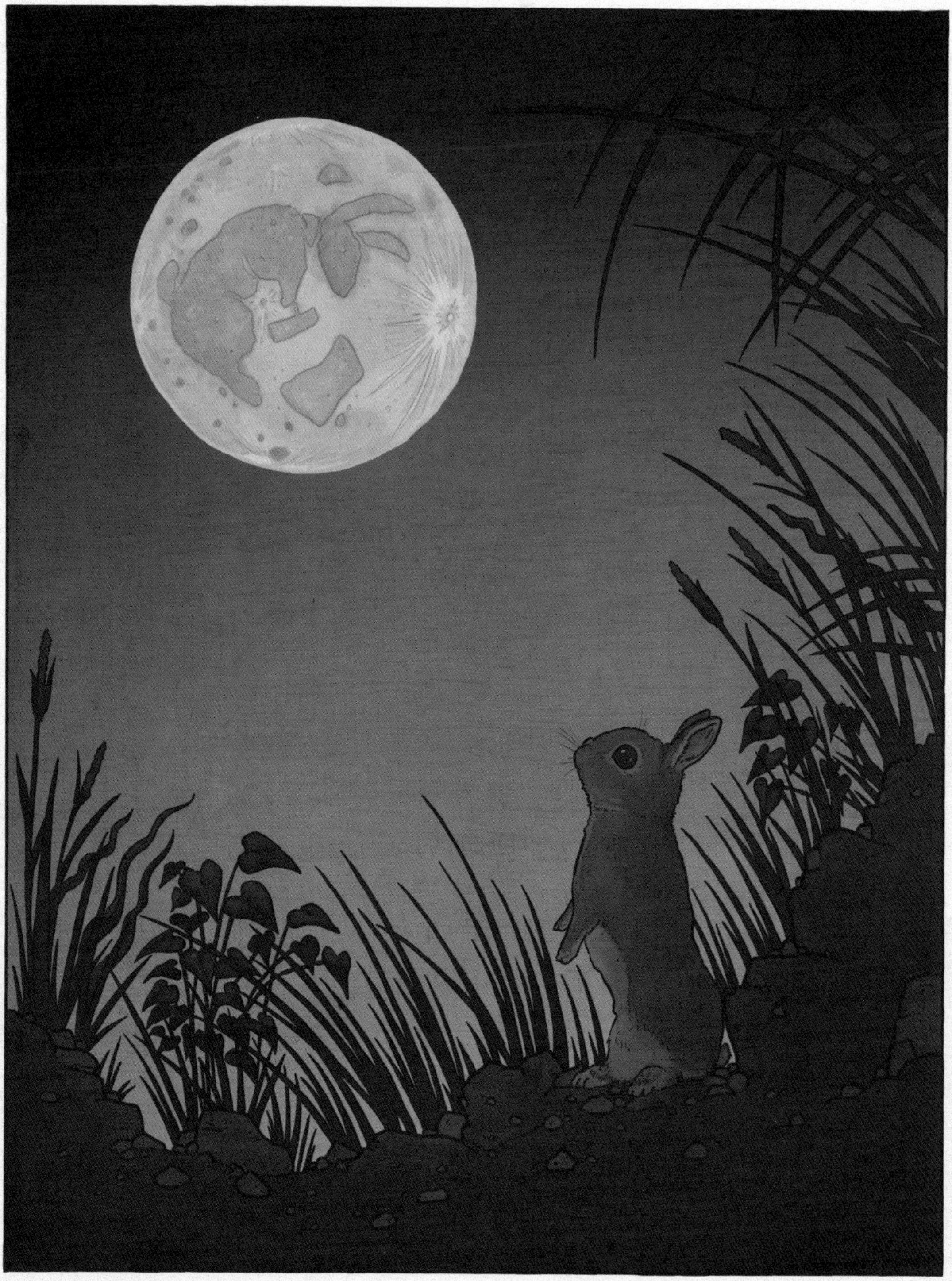

YATAGARASU 八咫烏

TRANSLATION: eight-span crow
ALTERNATE NAMES: sansoku'u (three-legged crow), kin'u (golden crow)
HABITAT: the sun
DIET: unknown, but probably omnivorous

APPEARANCE: Yatagarasu is a three-legged crow which inhabits the sun. It is found across East Asian folklore.

ORIGIN: A three-legged crow has been used as a symbol of the sun since Neolithic times in East Asia. It may have originated as a personification of sunspots by ancient astronomers. In Japan, the crow has also been a symbol of the sun since ancient times, appearing in Japan's earliest written works. It is a holy creature and a servant of the sun goddess, Amaterasu. Yatagarasu means "eight-span crow." One span was the length between the outstretched thumb and middle finger—roughly 18 centimeters—but this moniker is mainly a poetic way to say "very large." Originally Yatagarasu was depicted with two legs, but in the 930s CE, the Chinese myth of the three-legged crow blended with the story of Yatagarasu. Since then, Yatagarasu and the three-legged crow have been synonymous.

The three-legged crow has long been used in religious and astrological symbolism across China and Japan, particularly among those involved with sun worship and onmyōdō. The three legs of the bird represent heaven, the earth, and humanity, while the crow itself represents the sun. This symbolizes that heaven, earth, and mankind all come from the same sun. They are like brothers to each other. They are also said to represent the three virtues of the gods: wisdom, benevolence, and valor. The three legs may represent the three powerful clans of ancient Kumano—Ui, Suzuki, and Enomoto. These clans use a three-legged crow as their crest.

LEGENDS: Yatagarasu is an important figure in the mythical history of Japanese. According to the *Kojiki*, Japan's oldest written history, Yatagarasu is an incarnation of the god Kamo Taketsunumi, a deity today enshrined in Kyoto's Shimogamo Shrine. As Yatagarasu, he led Jimmu, the first emperor of Japan, through the mountains of Kumano to establish his country.

Jimmu's clan originated in Kyushu, in present-day Miyazaki Prefecture. He and his brothers led an eastward migration from along the Seto Insland Sea. They went in search of a better homeland, subduing the various tribes they encountered along the way. They suffered many hardships. When they reached Naniwa (present-day Osaka), Itsuse, Jimmu's older brother and leader of the expedition, was killed in battle. Jimmu realized that they had lost because they were fighting facing eastwards, against the sun. He led his troops around the Kii peninsula to Kumano (present-day Mie Prefecture). From there they began a westward push. His expedition became lost in the mountains of Kumano. Seeing this, Amaterasu, the sun goddess, and Takamimusubi, one of the creator gods, ordered Kamo Taketsunumi to act as a guide to Jimmu. Kamo Taketsunumi took the form of a giant crow and flew to Jimmu's side to show him the way. With Yatagarasu leading the way, Jimmu was able to navigate the mountains of Kumano and reach Yamato (in present-day Nara Prefecture). There he found his capital and become Japan's first emperor.

According to legend, Jimmu's great-grandfather Ninigi was the grandson of Amaterasu. Thus, Jimmu and the entire Japanese imperial line are the direct descendants of the sun goddess. Yatagarasu, as a guide to Jimmu, played a small roll in an event with a big impact on the future of the Japanese identity.

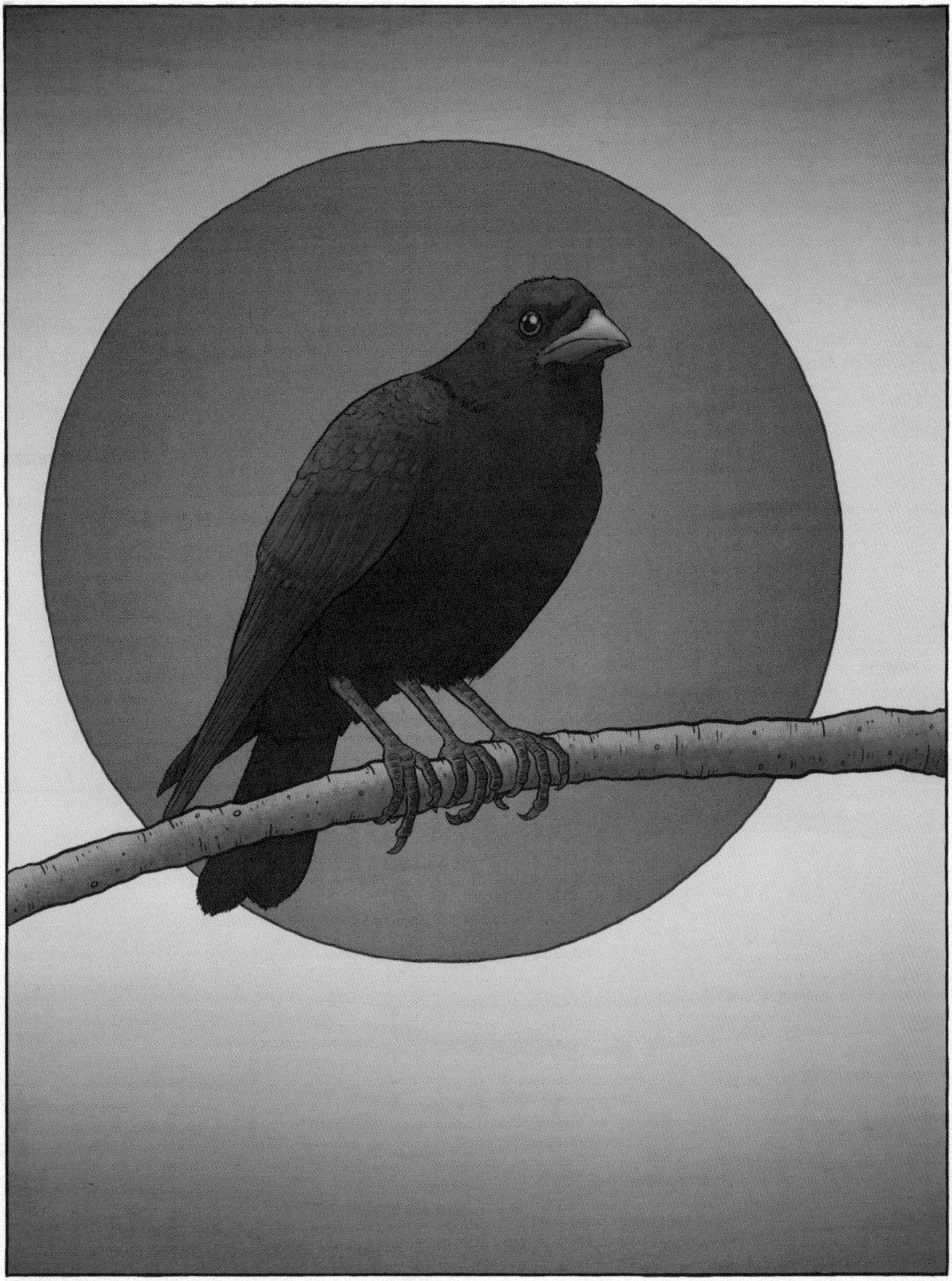

Fūri 風狸

Translation: wind tanuki
Alternate names: fūseijū, fūbo, heikō
Habitat: mountains and cliffs
Diet: omnivorous; feeds primarily on spiders and incense wood

Appearance: Fūri are wild beasts from the mountains of China. They are about the size of a tanuki or a river otter with bodies resembling monkeys. They have red eyes, short tails, black fur with a leopard-like pattern, and blue-greenish manes which run from nose to tail.

Behavior: Fūri are nocturnal and spend the daylight hours sleeping. At night they leap from tree to tree, or cliff face to cliff face, with soaring jumps. They can move as quickly as the wind and resemble flying birds when they leap. They can clear the distance between two mountains in a single leap.

A fūri's diet consists of spiders and the fragrant wood from incense trees. However, they have also been observed hunting. They use a special kind of grass (the species is unknown) and climb to the top of a tree. They hold the grass out in their hands to try to attract a bird. When a bird comes for the grass, the fūri is able to catch and eat the bird.

Interactions: Fūri are extremely fast, but Chinese records say that it possible to capture one with a well-placed net. A captured fūri will act embarrassed, lowering its head and looking up with big, pitiful eyes in an attempt to convince a person to release it. They are extremely fragile and die immediately if they are struck. However, if you try to slice them up with a sword or knife, the blade will not cut through their skin. If you try to roast them with fire, their bodies will not burn. They have the amazing ability to revive from death merely if wind blows into their open mouths. However, they cannot revive if their skull has been broken, or if their nose is stuffed with leaves of Japanese rush (*Acorus gramineus*), a wetland shrub.

Origin: Fūri appear in various Chinese atlases of herbology and medicine. These were referenced by Japanese authors during the Edo period, which is how fūri entered Japanese folklore. The original description of the fūri is most likely based on the colugo—a gliding mammal native to Southeast Asia. There are no colugo in Japan, which is likely why Japanese folklorists described them as a subspecies of tanuki.

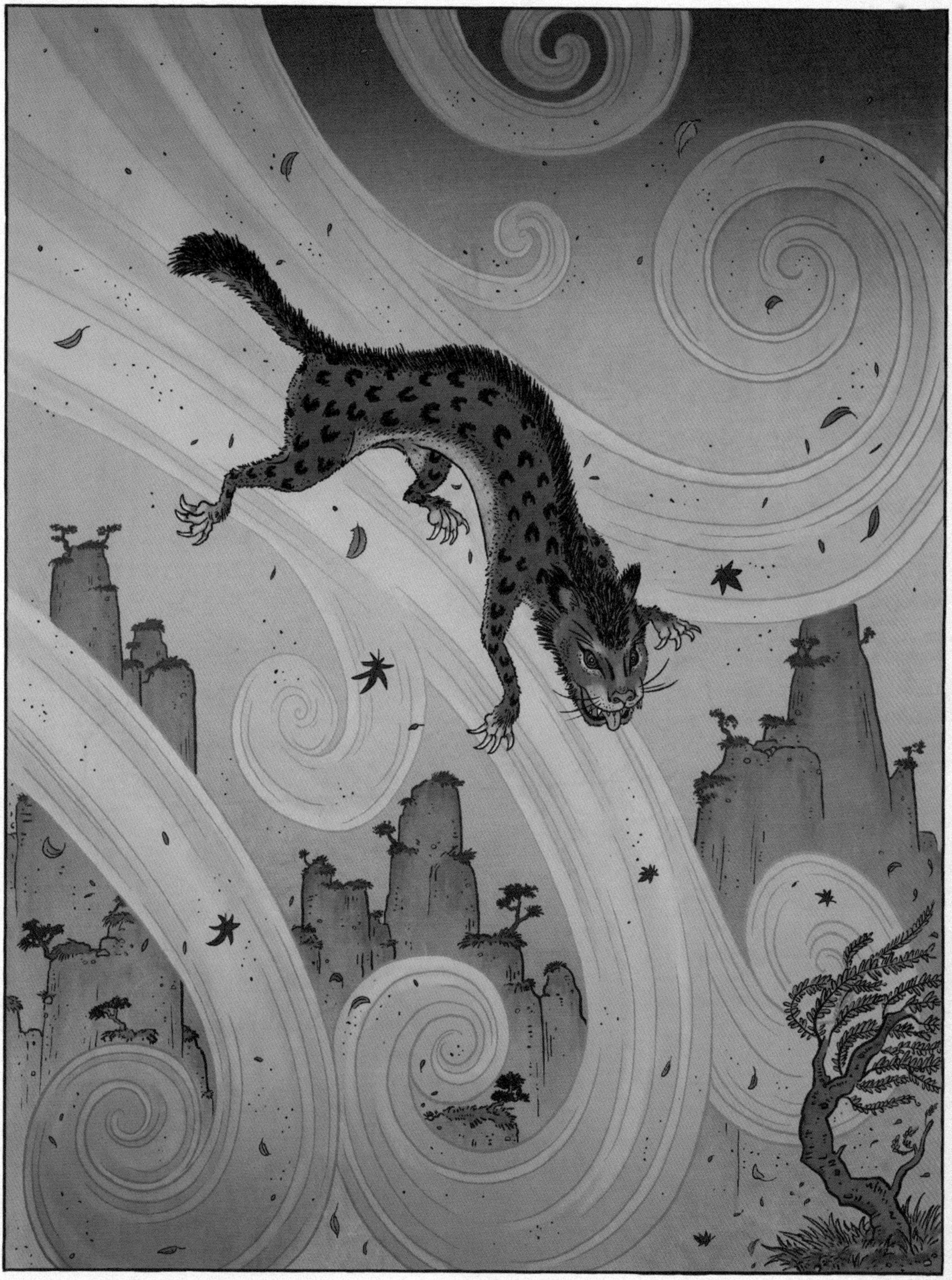

Raijū 雷獣

TRANSLATION: thunder beast
HABITAT: thunderbolts

APPEARANCE: Raijū are the embodiment of lightning in an animal form. They have long, sharp claws and ferocious faces. They are thought to look like wolves, dogs, tanuki, or even weasels or cats. Far more fanciful forms exist. Some raijū look like dogs with four rear legs and two tails. Some look like insects or crustaceans. Others look like miniature dragons. There are even chimerical raijū composed of many different animal features.

BEHAVIOR: Raijū live in the sky—a world which was off limits to humans before the 20th century. Because of this, not much was written about their true nature or behavior. They ride bolts of lightning to earth when thunder claps and create mayhem wherever they land. For seemingly no reason at all they attack buildings, start fires, and cause mass destruction.

INTERACTIONS: Raijū were once seen as divine beasts, akin to the thunder gods (*raijin*). Nothing was known about them except that they were fast and deadly. When lightning struck, people believed that a raijū had been sent by the gods to punish them for some reason or another.

Small raijū like burrow into humans' belly buttons to hide from angry thunder gods. This is the origin of a Japanese superstition which says to cover your belly button when you hear thunder.

ORIGIN: Once, the raijū was one of the most well-known and feared supernatural creatures in Japanese folklore. Yet today it is relatively minor, practically unknown to the average person. This dramatic reversal is due to advances in science during the 19th and 20th centuries. Long ago, lightning was believed to be the work of the gods. Only gods had the power to shake the earth and send fire from the sky. Lightning strikes so quickly and so randomly that it is impossible to observe. But it has observable effects: the terrible booms that shake the ground; the odd burn patterns on the things it strikes; and the fires that it ignites. When buildings were all made of wood and packed closely together, a single lightning strike could cause mass destruction. The damage caused by lightning was indiscriminate—it destroyed everything from peasant hovels to imperial palaces. Lightning was rightly feared by all.

During the Edo Period, "real" raijū were popular sideshow attractions. Mummified and taxidermized remains of cats, monkeys, and dogs were presented as raijū and displayed in traveling shows. Anyone could pay a small fee to get a safe, close up look at a dead raijū.

During the Meiji Period, society was rapidly transformed due to the influx of foreign science and technology. Yōkai like raijū were one of the first victims of this modernization. People were actively discouraged from holding on to superstitions because they were perceived as an embarrassment to the country. New understandings about electricity and inventions like the airplane took away the raijū's most powerful mysteries. Its life in the unreachable sky and the god-like power of lightning were commonplace. Once those were gone, the raijū held no more power over peoples' imaginations. It was quickly forgotten.

LEGENDS: Raijū in literature are beasts meant to be slain by brave heroes. The most famous example is probably the nue, which attacked Kyōto and was slain by Minamoto no Yorimasa in 1153. Another legend involves the samurai Tachibana Dōsetsu. One night he was taking shelter from a storm under a tree when lightning struck. He drew his sword just in time to strike the bolt. When the smoke had cleared, there was a dead raijū on the ground next to him. Afterwards, he named his sword *Raikiri*, or "lightning cutter."

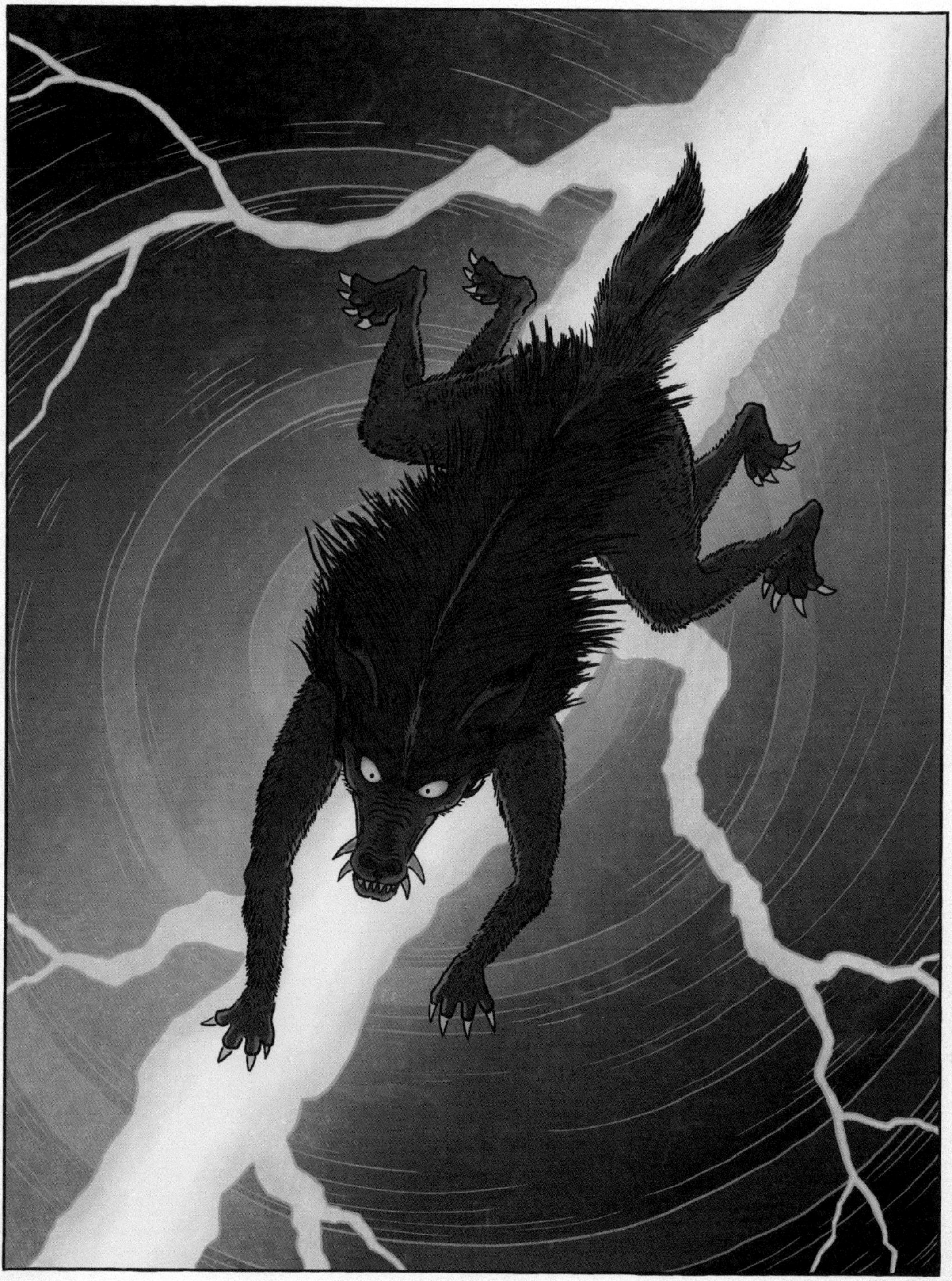

Tatarimokke 祟り蛙

TRANSLATION: curse child
ALTERNATE NAMES: tatarimoke
HABITAT: lives inside of owls
DIET: none

APPEARANCE: Tatarimokke are the spirits of dead babies which inhabit the bodies of owls. Visually they appear no different than ordinary owls.

BEHAVIOR: Tatarimokke (or rather, the owls who serve as hosts to tatarimokke) remain near the homes of their families. The hooting of these owls is said to be the crying of the dead children's spirits.

INTERACTIONS: Like zashiki warashi and other house ghosts, tatarimokke are treated with respect. Families which have lost children recently will take care of owls that appear near their homes and treat them as if they are the spirit of the lost child. In most cases, these spirits are beloved by the families they haunt. They cause no harm.

In some cases, however, tatarimokke can be dangerous to people. The souls of babies whose bodies were carelessly discarded into rivers, babies who were killed by their parents to reduce the number of mouths to feed, and even the spirits of aborted fetuses could retain a grudge against the living. People passing through the places where these resentful spirits haunt might hear eerie sounds and feel unsettling sensations, see strange phenomena like floating fireballs, or may stumble on a rock and hurt themselves.

In the most extreme cases, tatarimokke truly do bring terrible curses upon those who are perceived as having wronged them. Particularly in the case of people who were murdered in violent and gruesome fashion. In these cases, the tatarimokke is born not from the spirit of a newborn baby, but instead from the spirit of the murder victim. These tatarimokke lay a curse on their assailant so powerful that it not only brings ruin to the murderer, but to his entire family for generations to come.

ORIGIN: The name tatarimokke comes from *tatari* (curse) and *moke*, which means "infant" in some northern dialects. It is usually written phonetically but is sometimes also written with characters that mean "curse" and "frog." In this case, the character for frog is pronounced "moke" and refers to a newborn baby.

In ancient Japan, babies were not considered fully human until sometime after they were born. Therefore, when a newborn died, it was not usually given a proper funeral and placed in a cemetery. Instead it was buried quietly in or around the house. The spirits of these children would float out and were believed to easily get "stuck" in owls, creating a tatarimokke.

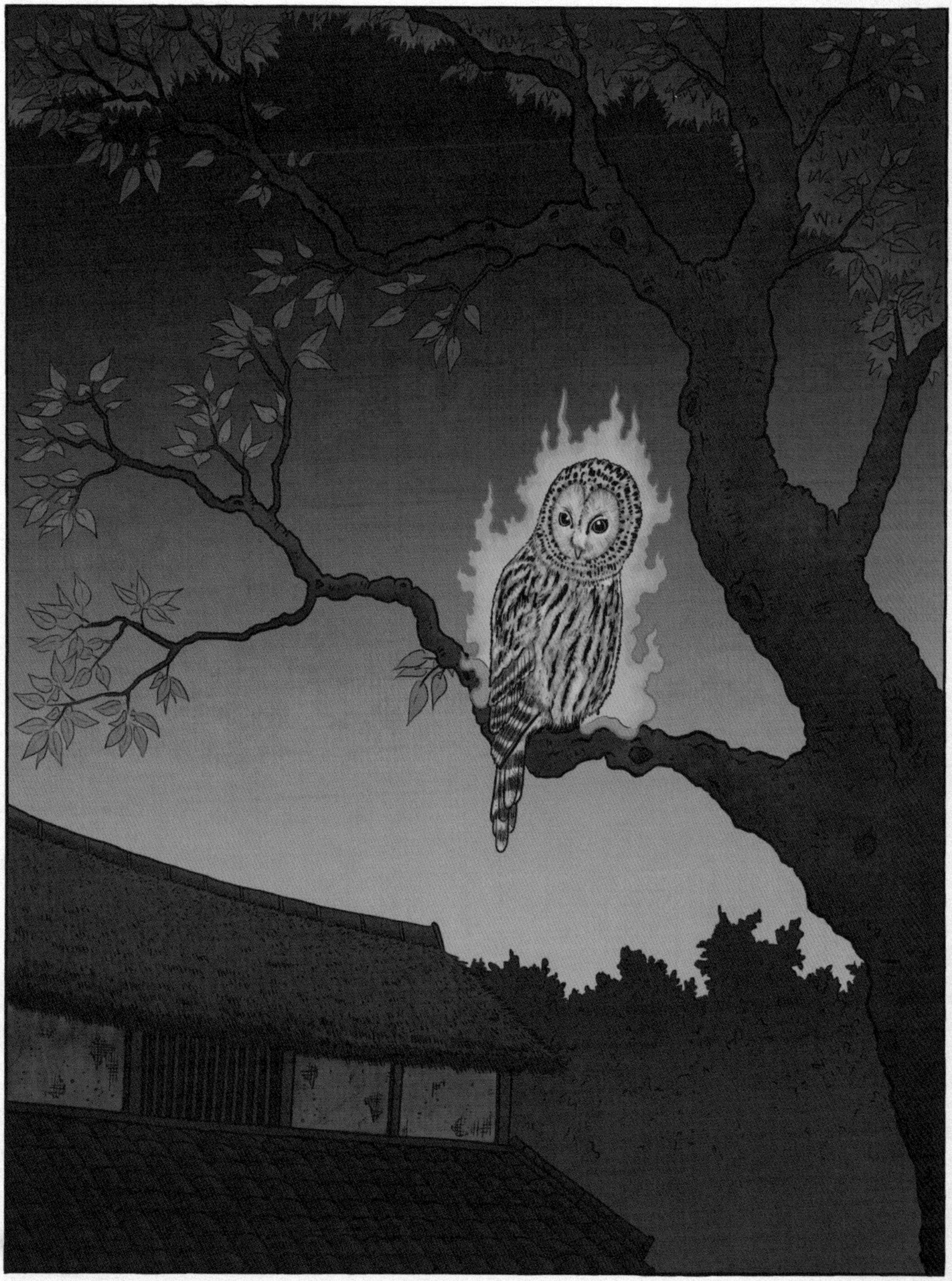

SHIRO UKARI 白うかり

TRANSLATION: white floater
HABITAT: the sky
DIET: unknown

APPEARANCE: Shiro ukari are ghost-like spirits with long tails. They are white, with large eyes that stare off into the distance as if lost in thought. They float about in the air, aimlessly wandering.

BEHAVIOR: Shiro ukari appear on a few Edo period scroll paintings and nowhere else. They were invented by an artist rather than recorded from folklore. Aside from the name, nothing is written about them. Everything about them, including their behavior and origins, is unknown and unexplained. However, their name may hold a clue to their identity.

ORIGIN: Shiro ukari literally means "white floater." Both of these words carry a number of nuances. *Shiro* not only refers to the color white, but to a state of total innocence or naivety. While *ao* (blue) is used in many yōkai names to refer to a novice or an apprentice, shiro can refer to a state of total, absolute naivete. It has a negative connotation, akin to "fool" or "country bumpkin" in English. The urban socialites of Edo looked down on the rural people who lived far outside of the capital as naive, uneducated, and unsophisticated. While not specifically stated, the vacant expression on this yōkai's face could be an allusion to this alternate meaning of shiro.

Ukari comes from the word for floating, which has a number of different implications. The most literal meaning is to float about from place to place. This carries a nuance of absentmindedness or disconnect from others. Tourists who feel out of place in a strange city might be described as floating about in this way. It can also refer to merrymaking, particularly in a way that is in disconnect with the realities of the world. This has the same origins as the word ukiyo, which refers to the "floating world"—the urban, ephemeral pleasure-seeking lifestyle of old Edo. In a spiritual sense, it can also refer to ghosts which have not been able to pass on to the next world due to the weight of their ignorance and sin. They float about, but never ascend to heaven. They are doomed to haunt this world forever.

Perhaps shiro ukari is a pun describing the uncouth, naive rural bumpkins who Edo urbanites thought had no business being in their city. Their experience in the capital might be something like a wide-eyed ghost floating from place to place. Or perhaps they are yōkai which seek out the impermanent pleasures of life as the humans of old Edo's pleasure districts did. Or perhaps they are the spirits of people who were unable to ascend into the next world, burdened by the weight of their ignorance to float about and wander aimlessly for the rest of time.

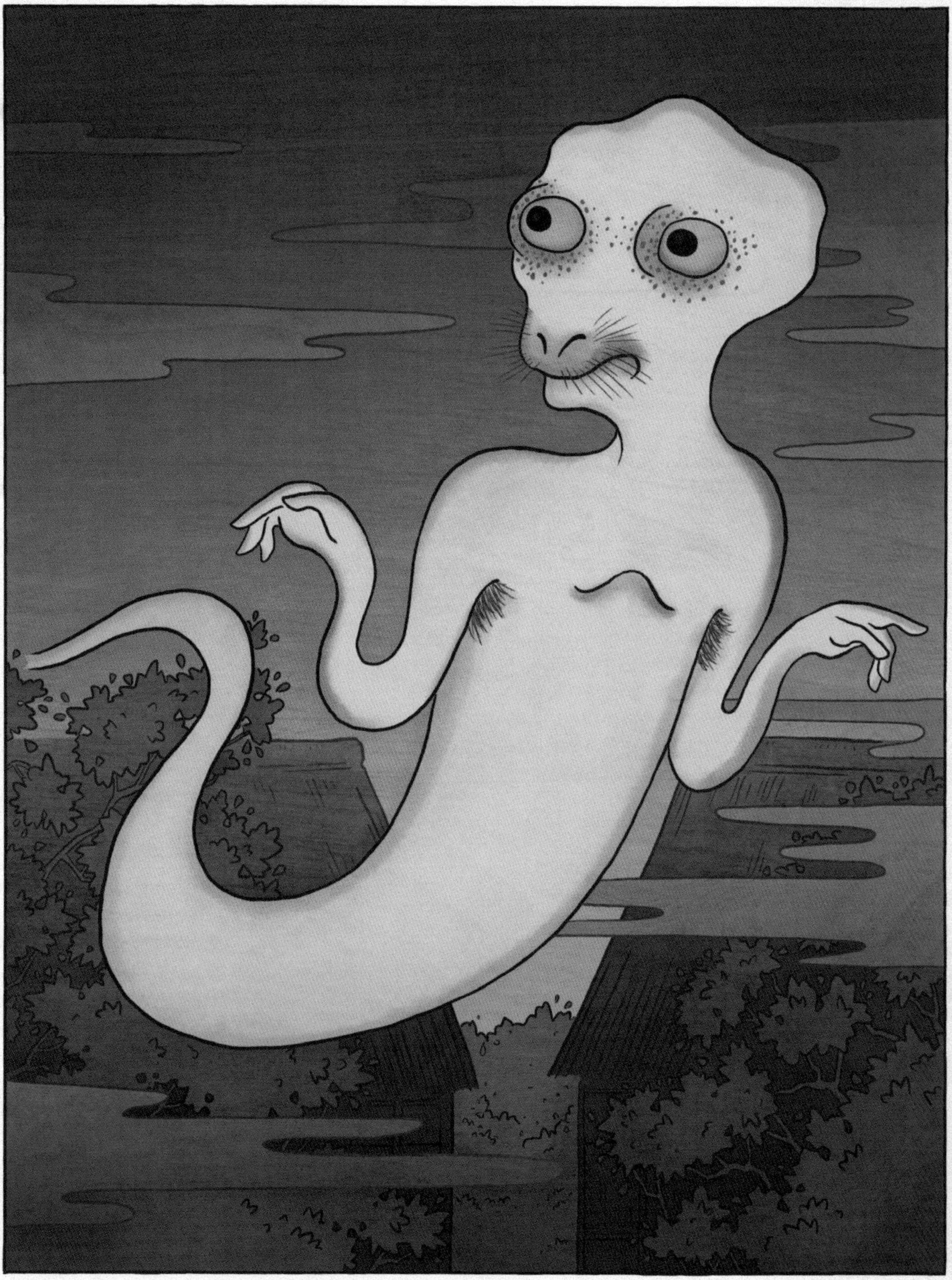

Tennyo 天女

TRANSLATION: heavenly woman, celestial woman
HABITAT: Tendō, the realm of heaven in Buddhist cosmology
DIET: vegetarian (as required by Buddhism)

APPEARANCE: Tennyo are extraordinarily beautiful creatures who resemble human women. They have unparalleled grace and elegance, and supernaturally attractive faces and figures. They wear beautiful gowns called *hagoromo* ("feather cloth") which allow them to fly.

BEHAVIOR: Tennyo are servants and courtesans for the emperor of heaven, and companions of buddhas and bodhisattvas. They sing, dance, play music, recite poetry, and do much of the same things as the women in human imperial courts; though they have far more grace, refinement, and beauty.

ORIGIN: Tennyo are a female-only subgroup of *tennin*, one of many celestial races native to Tendō. They are based on the Indian apsaras, celestial nymphs from Indian mythology. They were brought to China with Buddhism, where they developed into the tennyo we know today, which was later brought over to Japan.

LEGENDS: Tennyo legends often involve love stories and marriage between tennyo and human men. A famous story is told in the Noh play *Hagoromo*.

Long ago, a fisherman named Hakuryō was walking along the pine-covered beaches of the Miho Peninsula. It was a beautiful spring morning, and Hakuryō stopped for a moment to admire the beautiful white sand, the sparkling waves, the fluffy clouds, and the fishing ships on the bay. A pleasant fragrance filled the air, and it seemed that ethereal music was dancing on the winds. Something caught his eye; draped over a nearby pine branch was a robe of the most splendid fabric he had ever seen. It was made of a soft, feathery material, and was woven in fantastic colors. He decided to take it home and keep it as a family heirloom.

Just as Hakuryō was preparing to leave, a young woman of breathtaking beauty appeared in the nude. She had flowers in her hair and smelled just as beautiful as she looked. She asked him to return her hagoromo robe. Hakuryō realized that this beautiful maiden was a tennyo. He refused to return to robe, saying it would bring good luck and fortune to his village.

The woman grew sad and lamented that she would not be able to fly home to heaven without her robe. She dropped to her knees and cried, her tears falling like beautiful pearls into the sand. The flowers in her hair wilted. She looked up at the clouds above, and heard a flock of geese flying by, which only saddened her more as they reminded her of the celestial birds of heaven.

Hakuryō was moved by the beautiful maiden's sadness. He told her that he would return her robe, but first she must perform a celestial dance for him. She agreed, but she needed her hagoromo to perform the dance. Hakuryō refused to return the robe, thinking she would fly off to heaven without performing for him. The tennyo replied to him that deception was a part of his world, not hers. She said that her kind do not lie. Hakuryō felt shame and returned the dress to her.

The tennyo donned her hagoromo and performed the dance of the Palace of the Moon. She was accompanied by celestial music, flutes, koto, and the wind in the pines. The moon shown through the trees and sweet fragrances filled the air. The waves grew calm and peaceful. Her long sleeves played upon the wind, and she danced in sheer joy. As she danced, she slowly floated up into the sky. She flew over the beach, higher and higher, above the pines, through the clouds, and beyond the top of Mt. Fuji, then disappeared into the clouds.

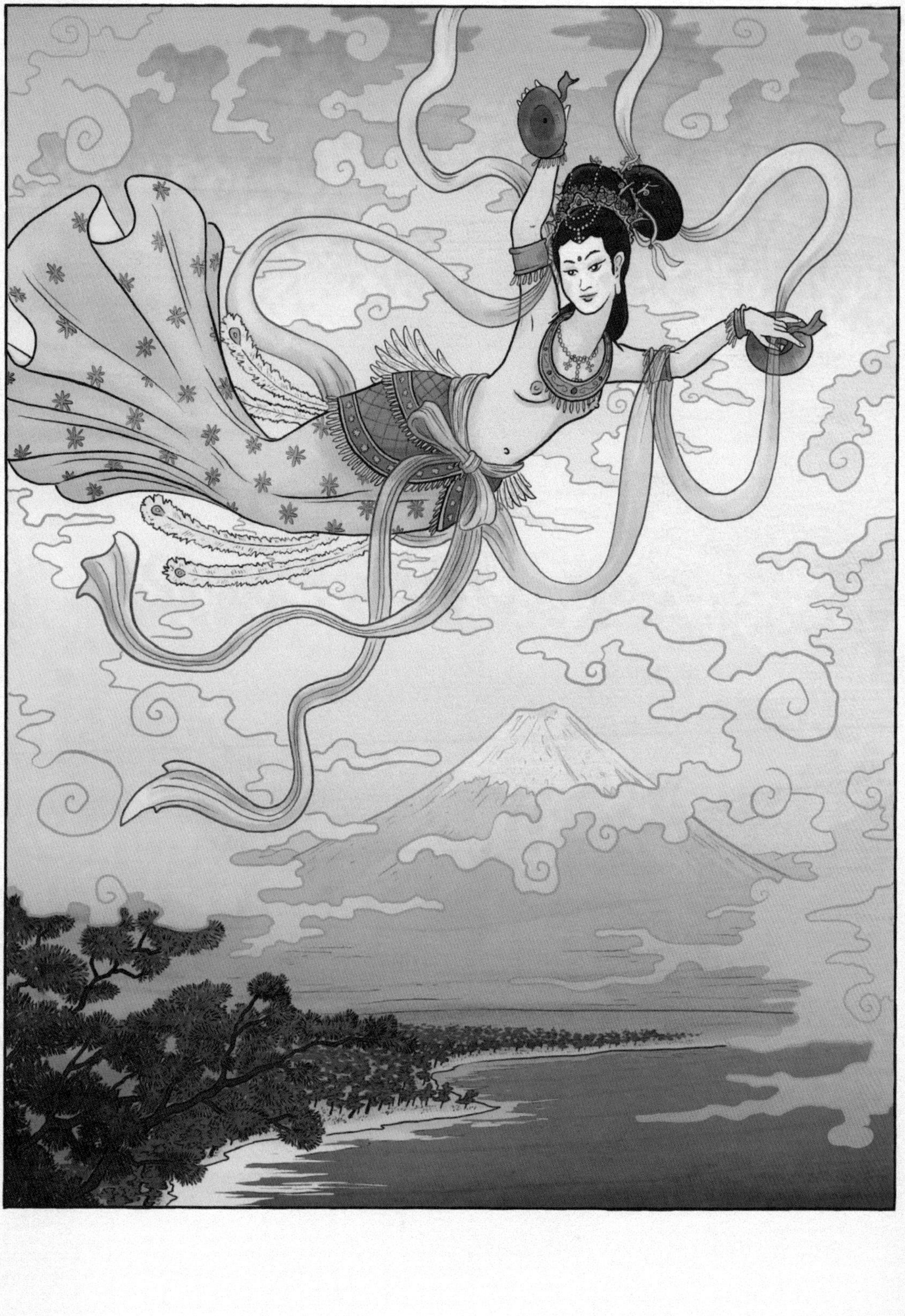

KARYŌBINGA 迦陵頻伽

TRANSLATION: a phonetic rendition of its sanskrit name, kalaviṅka
ALTERNATE NAMES: myōonchō (exquisite sounding bird)
HABITAT: Gokuraku jōdo, a realm of paradise
DIET: vegetarian (as required by Buddhism)

APPEARANCE: Karyōbinga are celestial beings from Buddhist cosmology. They have the head and arms of a bodhisattva, the body of a bird, and long, flowing tail feathers similar to that of a hōō. They live in a realm of paradise called Gokuraku jōdo.

BEHAVIOR: Karyōbinga possess voices of incomparable beauty. They begin singing while still inside of their eggs. After they hatch, they dance and play heavenly musical instruments as well. They sing holy scriptures and the words of the buddhas.

ORIGIN: Karyōbinga come from Indian mythology. They originated in Buddhist scripture, which was brought to Japan from China. They differ little from their Indian counterparts. They are usually used in paintings and sculpture as symbols of paradise and the Buddha's words. They are a reminder that by living a holy life, one can be reborn into Gokuraku jōdo after death. Practitioners of Pure Land Buddhism make reaching this paradise their goal. Gokuraku jōdo is a pure land of utter bliss—a celestial kingdom created by Amida Buddha. Its inhabitants can practice Buddhism directly under Amida's tutelage, listen to the songs of karyōbinga, and achieve enlightenment themselves.

A PURE LAND

One of the largest denominations of Buddhism in Japan is Pure Land Buddhism. Pure Land teaches that our earthly world will never be peaceful or perfect enough for its inhabitants to attain enlightenment. Thus, the goal of Pure Land practice is not to achieve Buddhahood, but to be reborn in the paradise of Amida Nyōrai, where enlightenment is possible.

The pure land of Amida is known as Gokuraku jōdo in Japanese. It is a heaven-like world created by Amida, where conditions are perfect for attaining Buddhahood. Those who are reborn in Amida's Pure Land experience a life free from suffering and ignorance. They spend their days in bliss, listening to the sermons of Buddha and the songs of the karyōbinga, and focus on achieving Buddhahood free from the distractions of Earth.

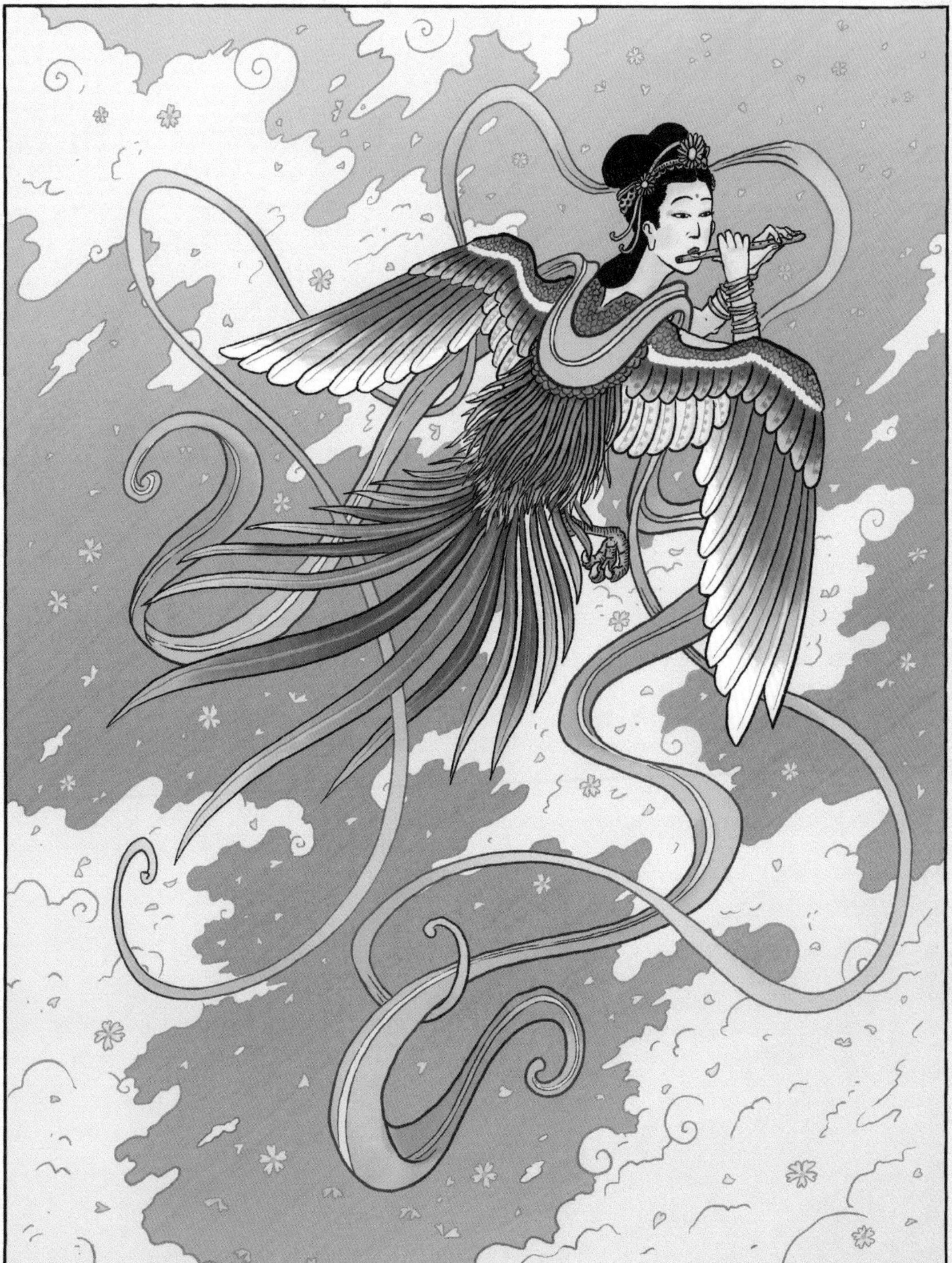

GUMYŌCHŌ 共命鳥

TRANSLATION: interconnected lives bird
ALTERNATE NAMES: kyōmeichō
HABITAT: Gokuraku jōdo, a realm of paradise
DIET: vegetarian

APPEARANCE: Gumyōchō are beautiful two-headed birds that resembles pheasants. Occasionally they are depicted as having two human heads instead of two bird heads. Their home is Gokuraku jōdo, the realm of utter paradise created by Amida Buddha.

BEHAVIOR: The gumyōchō is one of six bird species which are said to inhabit nirvana—the others being white swans, peafowl, parrots, mynah birds, and karyōbinga. Like karyōbinga, gumyōchō are said to have exceedingly beautiful voices. They and the other heavenly birds sing the holy scriptures in nirvana. Those who listen to their songs achieve enlightenment.

ORIGIN: Gumyōchō originate in the cosmology of Pure Land Buddhism. They were brought to Japan in the 6th century along with Buddhism. They are often used as ornamentation on Buddhist temples. Their story is a parable for the interdependence of all humans on one another.

LEGENDS: Long ago, a gumyōchō lived in the snowy mountains of India. It had two heads and one body. One head was named Karuda, and the other head was named Upakaruda. The bird's two heads had different personalities and desires. When one head was sleepy, the other one wanted to play. When one head was hungry, the other one wanted to rest. Eventually, the two heads began to resent each other.

One day while Upakaruda was sleeping, Karuda feasted on delicious fruits and flowers until he was stuffed and could eat no more. When Upakaruda woke up, he wanted to eat too, but he was already full because they shared one stomach. He could not enjoy any of the food.

Upakaruda decided to punish Karuda. While Karuda slept, Upakaruda found a tree with poisonous fruit. Because they shared one stomach, Upakaruda ate the fruit in order to make Karuda sick. Sure enough, when Karuda woke up, the poison had already taken effect. Karuda writhed and suffered, and then died. Of course, because they shared one body, Upakaruda also became sick, collapsed in agony, and then died.

Just before dying, Upakaruda realized how foolish he had been. When he resented his other head, he failed to recognize that his own life depended on it. Just the same, by harming his other head, he was also harming himself. When he realized this, he understood one of the core tenets of Buddhism: interconnectedness. The birds became enlightened and were reborn in nirvana.

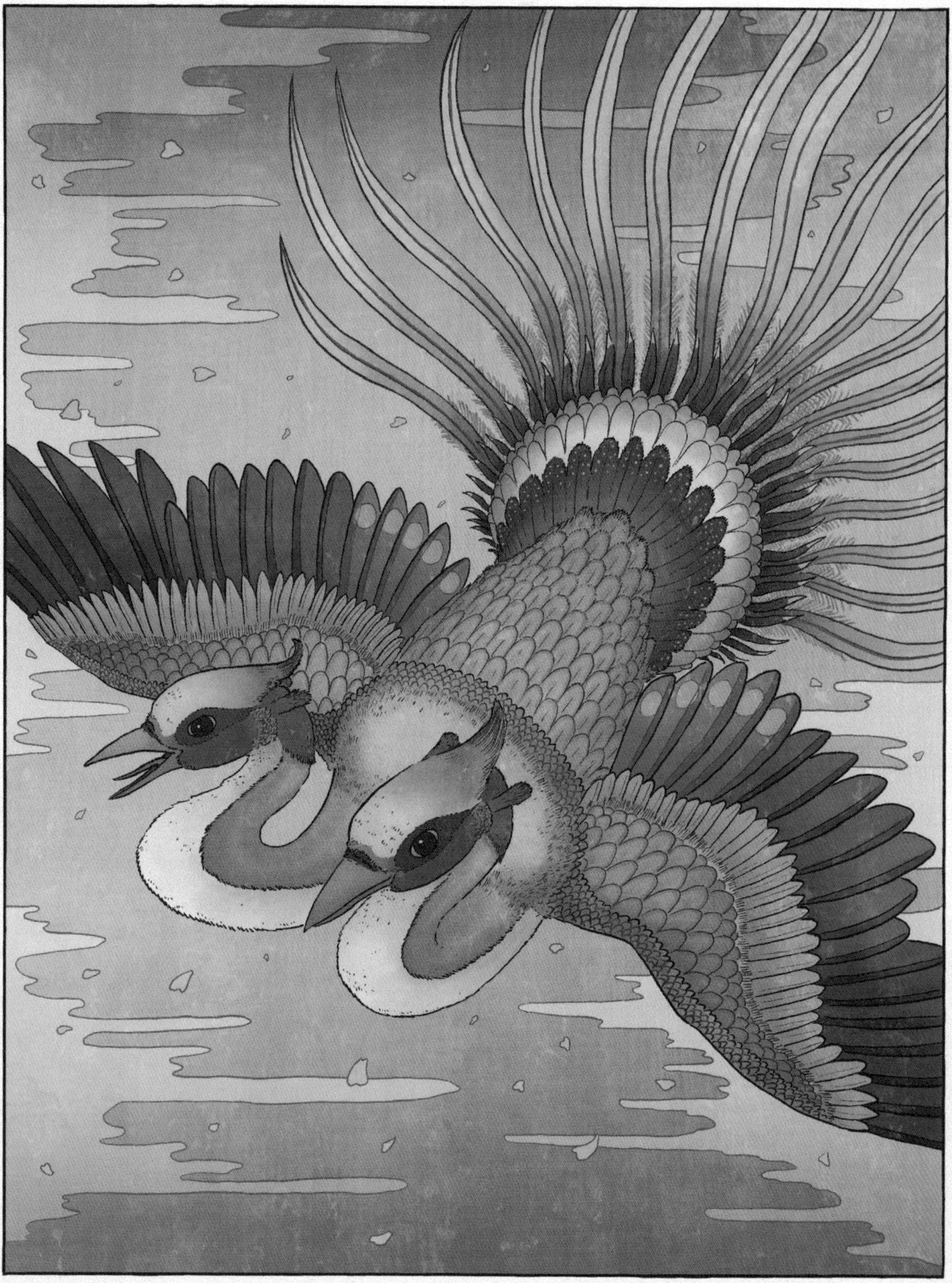

Karura 迦楼羅

TRANSLATION: derived from the Hindu deity Garuda
ALTERNATE NAMES: konjichō (golden winged bird)
HABITAT: Shumisen (aka Mount Meru, a holy mountain in Buddhism)
DIET: mainly dragons

APPEARANCE: Karura are a race of enormous, fire-breathing demigods. They are humanoid in appearance, with the heads and wings of eagles. They have red skin, and red and gold feathers. Karura are fearsome. They breath fire from their beaks. The flapping of their wings sounds like thunder and creates gusts of wind which can dry up lakes, knock down houses, and cover entire cities in darkness. Their gigantic wingspans are 330 *yojanas* wide, and they can leap 3,360,000 *ri* in a single bound. (The lengths of one yojana and one ri vary greatly from country to country and era to era. A yojana can measure anywhere between 1.6 km to over 13 km long. One ri can measure anywhere between 400 m and 3.9 km.)

BEHAVIOR: Karura inhabit Tendō, the realm of heaven. They are found on Shumisen (known as Mount Meru in English), a sacred mountain with five peaks which exists at the center the universe. They make their homes in trees and live in cities rules by kings. They are the mortal enemies of the naga—a group of beings which includes dragons and serpents—and feed upon them as their main diet.

INTERACTIONS: Karura are worshiped in some branches of esoteric Buddhism. Because karura are the enemies of dragons and serpents, they are seen as a counter to things associated with these creatures. They are guardians who keep venomous snakes and dragons away. They protect against poison and disease. They are even helpful against excessive rains and typhoons. Because they are such fierce predators, they are also viewed as destroyers of sin, devouring the spiritual impurities of the faithful in the same way they devour dragons.

ORIGIN: Karura comes from the Hindu deity Garuda, a giant eagle who served as the mount of Vishnu. Garuda was incorporated into Buddhist folklore where he became an entire race of powerful eagle-like devas. They were then later brought along with Buddhism to China, and finally to Japan. The name karura comes from the Japanese pronunciation of Garuda.

Karura are one of the *hachi bushū*—the Eight Legions. These are the eight classes of supernatural beings who were converted to Buddhism by Buddha. The eight races of the hachi bushū are ten (*deva* in Sanskrit), tatsu (*naga*), yasha (*yaksa*), kendatsuba (*gandharva*), ashura (*asura*), karura (*garuda*), kinnara (*kinnara*), and magoraka (*mahoraga*). All of these creatures are inhabitants of Tendō (the highest state of existence) except for the ashura, who live in Ashuradō (the third highest state of existence).

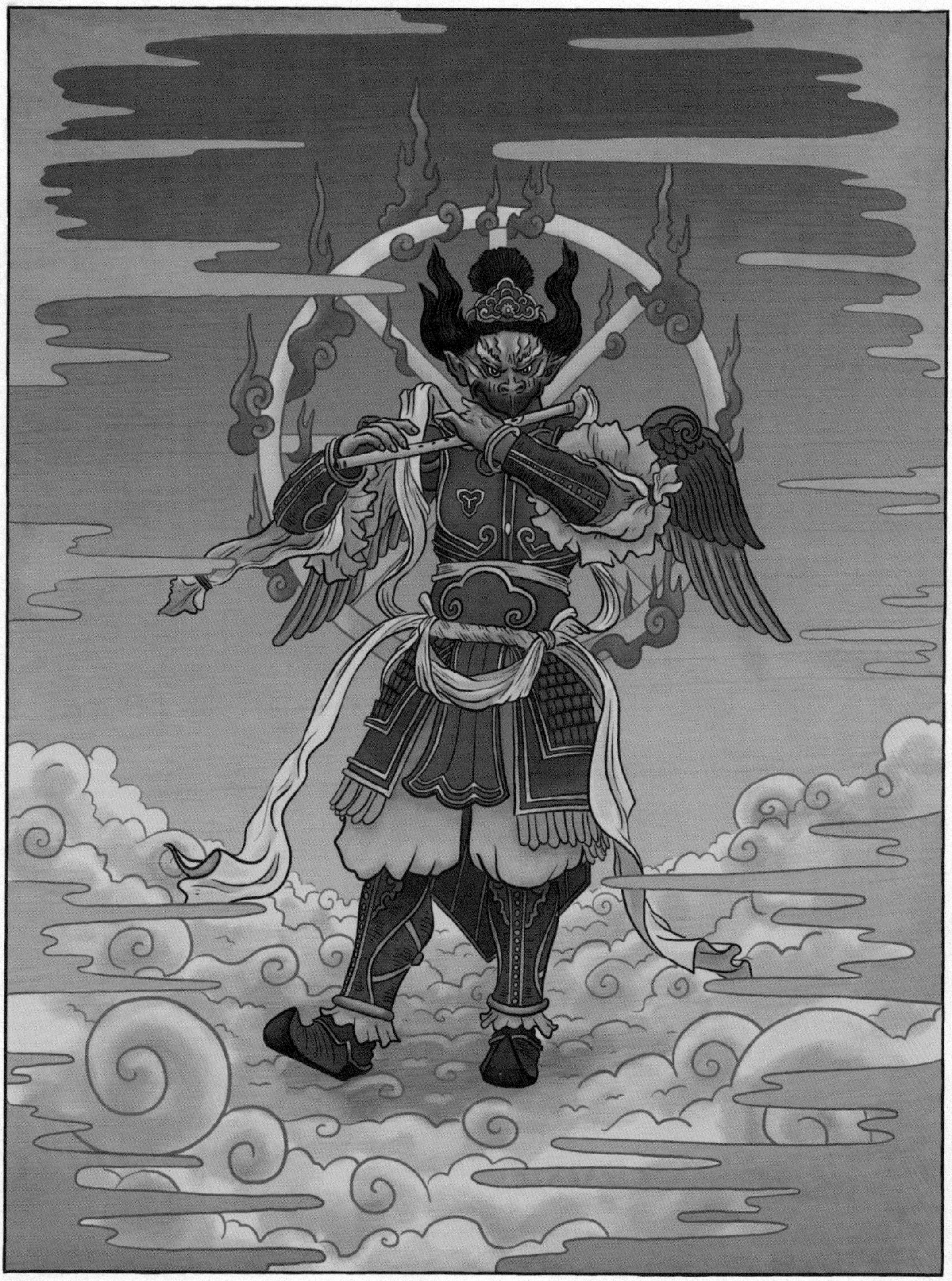

YASHA 夜又

TRANSLATION: yaksha; demon gods from Buddhist cosmology
HABITAT: rivers, forests, and mountains
DIET: omnivorous; occasionally man-eating

APPEARANCE: Yasha are a race of powerful, high ranking nature spirits which appear in Buddhist cosmology. They are a type of *kijin* (demon god) both worshiped for their benevolence and feared for their wrath. They are terrifying warriors and serve as guardians of the treasures of the earth. They have varied forms, but generally are humanoid in appearance. They have brightly colored skin, spiked hair, sharp teeth, and fierce eyes. They are usually depicted carrying weapons and wearing ornate armor.

BEHAVIOR: Yasha are one of the members of the Eight Legions—eight supernatural races who listened to the sermons of Shaka Nyōrai and converted to Buddhism. Along with the ten, tatsu, kendatsuba, ashura, karura, kinnara, and magoraka, they serve as guardians of the Buddhist teachings.

Yasha serve Buddhism in a number of ways. Most importantly, the Twelve Heavenly Generals (the twelve most fearsome yasha), serve as the personal bodyguards of Yakushi Nyōrai, the buddha of medicine. They wage war on sickness and fight the enemies of Buddhism. They are also important in astrology. The twelve of them are associated with the twelve animals of the Chinese zodiac, the hours of the day, the months, and the directions. Their leader, General Kubira, is also an important kami in the Shinto faith. He is believed to be the Buddhist manifestation of Konpira, god of fishing, seafaring, and farming. He is enshrined as Ōmononushi in the Kotohira shrine of Kagawa Prefecture, alongside Sutoku Tennō.

Yasha, along with another kind of demon called rasetsu, are used as soldiers in the armies of Bishamonten, one of the Four Heavenly Kings. Bishamonten is often depicted trampling a tiny, evil yasha (called a jaki or amanojaku) under his feet. His armor is also often decorated with scowling yasha faces. In this way yasha also serve as a symbol the triumph of virtue over wickedness.

ORIGIN: Yasha come from Hindu mythology. They were originally benevolent nature spirits and caretakers of the trees and earth. In Buddhism, they were interpreted as evil, ghost-like spirits who preyed upon travelers. They later gave up their wicked ways upon hearing the sermons of the Buddha. The Buddhist version of yasha is similar to another class of Hindu spirits: the ogrish, man-eating demons known as rasetsu. When Buddhism was brought into China, it mixed with Chinese folk religion and astrology. Yasha grew even further away from their Hindu origins.

When Buddhism was brought to Japan from China, the Chinese interpretation of yasha was brought along with it. In Japan, yasha were often viewed as Buddhist manifestations of local evil spirits, like amanojaku and oni. Yasha took on some of the characteristics of these spirits, and sometimes even became synonymous with them.

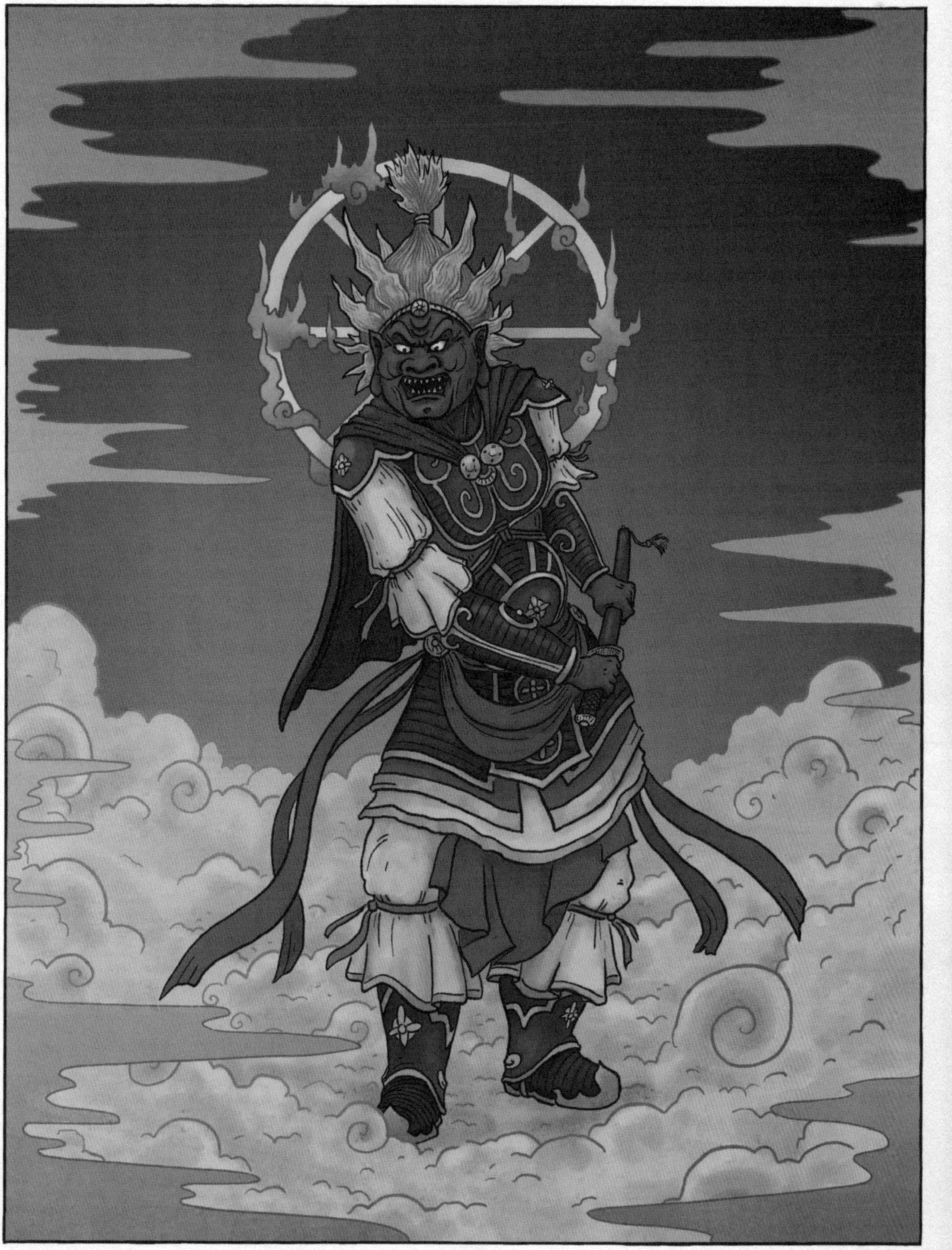

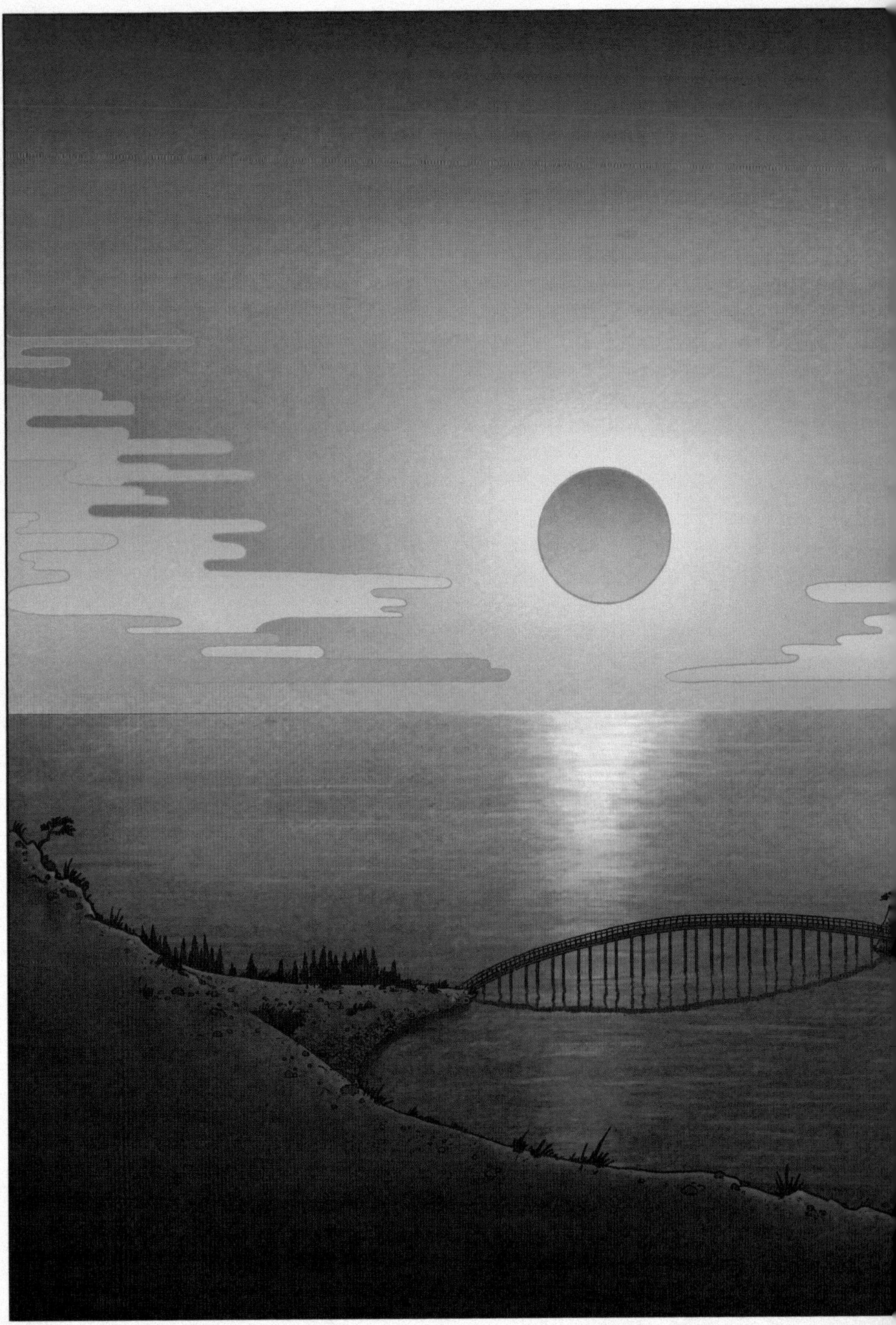

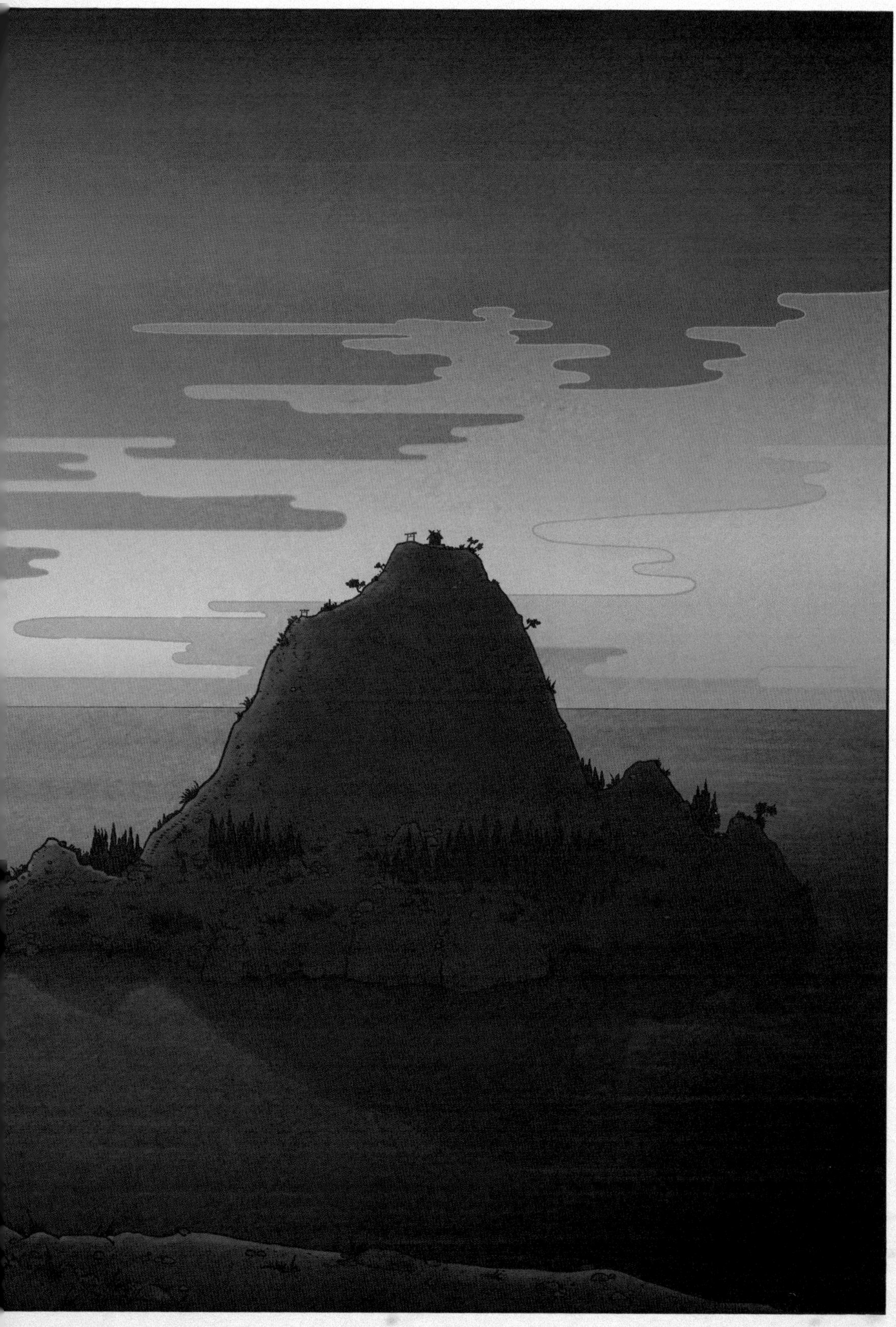

JINJA HIME 神社姫

TRANSLATION: shrine princess
HABITAT: deep lakes and oceans
DIET: unknown; probably omnivorous

APPEARANCE: Jinja hime are serpentine creatures roughly six meters long. They have two horns on their heads, long tails, dorsal fins, and flippers. Their faces are those of human women. They resemble ningyo, the Japanese mermaid.

BEHAVIOR: Jinja hime spend most of their lives underwater, and as a result rarely interact with humans. They are the servants of Ryūgū, the palace of the sea dragon king.

ORIGIN: Jinja hime was first sighted in Hizen Province (present-day Saga and Nagasaki Prefectures) in 1819 by the Edo period scholar Katō Ebian. He recorded the encounter in his book *Waga koromo*. According to Katō, he encountered a fish-like creature on a beach in Hizen. The creature spoke to him: "I am a messenger from Ryūgū, called jinja hime. For the next seven years there will be a bumper crop. After that, there will be an epidemic of cholera. However, those who see my picture will be able to avoid hardship and instead will have long life." After delivering her prophecy, the jinja hime disappeared into the sea. Katō printed an illustration of the jinja hime in *Waga koromo* so that all could see it and be protected.

The news of the jinja hime and her prognostication became so popular that it spawned numerous copycat stories across Japan. Not long after the sighting of jinja hime other stories about yōkai with foresight—such as kudan and amabie—began popping up all over Japan. Jinja hime is thought to be the basis for all of these stories.

The jinja hime resembles a real-world animal called the giant oarfish. Its name in Japanese is *ryūgū no tsukai*, which means "servant of Ryūgū"—the same title this yōkai used for itself.

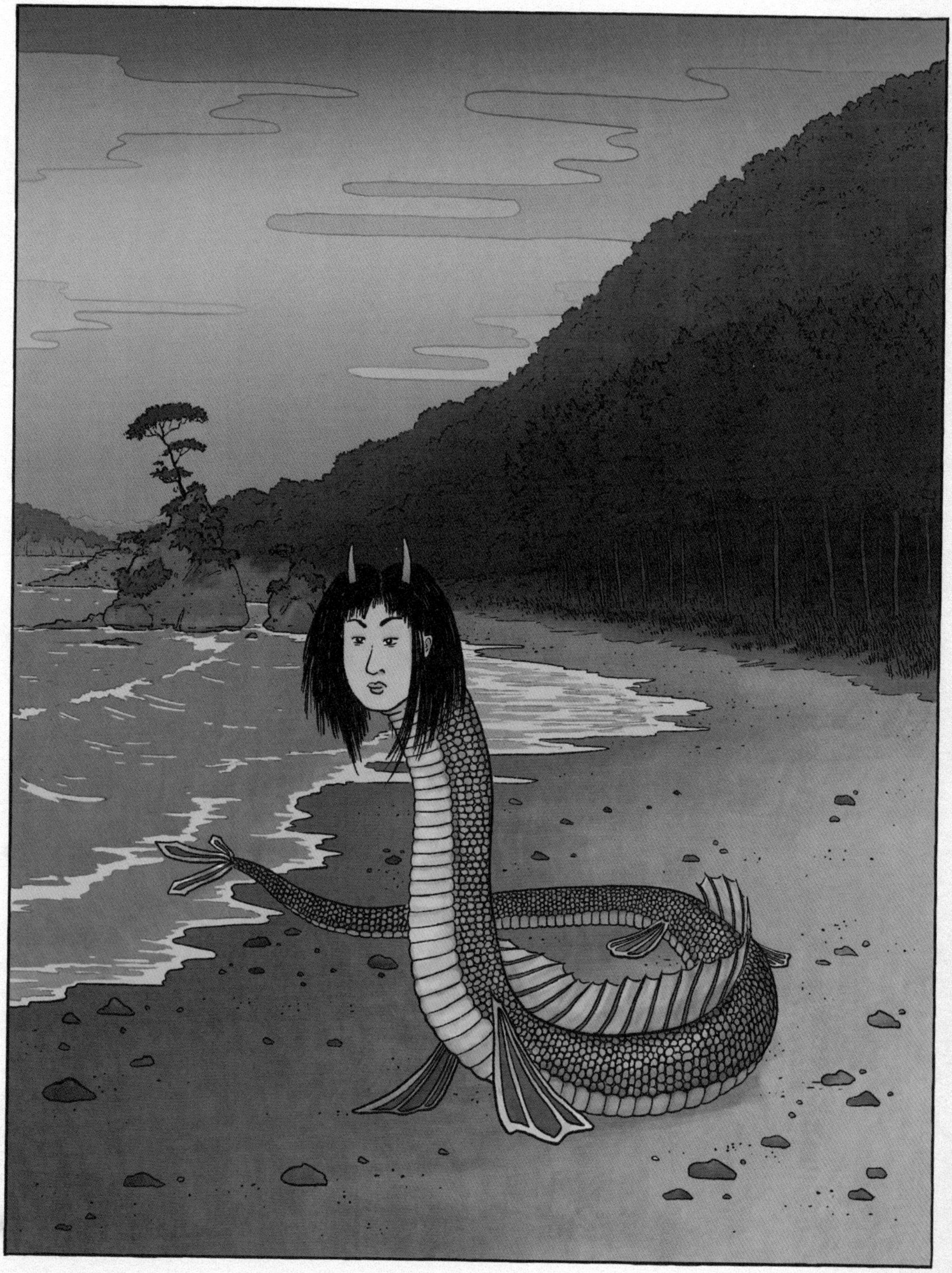

Gangi kozō 岸涯小僧

TRANSLATION: riverbank priest boy
HABITAT: rivers and riverbanks
DIET: fish

APPEARANCE: Gangi kozō are hairy, monkey-like water spirits which inhabit rivers. They live along the riverbanks where they hunt fish. Their bodies are covered in hair. The hair on their head resembles the bobbed *okappa* hair style once popular among children in Japan. They have webbed hands and toes, and long teeth which are sharp and jagged like files. They are close relatives of the much more well-known kappa.

BEHAVIOR: Gangi kozō are not encountered outside of riverbanks. There may be a good reason for this; according to one theory, they are a transitional form of kappa. Kappa are said to transform from river spirits into hairy mountain spirits when the seasons change. Different regions of Japan have different names for these different forms of kappa. In Yamaguchi Prefecture, there is a hairy mountain spirit called a takiwaro which transforms into a water spirit called an enko (a variety of kappa). Some folklorists believe that the gangi kozō is a kind of takiwaro, and thus is a transitional form of a kappa. This explains why so little is known of their natural behavior.

INTERACTIONS: Gangi kozō normally stay away from people, but occasionally encounter fishermen along the rivers they inhabit. When fishing near a place where gangi kozō live, fishermen often leave their largest, cheapest fish on the riverside as an offering.

ORIGIN: Though there are stories of similar-looking yōkai, gangi kozō do not appear by name in any local legends. The first written record of them is in Toriyama Sekien's yōkai encyclopedias. It is therefore possible that gangi kozō was made up by Toriyama Sekien based on the numerous legends of transforming kappa.

According to Mizuki Shigeru, the name gangi kozō can be written with another set of kanji: 雁木小僧. These characters can mean "stepped pier" or "gear tooth" depending on the context. This writing reflects both the riverside habitat of the gangi kozō as well as its mouth full of sharp teeth, which resemble toothed gears.

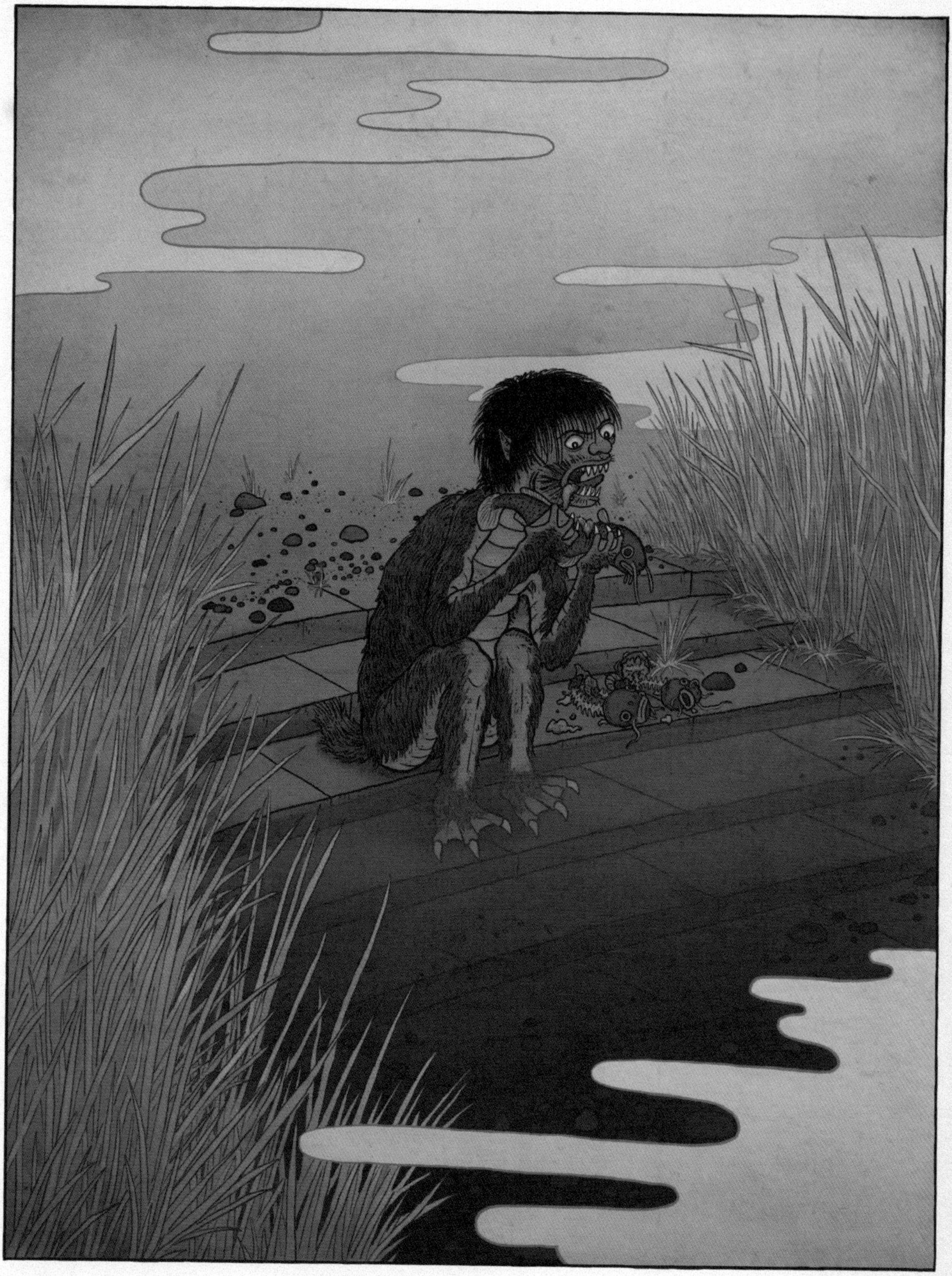

Tako nyūdō 蛸入道

TRANSLATION: octopus priest
ALTERNATE NAMES: tako bōzu
HABITAT: the Sea of Japan; particularly near Shimane Prefecture
DIET: carnivorous

APPEARANCE: Tako nyūdō is an octopus yōkai which takes on a humanoid form. It has a bulbous head and the face of a bearded, old priest. It has eight tentacles and wears human clothing.

BEHAVIOR: The *Bakemono emaki* depicts a tako nyūdō dangling a fish above the head of an unagi hime. It appears to be teasing or seducing her, however no description accompanies the painting. This yōkai's natural habitat is hidden from the human world, leaving its lifestyle a mystery.

INTERACTIONS: In Shimane Prefecture along the Sea of Japan, tako nyūdō are feared. They attack boats, grabbing fishermen and dragging them down beneath the waves.

ORIGIN: The phrase tako nyūdō is sometimes used to mockingly refer to bald-headed old men, as their smooth scalps resemble the heads of octopuses.

Unagi hime 鰻姫

TRANSLATION: eel princess
ALTERNATE NAMES: ōunagi (giant eel)
HABITAT: lakes and deep ponds, especially in Miyagi Prefecture
DIET: carnivorous

APPEARANCE: Unagi hime are large, shape-shifting eels which take on the appearance of beautiful women.

BEHAVIOR: Unagi hime live at the bottom of lakes and ponds. They are said to weave clothing on looms at the bottom of their ponds. The loom's clacking sound can be heard near the banks of ponds where an unagi hime lives.

INTERACTIONS: Unagi hime rarely interact with humans due to the fact that they live deep underwater. When fishermen discover one, they usually leave the area where it was encountered and try not to disturb it. People who catch eels near ponds inhabited by unagi hime are scolded by their peers.

ORIGIN: In Miyagi Prefecture, eels were believed to be guardians of the ponds they inhabit. They battle with other pond guardian animals such as crabs and spiders. These eels usually take the form of beautiful women and request the help of humans. Sometimes they find a famous warrior or priest who is willing to aid them, but in many stories the eel loses the battle.

LEGENDS: A warrior named Genbē lived near a deep pond. One rainy summer night, he took a walk around the pond. An eel who lived there appeared before Genbē in the form of a beautiful woman. She told him that on the following night, a spider who owned a nearby pond would come to fight her. She begged the warrior to stay by the pond and protect her, for with his help she would surely win the battle. Genbē promised to help. However, on the following evening, he grew cowardly and stayed at home, shaking. The next morning, he returned to the pond and found the severed head of a giant eel. Its unblinking eyes stared at him with such hatred that he lost his mind. He threw himself into the pond and drowned.

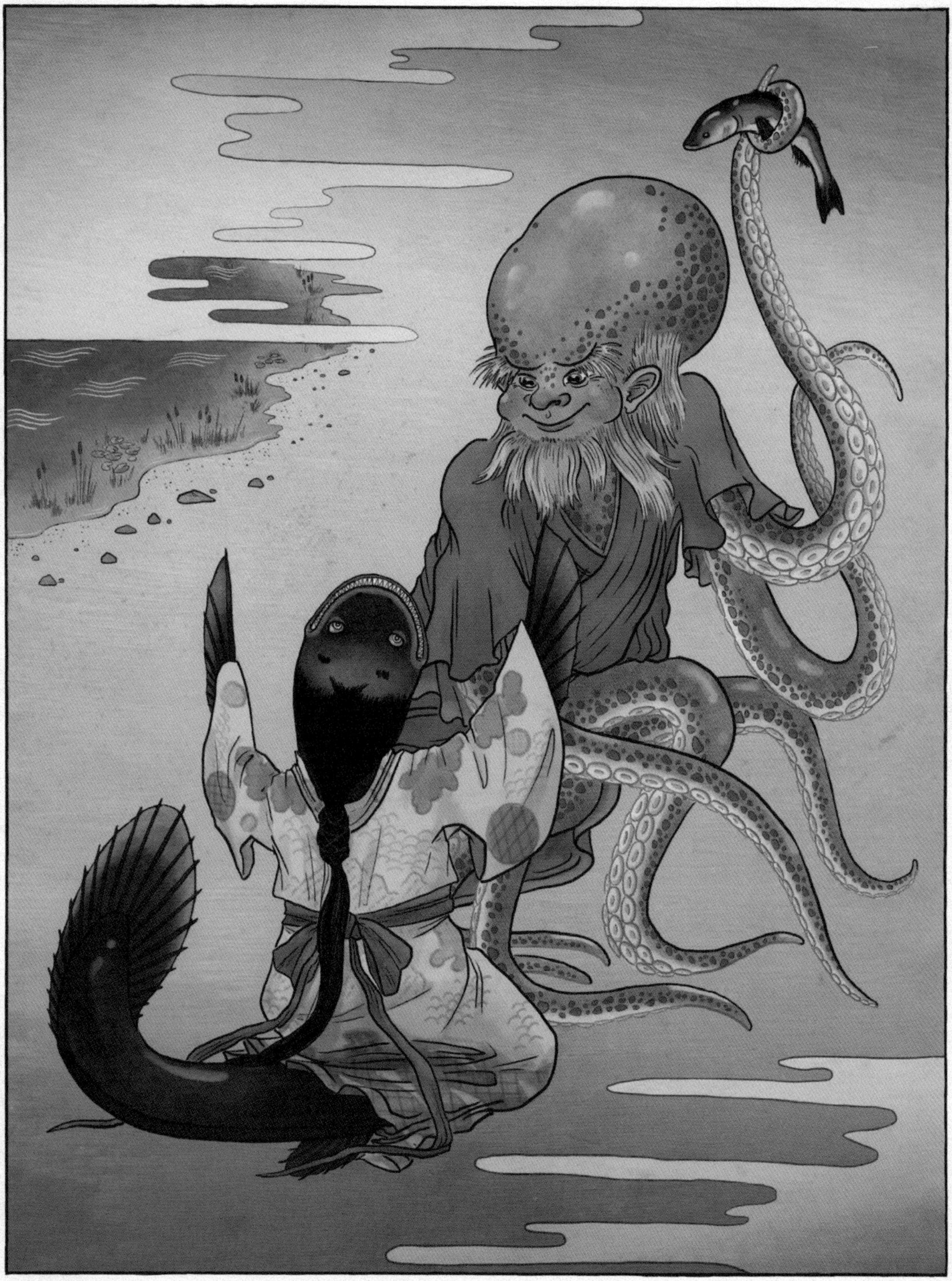

HANZAKI 鯢魚

TRANSLATION: giant salamander (*Andrias japonicus*)
ALTERNATE NAMES: ōsanshōuo, hanzake, hazako
HABITAT: rivers and streams
DIET: mainly insects, frogs, and fish

APPEARANCE: Hanzaki are monstrous versions of the Japanese giant salamander. These animals normally grow up to one and a half meters long. However, the yōkai versions can grow much larger. They have rough, mottled, brown and black skin, tiny eyes, and enormous mouths which span the entire width of their heads. They live in rivers and streams far from human-inhabited areas.

INTERACTIONS: Hanzaki and humans rarely come into contact with each other. When they do, it is usually because the hanzaki has grown large enough to start eating humans or livestock and is causing trouble for nearby villages.

ORIGIN: The name hanzaki is a colloquialism for the Japanese giant salamander. They are called hanzaki for their regenerative powers; it was believed that a salamander's body could be cut (*saku*) in half (*han*) and it would still survive. The call of the salamander was said to resemble that of a human baby. So, their name is written with kanji combining fish (魚) and child (兒).

LEGENDS: There was once a deep pond in which a gigantic hanzaki lived. The hanzaki would grab horses, cows, and even villagers, and drag them into the pond. It would then swallow them in a single gulp. For generations, the villagers lived in fear of the pond and stayed away from it.

During the first year of Bunroku (1593 CE), the villagers called for help asking if there was anyone brave enough to slay the hanzaki. A young villager named Miura no Hikoshirō volunteered. Hikoshirō grabbed his sword and dove into the pond. He did not come back up; he had been swallowed by the hanzaki in a single gulp! Moments later, Hikoshirō sliced through the hanzaki and tore it in half from the inside out, killing it instantly. The slain creature's body was 10 meters long, and 5 meters in girth.

The very day the hanzaki was slain, strange things began to happen at the Miura residence. Night after night, something would bang on the door. A screaming and crying voice could be heard just outside the door. However, when Hikoshirō opened the door to check, there was nothing there at all. Strange things began to occur all through the village as well.

Not long after that, Hikoshirō and his entire family died suddenly. The villagers believed the angry ghost of the dead hanzaki had cursed them. They built a small shrine and enshrined the hanzaki's spirit as a god, dubbing it Hanzaki Daimyōjin. After that, the hanzaki's spirit was pacified. The curse was laid to rest.

A gravestone dedicated to Miura no Hikoshirō still stands in Yubara, Okayama Prefecture. The villagers of Yubara still honor Hanzaki Daimyōjin by building giant salamander shrine floats and parading them through town during the annual Hanzaki Festival.

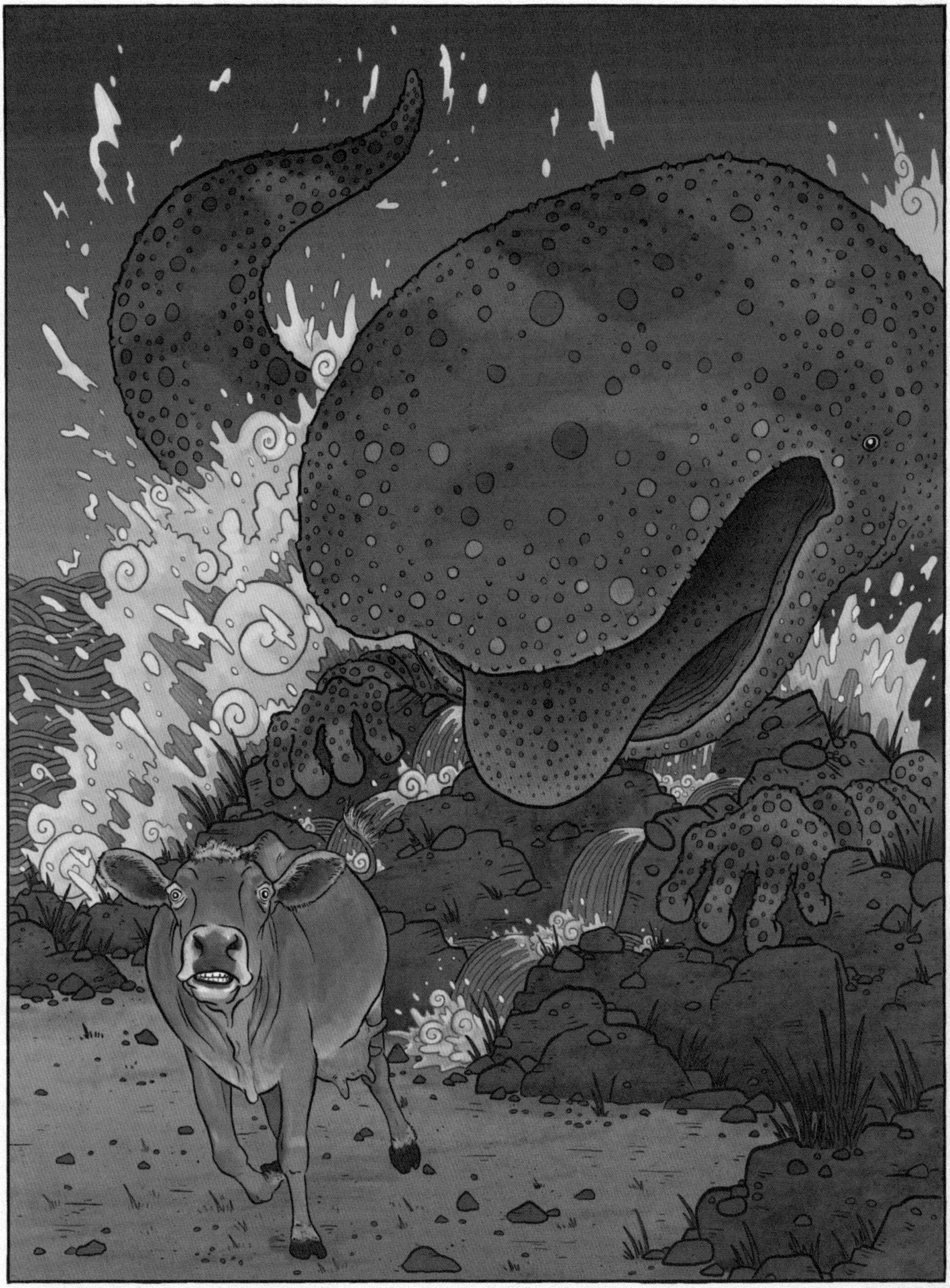

Kōjin 鮫人

TRANSLATION: shark person
ALTERNATE NAMES: samebito
HABITAT: oceans; particularly the South China Sea
DIET: carnivorous

APPEARANCE: Kōjin are aquatic humanoids that resemble mermaids. They have black, scaly shark-like bodies, and ugly, human-like faces and arms.

BEHAVIOR: Kōjin are well known for their weaving skills, and they spend much of their lives working on their looms. The sea silk that they weave is of the finest quality and doesn't get wet even in the water. Kōjin are emotional, and cry frequently. When they cry, pearls and gems fall from their eyes instead of tears.

LEGENDS: Long ago, a man named Tawaraya Tōtarō came across a strange looking creature crouching at the base of a bridge near Lake Biwa. It resembled a man, but its body was inky black, it had the face of a demon, the beard of a dragon, and its eyes were like green emeralds. It had served as an officer under the Eight Great Dragon Kings in the dragon palace of Ryūgū-jō but was banished from the palace and exiled from the sea due to a small mistake he had made. Since then, it had been wandering, unable to find food or shelter. It begged Tōtarō for help.

Tōtarō took the kōjin back to his home where he had a small garden with a pond. He allowed the kōjin to live there for as long as it wanted. For six months they lived together. Every day Tōtarō brought the kōjin fresh food fit for a sea creature.

During the seventh month, Tōtarō met a woman of extraordinary beauty and refinement. Her skin was white as snow, and her voice like a nightingale's. Her name was Tamana. Tōtarō fell in love with her at first sight. She was unwed and her family wanted her to marry a man of rank. They demanded as a betrothal gift a casket of ten thousand jewels from whomever wished to marry Tamana.

Tōtarō fell into despair. Even if there were ten thousand jewels in all of Japan, he would never be able to procure them. It seemed impossible that he could ever make Tamana his wife. Yet he could not get her out of his mind. He refused to eat or sleep and became so ill that he could not even lift his head from his pillow. It seemed that he would die of a broken heart. The kōjin cared for Tōtarō in this time. Tōtarō apologized to the kōjin, for if he died, it would surely die as well. The kōjin was so touched by Tōtarō's concern that it began to cry. Great tears of blood spilled from its eyes, and when they hit the floor they hardened into splendid rubies.

Tōtarō instantly found new strength and gathered up the jewels. Seeing Tōtarō recover, the kōjin stopped crying. The flow of jewels stopped. Tōtarō begged it to continue crying until he had ten thousand jewels, but seeing that Tōtarō's sickness was cured, the kōjin was filled with relief and could not cry anymore. He suggested that they visit the bridge where they had first met to reminisce, and perhaps it could cry again.

The next day, they visited the bridge. They ate fish and drank wine and watched the sunset. The kōjin thought about its life in the sea and its happy days in the dragon palace. Overcome with homesickness, it began to weep profusely. A great shower of jewels covered the bridge. Tōtarō gathered them up. When he had collected ten thousand jewels he shouted for joy. Suddenly, a song was heard far away in the sea. A glorious palace made of coral the color of the setting sun rose like a cloud out of the water. The Eight Great Dragon Kings had granted the kōjin amnesty and were calling it back home. The kōjin leaped with joy. It bade farewell to Tōtarō, thanked him for his friendship, and then dove into the sea.

Tōtarō never saw the kōjin again. He brought the casket of ten thousand jewels to Tamana's family and presented them as a betrothal gift. Shortly after, Tōtarō and Tamana were married.

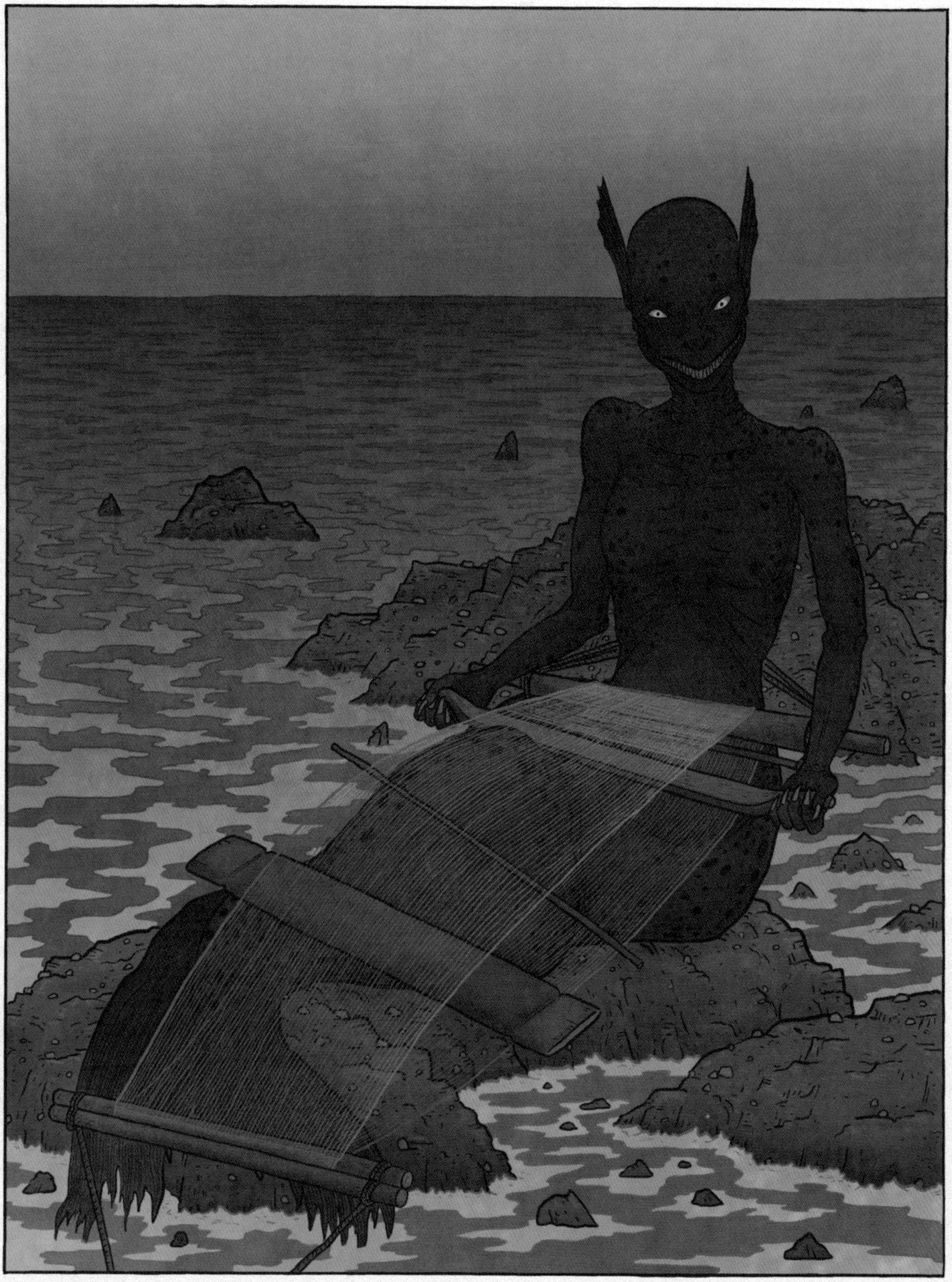

Amabie アマビエ

TRANSLATION: unknown; possibly a misspelling of "amabiko"
HABITAT: oceans
DIET: unknown

APPEARANCE: Amabie are mermaid-like yōkai with a mixture of human and fish features. They have long hair and scaly bodies. They have beak-like mouths and three legs. Amabie glow with a bright light that can be seen from the shore. Amabie are auspicious yōkai—keeping a picture of an amabie can protect you from disease.

ORIGIN: Little is known of the amabie's characteristics. However, their story is similar to other prophetic yōkai such as jinja hime and kudan, which deliver a prognostication and then disappear. These yōkai first appeared during periods when epidemics like cholera were spreading around the world. Fear of disease was widespread, and images of protector yōkai that could be used as charms against sicknesses were in high demand. It is possible that amabie were a sort of copycat yōkai, following the trends of the time.

The origin of the name amabie is a mystery. There is only one recording of an amabie sighting and it appears similar to another yōkai with a similar sounding name: amabiko. There are numerous recorded amabiko sightings. All of them are minor variations on the same theme: a three-legged creature that appears on the water to deliver a prophecy about abundant harvests and disease. Similarly, amabiko instructs people to spread its image around to protect them from the disease. "Amabie" may have been a simple typographical error, or else it may be a regional variation of the amabiko.

LEGENDS: The only recorded sighting of an amabie comes from Higo Province (present-day Kumamoto Prefecture) in April of 1846. For some nights in a row, a bright light could be seen in the waters off shore. One night, a government official went out to see to investigate the light. When he approached, a strange creature appeared before him. The creature introduced itself as an amabie. It told the government official that a six-year bumper crop was coming. It also said that should there be an outbreak of disease, he should immediately show the amabie's picture to people everywhere as it would protect them against harm. After that, the creature returned to the sea. Shortly after, the amabie's story along with an illustration of it was featured in the newspaper to be distributed to as many people as possible.

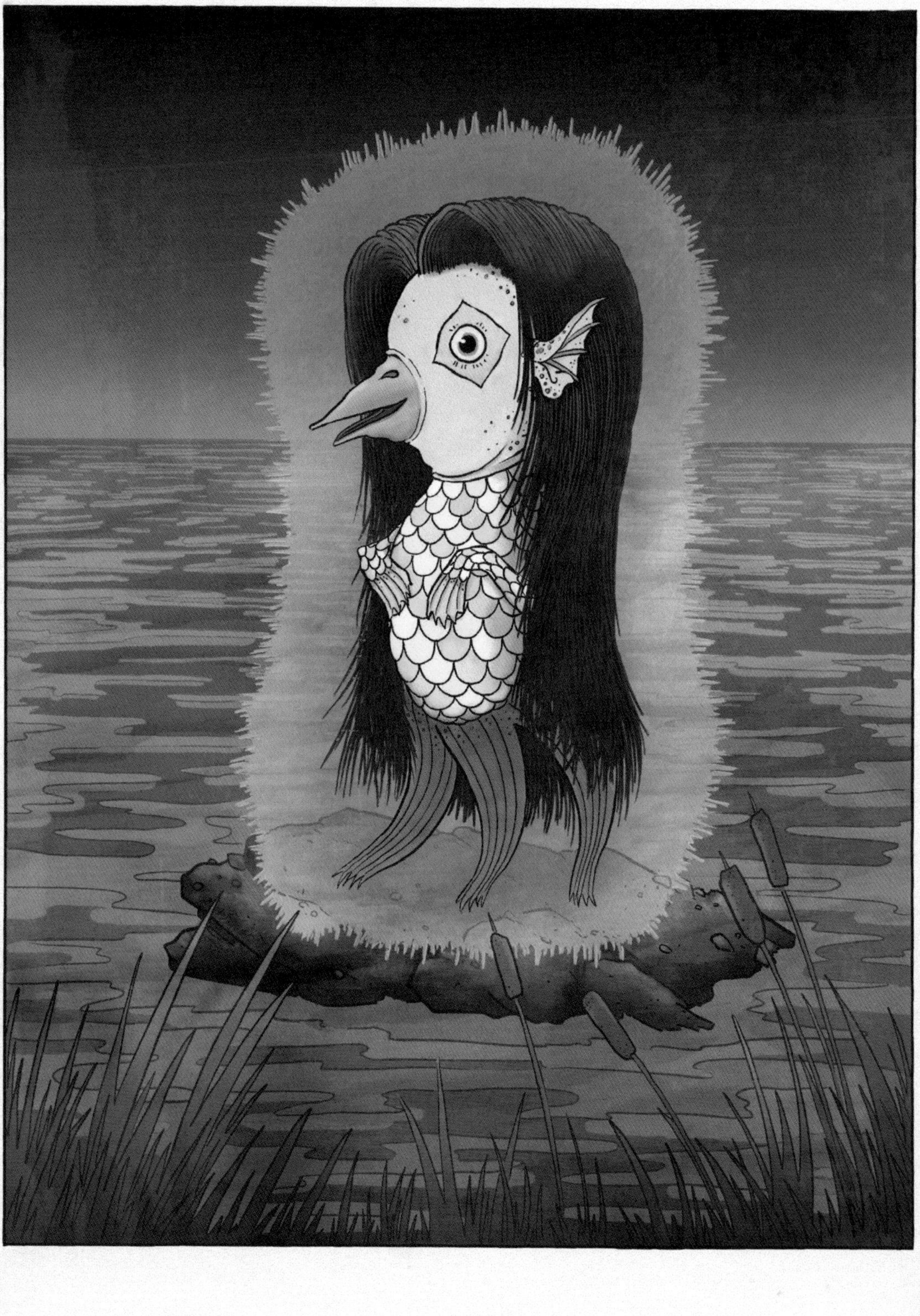

AKKORO KAMUI アッコロカムイ

TRANSLATION: string-holding god
HABITAT: Uchiura Bay in Hokkaido
DIET: omnivorous; it can swallow ships and whales whole

APPEARANCE: Akkoro kamui is a gigantic octopus god which resides in Hokkaido's Uchiura Bay. When it extends its legs, its body stretches over one hectare in area. It is so big that it can swallow boats and even whales in a single gulp. Its entire body is red. Akkoro kamui is so large that when it appears the sea and even the sky reflect its color, turning a deep red.

INTERACTIONS: Any ship foolish enough to sail too close to Akkoro kamui are swallowed whole. Therefore, for generations, locals have stayed away from the water when the sea and sky turn red. Fishermen and sailors who had no choice but to be on the waters would carry scythes with them for protection.

ORIGIN: Akkoro kamui comes from Ainu folklore, where it is known as Atkor kamuy. Its name can be translated as "string-holding kamuy." String-holding likely refers to the octopus's string-like tentacles, while *kamuy* is an Ainu term for a divine being—similar to the Japanese term kami. In Ainu folklore, Akkoro kamui is both revered and feared as a water deity, specifically as the lord of Uchiura Bay.

Legends: Long ago, in the mountains near the village of Rebunge, there lived a gigantic spider named Yaushikep. Yaushikep was enormous. His great red body stretched over one hectare in area. One day, Yaushikep descended from the mountains and attacked the people of Rebunge. He shook the earth as he rampaged, destroying everything in his path. The villagers were terrified. They prayed to the gods to save them. The god of the sea, Repun kamuy, heard their prayers and pulled Yaushikep into the bay. When the great spider was taken into the water, he transformed into a giant octopus and took over charge of the bay as its god. Ever since then, he has been known as Atkor kamuy, or Akkoro kamui in Japanese pronunciation.

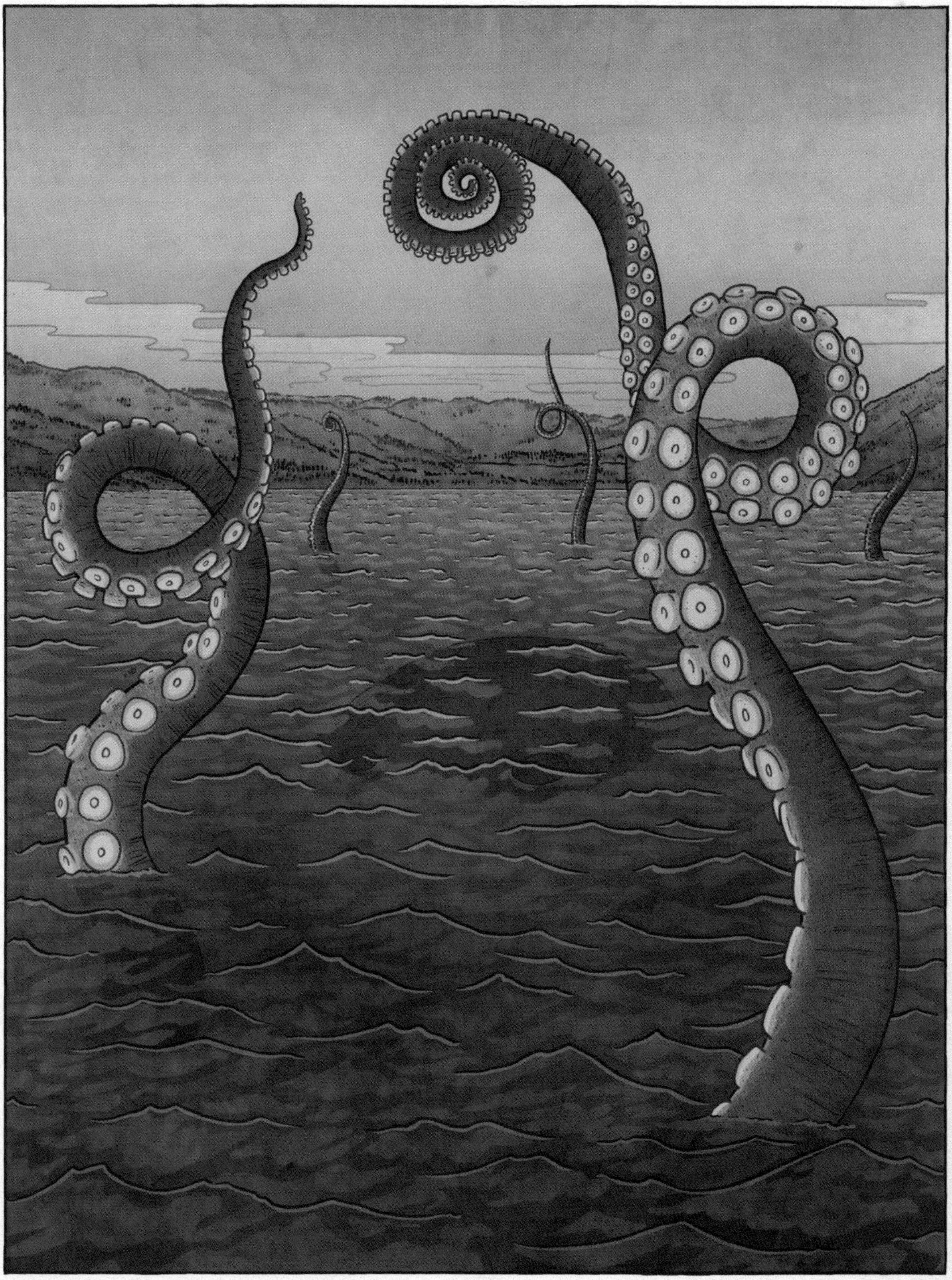

ATUI KAKURA アトゥイカクラ

TRANSLATION: ocean sea cucumber
ALTERNATE NAMES: atsuui kakura
HABITAT: Uchiura bay in Hokkaido
DIET: mainly a scavenger; occasionally eats ships

APPEARANCE: Atui kakura is an enormous sea cucumber which lives deep in Uchiura Bay in Hokkaido.

BEHAVIOR: Atui kakura is rarely seen due its underwater lifestyle. It spends most of its time deep in the water, occasionally attaching itself to chunks of driftwood and floating to other parts of the bay.

INTERACTIONS: Despite rarely being seen, Atui kakura can be dangerous to ships on the bay. When Atui kakura is startled, it thrashes about wildly, smashing or capsizing ships which happen to be near it. It also sometimes mistakes a wooden boat for a piece of driftwood, attaches its mouth to it, and drags the ship under the waves.

ORIGIN: Atui kakura is the Japanese transcription of its Ainu name, Atuy kakura. *Atuy* is the Ainu word for the sea, and *kakura* means sea cucumber. According to local legend, Atui kakura was formed when a *mouru*—the traditional undergarment of Ainu women—washed down a river and into the bay. The mouru settled at the bottom of Uchiura Bay and turned into a giant sea cucumber.

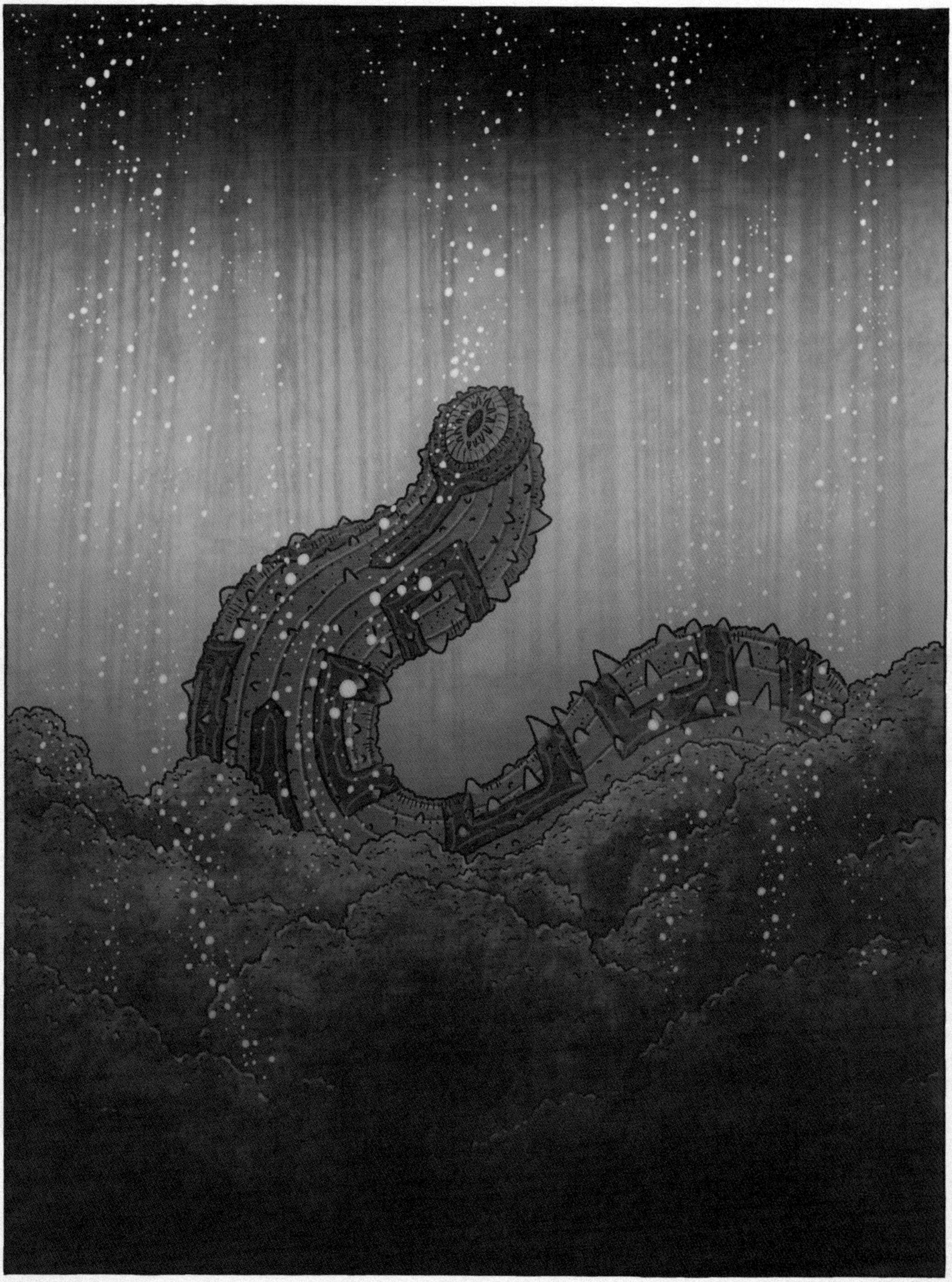

AMEMASU 雨鱒

TRANSLATION: white-spotted char; literally "rain trout"
HABITAT: cold streams and lakes, occasionally seagoing
DIET: carnivorous, ranging from small fish and plankton up to and including large boats

APPEARANCE: Amemasu is the Japanese name for the white-spotted char (*Salvelinus leucomaenis*), a species of trout which is found in Northeast Asia.

BEHAVIOR: Amemasu spend most of their lives in the water away from humans. They are found mostly in rivers and streams, but seagoing varieties also exist. They are more common in Hokkaido, the northern parts of Honshu, and along the Sea of Japan. However, legends of amemasu occasionally take place in the southern parts of Japan. They feed on whatever they can eat, from plankton to insects, to fish and any other aquatic lifeforms they can fit into their mouths.

Yōkai amemasu can grow to colossal sizes, sometimes spanning an entire lake from head to tail. These gigantic fish also occasionally thrash and sink ships, devouring any poor souls who happened to be on the ship. In Ainu folklore, the wild thrashing of giant amemasu is believed to be what causes earthquakes—much like giant catfish are thought to cause earthquakes in the rest of Japan.

INTERACTIONS: Ordinary amemasu are a popular target of game fishing and are also raised in fisheries. Amemasu that have become yōkai can transform into human shape and walk about on land. They usually take the form of young, beautiful women in order to seduce young men. Shape-changed amemasu can be identified by their skin, which feels cold and clammy like that of a fish.

LEGENDS: A number of lakes in Hokkaido are believed to be the home of giant amemasu. According to Ainu folklore, these amemasu are the guardian deities of their lakes. Lake Mashū is home to an amemasu the size of a whale. Lake Shikotsu contains an amemasu so large that its head touches one end of the lake and its tail touches the other.

A legend from Minabe, Wakayama Prefecture tells of a mysterious whirlpool that appeared in a deep pond. A giant amemasu lived in the pond. Every spring, she would emerge from the pond in the form of a beautiful woman. For two or three days she would catch young men and take them away—where to nobody knows, but they were never seen again. The only way to know this woman was a fish and not a human was from her cold, clammy skin. One day, a cormorant dove into the pond to go hunting. The giant amemasu swallowed the bird in a single gulp. However, after a short time, the amemasu's body floated up to the surface of the pond, dead. The cormorant burst out of its stomach. Afterwards a shrine was built at that spot in honor of Konpira, the god of seafaring. It still stands there today.

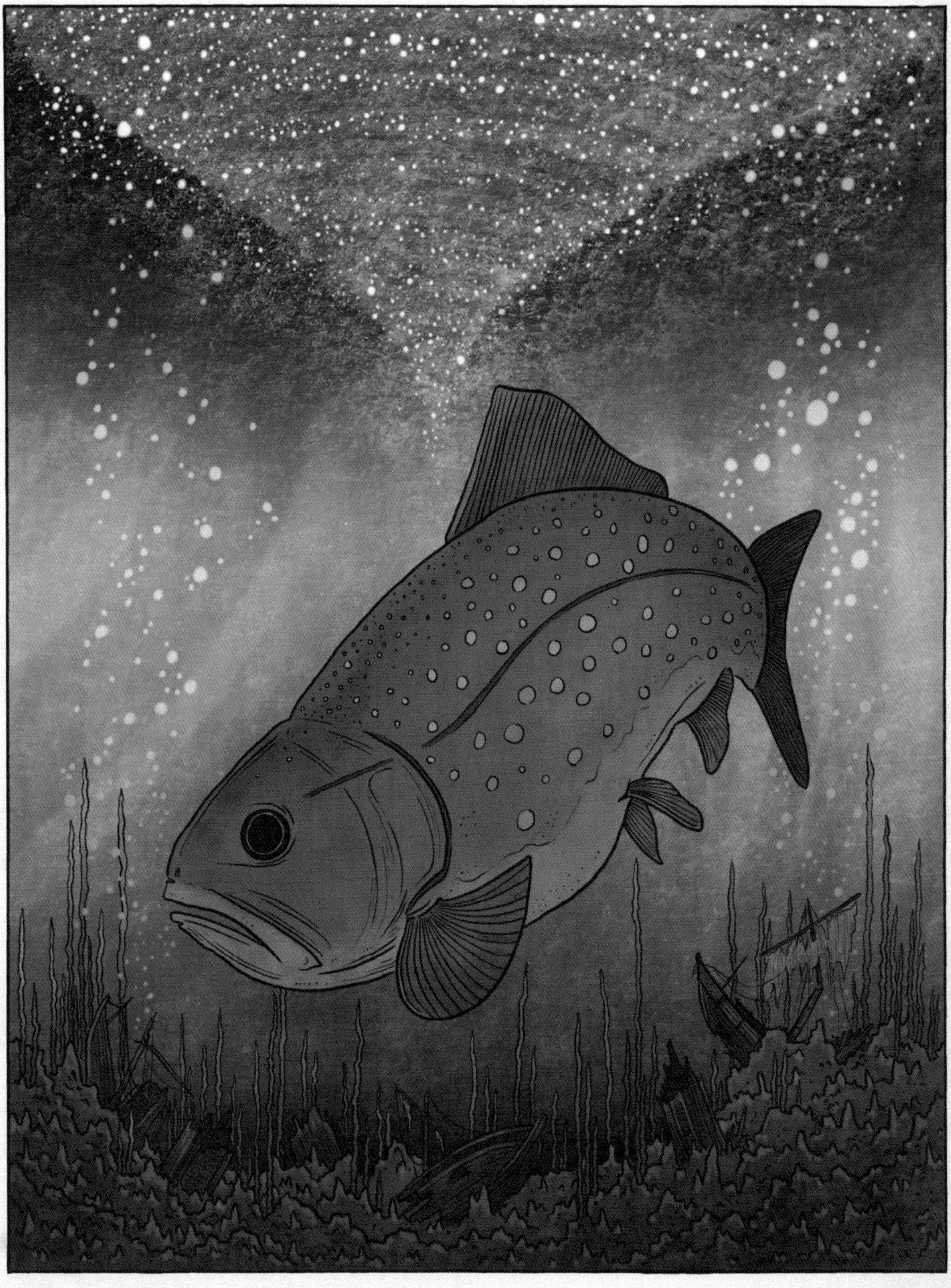

Tomokazuki トモカヅキ

TRANSLATION: diving together
ALTERNATE NAMES: umiama
HABITAT: coastal areas where shellfish are found
DIET: unknown

APPEARANCE: Tomokazuki are aquatic yōkai found underwater that appear to *ama*, the deep-diving women who gather oysters, urchins, and other sea creatures. They appear on cloudy days. They are a kind of diving doppelganger; they take on the appearance of the ama who see them. The only way to tell them apart from actual women is the length of the headbands they wear; tomokazuki have much longer headbands.

INTERACTIONS: Tomokazuki appear to divers deep underwater. They beckon the divers closer to them, offering shellfish and sea urchins as a way to lure them deeper. They continue to lure the divers deeper and farther away from safety. Eventually the divers are lured too deep or too far from the shore, and they drown.

In order to protect themselves from tomokazuki, superstitious ama will carry magic charms with them while diving; usually in the form of the *seiman* and *dōman* symbols on their headbands.

ORIGIN: Since tomokazuki are only ever seen by ama deep under the water, belief in them is not widespread. Most of the time, tales of tomokazuki encounters are written off as hallucinations or delirium brought on by the stresses of deep diving—high pressure, lack of oxygen, physical exhaustion, and the fear of being swept away. One popular explanation among believers is that tomokazuki are the ghosts of drowned ama.

In one story from Shizuoka Prefecture, an ama and her husband took a boat out to sea to dive for shellfish. While deep underwater, the ama saw a tomokazuki and quickly surfaced to tell her husband. He mocked her for believing in stupid things and told her to keep working. The ama dove back down as her husband commanded. She was never seen again.

In Fukui Prefecture there is yōkai called an umiama, which is similar to a tomokazuki. When an ama dives down to the sea floor, the umiama surfaces. Then, when the ama surfaces, the umiama dives down to the sea floor. Because of this, it is difficult to spot this yōkai. However, those unlucky few who do manage to see it become gravely ill shortly afterwards.

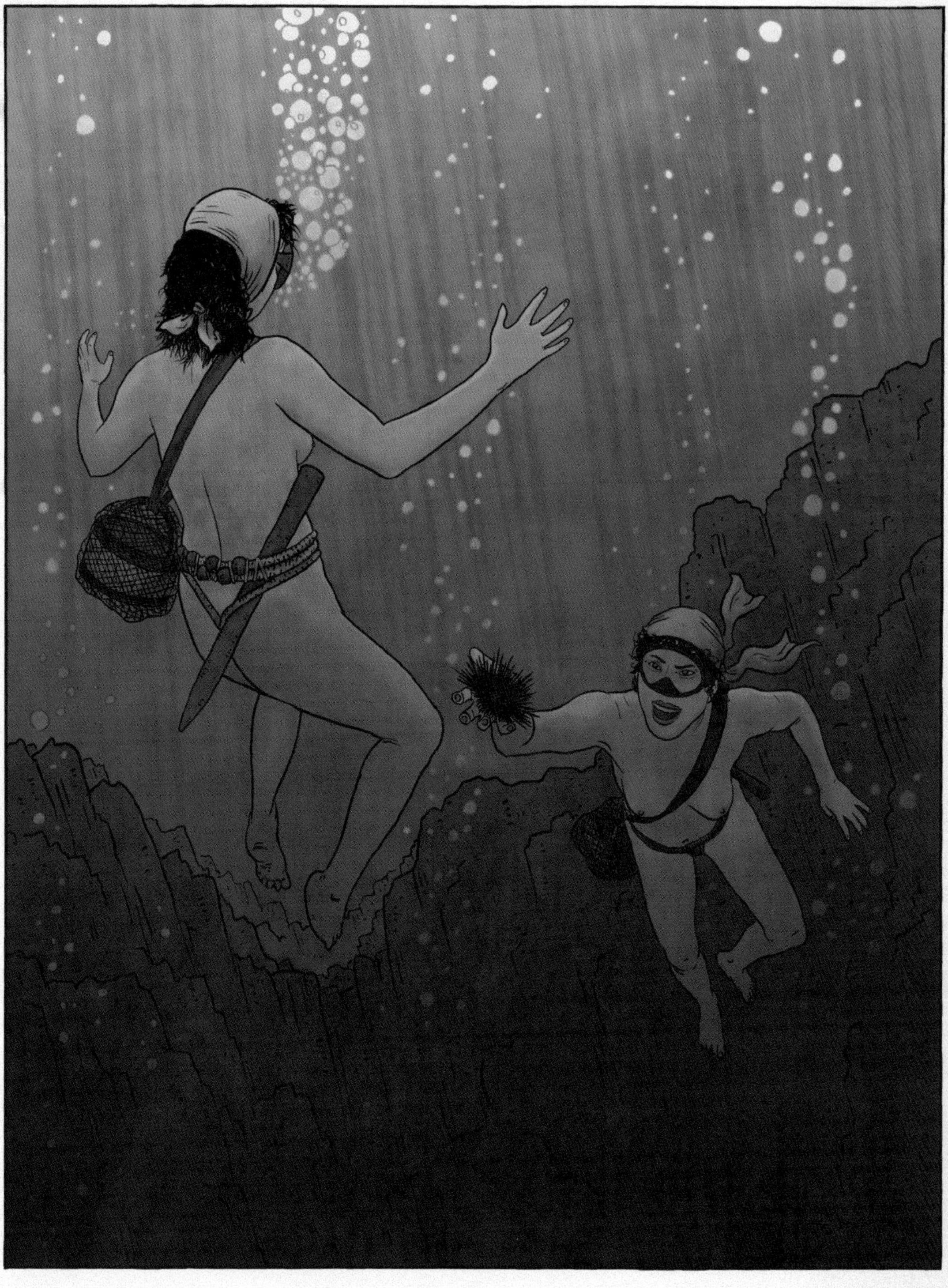

Ōnamazu 大鯰

TRANSLATION: giant catfish
ALTERNATE NAMES: jishin namazu (earthquake catfish)
HABITAT: rivers, seas, oceans, and subterranean caverns
DIET: omnivorous

APPEARANCE: Ōnamazu are gigantic catfish which live in the muck and slime of the waterways around Japan. They also inhabit large caverns deep underground, working their way into the cracks in the earth.

BEHAVIOR: Ōnamazu behave much like ordinary catfish. They dig in the muck, and thrash about when disturbed or excited. Due to their titanic mass, the thrashing of ōnamazu is considerably more violent than that of ordinary catfish, to the point where they are dangerous. When these monstrous fish get excited, they shake the earth with their violent thrashing. Ōnamazu cause devastating earthquakes in the areas near where they live.

INTERACTIONS: Ōnamazu do not normally encounter people. However, during the Edo period they were frequently depicted in newspaper illustrations. Usually these pictures showed a huge, grotesque catfish being subdued by a large number of people, gods, or even other yōkai desperately trying to calm its thrashing.

ORIGIN: Long ago, common belief was that earthquakes were caused by large dragons which lived deep in the earth. During the Edo period, the idea of catfish causing earthquakes gradually began to displace dragons in popular lore as the origin of seismic activity. By the 1855 Great Ansei Earthquake, the ōnamazu had become the popular culprit to blame for earthquakes. This was due mostly to the hundreds of illustrations of thrashing catfish which accompanied newspapers reporting the news of that disaster. They were so popular they spawned an entire genre of woodblock print: namazue (catfish pictures).

The reason catfish came to represent earthquakes was due to a large number of witnesses observing catfish behaving oddly just before tremors, thrashing about violently for seemingly no reason. Rumor quickly spread that that catfish had some kind of ability to foresee the coming disaster. Since then, the catfish has regularly appeared as a symbol for earthquakes—either as the cause or as a warning sign of the coming disaster. Studies have shown that catfish are in fact electrosensitive and do become significantly more active shortly before an earthquake.

LEGENDS: The Kashima Shrine in Ibaraki Prefecture has a famous story about ōnamazu. The deity of the shrine, a patron deity of martial arts named Takemikazuchi, is said to have subdued one. He wrestled and pinned it down underneath the shrine, piercing its head and tail with a sacred stone which still remains in the shrine today. The tip of the stone protrudes from the ground. Earthquakes that take place during the 10th month of the lunar calendar—known as "the godless month," when the gods all travel to Izumo—are said to be due to Takemikazuchi's absence from the shrine.

During the 2011 Tōhoku disaster, the Kashima Shrine was badly damaged by an earthquake. The large stone gate was destroyed, stone lanterns were knocked down, and the water level in the reflecting pond changed. The gate was rebuilt in 2014.

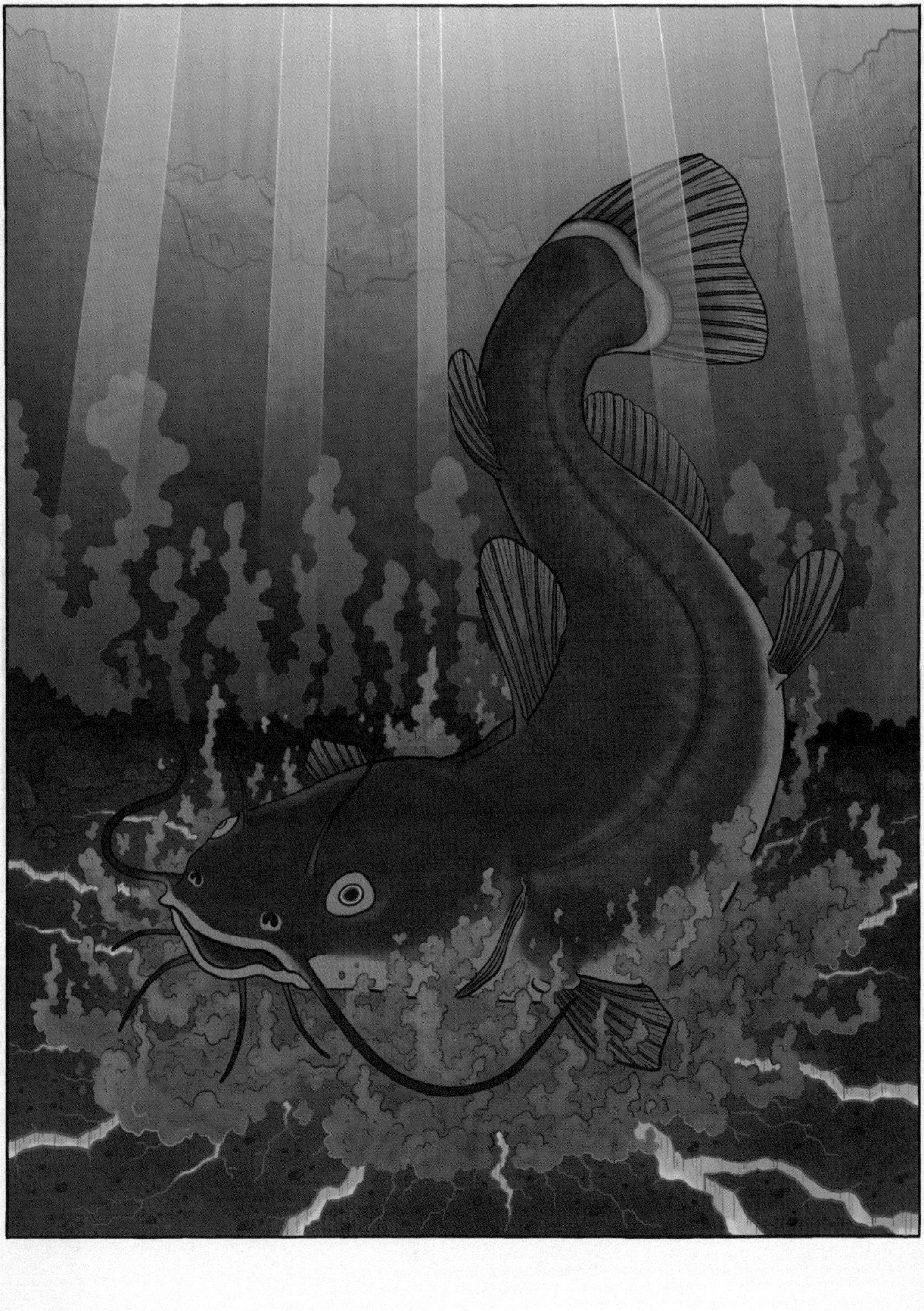

SHACHIHOKO 鯱

TRANSLATION: none; this is the creature's name (written with kanji that mean fish and tiger)
ALTERNATE NAMES: shachi
HABITAT: cold oceans
DIET: carnivorous

APPEARANCE: Shachihoko are fearsome sea monsters. They have the body of a large fish and the head of a tiger. Their broad fins and tails always point towards the heavens, and their dorsal fins have numerous sharp spikes. Shachihoko live in colder, norther oceans. They are able to swallow massive amounts of water with a single gulp and hold it in their bellies. They are also able to summon clouds and control the rain.

INTERACTIONS: Shachihoko are often found adorning the rooftops of Japanese castles, temples, gates, and samurai residences. They are placed facing each other on opposite ends of a roof. They serve as protector icons, similar to the oni roof tiles also commonly found on castles. It was believed that in the event of a fire, the shachihoko could protect the building by summoning rain clouds or by spitting out massive amounts of water which they had previously swallowed.

ORIGIN: Shachihoko as an element of architecture evolved from *shibi*–large, ornamental roof end tiles. Shibi originated in China during the Jin dynasty and were popularized in Japan during the Nara and Heian Periods. During the Sengoku Period, when castles rapidly began appearing all over Japan, shibi were reimagined as large fish, and the current image of the shachihoko was popularized. From them on, shachihoko have remained popular elements of Japanese roof construction.

Shachihoko's origins may go even further back to India. In Hindu mythology, there is a large sea monster named Makara who is half-fish and half-beast (sometimes depicted as an elephant, a deer, a crocodile, or another animal). Makara was a powerful protector and servant of various deities. Images of Makara were commonly used in temple architecture, particularly over archways and doorways, or as rain spouts. Japanese versions of Makara tend to resemble the shachihoko more than they resemble the original Hindu creature.

Today, the Japanese word for the orca is *shachi* because of its similarity to this mythical creature.

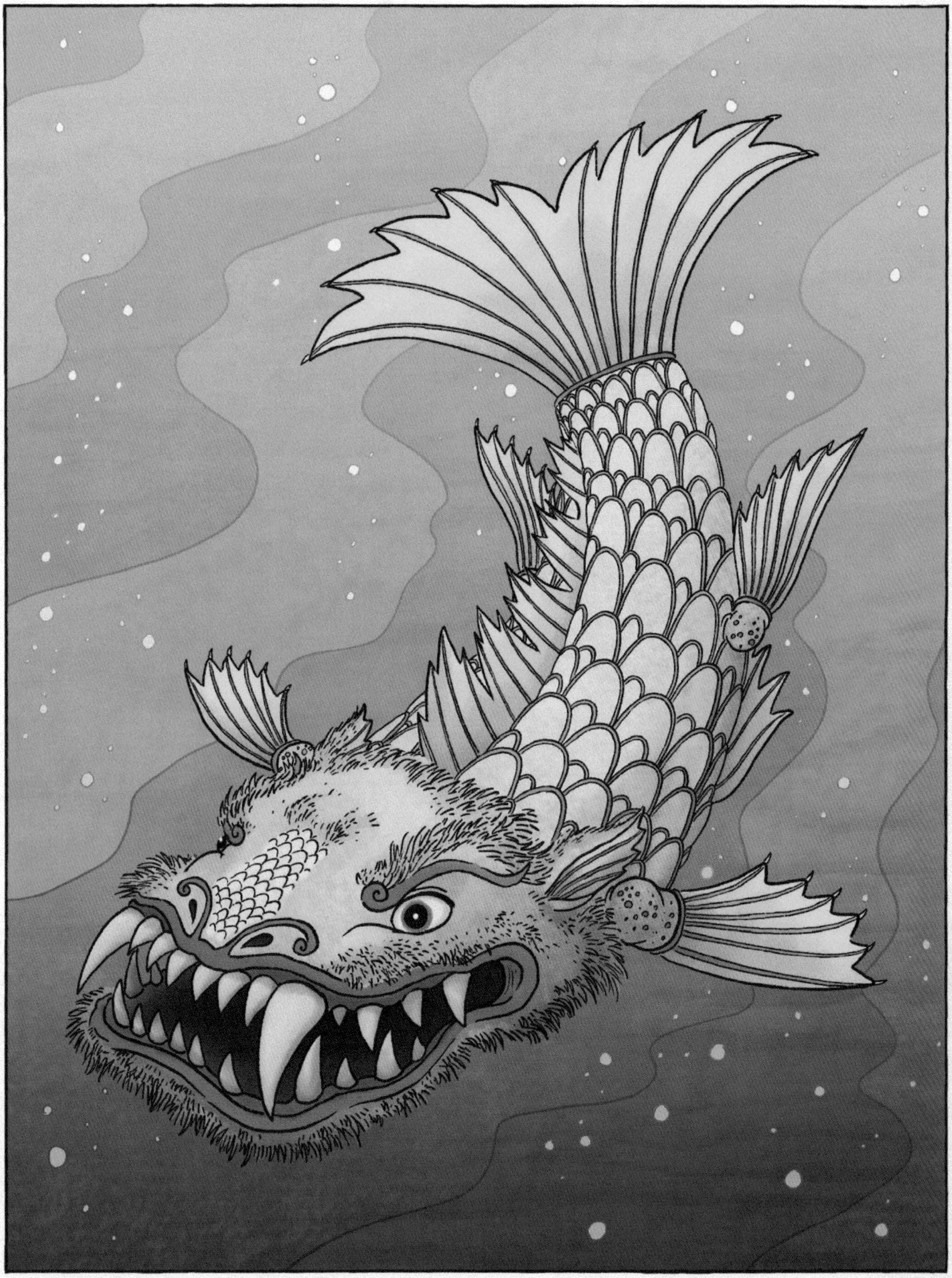

SHUSSEBORA 出世螺

TRANSLATION: eminent giant triton
HABITAT: migrates from mountains, to valleys, and finally to seas
DIET: omnivorous

APPEARANCE: Like many animals, giant tritons (*Charonia tritonis*)—a kind of sea snail similar to a conch—can turn into yōkai after living for an extraordinarily long time. When giant tritons reach an age of several thousand years old, they transform into draconic creatures called shussebora.

BEHAVIOR: Long ago, it was believed that giant tritons started their lives deep in the mountains. They spent many years buried under the earth, growing larger and larger. After three thousand years they exited the mountains and descended into the valleys in great landslides. Then they spent three thousand more years living near human villages, until they finally burrowed down into the sea. After three thousand more years underwater, they transformed into mizuchi—a kind of sea dragon.

INTERACTIONS: Because they spend their years buried in the earth or deep in the sea, shussebora very rarely ever encounter humans. However, the caves they leave behind during their migrations serve as a testament to their existence. All over Japan, after landslides people have discovered large caves in which shussebora were thought to have lived. These discoveries were even documented in newspapers during the Meiji period.

The flesh of a shussebora was said to bring long life to anyone who ate it. However, the rareness of these creatures made confirmation of this rumor difficult. Nobody who has eaten a shussebora has come forth to tell their story.

ORIGIN: Because of the ambiguous nature of these creatures, the rumors about their life-giving meat, and the lack of any evidence other the caves they allegedly lived in, the phrase *hora wo fuku* ("to blow a conch shell," meaning to brag), is said to have originated from this yōkai.

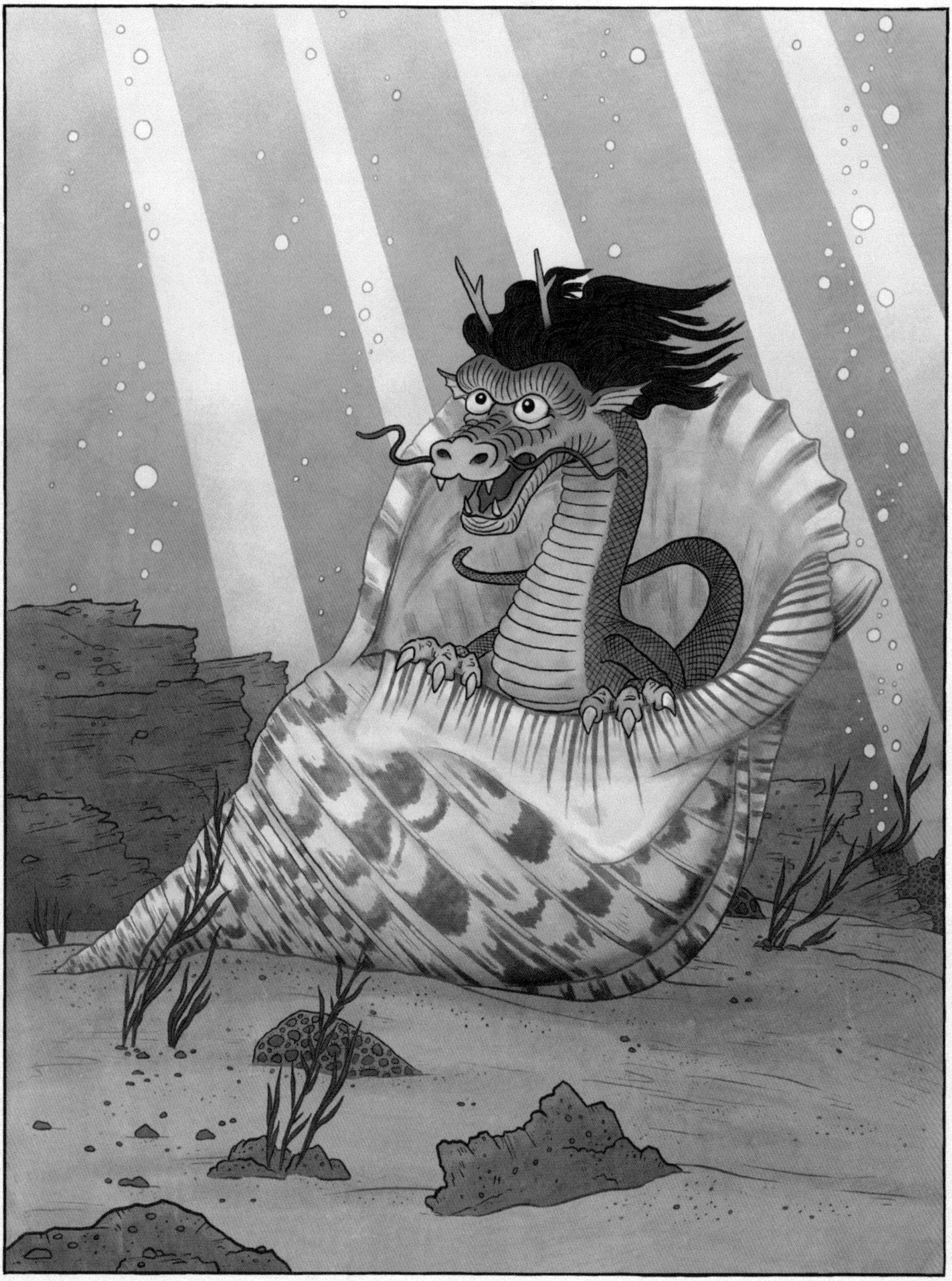

WANI 和邇

TRANSLATION: none; this is the creature's name
HABITAT: oceans, seas, and lakes
DIET: omnivorous

APPEARANCE: Wani are sea dragons that live in deep bodies of water. They have long serpentine bodies, fins, and can breathe both air and water. They are able to shapeshift into humans. There are even tales of wani and humans falling in love.

BEHAVIOR: Wani are the rulers of the oceans and gods of the sea. They live in splendid coral palaces on the ocean floor. Wani have a complex political hierarchy which mirrors that of the surface world. There are kings and queens, princes and princess, courtesans, servants, and so on. Ōwatatsumi, also known as Ryūjin, is the greatest of them all. He rules the sea from his palace Ryūgū-jō. He controls the ebb and flow of the tides using the magic jewels *kanju* and *manju*.

ORIGIN: Wani appear in the earliest written records of Japanese myths, the *Kojiki* and *Nihon shoki*. They almost certainly go back even further, into the mists of prehistory. Scholars disagree over whether the earliest legends of wani originated in Japan or were imported from other cultures, citing similarities between wani and the Chinese long or the Indian naga. Wani play an important role in Japanese mythology, including in the mythological founding of Japan.

The word wani first appears written in man'yōgana, an ancient phonetic syllabary. Later it came to be written with the kanji 鰐. Wani came to refer to sharks and other sea monsters that sailors and fishermen might encounter out at sea. The sea was a dangerous and mysterious place. Sailors may have thought that sharks were the powerful monsters they had heard about legends. Over time, the meaning of the word expanded to include to crocodiles as well as sharks, and then later shifted exclusively to mean crocodiles. Today both the kanji and the word wani mean crocodile. They are rarely used to refer to sea dragons.

LEGENDS: One of the most famous wani legends is the story of Toyotama hime, the daughter of Ōwatatsumi. She married a surface dweller named Hoori. Hoori and his brother Hoderi were grandchildren of Amaterasu, the goddess of the sun. One day Hoori borrowed Hoderi's fish hook and then lost it. Hoderi demanded that Hoori return the lost hook. Hoori went into the ocean to look for it. He was unable to find it, but instead he discovered the palace where the dragon king of the sea lived. Hoori visited the palace and asked Ōwatatsumi for help finding the hook. With the dragon god's help, he found the hook. However, by the time it was found, he had fallen in love with Toyotama hime, the dragon god's daughter.

Hoori and Toyotama hime were married, and they lived together at the bottom of the sea for three years. Eventually, Hoori became homesick and longed to see country again. Together, he and his wife returned to the surface world with Hoderi's lost hook. While on land, Toyotami hime gave birth to a son. When she went into labor, she asked Hoori not to look upon her because she had to change into her true form in order to bear her child. Hoori became curious and could not resist looking. He was shocked to see that, instead of his wife, a huge wani was cradling their newborn son. The wani was Toyotama hime's true form. She was ashamed and unable to forgive Hoori's betrayal. She fled back into the ocean and never saw Hoori or her son again.

Although Toyotama hime abandoned her son, her sister Tamayori came to raise him in her absence. The boy, Ugayafukiaezu, grew up to marry Tamayori, and together they had a son. Their son was Jimmu, who became the first emperor of Japan.

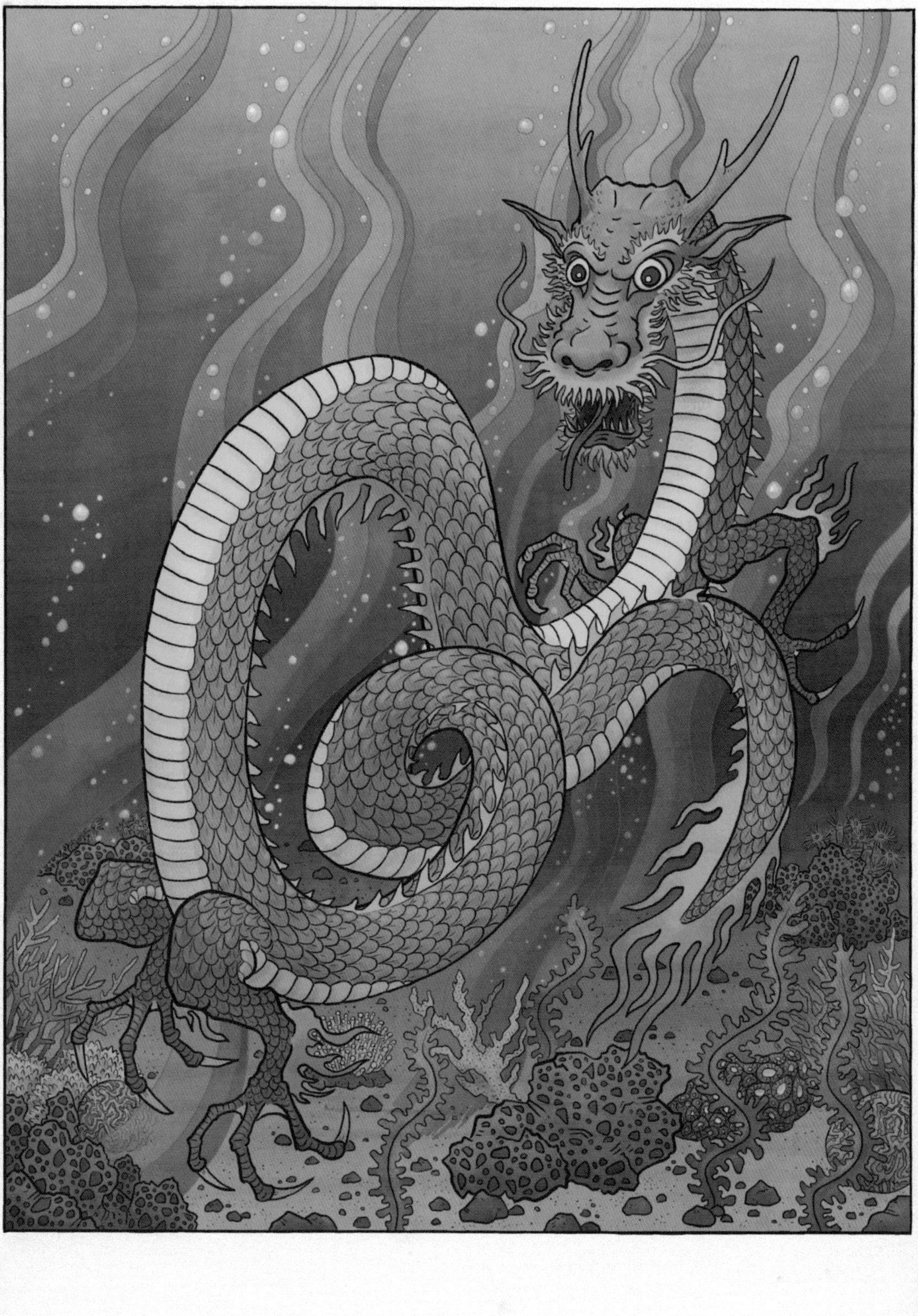

SHIOFUKI 汐吹

TRANSLATION: tide sprayer
HABITAT: oceans and coastal areas
DIET: unknown; probably fish

APPEARANCE: Shiofuki are elusive aquatic yōkai with elephantine ears and a trunk-like mouth. They have human-like arms, but their hands are webbed and resemble the fins of a fish. Their bodies are covered in fine hairs which the salt in the ocean sticks to.

BEHAVIOR: Shiofuki live in the oceans, far away from human civilization. They are only seen when they rise up from the waves to spray salty water into the air. Everything else about the lifestyle and habits of these creatures is a mystery.

ORIGIN: Shiofuki is not well known. In fact, the only reference to it anywhere is the *Bakemono tsukushi emaki*, a yōkai scroll painted in 1820 by an anonymous author which depicts unique yōkai found nowhere else in folklore. No text accompanies its illustration, so everything about this yōkai is purely speculative.

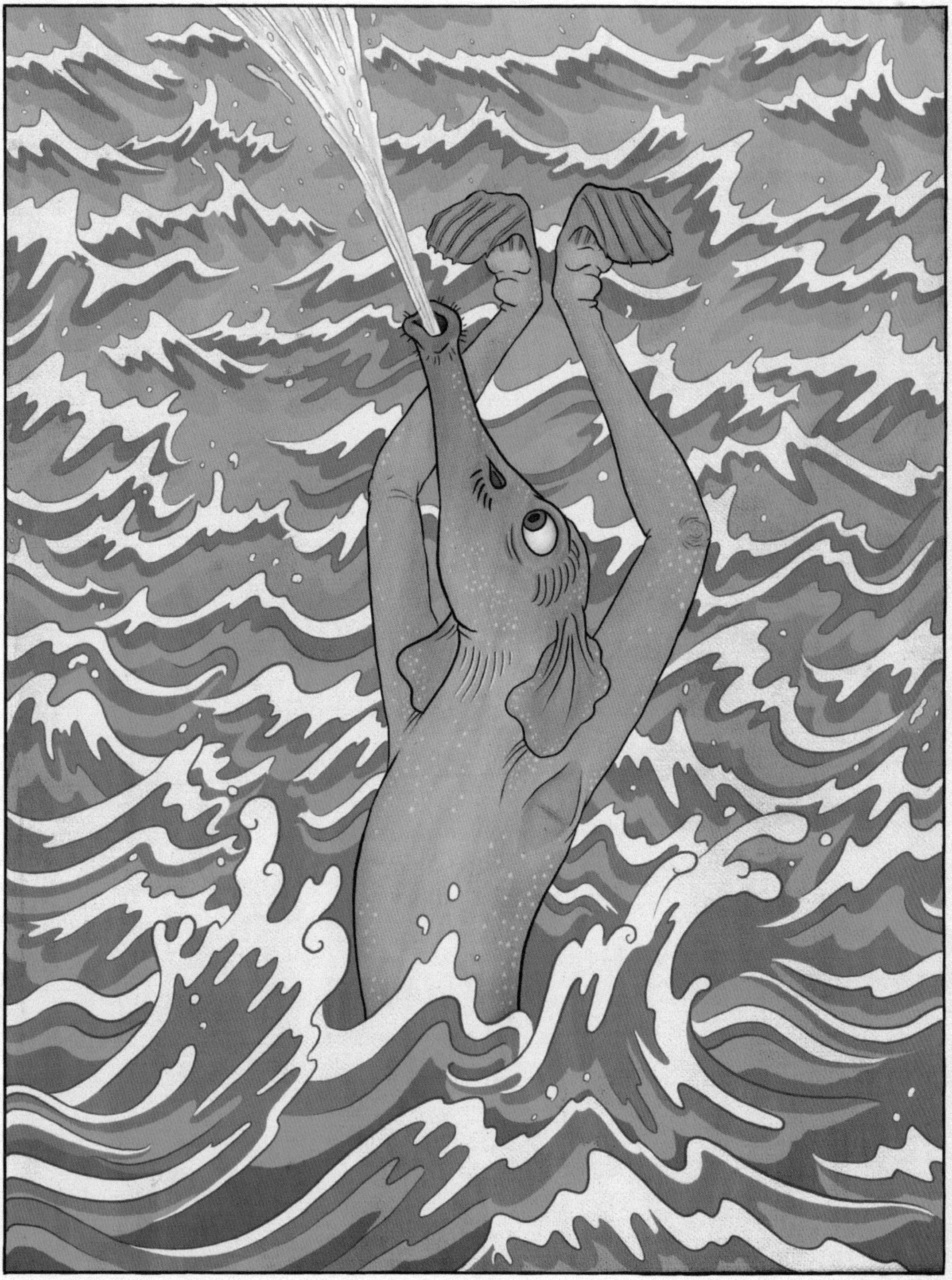

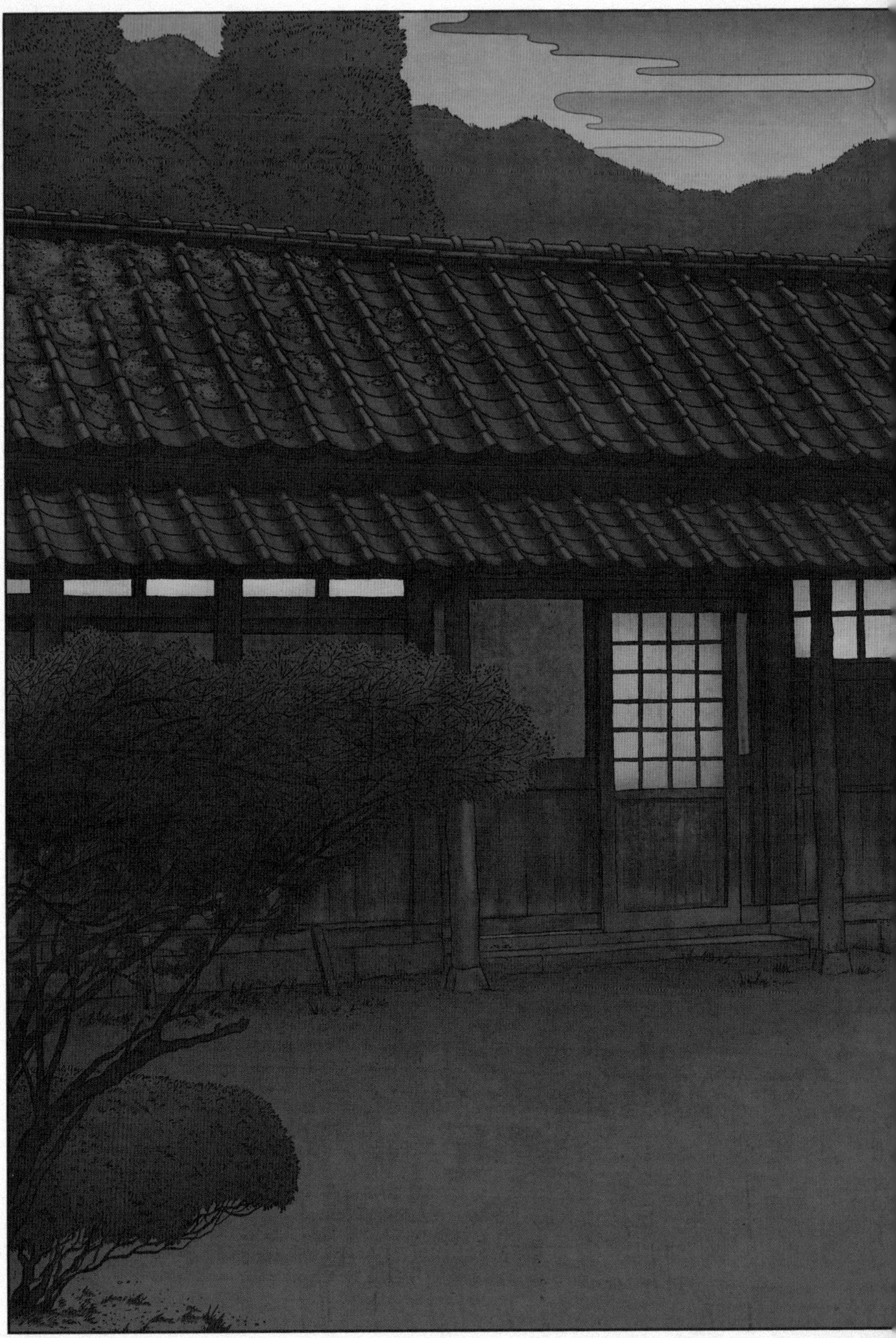

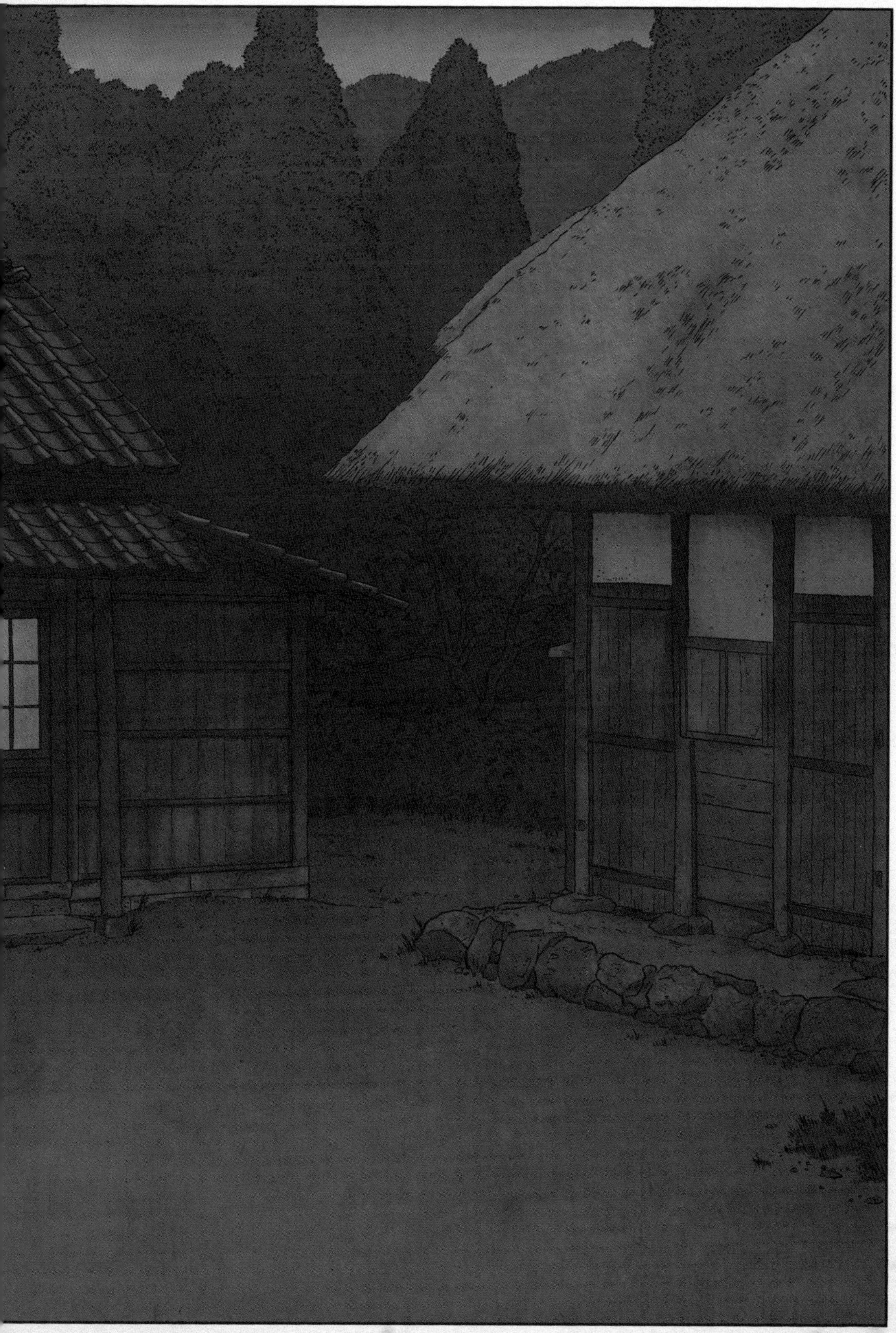

NAMEKUJIRA なめくじら

TRANSLATION: slug whale
HABITAT: homes and gardens
DIET: herbivorous

APPEARANCE: A namekujira is a slug of monstrous proportions. Its body is reddish-brown in color. It has a long stripe which runs down its back, and from its head to its neck it is covered in black spots.

BEHAVIOR: Namekujira live in gardens and behave like ordinary slugs. It is their size that makes them so strange. They crawl across doors and fences, leaving behind enormous, silvery slime trails up to 100 *hiro* in length—almost 182 meters.

ORIGIN: The namekujira is described in the *Kujirazashi shinagawa baori*, a comical Edo-period book featuring different types of fantastic whales based on puns. The name namekujira is a portmanteau, combining the *namekuji* (slug) and *kujira* (whale).

This yōkai's description contains an additional pun. There is a dish made from whale intestines called *kujira no hyakuhiro*. The name literally means "whale's 100 hiro," which comes from the great length of the whale's intestines. The joke is that while kujira no hyakuhiro refers to a delicious meal, *namekujira no hyakuhiro* is just a 182-meter-long slime trail.

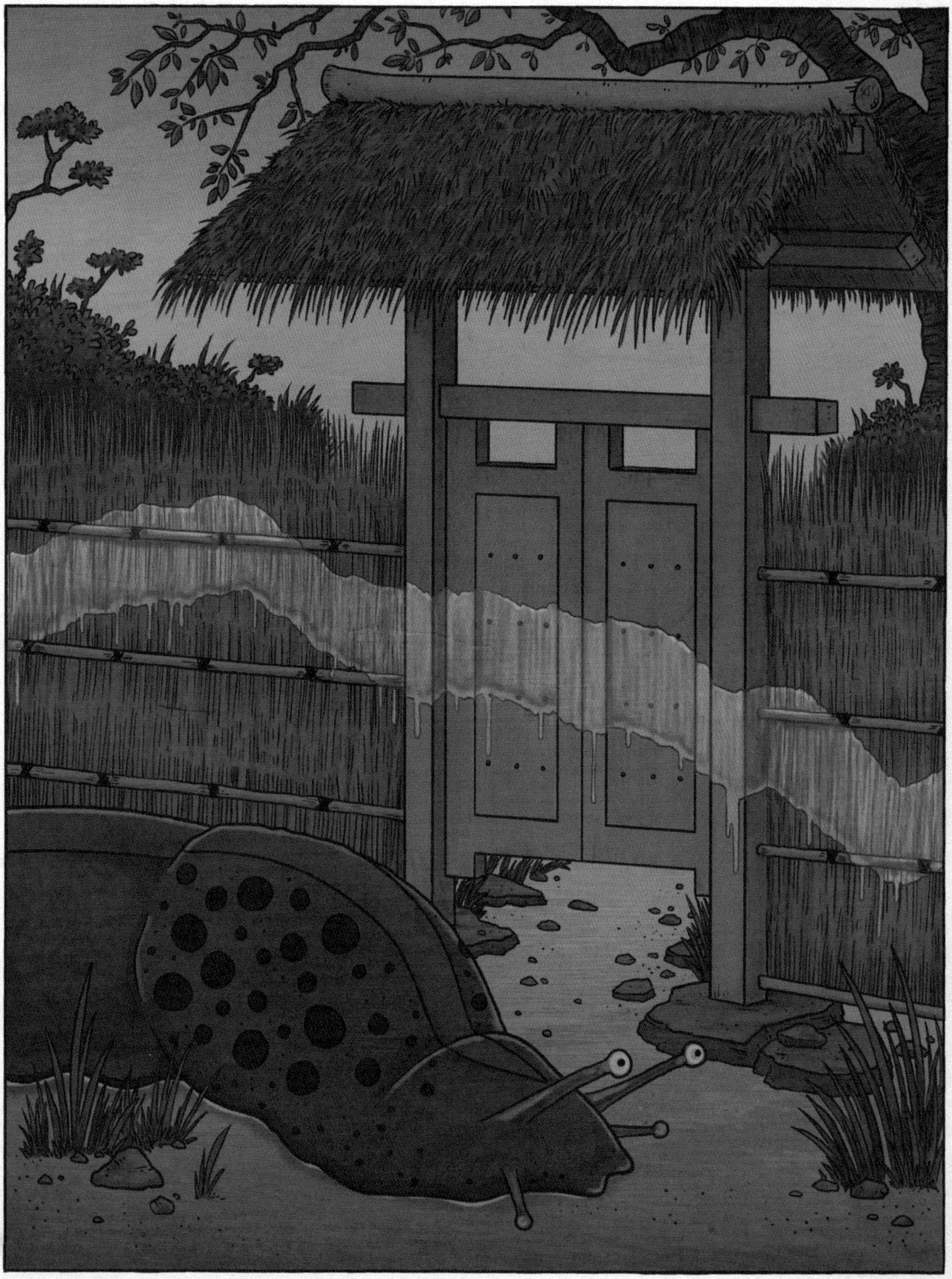

KYŌKOTSU 狂骨

TRANSLATION: crazy bones
HABITAT: wells
DIET: none; it is powered solely by vengeance

APPEARANCE: A kyōkotsu is a ghostly, skeletal spirit which rises out of wells to scare people. It is wrapped in a ragged shroud, with only its bleached skull and tangled hair emerging from its tattered clothes.

BEHAVIOR: Kyōkotsu are formed from bones which were improperly disposed of by being discarded down a well. The bones may belong to a murder or a suicide victim, or someone who died after accidentally falling into a well. The lack of a proper burial combined with the egregious disrespect shown by discarding remains in this manner creates a powerful grudge in those bones. This transforms the deceased into a shiryō—a spirit of the dead. Like other ghosts, they inflict their grudge on to those they come in contact with. A kyōkotsu lies at the bottom of its well until it is disturbed. Then it rises up to curse anyone unfortunate enough to be using the well.

ORIGIN: The kyōkotsu was invented by Toriyama Sekien for his book *Konjaku hyakki shūi*. In his description, he writes that this yōkai's name is the origin of the word *kyōkotsu*, which means fury and violence. While there is a word in a local dialect of Kanagawa which does match this description, there is no evidence actually linking it to this yōkai. It is just as likely that Toriyama Sekien—who was fond of wordplay—actually created this yōkai based on words in local dialects and made up a false etymology to add authority to his tale.

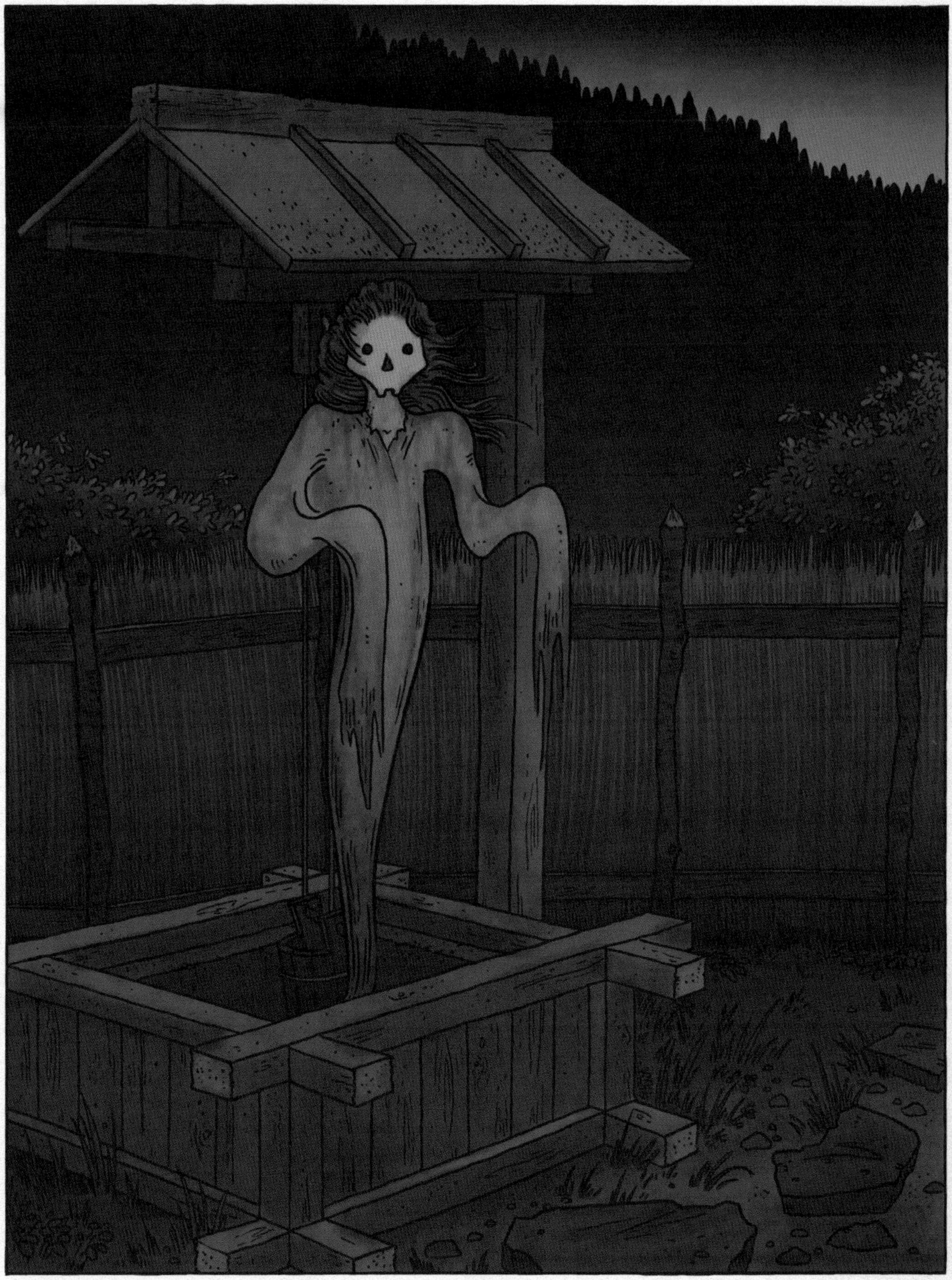

KOSODATE YŪREI 子育て幽霊

TRANSLATION: child-rearing ghost
HABITAT: towns, cities; anywhere it can find people to haunt
DIET: none; they exist only to see that their children are tended to

APPEARANCE: Kosodate yūrei are the ghosts of mothers who died in childbirth or shortly after childbirth. They return to the world of the living because of their strong attachment to their child and their lingering motherly duties. They look like faint versions of their former selves, wearing burial clothing or the clothes that they wore during life. They appear to shopkeepers or travelers on the road at night, and often return to the same place over and over again.

INTERACTIONS: Kosodate yūrei exist to fulfill one purpose: to see to the well-being of their child. They try to buy candy or toys for their children with whatever money they have—they even try to pay with dead leaves. When the mother died in childbirth, these ghosts seek out living people and try to lead them the baby. If the baby is discovered and taken care of, the kosodate yūrei can finally rest. Until then, though, she will appear every night to seek help for her child.

LEGENDS: One rainy night, a shopkeeper was closing up his shop when he heard a tapping sound at the window. A woman was standing in the rain, cold and drenched. When he asked what she needed, all she said was, "One candy please." Though the shop was closed, the shopkeeper felt sorry for the woman, so he sold her the candy. She paid him one *mon*—a low denomination coin—and vanished into the night.

The next night she came at the very same time. Again, she asked the shopkeeper in a voice almost too faint to hear, "One candy please." The shopkeeper gave her the candy, and again she paid with one mon. She left as quietly as she had come.

For six nights, the same scenario played out. On the seventh night, the woman had no money left. Instead, she presented a handful of leaves as payment. The shopkeeper would not accept the leaves, so she offered him her coat instead. He protested, but she insisted until he finally accepted the coat.

The next day, a traveling merchant stopped by the shop. The shopkeeper told him of the strange woman who came visiting every night and showed him the coat that she gave him as payment. When the merchant saw the coat, he went pale. "That is the coat of my friend's wife! She died one week ago. She was buried in this coat!"

The merchant and the shopkeeper went to the temple where she was buried. When the told the story to the priest, he scolded them for believing in such superstitions. Afterwards he took them to the woman's grave to show them that all was okay. When they reached the grave, however, the unmistakable screaming of a newborn baby could be heard under the earth!

They dug up the grave and discovered the body of the woman who had been visiting the shop. Entwined in her arms, there was a living baby wrapped up in cloth. She had given birth posthumously in her coffin. Wrapped up with the baby were six mostly-eaten pieces of candy, which had kept it from starving during the week. Its mother had bought the candy with the six mon traditionally buried with a corpse to pay the guardians of the underworld.

They took the baby from the grave and returned it to its family. When they reburied the woman's body, she had a serene expression on her face. The ghostly visitor to the candy store was never seen again.

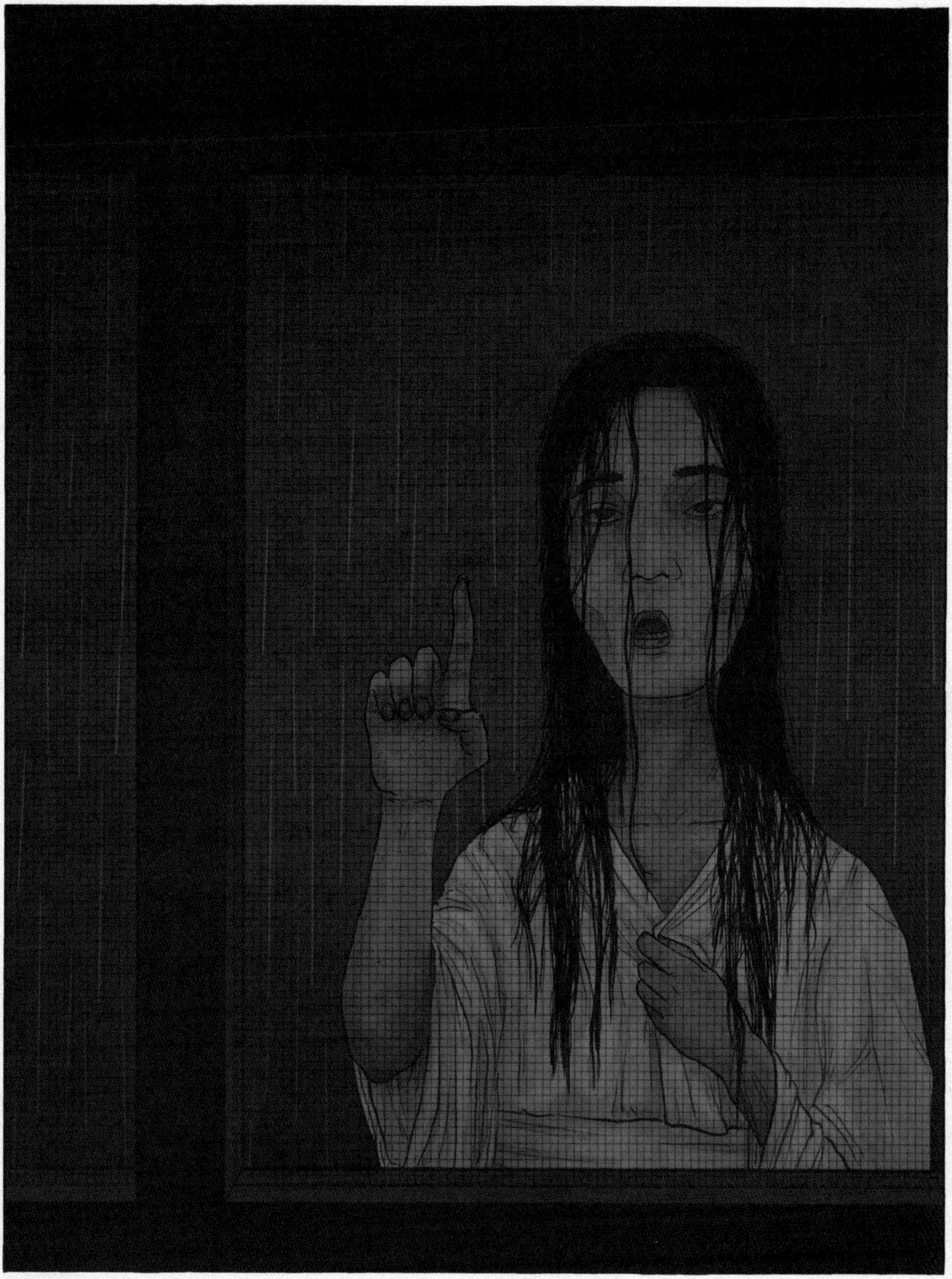

APPOSSHA あっぽっしゃ

TRANSLATION: a phrase from a local dialect meaning "give me mochi"
HABITAT: underwater, in the Sea of Japan
DIET: omnivorous; fond of mochi

APPEARANCE: Appossha are fearsome monsters which appear in the village of Koshino in Fukui Prefecture. They resemble red oni, with large heads and dark, kelp-like hair. They wear the clothing typical of workmen.

INTERACTIONS: Appossha live in the Sea of Japan. They appear on land once a year, on Koshōgatsu—a holiday celebrating the first full moon of the lunar new year. On this night, appossha crawl out of the sea and wander the village streets, banging iron tea kettles and chanting, "Appossha!" They travel from house to house, demanding food and threatening children. They ask each household if there are any ill-mannered children living there, and if there are they will take them back to the sea. Once a household's children have been thoroughly scared, the parents give a gift of mochi to the appossha and they leave.

ORIGIN: The appossha tradition comes from long ago, when a sailor from a foreign country was shipwrecked and swam ashore in Koshino. He traveled from door to door begging the villagers for food. The name appossha is thought to be based on the foreigner's words, a heavily accented attempt to ask for some mochi to eat: "*Appo* (mochi) *hoshiya* (want)."

The appossha is part of a family of oni-like yōkai which are found all over Japan, but especially along the Sea of Japan coast in the Hokuriku region. The namahage of Akita Prefecture is the most famous example. In nearby Ishikawa and Niigata Prefectures, similar yōkai named amamehagi can be found. In Yamagata they are known as amahage. Although details and origins differ, a key part of each story is the same: these yōkai come from the wilderness on or around the new year, scare young children, and leave once offered a gift from the villagers.

VISITORS FROM THE OTHER WORLD

Appossha are an example of a type of creature called a *marebito*. In Japanese folk religion, marebito are divine spirits—demons, gods, or otherwise—which come from the world of the dead to visit our world at times when the border between the worlds has become weak. Some marebito deliver prophecies or bring gifts. Others bring disaster. These strange foreign spirits are welcomed as honored guests. They are fed, sheltered, and treated kindly and respectfully by those they visit. Sometimes they are even revered as gods; their coming is welcomed in the form of festivals and rituals. Although the marebito-centered folk religion is no longer practiced today, aspects of it are still a visible part of Japanese culture. Yōkai like the appossha and namahage and festivals like Obon have preserved many of the elements of this ancient folk religion.

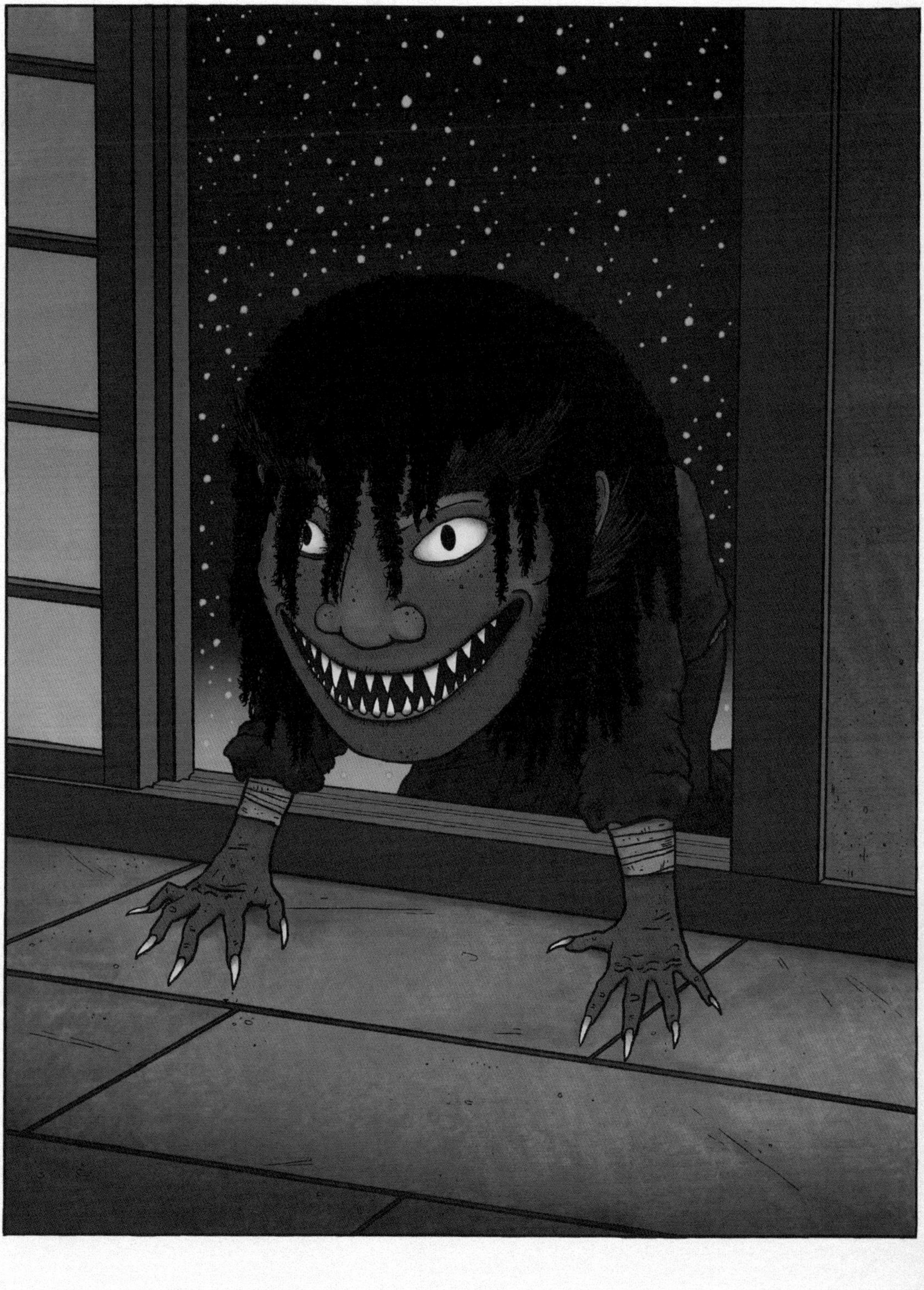

JIKININKI 食人鬼

TRANSLATION: human-eating ghost
HABITAT: old temples and ruins
DIET: human corpses

APPEARANCE: Jikininki appear as ordinary humans for the most part, except their features are ugly and monstrous. They have sharp, pointed teeth which they use to peel off and eat the flesh of the recently deceased.

BEHAVIOR: Jikininki usually live in abandoned temples and old ruins. They avoid contact with humans. However, they remain close to human settlements as corpses are their main source of food. They do not enjoy their existence. They do not find pleasure in eating the dead; it merely temporarily relieves some of the pain of their eternal hunger.

Jikininki exist somewhere between the living and the dead. They and their dwellings are often invisible during the day. They appear only to unsuspecting travelers at the night. Jikininki usually hunt their prey at night, slipping into temples when the dead are placed there for funerals.

ORIGIN: Jikininki are closely related to gaki—hungry ghosts of Buddhist cosmology who are constantly starving but unable to eat anything. A jikininki is born when a person commits evil deeds, tainting their soul. Some jikiniki were corrupt priests who did not properly pass on after death. Others were humans who developed a taste for human flesh. As they continued to eat human meat, they gradually transformed into these monsters.

LEGENDS: Long ago, a monk named Musō Soseki was traveling on a pilgrimage when he became lost in the mountains. As day faded, he came across a dilapidated hermitage. An elderly monk there gave him directions to a nearby village. Soseki arrived in the village just as night fell.

The son of the village chief welcomed the monk and invited him to stay in his house as a guest. "However," he said, "my father passed away earlier today. Our village has a custom: when one of us dies, we must spend the night away from the village. If we do not, we will be cursed. But you are tired and are not a member of this village. I see no reason why you must leave. Please, stay in my house tonight while the rest of us depart." Soseki was grateful. The villagers left town and Soseki was alone.

That night, Soseki recited funerary prayers over the body of the village chief. Suddenly, he felt a presence nearby. His body froze in fear. A dark, hazy shape crept through the house and up to the body. The creature devoured the remains of the chief, then slipped away as quietly as it had come.

The following morning the villagers returned. Soseki told them what he had seen during the night. He asked why the monk living in the nearby hermitage did not perform funerals for the village. The village chief's son was confused. "There is no hermitage nearby. What's more, there haven't been any monks in this region for several generations..."

Soseki traced his steps to the old hermitage. The monk welcomed him into the hovel and said, "I apologize for what you sight last night. The monster in the chief's house was me. Long ago I was a priest. I lived in the village and performed funeral prayers for them. However, all I ever thought of was money. I disdained the souls of the deceased. Because of my lack of conviction, when I died I was reborn as a jikininki. Now, I am forced to feed off the bodies of the dead. Please, save my soul and release me from my torment!"

In that instant, the elderly monk and the dilapidated old hermitage disappeared. Soseki was sitting on the dirt, surrounded by tall grass. The only feature nearby was an ancient, moss-covered gravestone.

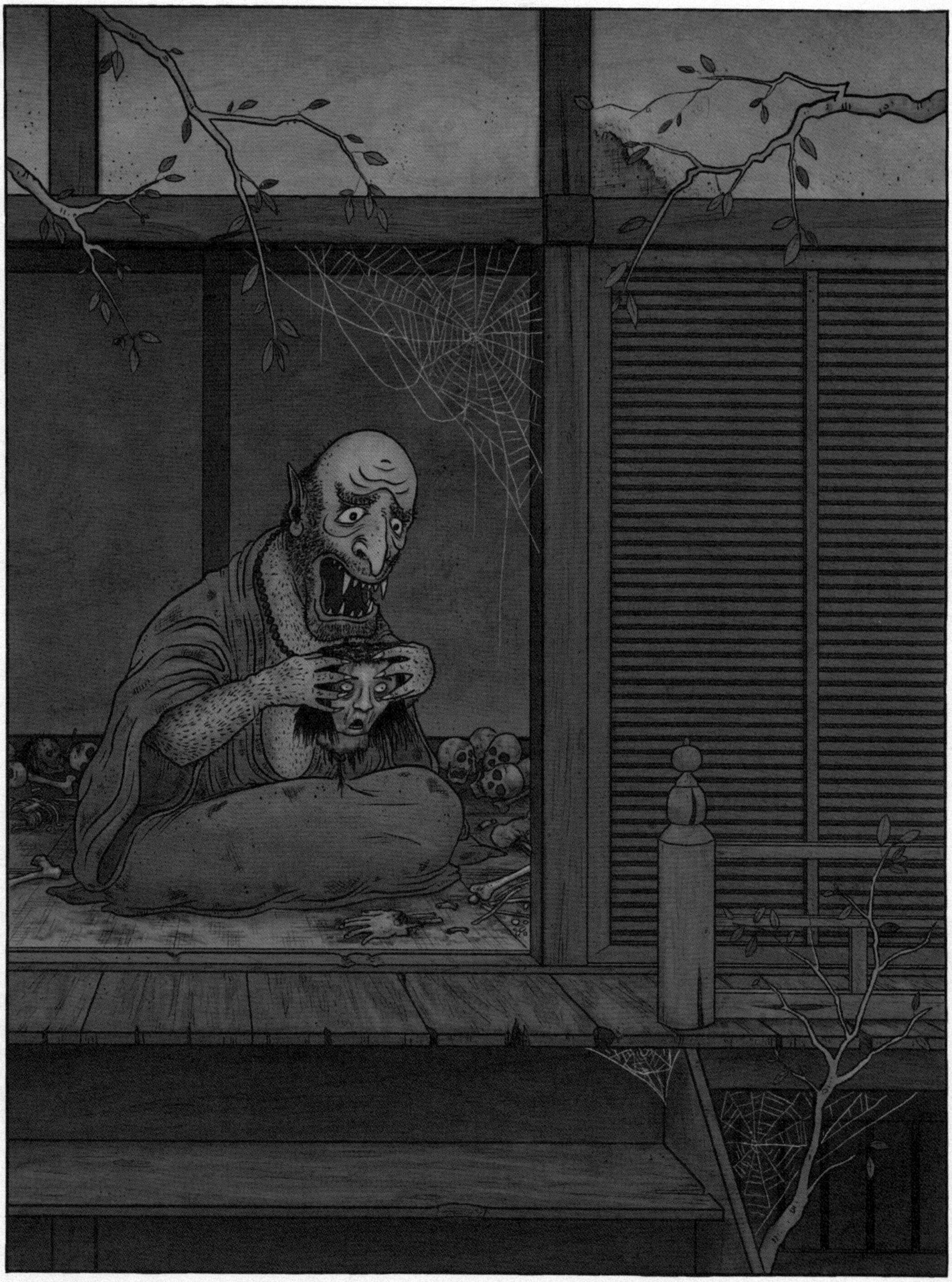

KOKURI BABĀ 古庫裏婆

TRANSLATION: hag of the old temple living quarters
HABITAT: old, dilapidated temples
DIET: human flesh

APPEARANCE: Kokuri babā are old hags which haunt temples deep in the mountains.

BEHAVIOR: Kokuri babā hide themselves away in the backs of the temples they used to work in. They feed themselves by carving up the bodies of those dead placed in the temple for funeral services. When there are no fresh corpses available, they unearth previously buried corpses from the temple's graveyard, peeling off chunks of rotting flesh to gnaw on.

INTERACTIONS: Kokuri babā do not usually interact with people. They prefer to stay hidden away in the back rooms of their temples. However, when traveling monks pay a visit, they do not pass up the chance for some fresh meat. People who encounter a kokuri babā don't realize they are in danger until it is too late.

ORIGIN: Kokuri babā was once a priest's widow at a remote, rural temple. While her husband lived she was a dutiful wife. She helped run the temple and tended to the needs of the parishioners by cooking, cleaning, washing, and taking care of the temple grounds. However, after her husband's death, she retreated into the temple's living quarters. There she became a shut in. When her food stores ran out she began to steal the offerings left behind by people visiting the temple. Because of this grave sin, she was unable to die and pass on to the next life. Instead she transformed into a yōkai. From then, she developed a taste for human flesh.

Kokuri babā was invented by Toriyama Sekien for his book *Konjaku hyakki shūi*. Although it is written with words that literally mean "hag of the old temple living quarters," Sekien was well known for using wordplay in his yōkai names. This yōkai is no exception.

Kokuri is reminiscent of a popular folk phrase *"mukuri kokuri,"* which is a metaphor for something scary. Indeed, Sekien points out in his description that kokuri babā is even more fearsome than Datsueba, the skin-flaying hag of the underworld. Parents would scold misbehaving children with "Mukuri kokuri, a demon will come (if you don't stop misbehaving)!"

MUKURI KOKURI

Mukuri kokuri has a long history, originating in the Mongol invasions of the 13th century. The Mongols under Kublai Khan conquered China and Korea. From there they set their sights on Japan. The invaders were viewed by most people as the living embodiment of demons due to their ferocity and advanced technology. Japan's victory against the them ended the expansion of the Mongol empire—thanks in no small part to two typhoons believed to be kamikaze, or "divine winds" sent from the gods. These typhoons eradicated two massive invasion fleets. The invasions had a profound impact on world history as well as the identity of the Japanese nation. Their memory remained strong for generations and became part of folklore. The fear of invading Mongols was the basis for the phrase *"Mōko Kōkuri no oni ga kuru"* ("The Mongolian-Korean demons are coming!"), which over the centuries was corrupted down to just mukuri kokuri.

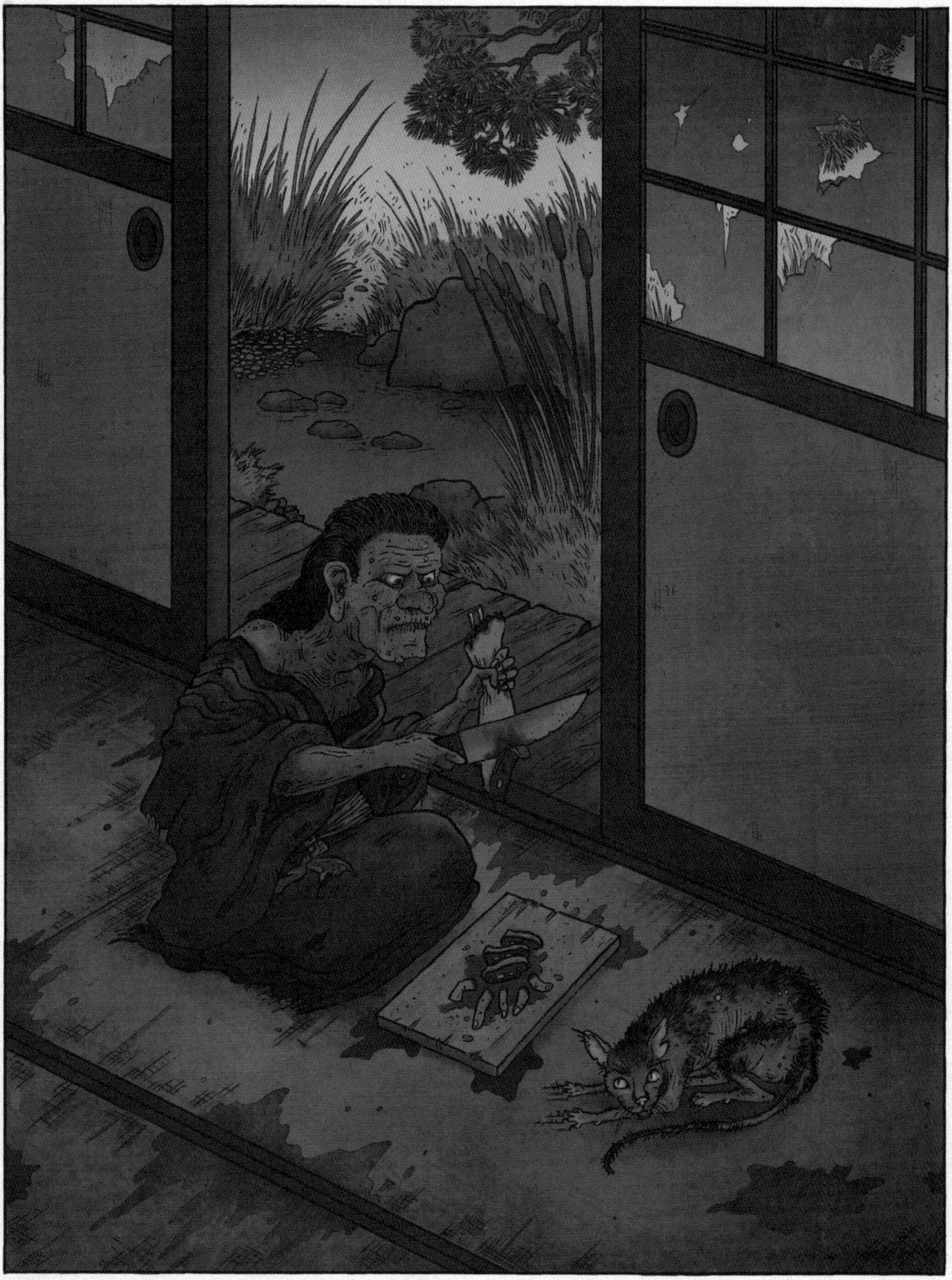

CHIRIZUKA KAIŌ 塵塚怪王

TRANSLATION: strange king of the dust heap
HABITAT: dirty, cluttered places
DIET: unknown

APPEARANCE: Chirizuka kaiō is a red, hairy demon who resembles a small oni. His clothing is old and tattered. He has wild hair and wears a crown on his head. He is called the king of the dust heap but is often thought of as the king of the tsukumogami—the animated spirits of discarded objects.

BEHAVIOR: Chirizuka kaiō appears in picture scrolls of the night parade of one hundred demons. In these scrolls he is prying open a Chinese-style wooden chest and releasing a horde of tsukumogami—presumably objects that were stored in the chest and forgotten.

ORIGIN: Chirizuka kaiō's earliest appearance comes from the Muromachi Period (1336 to 1573 CE). In the earliest scrolls he is depicted without name or explanation. He was given his name in the Edo period, in Toriyama Sekien's tsukumogami encyclopedia *Hyakki tsurezure bukuro*. This book contains a number of yōkai based on puns. Chirizuka kaiō's name appears to be a pun based on essay seventy-two from *Tsurezure gusa*, a popular collection of essays from the 14th century. This essay discusses the folly of having too many things—too much furniture in your home, too many pens at your inkstone, too many Buddhas in a temple, too many rocks and trees in a garden, too many children in your home, and so on. However, there is no such thing as having too many books on your book stand, or too much dust upon your dust heap. (In other words, the pursuit of knowledge and cleanliness can never be overdone.)

In his description of chirizuka kaiō, Sekien explains that there is nothing in creation which does not have a leader: the kirin is king of the beasts, the hōō is king of the birds, and so this chirizuka kaiō must be the king of the yama uba. The phrase is yet another pun and refers to a line from the noh play Yamanba. It explains that worldly attachments pile up like motes of dust, and if you let them build up into a dust heap then you may turn into a yama uba.

Despite the phrasing, chirizuka kaiō has come to be interpreted as the king of tsukumogami rather than yama uba. This is probably because he appears in *Hyakki tsurezure bukuro*, which is full of tsukumogami. There is no other connection between chirizuka kaiō and yama uba, as chirizuka kaiō has only ever been depicted releasing yōkai from a chest. Perhaps Sekien was merely using the yama uba as an allusion to yōkai born out of worldly attachment and ignorance. Yama uba are born when one's improper attachments pile up like a dust heap. Tsukumogami are born out of forgotten household objects whose owners could not bring themselves to properly dispose of. The same kind of attachment forms both of these types of yōkai.

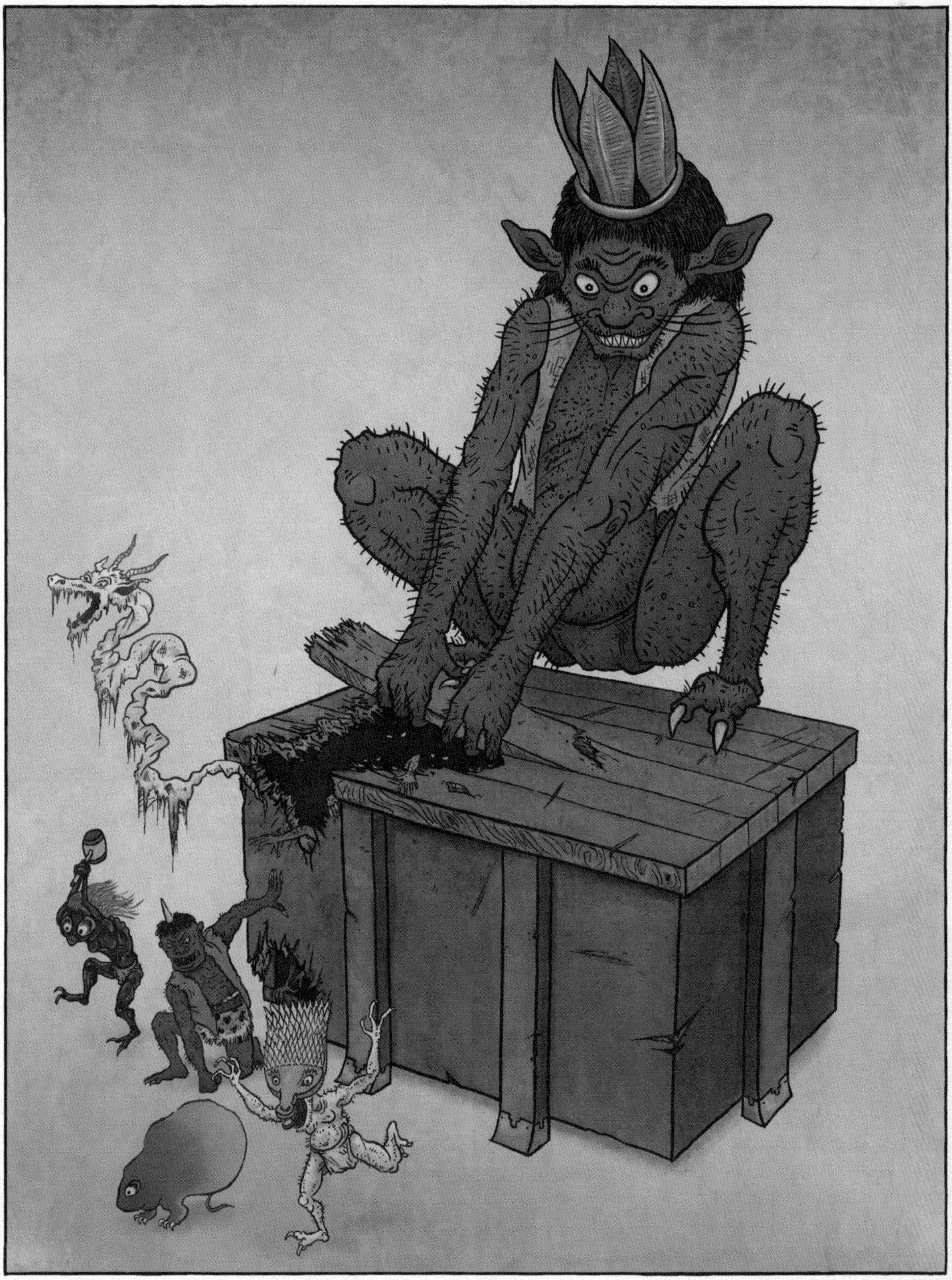

FUGURUMA YŌHI 文車妖妃

TRANSLATION: strange queen of the book cart
ALTERNATE NAMES: bunshō no kai (essay spirit)
HABITAT: libraries, temples, and noble houses; anywhere with book collections
DIET: none; she is fueled by the emotions contained in her letters

APPEARANCE: Fuguruma yōhi is a spirit which resembles an ogrish human woman in tattered clothing. She is a kind of tsukumogami–an artifact spirit–which manifests out of old-fashioned book carts called *fuguruma*. In this case, it is the emotions built up in piles of love letters which give birth to this yōkai.

ORIGIN: Fuguruma yōhi appears opposite of chirizuka kaiō in Toriyama Sekien's collection of tsukumogami *Hyakki tsurezure bukuro*. Like chirizuka kaiō, her name is a pun based on essay 72 from the medieval essay collection *Tsurezure gusa*.

Essay seventy-two discusses the folly of overabundance. Having too many possessions is a bad thing which distracts you from that which is important; however, there is no such thing as having too many books on your book cart. The fuguruma yōhi is what Toriyama Sekien imagined might appear if you actually did have too many books on your book cart. The emotions and attachments poured into a single love letter may not amount to much sin, but if there are enough letters, enough sin might pile up that a yōkai can be born from them.

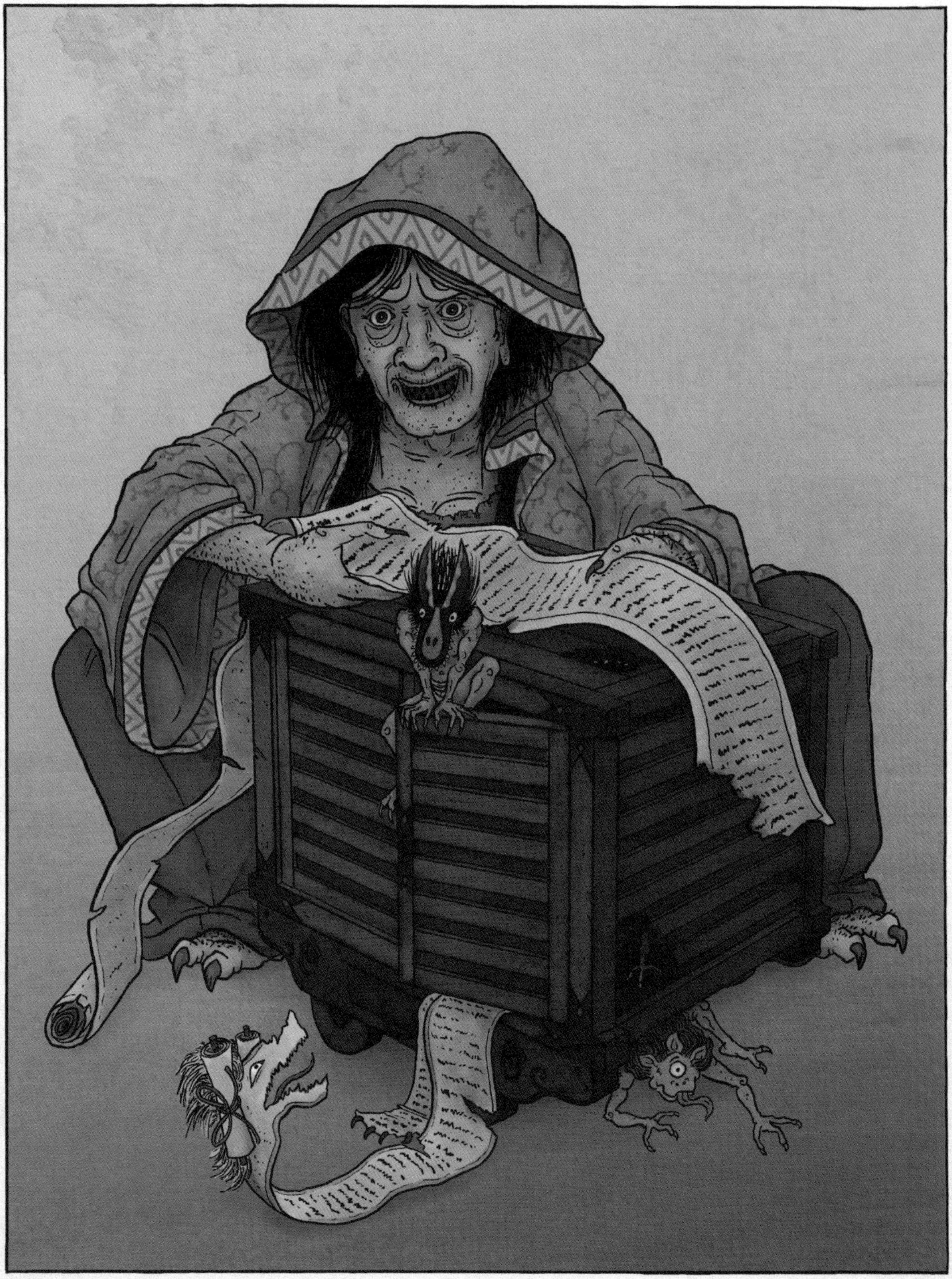

Hasamidachi 鋏裁

TRANSLATION: scissors cutter
ALTERNATE NAMES: hasami no bakemono, hasami
HABITAT: houses

APPEARANCE: Hasamidachi are small yōkai with wild hair, buggy eyes, and a pair of scissors sprouting from their heads.

ORIGIN: Hasamidachi appear in the earliest yōkai picture scrolls and have been copied many times from these early depictions. They appears over and over again in many different scrolls. Despite this, no name or description has ever been recorded. The name hasamidachi was given to them in recent years by yōkai researcher Aramata Hiroshi. They are also known by less descriptive names such as hasami no bakemono (scissors monster) or just hasami (scissors).

Furuōgi 古扇

TRANSLATION: old folding fan
HABITAT: houses

APPEARANCE: Furuōgi are squat, hairy yōkai with old, worn out folding fans sprouting from their backs.

ORIGIN: Furuōgi appear in some of the earliest *Hyakki yagyō emaki*, pictures scrolls of the night parade of one hundred demons, along with a number of other tsukumogami. Early yōkai scrolls did not give names or descriptions, so nothing about furuōgi is known other than their appearance. Even the name was added much later. Presumably, they are the spirits of old, ruined folding fans which have come to life to cause mischief.

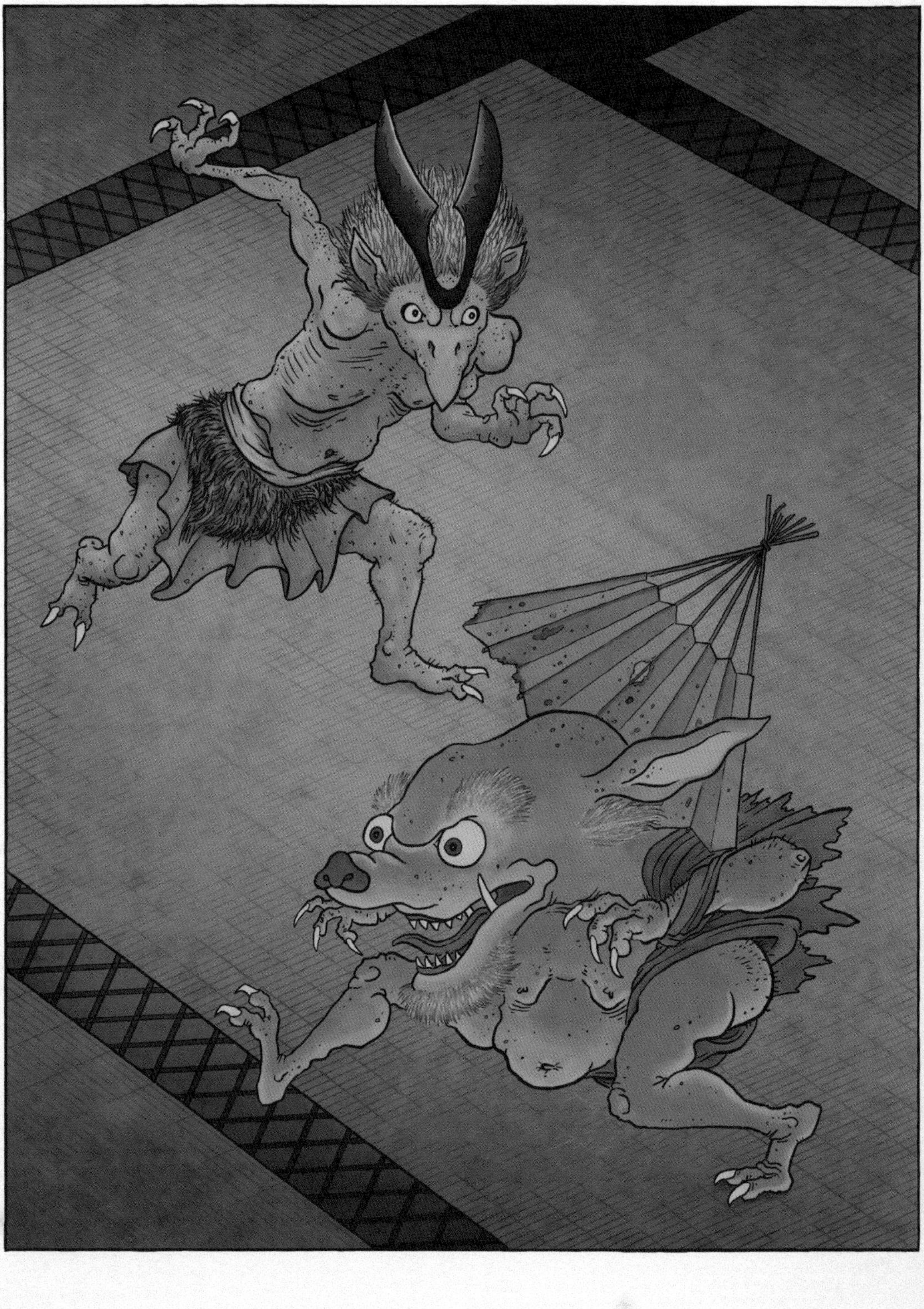

KAICHIGO 貝兒

TRANSLATION: shell boy
HABITAT: decorative shell boxes
DIET: none

APPEARANCE: Kaichigo are the spirits of shell boxes come to life. They take the form of small, doll-like boys in kimono.

BEHAVIOR: Kaichigo haunt the shell boxes used to store beautiful and expensive painted shells. They come out when nobody is around and play with the shells, flipping them over and moving them around into different positions.

ORIGIN: Kaichigo's origins lie in *kaiawase* (shell matching), a popular Heian Period game which uses painted seashells. Beautiful shells of the right size and color were collected and decorated, their insides lined with gold and painted with scenes from popular stories, such as *The Tale of Genji*. The two halves of the same shell would be painted with the same scene, and players of the game would try to match the two sides. Beautifully decorated shell boxes, or *kaioke*, were used to store the shells while not in use.

Kaiawase gradually was replaced by other matching games, such as karuta, which use less expensive playing pieces. The kaioke and shells themselves came to be viewed as precious art objects instead of toys. Because each shell half will perfectly fit its matching half and no other, expensive kaiawase sets came to be used as wedding dowries—symbolizing a perfect and unique match between bride and groom. Some boxes have been passed down from mother to daughter over and over for centuries. Those kaioke which have been around for a very long time and are no longer used as games begin to resent their existence. They grow restless and want to be played with once again and develop a soul which manifests as a kaichigo.

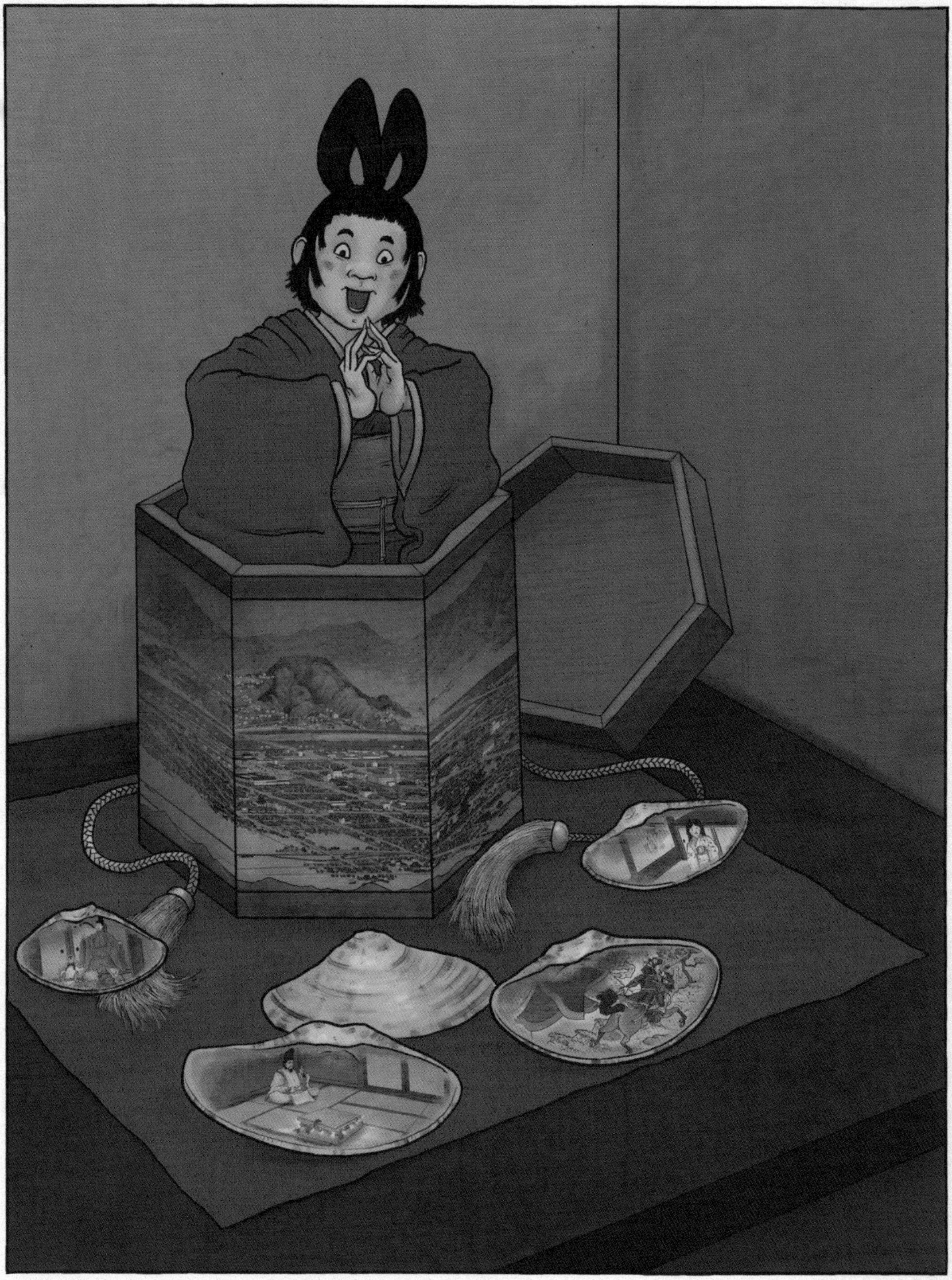

Byōbu nozoki 屏風闚

TRANSLATION: folding screen peeper
HABITAT: wealthy homes
DIET: thrives on others' lust

APPEARANCE: Byōbu nozoki are depraved spirits which emerge from the decorative folding screens known as byōbu. They are very tall, stretching well over two meters (tall enough to peer over any sized folding screen). Their bodies are long and lithe, and they wear white robes resembling those of ghosts. They have long black hair and blackened teeth. Despite the resemblance, byōbu nozoki are not yūrei, but are actually tsukumogami of folding screens.

INTERACTIONS: As its name suggests, a byōbu nozoki's chief activity is leering over folding screens at the people on the other side—particularly if the people are engaged in romantic activities.

ORIGIN: Byōbu nozoki were invented by Toriyama Sekien for his book *Konjaku hyakki shūi*. According to him, these spirits manifest from ancient folding screens which have witnessed many years of sexual activity.

Sekien invented a fake history linking this spirit to ancient Chinese history. Sekien describes the byōbu nozoki as tall enough to peer over a folding screen seven *shaku* (a unit of length approximately 30 cm) high. This recalls a story about the Chinese emperor Qin Shi Huang, in which he leaped over a seven shaku tall byōbu to escape an assassination attempt. This legend would have been well known to his readers during the Edo period. With this reference, Sekien both invents a silly narrative and finds a way to connect this amusing yōkai with literature and history, seemingly legitimizing it as more than something he just made up.

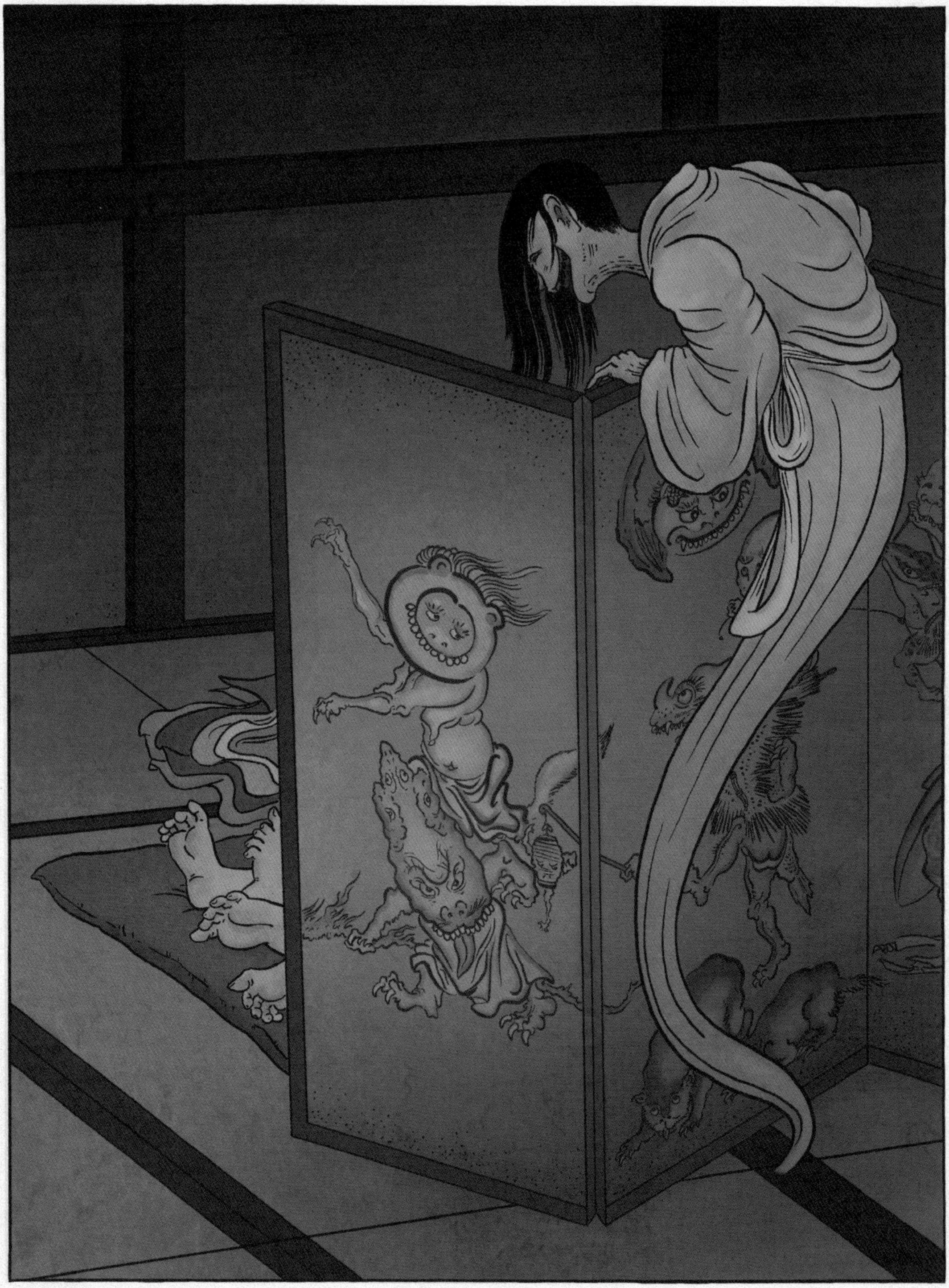

Tenjōname 天井嘗

TRANSLATION: ceiling licker
HABITAT: cold, dark homes with tall ceilings
DIET: dirt, dust, and ceiling grime

APPEARANCE: Tenjōname are tall yōkai with long tongues. Their bodies are covered with strips of paper which resemble a *matoi*—the paper flags carried by Edo period firemen. Tenjōname appear in houses with high ceilings, particularly in the cold months. The weak winter light cannot reach the ceilings, and weird shadows are cast upon the rafters.

BEHAVIOR: Tenjōname are named for their primary activity: licking ceilings. The older a house gets, the more dust and grime collects in hard-to-clean places such as the ceiling. This attracts tenjōname, who lick the dirty ceilings to feed on the filth. The telltale sign that a tenjōname has come calling is the appearance of dark stains and splotches on ceilings, walls, and support pillars.

ORIGIN: Although their appearance seems to be inspired by earlier yōkai scrolls, tenjōname first appear in Toriyama Sekien's *Hyakki tsurezure bukuro*. It is not specifically stated, but based on its appearance and the fact that most of the yōkai in that book are tsukumogami, it is likely that tenjōname is a transformed matoi.

Like many of the entries in *Hyakki tsurezure bukuro*, tenjōname appears to be a pun based on one of the essays in Yoshida Kenkō's *Tsurezure gusa*. Essay number fifty-five gives advice on building a house. It states that too high a ceiling would make winters feel cold and lamplight dark. Toriyama Sekien references this essay in his description of tenjōname.

LEGENDS: Tenjōname were created in the 18th century so older folktales do not exist. However, since then a number of stories have been invented. One such story claims that a samurai from Tatebayashi Castle—the ruins of which are in present-day Gunma Prefecture—captured a tenjōname. He used it to clean all the spiderwebs and grime from the ceilings of the castle.

More recently, it is thought that the stains left by tenjōname take the form of hideous human faces. Staring too long at these stains—particularly when they appear above your bed—can lead to madness and even death.

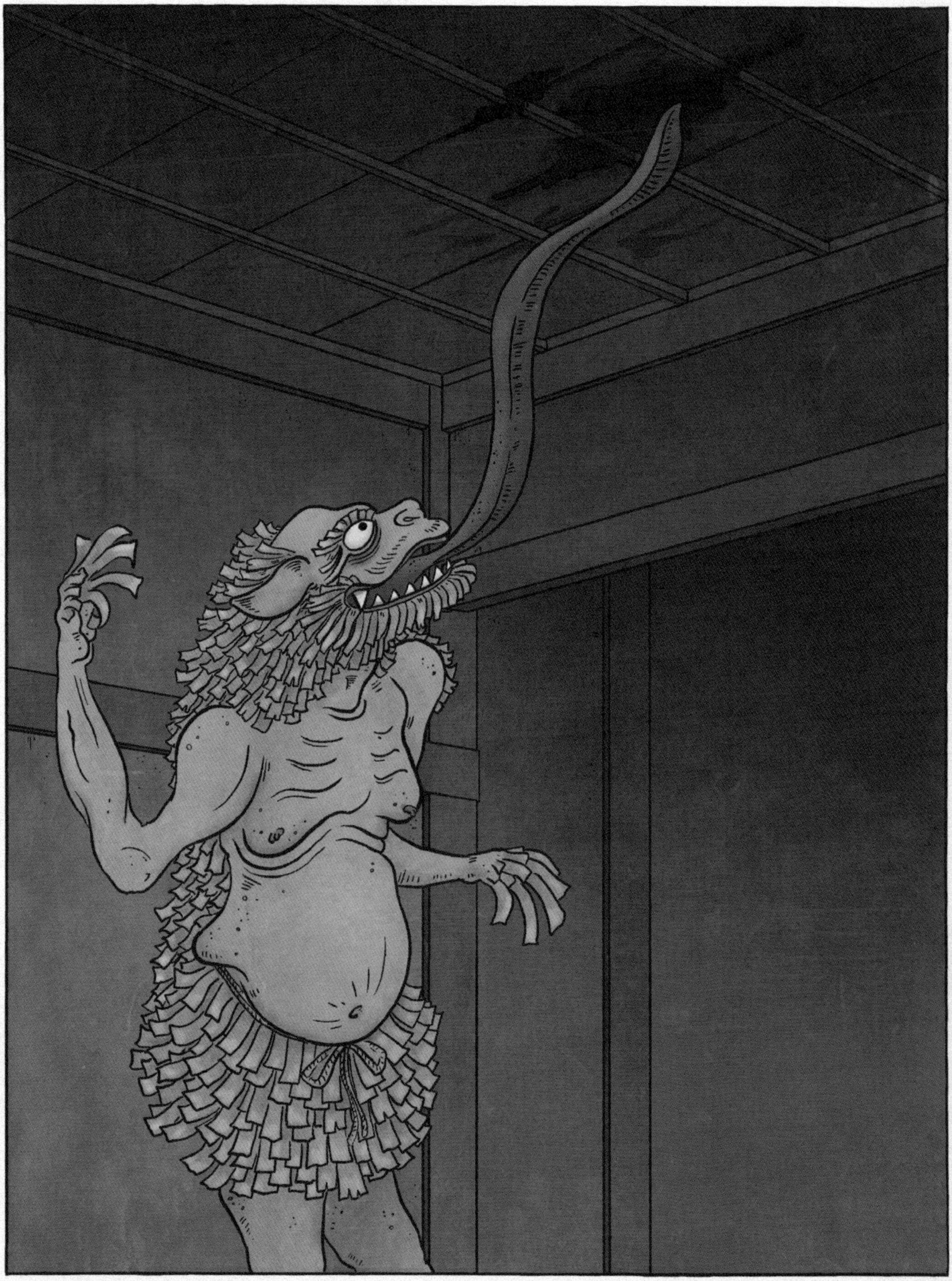

HARADASHI 腹出し

TRANSLATION: belly exposer
HABITAT: old temples and homes
DIET: unknown, but has a fondness for sake

APPEARANCE: Haradashi are goofy looking yōkai that can change into various forms. Occasionally, haradashi will appear as headless torsos with arms, legs, and comical facial features on their bellies. Others look like kind, elderly nuns. Still others look like female monsters with long black hair. Whatever form they take, the defining characteristic of haradashi are the large, silly-looking faces which appear on the creatures' enormous stomachs.

BEHAVIOR: Unlike most yōkai, haradashi do not do anything harmful. They are cheerful and agreeable. They enjoy amusing others and cheering sad people up. They frequently disguise themselves as ordinary humans and then suddenly reveal their belly faces to surprise people and make them laugh.

INTERACTIONS: Haradashi appear before sad and lonely individuals, particularly those who are at home drinking alone. Haradashi slip into these peoples' houses and join the lonely person. When offered a drink, a haradashi happily accepts. It then bares its belly and performs a ridiculous dance. Those who entertain a haradashi in their homes find that their troubles and worries vanish. They become filled with hopes and dreams.

Haradashi don't only perform house calls. They make their homes in old temples and invite in those who need help. They call out to people who are lost or seeking shelter from the snow or rain and invite them to stay the night in their temple. A haradashi will present its guest with a warm room and a hearty meal. And of course, it will entertain its guest with its signature belly dance.

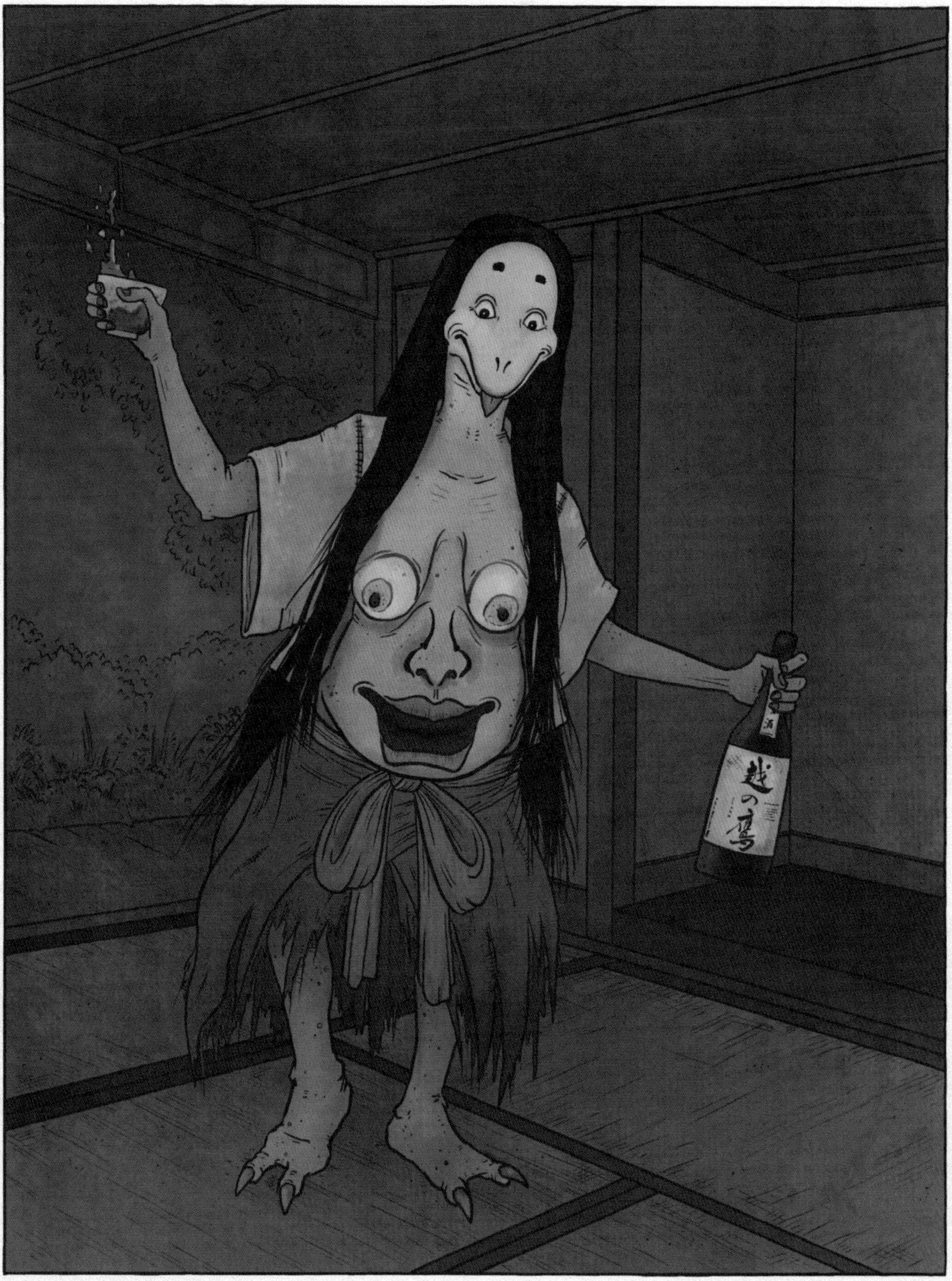
酒
越の

Aka manto 赤マント

TRANSLATION: red cloak, red vest
ALTERNATE NAMES: aoi manto, akai kami, akai hanten, akai chanchanko, akai te
HABITAT: school toilets
DIET: school children

APPEARANCE: Aka manto is an urban legend related to elementary school toilets. It usually takes place in a specific stall in a specific bathroom in the school—usually it is an older or disused bathroom. Often the fourth stall is the cursed one. This is because the number four is associated with death.

INTERACTIONS: Most stories follow the same pattern. While at school late in the evening, a student suddenly finds themself in desperate need of a toilet. The closest restroom is one that is normally avoided by the students. Older and less well-kept, separated from the rest of the school, the stall is rumored to be haunted. With no time to find another restroom, the student goes in. After they have finished, they realize that there is no toilet paper. Then a strange voice asks, "Do you want red paper or blue paper?" The student answers, "Red paper." A moment later, they are stabbed and sliced up violently. Blood sprays everywhere, soaking their body and making it look as if they were wearing a bright red cloak.

Some time later, a different student finds him or herself in need of a toilet in a similar situation. They know the story of the kid who died in the restroom but they use the bathroom anyway. Sure enough, a voice asks them, "Red paper or blue paper?" Remembering the legend, they say, "Blue paper." Then all of the student's blood is sucked out of their body. They are left dead and blue-faced on the bathroom floor.

Aka manto's identity varies from place to place. Sometimes it is a serial killer hiding in the adjacent stall. Other times it is the ghost of a tall man with a sickly, bluish-white face. Sometimes it is even blamed on a hairy yōkai called a kainade who lives in the toilet and likes to stroke people's rear ends with its hand. In this case, the result is markedly less violent; a hairy arm of the chosen color rises out of the toilet to stroke the student's behind.

In some versions, choosing "blue paper" gets you strangled until your face turns blue. In some, answering "red paper" gets your skin flayed so that it hangs off of your back like a red cape. Other versions are less lethal, with the students' skin color changed permanently to whatever color they chose. Sometimes the consequences are worse than death. Students are dragged into the netherworld, never to be seen again.

There is usually no escape from aka manto. Clever students who bring extra toilet paper with them discover that it vanishes before they are able to use it. They still find themselves having to answer the question. People who choose a different color other than those offered are met with an equally horrible death. (One version has a student say, "yellow paper." The result is that their face is pushed down into the dirty toilet water and held there until they drown.) In some instances, students have been able to escape by saying "I don't need any paper." This buys them just enough time to flee the bathroom. Those who survive and tell the story to others fall terribly ill and die shortly after.

ORIGIN: Aka manto has been a popular schoolyard rumor since as early as the 1930s. One explanation for its continued popularity is that it reflects the anxieties in a student's daily life. Aka manto asks a question with no good outcome. That feeling is not too different from having to answer a problem on a test that you don't know, or being singled out by a teacher in front of the whole classroom when you don't know the answer.

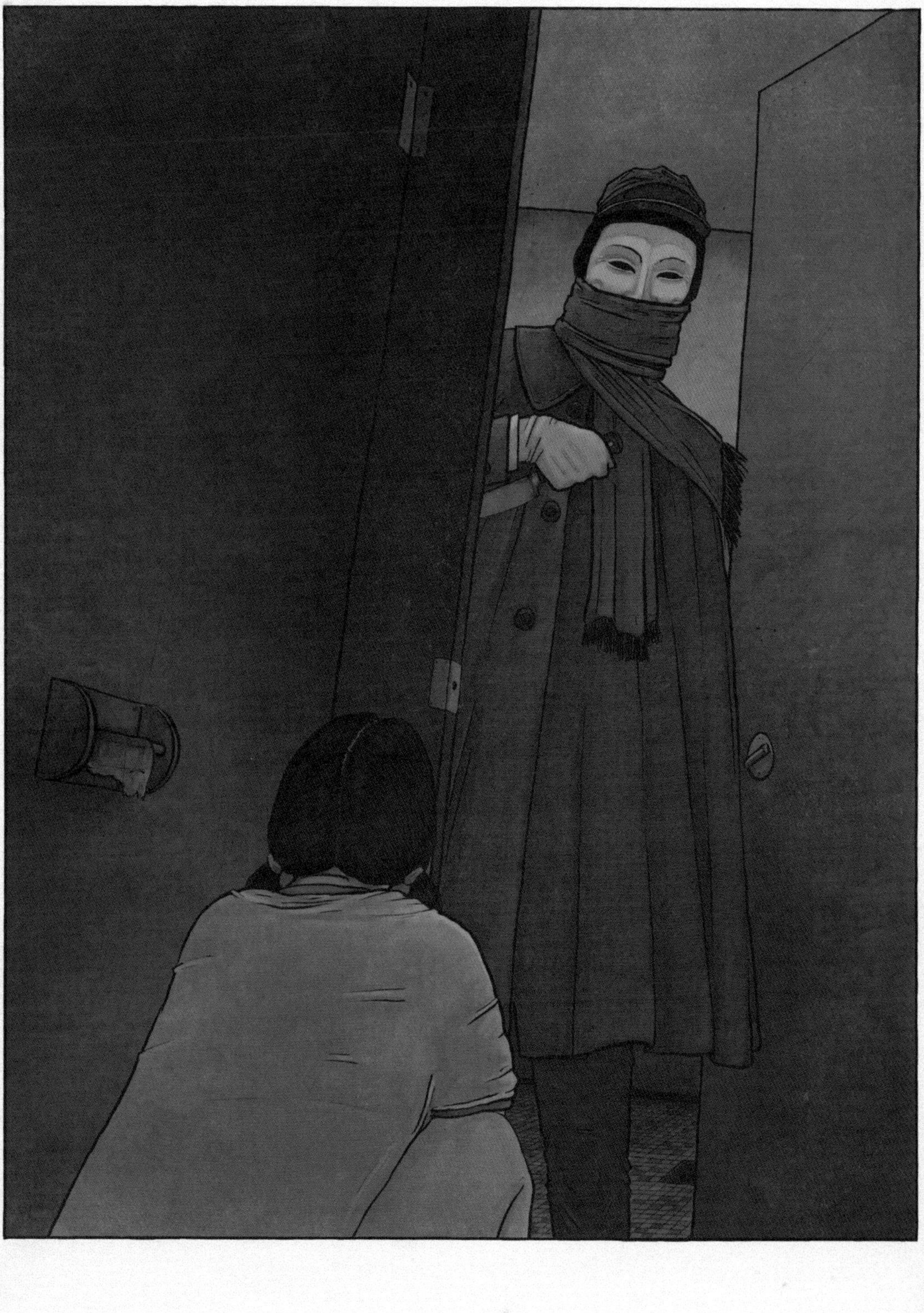

Maneki neko 招き猫

TRANSLATION: inviting cat, beckoning cat
HABITAT: towns and cities
DIET: carnivorous; as an ordinary cat

APPEARANCE: The maneki neko is a cat which brings good luck and fortune. It is most commonly seen in the form of decorative statues in homes and stores. It is usually depicted with one or both paws in the air in a beckoning motion.

ORIGIN: Cats have long been connected with the supernatural in Japan. While some superstitions link cats with bad luck, curses, and strange fires, there is also a long tradition of cats being revered. Cats are particularly seen as beneficial in agricultural and sericulture, where they eat mice and other pests which destroy crops and silkworms. In these areas cats were lucky creatures. Images of cats were used as charms.

Statues of maneki neko were popular items in the urban areas of Japan towards the end of the Edo Period. Cats with their right hand raised were said to bring economic fortune, while cats with their left hand raised were said to attract customers. The color of the cats' fur can be significant as well. Long ago, black cats were said to be lucky due to their ability to see in the dark. Black maneki neko were used as talismans against evil spirits. Red was believed to repel smallpox and measles, so red maneki neko were used as talismans against sickness.

The origins of these statues lie in folkloric tales about strange cats who brought riches to their owners, or who saved their owners from disaster.

LEGENDS: In the Yoshiwara pleasure district of Edo, there lived a famous courtesan named Usugumo. Usugumo was a *tayū* (the highest rank of oiran) in the esteemed brothel of Miura Yashirōzaemon. Usugumo was a cat lover and was particularly fond of her tortoiseshell cat. She always carried her cat with her wherever she went. So great was her love for her cat that rumors began to spread that Usugumo had been possessed or bewitched.

One day, as Usugumo went to use the restroom, her tortoiseshell cat began acting strangely. It refused to leave her side, clawing at her dress and meowing noisily. The brothel owner saw this and thought that the cat was attacking Usugumo. He drew his sword and slashed at the cat, slicing its head off. The cat's head flew across the room and sunk its teeth into a large venomous snake which was hiding out of sight near the toilet.

Usugumo was overcome with grief for her cat. It had given its life to save hers. To ease her sadness, the brothel owner had a statue in the likeness of her cat made by the finest woodcarver out of the finest wood. The carving was so masterfully done and so lifelike that Usugumo was overjoyed. She found happiness once again.

Everyone who saw the carving of the cat wanted one just like it. That year, copies of the figure were sold in the Asakusa markets. This is often told as the origin of maneki neko statues.

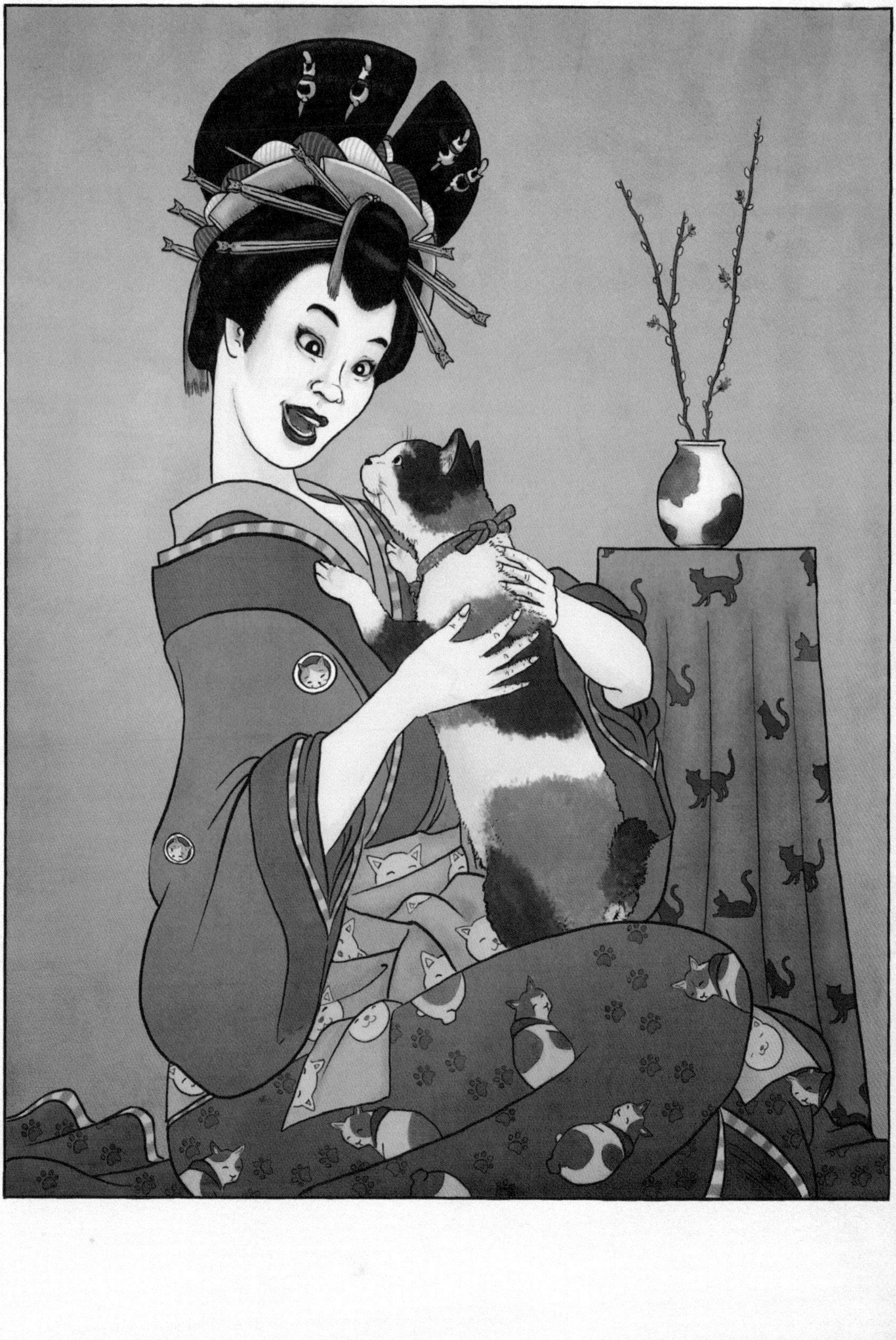

SHUKAKU 守鶴

TRANSLATION: none; this is his name

APPEARANCE: Shukaku was a tanuki who lived in disguise as a human priest. For many decades he worked at Morinji, a Buddhist temple in Gunma Prefecture. Shukaku is best known for his miraculous tea kettle, known as the bunbuku chagama, which he left to Morinji as a gift.

ORIGIN: Shukaku's story has been told at Morinji for centuries. However, different versions and variations have sprung up over the years. The story's popularity spread during the Edo Period. Thanks to a booming publishing industry it became well known across Japan. Although Shukaku is associated with Morinji, the structure of his story—a magical animal presenting a wonderful gift to humankind—is a recurring motif throughout Japanese folklore.

LEGENDS: Morinji was founded in 1426 by a priest named Dairin Shōtsū. While he was traveling through various countries on pilgrimage, he befriended a priest named Shukaku. They traveled together. After Morinji was built, Shukaku stayed on to act as a head priest there for many years.

In 1570, an important religious gathering was held at Morinji. Priests from all over the country traveled to the temple. When it came time to serve tea, the priests realized that they did not have enough kettles to serve such a large gathering. Shukaku—still serving the temple 144 years after his arrival—brought his favorite tea kettle to help serve the priests.

This tea kettle was a miraculous object. No matter how many times you dunked a ladle in it, it was always brimming with enough hot water to make tea. It also stayed hot for many days after heating it. The kettle was given the name bunbuku chagama—*chagama* being the word for tea kettle, and *bunbuku* meaning "to spread luck." The name was a pun as well: the sound of boiling water is *bukubuku*, which sounds much like bunbuku. Thanks to Shukaku's marvelous tea kettle, the gathering was a great success. The bunbuku chagama continued to be used by the temple for many years. Shukaku, as well, continued to work at Morinji for years after that.

According to Morinji's records, On February 28, 1587, a monk walked in on Shukaku while he was taking a nap. During his sleep, the tanuki's disguise faltered just a bit, and the monk noticed that Shukaku had a tail! Shukaku's great secret was exposed: he was not a human priest, but a tanuki in disguise. He had been living among humans for thousands of years. Long ago he had traveled through India and China. Eventually he met Dairin Shōtsū, who befriended him and brought him to Morinji. There he used his magic to serve the temple as best as he could.

After his secret was uncovered, Shukaku decided it was time to leave. To make up for the great shock he had caused, he gave them a parting gift: he used his magic to present the story of the Battle of Yashima, one of the final clashes of the Genpei War. To show their gratitude for all that he had done, the priests built a shrine to Shukaku. He is still worshipped as a local deity. And the bunbuku chagama, which Shukaku left behind, remains on display at Morinji.

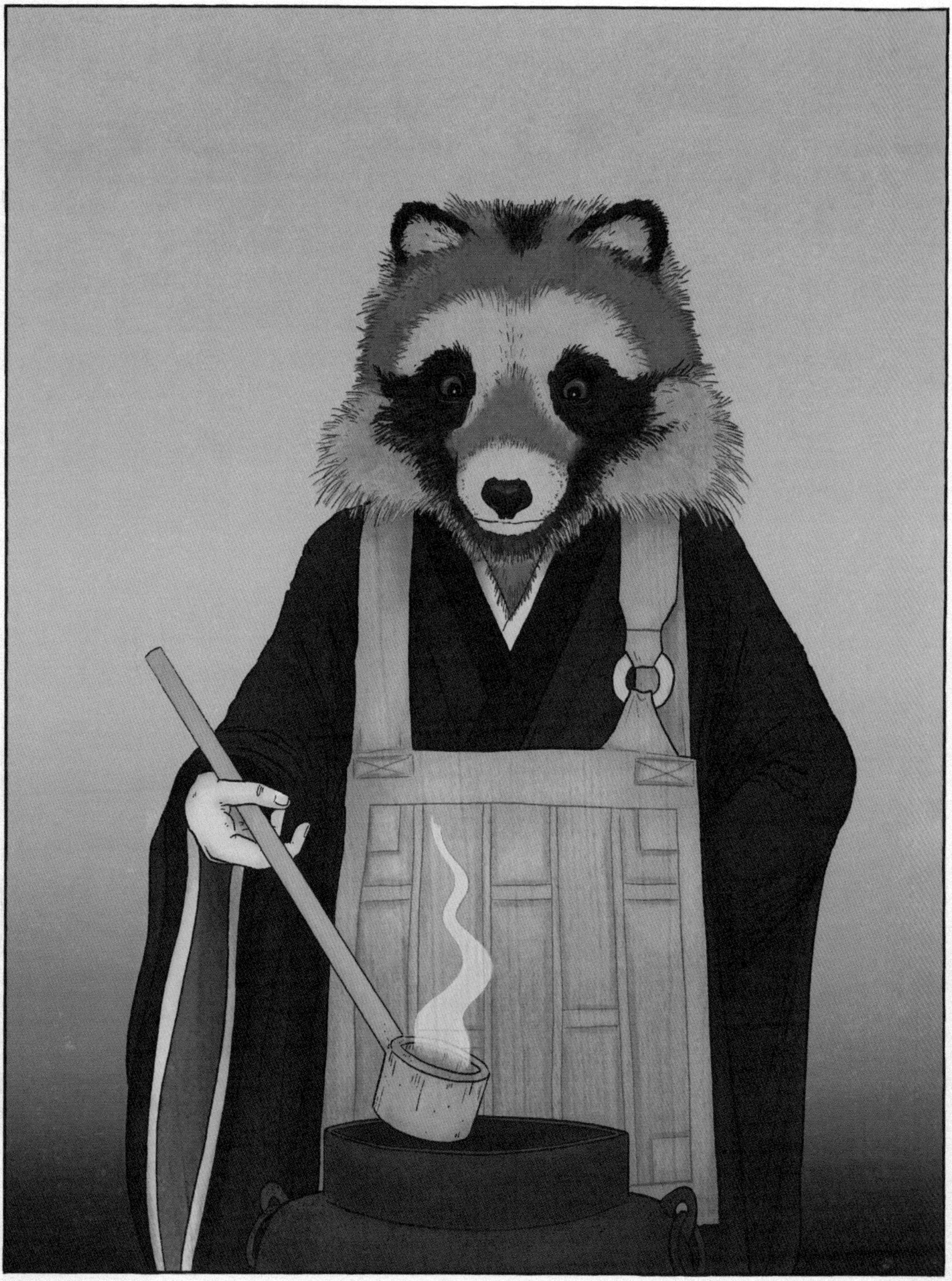

Kuzunoha 葛の葉

TRANSLATION: kudzu leaf
ALTERNATE NAMES: Shinodazuma (the wife from Shinoda)

APPEARANCE: Kuzunoha was a white-furred kitsune who is most famous for being the wife of Abe no Yasuna and the mother of Abe no Seimei. Her story is preserved in a number of kabuki and bunraku plays. The Inari shrine near where Abe no Yasuna first met Kuzunoha still stands today and is popularly known as the Kuzunoha Shrine.

LEGENDS: During the reign of Emperor Murakami (946–967 CE), the onmyōji Abe no Yasuna sought to rebuild his family house. The Abe family had been rich and powerful, but their lands and status were lost years before by Yasuna's father when he had been tricked by con men. While rebuilding his house, Yasuna regularly traveled to the Inari shrine in Shinoda, Izumi Province, to pray for the god's blessings.

One day, while walking through the woods of Shinoda, a beautiful white fox jumped in front of Yasuna's path. It was being chased by a hunter. The fox asked Yasuna to save it. Yasuna knew that white foxes were holy to Inari. He helped the creature to escape. Shortly afterwards, the hunter came to where Yasuna was and the two got into a fight. Yasuna was wounded in the fight and fell to the ground.

After the hunter left, a young woman came out of the forest to Yasuna's side. She told him her name was Kuzunoha. She took Yasuna back to his home and nursed him back to health. The woman continued to visit Yasuna, caring for him and checking up on his recovery. During the time she spent visiting him, Kuzunoha and Yasuna fell in love. When he finally recovered they decided to get married.

Eventually Kuzunoha became pregnant. She bore Yasuna a son. They three of them lived happily for some time. However, when their son was five years old, he witnessed something strange. Some say it was when she looked in a mirror, others say it was while she was sleeping; but his mother accidentally let her true form appear for a brief second: she was a white-furred kitsune!

Her secret discovered, Kuzunoha had no choice but to leave her beloved family. Holding a brush in her mouth, she wrote a farewell tanka on the paper door and vanished:

> *If you love me, come and visit*
> *in the forest of Shinoda in Izumi*
> *your resentful kudzu leaf*

When Yasuna read her poem, he realized that his beloved wife was the fox whom he had saved years earlier. He and their son traveled to the forests of Shinoda where Kuzunoha had first entered the world of humankind. There, Kuzunoha appeared before them one last time. She presented them with a crystal ball and a golden box as parting gifts. Then she left her human family forever.

Thanks to the magical gifts his mother had given him, her yōkai lineage, and his father's onmyōji training, Kuzunoha and Yasuna's son grew up to become a powerful sorcerer. He took the name Abe no Seimei and became the most powerful onmyōji in all of Japanese history.

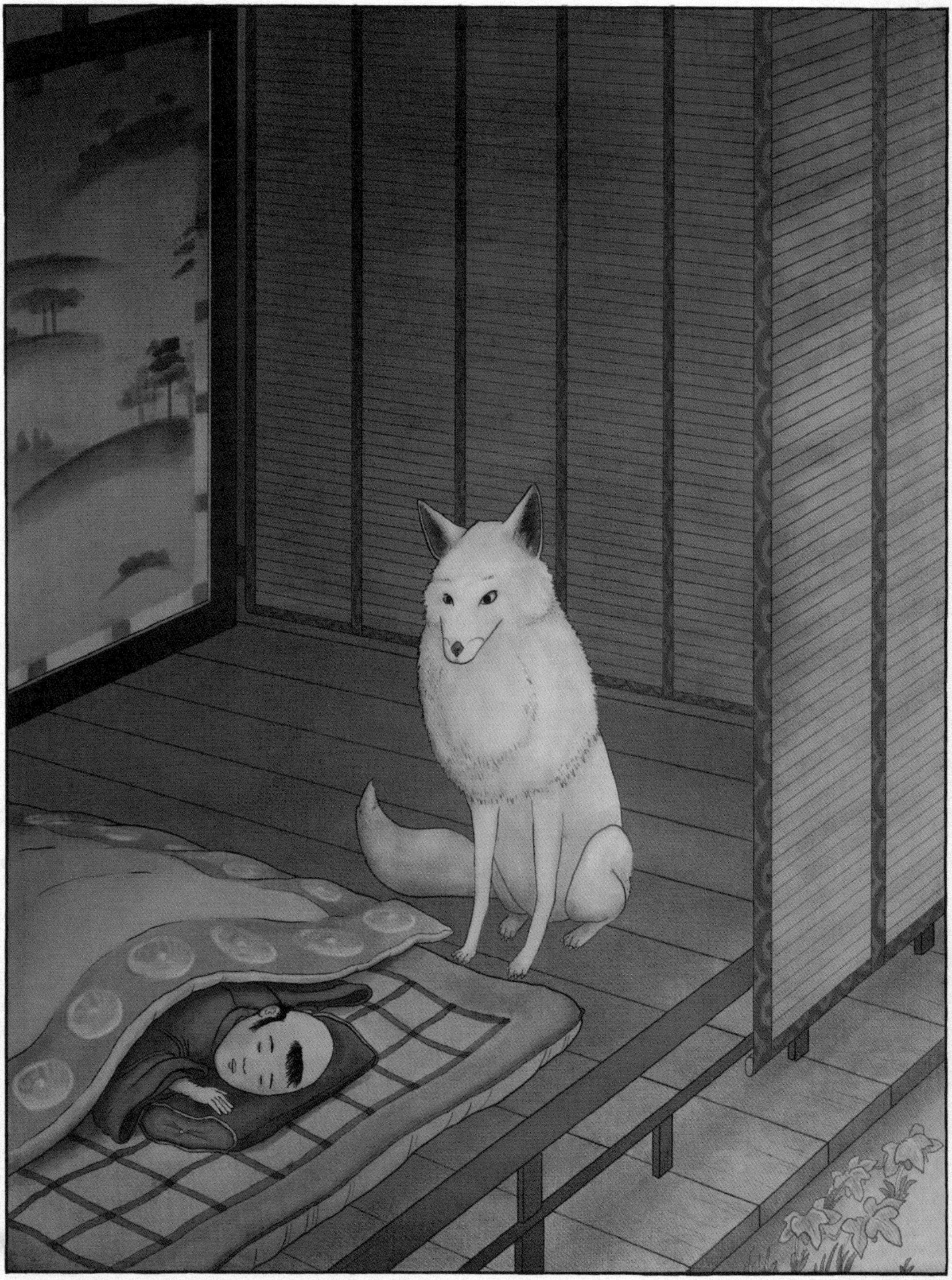

TŌDAIKI 燈台鬼

TRANSLATION: candlestick spirit, candlestick demon
DIET: none; it is sustained by dark magic

APPEARANCE: A tōdaiki is a magical lamp created using black magic and a living human being.

ORIGIN: Stories about people visiting strange lands and being transformed or disappearing into another world and never returning are not uncommon in Japanese folklore. Fanciful stories like these might have originated in true, but unsolved, disappearances of loved ones.

LEGENDS: The most famous tōdaiki story involves a real historical figure. Hitsu no Saishō was the nickname of Fujiwara no Arikuni, a Heian Period noble who lived from 943-1011 CE.

Long ago, during a period of great movement of culture and ideas between China and Japan, a government minister named Karu no Daijin was sent on a diplomatic mission to Tang China. He never returned. His family in Japan, including his young son Hitsu no Saishō, did not know whether Karu was alive or dead.

Many years later, when he was an adult, Hitsu no Saishō traveled to China to search for news of his missing father's whereabouts. He traveled far and wide. In a particular location he came across something he had never seen before—a candlestick fashioned out of a living human being! The man had been installed like a piece of furniture onto a fancy platform. A large candle had been affixed to his head. Every inch of his body was covered in strange tattoos. By some combination of drugs and sorcery, the man's throat had been blocked up and his ability to speak removed.

As Hitsu no Saishō looked in amazement at the strange object, the tōdaiki began to shed tears. Unable to speak, the man bit hard into his finger tip until it began to bleed. Then, using his finger, he wrote out a poem in his blood:

> *Long ago I came to China from Japan.*
> *I have the same family name as you.*
> *The bond between father and son transcends*
> *Even the seas and mountains that have separated us.*
> *For years I have cried in this horrible place.*
> *Every day I think of my parents.*
> *I have been transformed into a candlestick in this faraway land.*
> *I just want to go home.*

Upon reading this, Hitsu no Saishō realized in horror that the tōdaiki was his own father, whom he had come to China to find.

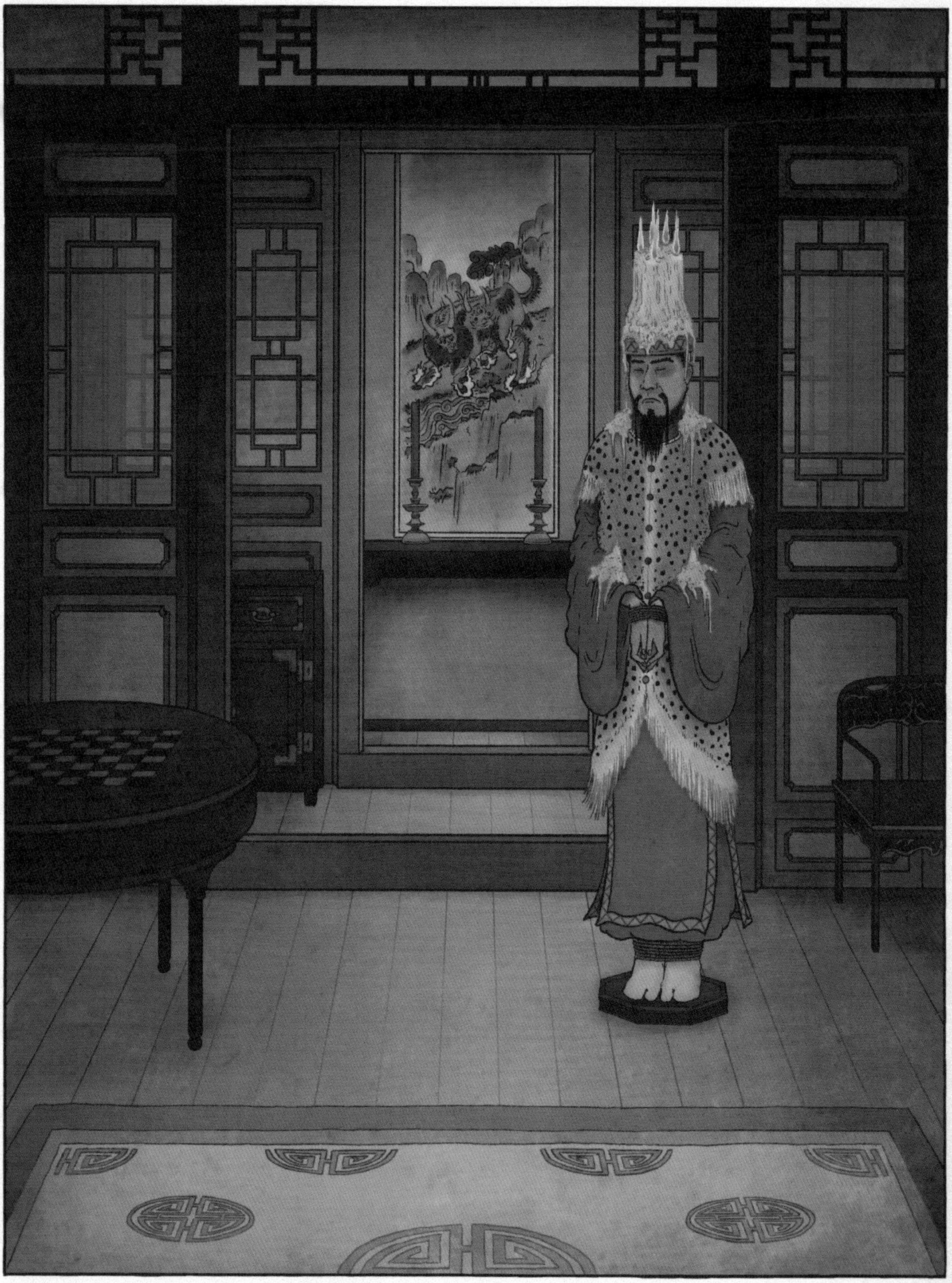

HIMAMUSHI NYŪDŌ 火間蟲入道

TRANSLATION: oven bug monk
HABITAT: under the floorboards
DIET: mainly lamp oil

APPEARANCE: Himamushi nyūdō are grotesque yōkai which live under floorboards and crawl out at night. They vaguely resemble Buddhist monks, but have long necks, sharp claws, and bodies covered in thick, dark hair. They have long tongues which they use to lap up the oil from lamps.

INTERACTIONS: Himamushi nyūdō bother people who are working hard or studying late at night. They jump out of the darkness towards them. Although they don't directly injure people, their presence is disturbing enough. They blow out the lights suddenly, and lick up the precious lamp oil, making it difficult to continue working.

ORIGIN: According to Toriyama Sekien's description of this yōkai in *Konjaku hyakki shūi*, himamushi nyūdō are born from those who were lazy in life, carelessly wasting time from birth to death.

The term "oven bug" in its name is probably a reference to cockroaches. The *hima* kanji in this yōkai's name can also be read *kama*—and likely refers to the *kamado*, a traditional Japanese oven. Cockroaches have quite a few nicknames in Japanese; among them *himushi* (fire bug) and *hitorimushi* (lamp bug), both of which sound similar to himamushi. Cockroaches and other pests would have fed on the fish oil used to power Edo Period lamps—just like this yōkai does. Cockroaches live in dark, warm spaces, such as underneath a kamado—just like this yōkai does. And they crawl out of the floorboards to scare those working late at night—again, just like this yōkai does.

Himamushi nyūdō's name contains a number of puns. According to Toriyama Sekien, it was originally called himamushiyo nyūdō (monk who wastes time at night). Over the years, the pronunciation gradually morphed. It became associated with hemamusho nyūdō—a popular Edo Period word doodle in which a monk is drawn using the characters in its name: ヘマムショ入道. The association of this yōkai with the word doodle would have amused readers during Sekien's time.

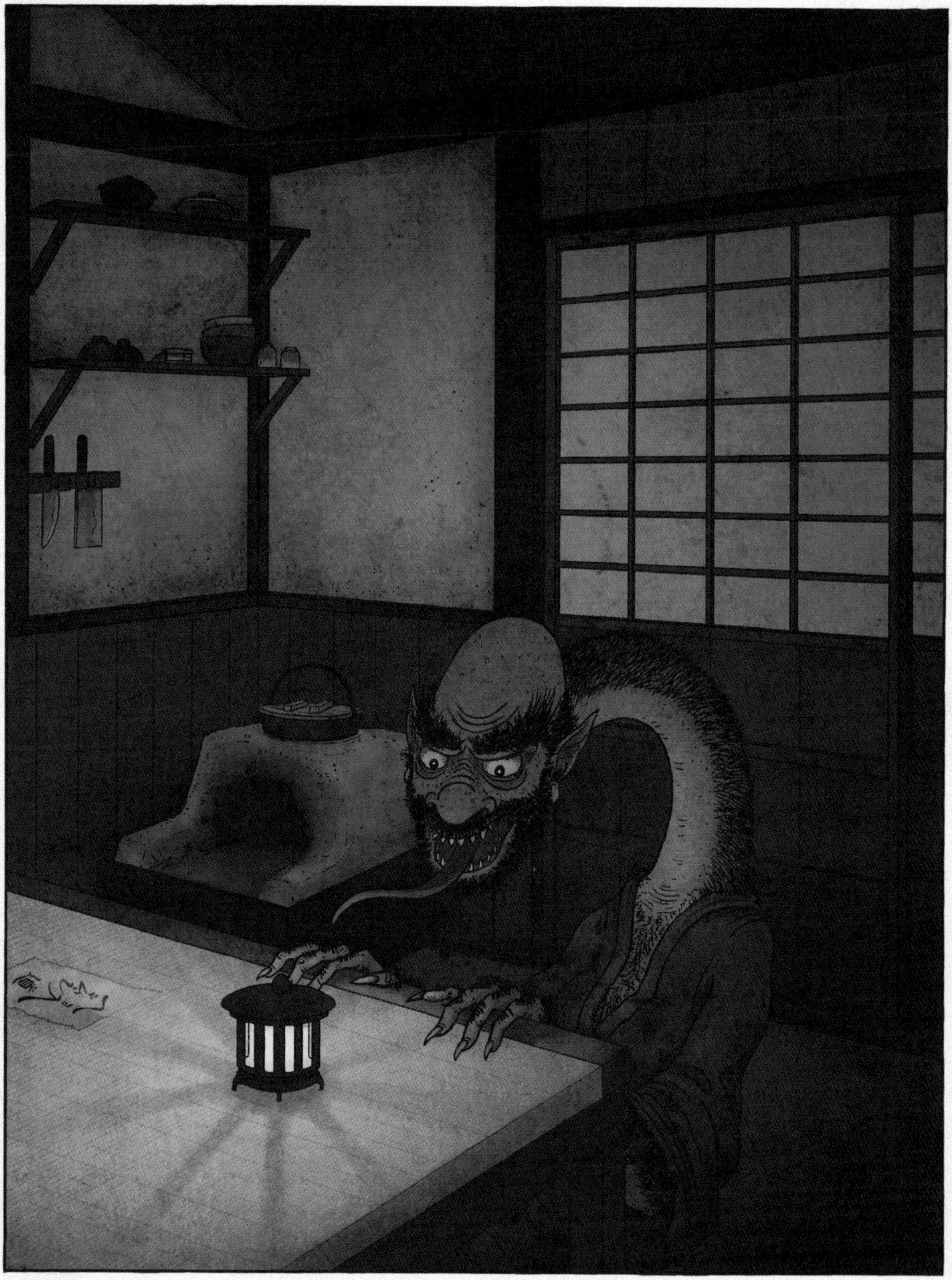

KURO BŌZU 黒坊主

TRANSLATION: black monk
HABITAT: human-inhabited areas
DIET: the breath of sleeping humans

APPEARANCE: Kuro bōzu are dark, shadowy yōkai which looks somewhat like dark, bald Buddhist monks. However, their exact appearance is vague and difficult to make out. Their bodies are entirely black. They wear black robes. Their faces have somewhat bestial features. Kuro bōzu have long tongues and reek of rotting fish. Their hands and feet are said to be indiscernible. They can change height rapidly, becoming towering monsters in an instant. They are extremely fast and can run as if they were flying.

INTERACTIONS: Kuro bōzu haunt areas inhabited by humans. They come out at night, sneaking into houses after everyone is asleep. They creep up to their victims—usually women—and suck the breath out of their mouths. They also slide their putrid tongues into the mouths, ears, and all over the faces of their victims. Those visited repeatedly by kuro bōzu fall deathly ill.

ORIGIN: Kuro bōzu didn't appear in folklore until the Meiji Period. They are relatively new by yōkai standards. Because of the wide variations in reports, it is hard to come up with a clear picture of this yōkai's identity. Due to their vague and indiscernible features, some experts believe they are a kind of nopperabō. Others compare them to yamachichi, who also sneak into houses to steal the breath of sleeping humans. Their size-changing abilities and monk-like appearance suggest that they may be a variety of taka nyūdō. Still others say that kuro bōzu are one of the forms taken by magical kawauso.

LEGENDS: The most well-known kuro bōzu report comes from the early Meiji period, from a newspaper article in the *Hōchi Shinbun*. The encounter took place at a certain carpenter's house in Kanda, Tokyo. At midnight, a black, shadowy figure shaped like a monk appeared in the house. The creature entered the bedroom where husband and wife were sleeping. It climbed over the carpenter's sleeping wife and stuck its tongue in her ears and mouth. Then it licked her all over. The creature smelled like foul garbage. The smell was so noxious that the family became ill.

Again and again, for several nights, the kuro bōzu returned to assault the carpenter's wife. Finally, she could not put up with it anymore. She left her husband and went to stay with some relatives. According to the carpenter, after his wife left, the black monk stopped coming.

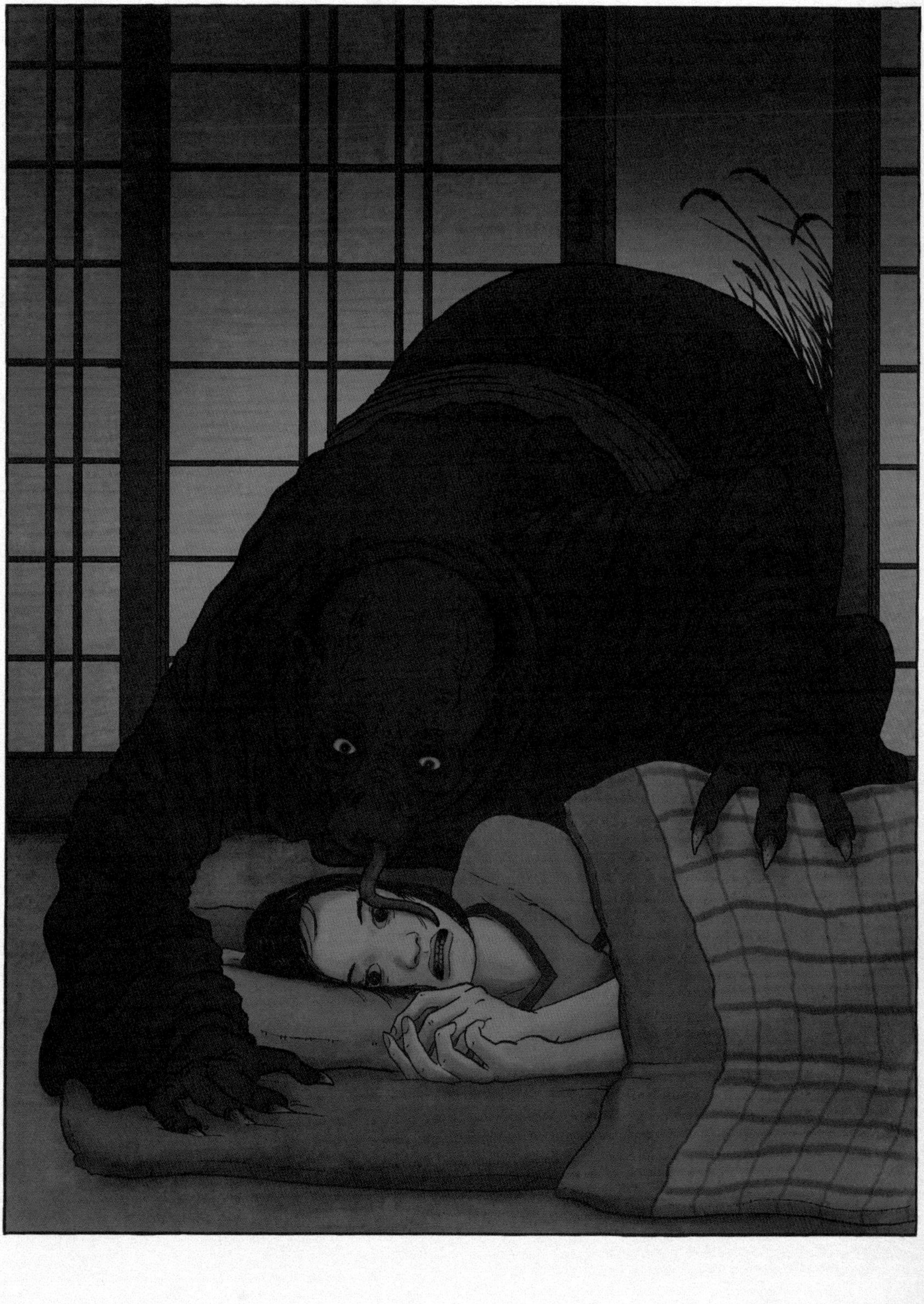

KEKKAI 血塊

TRANSLATION: blood clot, blood clump
ALTERNATE NAMES: kekke
HABITAT: under the floorboards of its birth house
DIET: its own mother

APPEARANCE: Kekkai are a kind of *sankai*—childbirth monster—from Saitama, Kanagawa, and Nagano Prefectures. They are small and ugly, resembling a monkey. Their hair is said to grow in backwards. They have two tongues—one red and one white. They are sometimes born from pregnant mothers instead of human babies.

BEHAVIOR: When a kekkai emerges covered in blood and amniotic fluid, it quickly scampers away from its mother and tries to escape. This is most often accomplished through the *irori*, or earthen hearth, a common feature in old country houses. It either burrows down beneath the floorboards or climbs up the long pothook which hangs above the irori and flees. If the kekkai is able to escape, it will return later to kill its mother while she sleeps. It does this by burrowing up through the floorboards and into its sleeping mother, tearing her apart from the inside.

INTERACTIONS: A few traditional precautions exist to protect against kekkai. The most important is preparation. A large *shamoji* (spatula) is placed by the irori. When the kekkai tries to climb up the pothook, it must be swatted down and caught before it has a chance to escape.

Another common precaution is to surround the floor around the mother with *byōbu* (folding screens) to prevent a kekkai from escaping. This practice is the source of a play on words surrounding this yōkai's name: the byōbu creates a spiritual barrier, or *kekkai* (結界), which prevents the kekkai (血塊) from escaping.

ORIGIN: Kekkai are almost certainly a way to explain the dangers surrounding childbirth and the existence of birth defects. Before modern medicine was invented, death from complications relating to childbirth was not uncommon. A grieving family might be easily convinced that a mother's death was caused by some evil spirit—spiritual punishment for the family's sins. Similarly, it is not hard to imagine how superstitious people might have seen premature, stillborn, or deformed babies as monsters. Referring to them as yōkai may have been an attempt to understand the unknown and explain the unexplainable.

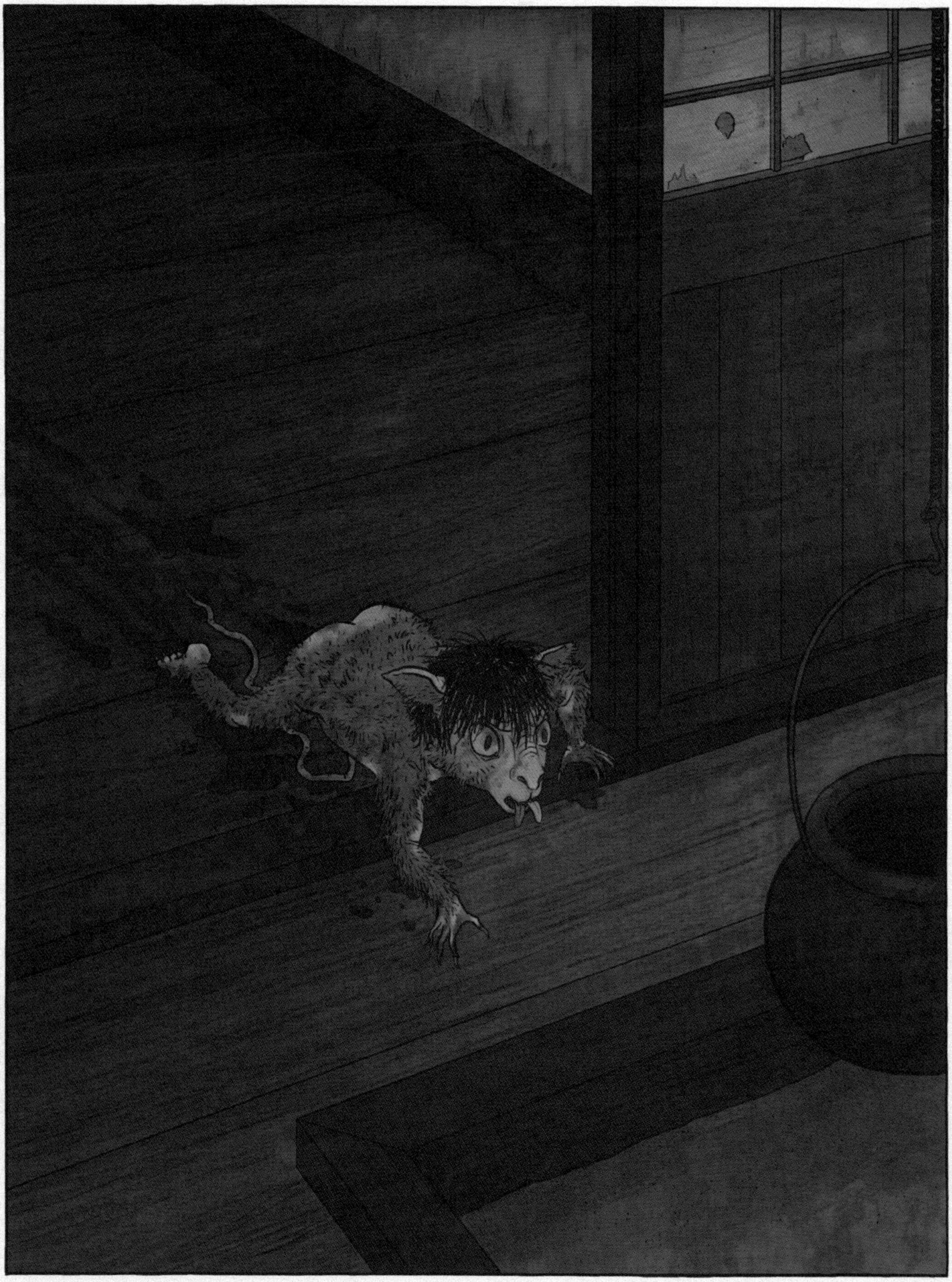

HINNAGAMI 人形神

TRANSLATION: doll god, doll spirit
ALTERNATE NAMES: kochobbo
HABITAT: homes

APPEARANCE: Hinnagami are powerful spirits from Toyama Prefecture. They reside in dolls and grant their owners' wishes.

INTERACTIONS: Hinnagami grant their owners any wish that they desire. Families who own hinnagami quickly become rich and powerful. People who become rich and famous too swiftly are suspected of owning hinnagami.

Hinnagami come with a catch: if a new request is not made as soon as a wish is granted, the hinnagami will demand, "What is next?" As soon as that request is fulfilled, the hinnagami demands another task. And another. And another. This pattern never ends. Because their creation comes out of human greed and desire, hinnagami cling to their creators obsessively and never leave their sides. A hinnagami's attachment is so powerful, in fact, that even death cannot separate it from its master. When a hinnagami's creator dies, the hinnagami will follow them to hell and haunt them for all of eternity.

ORIGIN: Hinnagami are created through a long and complicated ritual. There are a few variations depending on who you hear the story from.

In the most common ritual, the person who wishes to create a hinnagami must begin collecting grave earth that has been trampled on by people during the day. Grave earth must be collected in this way every night for three years. For an even stronger hinnagami, they should take earth from seven different graveyards in seven different villages. Once collected, the grave earth is mixed with human blood until it becomes clay-like. Then it is molded into a doll shape representing a god or a spirit that its creator worships. This doll is placed in a busy road and left there until it has been trampled upon by one thousand people. Then the creator retrieves the doll, which has become a hinnagami.

An alternative method is to collect graveyard stones and carve them into one thousand small dolls, each about nine centimeters long. These dolls are boiled in a large pot until only one of them rises to the surface. The doll that rises is said to contain the combined souls of all one thousand dolls. This type of hinnagami is called a kochobbo.

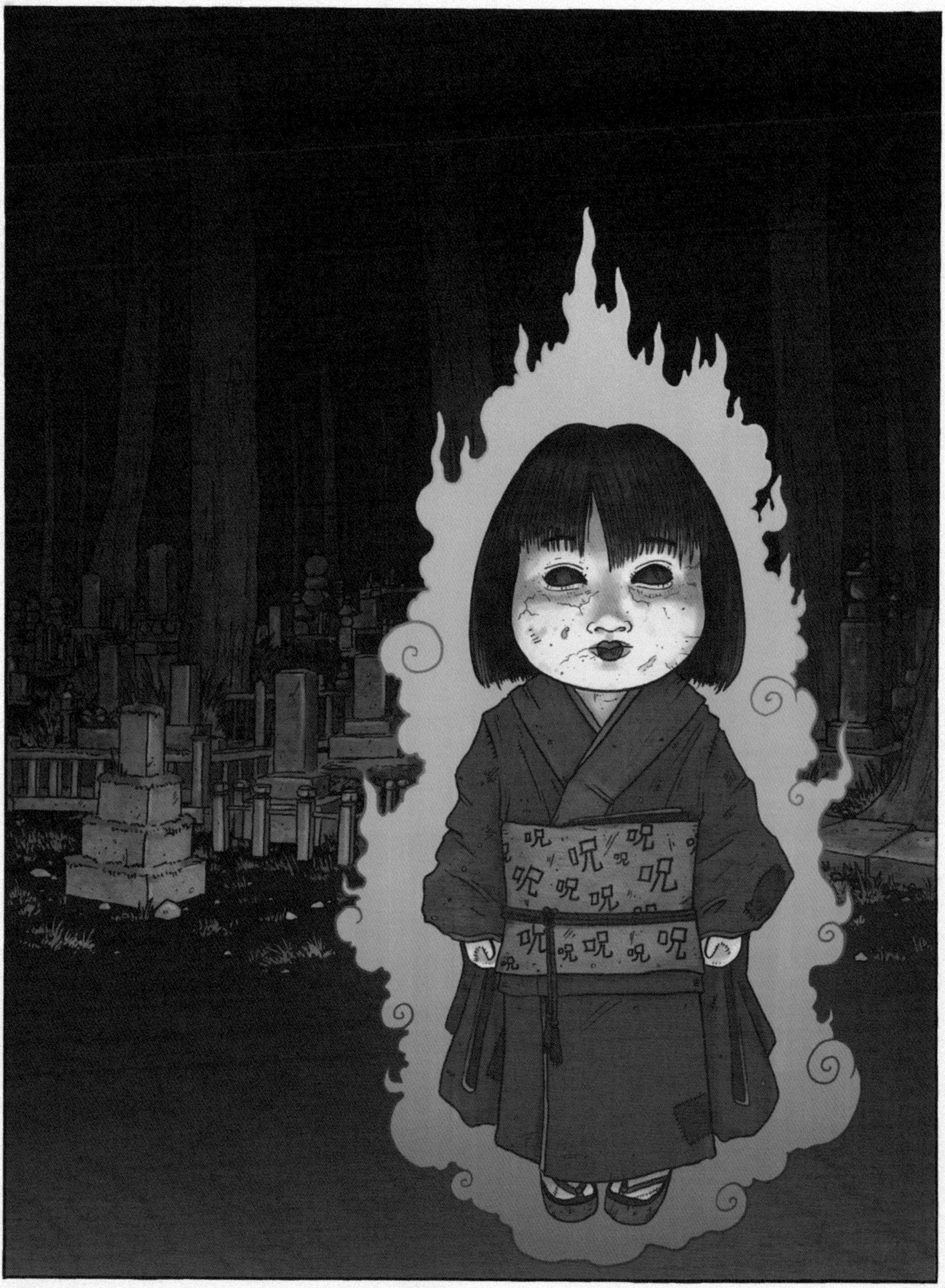
呪 呪 呪 呪 呪 呪 呪 呪 呪
呪 呪 呪 呪 呪 呪 呪 呪

HANGONKŌ 反魂香

TRANSLATION: spirit calling incense

APPEARANCE: Hangonkō is a special kind of incense from ancient Chinese legends which has the power to call forth the spirits of the dead. Those who burn the incense will see their loved ones' faces within the smoke of the incense.

ORIGIN: Hangonkō is made from the *hangonjū*, a magical tree with leaves and flowers that resemble those of a maple or Japanese oak. Its smell can be picked up from over 100 *ri* away. To make hangonkō, you steam the hangonjū's roots until the sap comes out. Then you knead the sap to make the incense. Even a small piece of this resin is strong enough to recall the spirits of those who died from sickness or disease. There is a catch, however. Hangonkō only returns the spirit for a short time and they only exist within the smoke of the burning incense.

LEGENDS: The incense was famously used by Emperor Wu of the Han dynasty in China. After his beloved concubine Li Furen passed away, the emperor fell into deep depression. A Taoist sorcerer, in an attempt to ease the emperor's grief, provided him with a bit of hangonkō that he might see Lady Li one more time.

Hangonkō was a popular subject in Japanese literature as well. It appears in a number of Edo Period works, from ghost story books to theater, kabuki, rakugo, and bunraku. The Japanese versions star famous characters from Japanese history. For example, in one story a man is overcome with grief at the death of his beloved prostitute. A hōkan (a male geisha) recommends he try recalling her spirit using a secret incense handed down by the onmyōji Abe no Seimei.

All the variations of the story have the same ending. After the person uses the incense to meet their lover's spirit, it only leaves them sadder and more grieved than before. Hangonkō doesn't alleviate their loneliness—it makes it worse. This story is a Buddhist allegory. Smoke can be a symbol of delusion, such as attachment to the material world, or the inability to let go of a loved one after death. In Buddhism, this delusion is the ultimate cause of all suffering. The smoke of this incense prevents people from properly letting go of their loved ones and moving on. They're stuck in the past, in a delusion, and will be forever miserable unless they learn to let go.

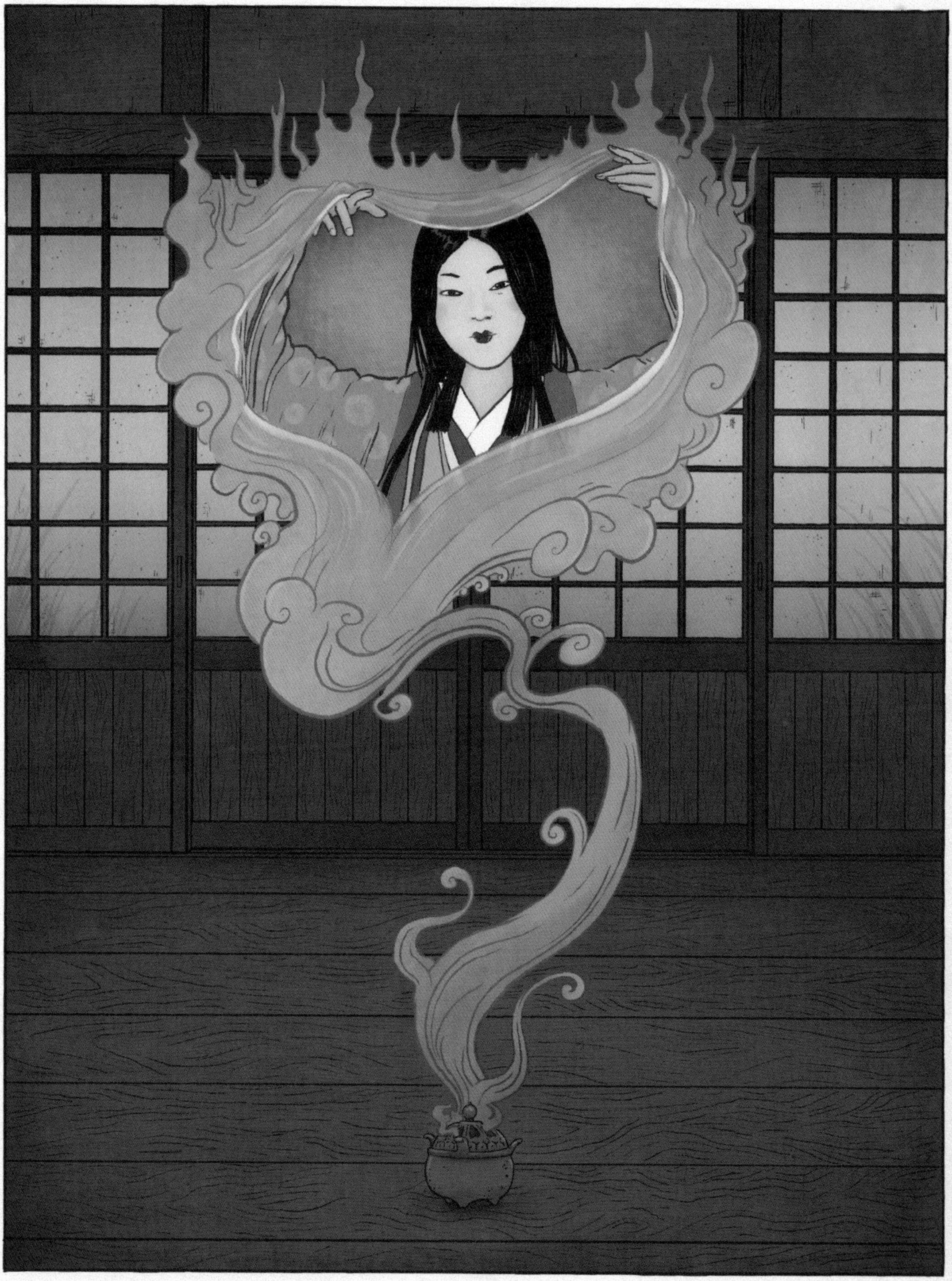

OIWA お岩

TRANSLATION: a girls' name meaning "rock"

APPEARANCE: Oiwa is the onryō from the ghost story *Yotsuya kaidan*. Her story is based on real-life events which took place in 17th century Edo. The real Oiwa died in 1636. It is rumored that her onryō still haunts the places she lived as well as those who perform her story. Mysterious disasters occurring around theater and film adaptations of her story have been blamed on her ghost. A small shrine and a temple dedicated were erected on the ruins of her family's house to appease her angry spirit. It is customary for actors and crews putting on a production of *Yotsuya kaidan* to visit Oiwa's grave and ask her permission.

LEGENDS: Oiwa was married to a samurai named Iyemon . He was a wasteful man and a thief. One day, Oiwa decided to leave her husband and return to her family. Iyemon followed her but was stopped by Oiwa's father, Yotsuya Samon. He knew of Iyemon's crimes. He demanded the bandit divorce Oiwa. Iyemon drew his sword and murdered Samon, then returned to Oiwa and told her that a stranger had killed her father on the road. He begged her to reconcile with him and promised to avenge her father's murder.

Times were hard. They had little money. Oiwa bore Iyemon a son, but she became sickly after giving birth, and Iyemon grew resentful of her. A rich doctor named Itō Kihei lived next door. He had a beautiful granddaughter named Oume. She was attracted to Iyemon, and so Kihei conspired to help her marry him. Kihei prescribed an ointment for Oiwa to help her recover from her sickness. In reality, it was a poison. After she applied it, her face was horribly disfigured. Iyemon's resentment grew into disgust. Kihei suggested to Iyemon that he leave Oiwa and marry his granddaughter; if he were to wed Oume, all the wealth of the Itō family could be his to inherit. Iyemon so hated Oiwa's face that he agreed to the scheme. Iyemon pawned Oiwa's possessions, her clothing, and even their son's clothing to save money to marry Oume. He needed a legitimate reason to divorce Oiwa, so he paid his friend Takuetsu to rape her so that he could accuse her of infidelity.

On a prearranged night when Iyemon was away, Takuetsu entered Oiwa's room. He was so shocked by her disfigurement that he abandoned the plan. He confessed everything to Oiwa. She had not known what the ointment had done to her face. Takuetsu showed her a mirror. When Oiwa saw her reflection, she cried. She tried to cover the disfigurement by brushing her hair over it, but it fell out in large, bloody clumps. She went mad. She grabbed a nearby sword and stabbed her own throat. As she bled to death, she cursed Iyemon's name until she could breathe no more.

Oiwa's body was discovered by Iyemon's servant Kohei. When Kohei delivered the sad news, Iyemon was overjoyed. Kohei became suspicious, but before he could act, Iyemon murdered him. He nailed Kohei's and Oiwa's bodies to a door and threw them in a river. He claimed that Kohei and Oiwa had slept together, justifying their deaths and freeing him to marry Oume.

On their wedding night, Iyemon had trouble sleeping. He rolled over in bed and next to him was the disfigured face of Oiwa! He slashed at the ghost with his sword, but Iyemon realized too late that it was not Oiwa, but Oume. His new bride lay dead on the floor. Iyemon ran next door to seek Kihei's help. However, when he got there, he was confronted by Kohei's ghost. Iyemon slashed at the ghost with his sword. As he did Itō Kihei's slain body fell to the floor.

Iyemon fled into the night but Oiwa's onryō pursued him. Everywhere he went, she was there. Her ruined face haunted his dreams. Her terrible voice cried out for vengeance. She even appeared in the paper lanterns that lit his way. Iyemon ran into the mountains and hid in an isolated cabin. But Oiwa followed him there too. Haunted by Oiwa's ghost, no longer able to separate nightmare from reality, Iyemon descended into madness.

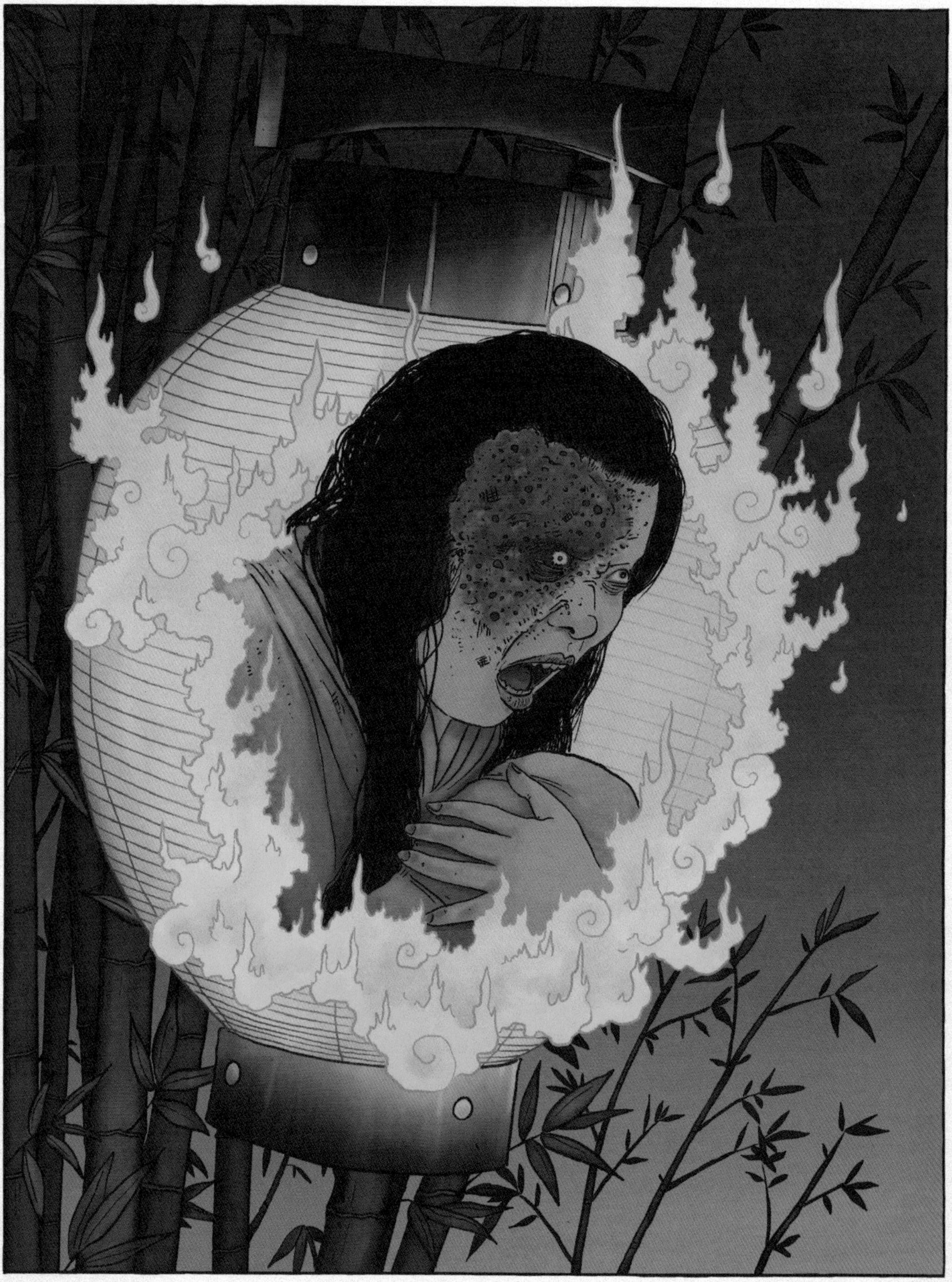

Okiku お菊

TRANSLATION: a girls' name meaning "chrysanthemum"

APPEARANCE: Okiku was the name of a servant girl who lost a precious plate, died a terrible death, and returned as a vengeful ghost. Her story is called *Bancho sarayashiki*: "The Dish Manor at Banchō." It has been retold countless times in folk tales, puppet theater, kabuki, film, and manga. Though the general outline of her story remains the same, the names, locations, and surrounding details vary quite a bit from telling to telling.

LEGENDS: Long ago, a woman named Okiku worked as a dishwashing servant at Himeji Castle. Okiku was beautiful. It was not long before she caught the eye of one of her master's retainers, a samurai named Aoyama. Aoyama tried many times to woo Okiku, but each time she rejected his advances.

Aoyama grew impatient with Okiku and decided to trick her into becoming his lover. In the castle there was a set of ten extremely expensive dishes. Aoyama stole one dish and then called for Okiku. He told her one of his master's fine dishes was missing. He demanded to know where it was. Okiku became frightened. Losing one of her lord's prized dishes was a crime punishable by death. She counted the dishes, "One... two... three... four... five... six... seven... eight... nine..." She recounted them. Again and again, each time she came up one dish short.

Aoyama told Okiku that he would tell his master that it wasn't her who lost the dish—but only if she would become his mistress. She again refused. This time Aoyama became furious. He ordered his servants to beat Okiku with a wooden sword. Afterwards, he had her tied up and suspended over the castle well. He tortured her, repeatedly dunking her into the well, then pulling her back up and beating her. He demanded one last time that she become his mistress. Okiku refused. So, Aoyama struck her violently with his sword and dropped her body down into the well.

Not long after, Okiku's ghost was seen wandering the castle grounds. Night after night, it would rise from the well and enter her master's house searching for the missing dish. It would count the plates: "One... two... three... four... five... six... seven... eight... nine..." After counting the ninth plate, the ghost would let out a blood curdling scream that could be heard throughout the castle. Okiku tormented Aoyama every night, robbing him of his rest. Those who overheard part of Okiku's counting became sick. Those who listened all the way to nine died.

Finally, the lord of the castle demanded that something be done about Okiku's ghost. He asked a priest to pray for her soul. The priest waited in the garden all night, chanting sutras. One again, Okiku's ghost rose out of the well. It began to count the dishes: "One... two... three... four... five... six... seven... eight... nine..." As soon as the ghost had counted the ninth dish, the priest shouted out: "TEN!" The ghost suddenly looked relieved. Someone had found its missing dish! After that, Okiku was never seen again.

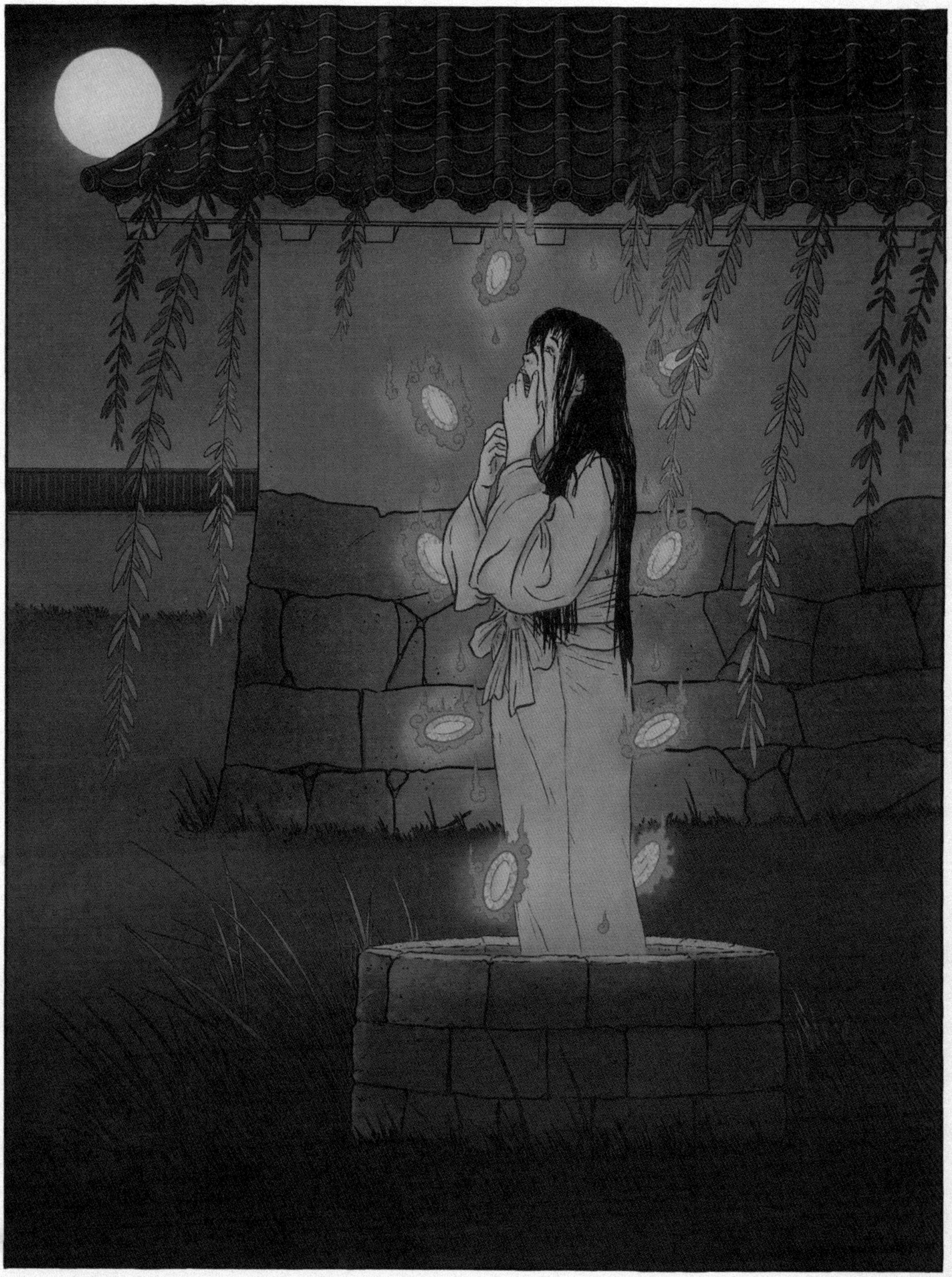

OKIKU MUSHI 於菊虫

TRANSLATION: Okiku bug
HABITAT: wells around Himeji Castle
DIET: herbivorous

APPEARANCE: Okiku mushi are caterpillar-like yōkai with the torso of a human woman. They are called Okiku mushi because it is believed they are born from the vengeance of Okiku's ghost.

ORIGIN: According to the story *Banchō sarayashiki*, the servant girl Okiku was murdered by her lover. Her body was tied up, she was tortured, and then her body was discarded into the well of Himeji Castle.

After her death, a number of strange occurrences were blamed on Okiku's ghost. One of these was the sudden proliferation of a certain type of caterpillar—specifically the Chinese windmill (*Byasa alcinous*). The chrysalis of this butterfly was thought to look like a woman's body tied up with ropes. The locals of Himeji immediately associated this with Okiku's story. It was believed that Okiku's spirit must have manifested as these bugs, spawned by whatever part of her grudge lingers in this world.

While this insect is commonly known as the *jakō ageha* in Japan today, it is sill also known by the nickname Okiku mushi. This is in part due to the popularity of Okiku's story across Japan as well as to the clever marketing of the local shopkeepers around Himeji Castle. During the Edo period, Himeji's souvenir shops sold the chrysalises of these insects to tourists at shrines near the castle.

THE "BIG THREE" GHOSTS

Japan has a love for "top three" lists. The Big Three Japanese Gardens, the Big Three Views of Japan, and the Big Three Mountains are common tourist destinations among Japanese and foreigners alike. Of course, folklore is no exception. There are numerous "big three" lists which rank yōkai, oni, and onryō by various criteria. One of these lists is *Nihon san dai kaidan*-Japan's Big Three Ghost Stories. These are *Yotsuya kaidan*, *Banchō sarayashiki*, and *Botan dōrō*—the tales of Oiwa, Okiku, and Otsuyu. These stories are singled out because of the profound influence they have had on Japanese culture.

A fourth tale is often included alongside these as one of the most famous *Japanese* ghost stories (replacing *Botan dōrō*, which originated in China). That is the story of Kasane, from *Kasane ga fuchi*. Kasane is held up alongside with Oiwa and Okiku as a paragon of the grudge-driven female ghosts of Japanese folklore.

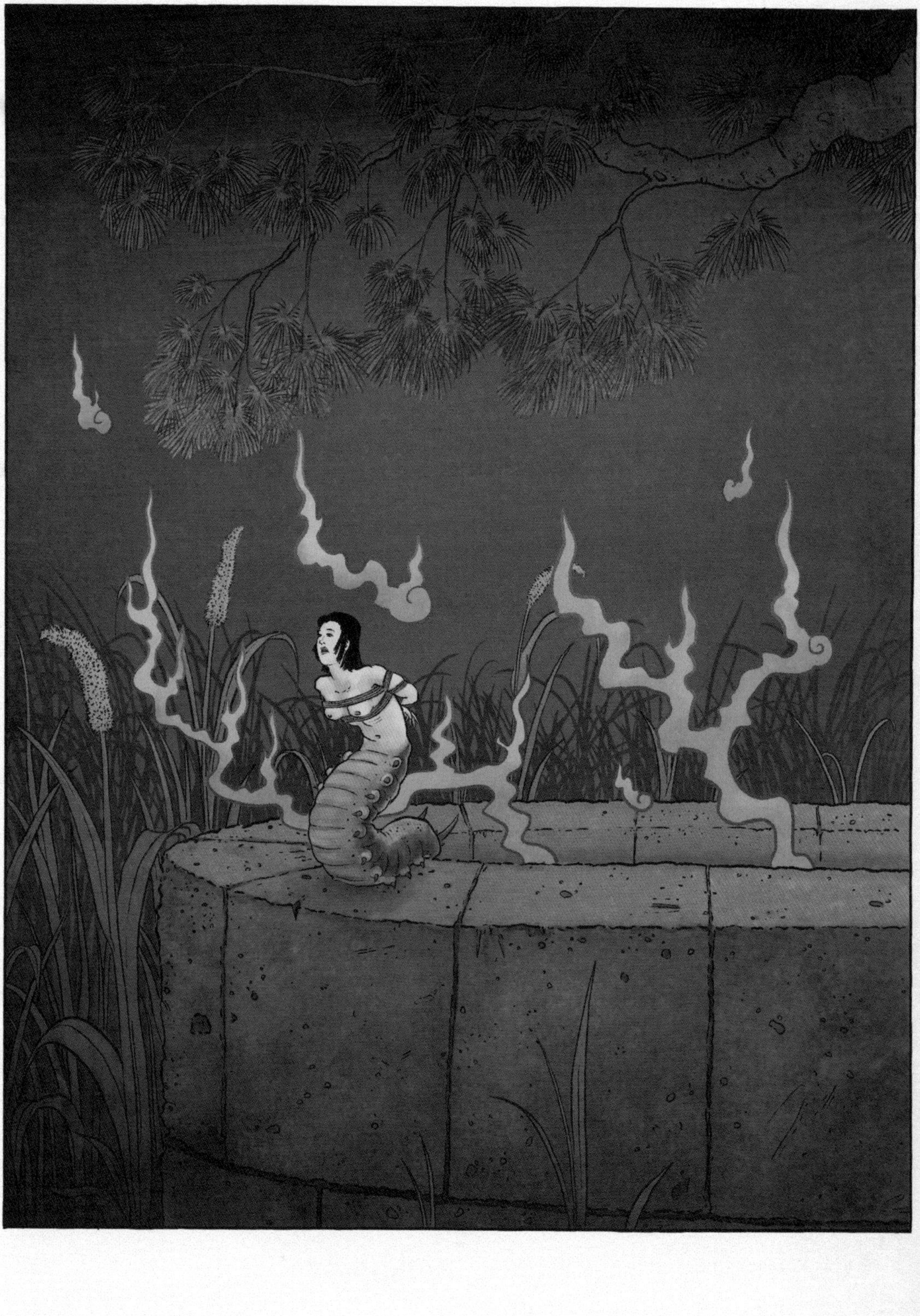

Otsuyu お露

TRANSLATION: a girls' name meaning "dew"

APPEARANCE: Otsuyu is the ghost from *Botan dōrō* (The Peony Lantern). Her story was originally a Chinese folk tale. It was adapted into Japanese in the 17th century. It has been adapted for rakugo and kabuki, with various changes, extra characters, and more details added to flesh out the story. Her story takes place during the Obon holiday, when the dead are believed to return to the land of the living. Unlike most Japanese ghost stories, Otsuyu's tale is one of love rather than of vengeance.

LEGENDS: Long ago lived a man named Ogiwara Shinnojō. He was recently widowed. On the first night of Obon, Ogiwara saw a beautiful woman and her servant walking down the street, carrying a lantern with a peony motif. Her name was Otsuyu. Ogiwara was instantly smitten by her beauty and invited her into his home. Otsuyu spent the night with him. Long after the moon had set and the lamplight had grown faint, she reluctantly bade him farewell and left before sunrise.

To Ogiwara's delight, Otsuyu and her servant returned the following evening, carrying the same peony lantern. Ogiwara fell deeply in love with Otsuyu. He lost interest in seeing anybody but her. He no longer left his house and stopped taking care of himself. Night after night, Otsuyu visited Ogiwara's house. Each night she left just before dawn.

Twenty days passed. The neighbors began to grow concerned for Ogiwara. An old man who lived next door heard laughing and singing coming from Ogiwara's house at night. He peeked through a hole in Ogiwara's wall. He saw Ogiwara ecstatically entwined in the boney arms of a skeleton. When Ogiwara spoke, the skeleton nodded its head and moved its arms and legs. When the skeleton's jaw opened, a haunting voice came from where its mouth should have been. The old man was frightened.

The next day, the old man called upon Ogiwara. He warned him that his guest was a ghost, and that he should visit to a temple at once. Ogiwara heeded the old man's advice. At the temple, Ogiwara discovered Otsuyu's grave. An old and tattered peony lantern was draped across it. The priest warned Ogiwara that he must resist Otsuyu's calls or he would surely die. He gave him a magical charm to place on his house. Ogiwara rushed home and attached the charm to his door. The charm worked perfectly: Otsuyu stopped visiting Ogiwara.

Although he was safe, Ogiwara was despondent. He missed Otsuyu dearly. Some days after her last visit, Ogiwara became drunk and left his house. He wandered to the temple where he had discovered Otsuyu's grave. At the temple gate, Otsuyu appeared and beckoned to him. She led him away, and they spent one more night together.

Several days later, the neighbors noticed that Ogiwara had been missing for some time. Fearing the worst, the priest opened up Otsuyu's grave. Inside was the dead body of Ogiwara, wrapped up in the boney arms of Otsuyu's skeleton.

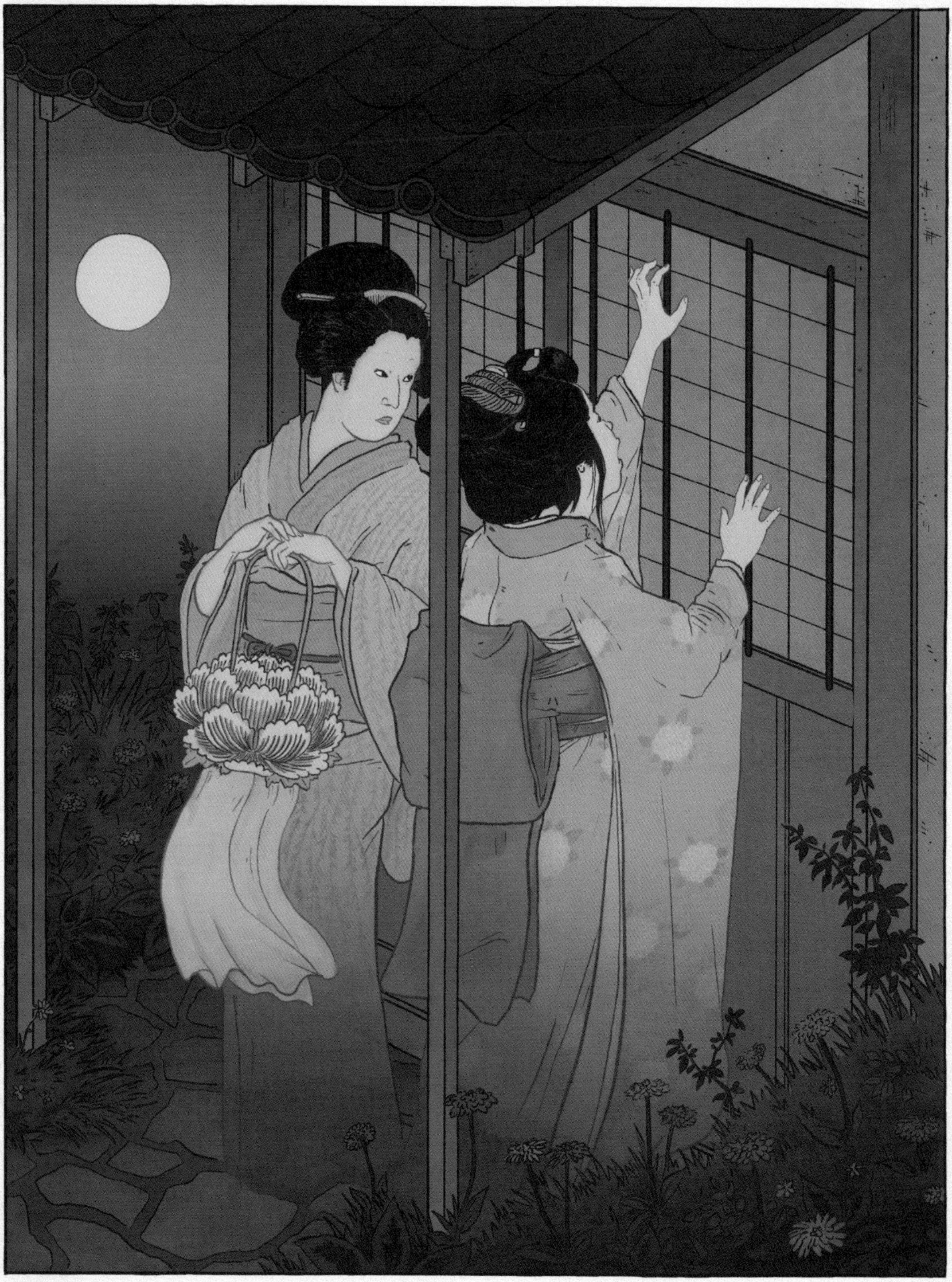

Kasane 累

TRANSLATION: to pile up, to overlap, to add on

APPEARANCE: Kasane is the ghost from *Kasane ga fuchi* (the pond of Kasane). Her tale is based on true events which happened in the 17th century.

LEGENDS: Long ago, a farmer named Yoemon and his wife Osugi lived in the village of Hanyū, Shimosa Province. Osugi had a child named Suke from a previous relationship. Suke's face was disfigured and his leg was malformed. Yoemon hated him. One day, while crossing a bridge over a deep pond, Yoemon pushed the child into the pond. Suke was unable to swim and drowned.

The next year, Yoemon and Osugi had a baby girl. They named her Rui. Rui looked so much like Suke, including the disfigured face, that the villagers believed she was haunted by his spirit. Instead of calling her Rui they referred to her as Kasane—an alternate reading of her name implying that Suke's soul had been reborn in her.

Years later, Yoemon and Osugi died. Kasane lived alone. One day she became sick. A man named Yagorō visited her and nursed her back to health. Out of gratitude, Kasane offered to marry Yagorō and make him the inheritor of her father's property. Yagorō found Kasane's face repulsive but he wanted her land and inheritance. He agreed.

One day, Yagorō and Kasane went out to the fields to collect beans. Yagorō made Kasane carry all of the beans herself. The burden was so heavy she could barely walk. As they crossed the pond, Yagorō pushed Kasane into the water. He jumped in after her and stepped on her chest, pinning her to the riverbed. He crushed and squeezed the air out of her lungs. He shoved rocks and river sand into her mouth. He stabbed her eyes with his thumbs. Then he wrung her neck until she could struggle no longer. Some townspeople witnessed this, but nobody tried to help her. She was so disliked for her ugliness that there seemed to be an unspoken agreement to leave things be.

Yagorō continued to live in Kasane's home and maintain her family's lands. He remarried quickly. However, his new wife died shortly after the wedding. He remarried again, and again his wife died. This happened over and over again. After Yagorō had remarried six times, his wife managed to survive long enough to bear him a daughter. They named her Kiku. Yagorō's sixth wife died when Kiku was thirteen.

One day Kiku suddenly became extremely sick. She collapsed to the floor. Her mouth foamed. Tears streamed from her eyes. She cried that she couldn't bear the pain and begged Yagorō to help her. Suddenly, a different person's voice spoke forth from her body: "I am not Kiku! I am the wife you murdered! I curse your family! I killed your wives! Don't you remember me? I am Kasane!"

Kiku lunged at Yagorō, but he escaped and ran to the village temple. Yagorō told everyone Kiku was lying. But the villagers, wanting to save poor Kiku, dragged Yagorō from the temple and confronted Kasane's ghost. Yagorō defiantly maintained his innocence even while Kasane's spirit cursed him. Kasane then cursed the villagers who witnessed her murder and did nothing to stop it. "All of your ancestors are here with me in Hell!" She named each of their ancestors and listed their sins. Then she listed the sins of the living villagers. The entire village's pride was shattered as their shame was made public.

Yagorō and the others confessed what they had done. Though Yagorō committed the act, through inaction the whole village was guilty of her murder. The villagers who didn't witness

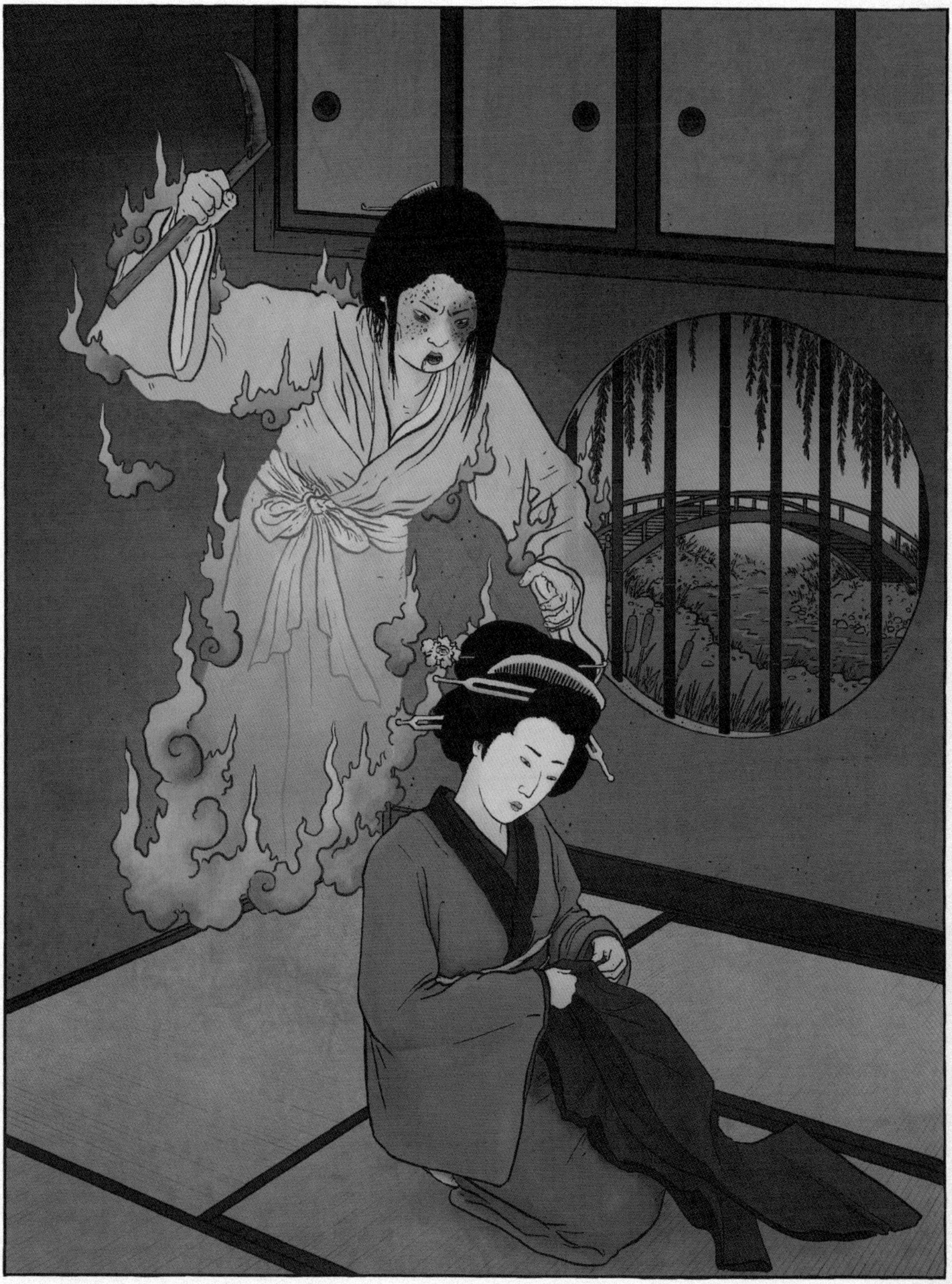

the murder but never asked about Kasane's disappearance were partially responsible too. It was their fault poor Kiku was possessed by Kasane's ghost.

Kasane demanded that the villagers hold a lavish funeral and erect a Buddha statue in her name to end her torment. The villagers balked at the cost to cover such a funeral. Kasane told them to sell her father's land to pay for it. The villagers told Kasane that her family's lands had already been sold away. Kasane's wrath exploded. Kiku's body twisted and floated high up into the air. The poor girl lost consciousness.

Word of Kiku's possession spread far and wide. A traveling priest named Saint Yūten visited the Yoemon household to offer his prayers and try to save Kiku. But his chanting and praying had no effect. Kasane taunted Yūten. He then tried to have Kiku recite the prayers, but Kasane's spirit interfered and Kiku was unable to speak. Finally, Yūten grabbed Kiku's hair, forced her into a bow, and told her to pray. Kiku was able to recite the sutra, and the spirit of Kasane grew quiet. Kiku appeared safe.

A few days later, however, Kiku's possession returned. Yūten returned to the Yoemon household, this time determined to subdue Kasane no matter what the cost. He grabbed Kiku's hair and with all of his strength forced her down onto the floor. As he held her down, demanding she pray, Kiku's voice could be heard faintly mumbling. Yūten bent down close to her mouth and listened. He asked Yagorō: "Does the name Suke mean anything to you?"

Yagorō had never heard of Suke, nor had anybody else present. Saint Yūten asked the villagers. An elderly man came forward, saying, "Some sixty years ago the first Yoemon's wife had a son. He was murdered and thrown into the pond. I think his name was Suke."

"Are you Suke?" Saint Yūten asked Kiku. Kiku's voice replied, "Yes. When you saved Rui, you left me behind. Now I possess her." Yūten blessed Suke and granted him a *kaimyō*—a posthumous Buddhist name. He wrote this name on the family altar. Suke's spirit left Kiku's body and entered the altar. Everyone present dropped to the floor and prayed. The spirits of Kasane and Suke were never heard from again.

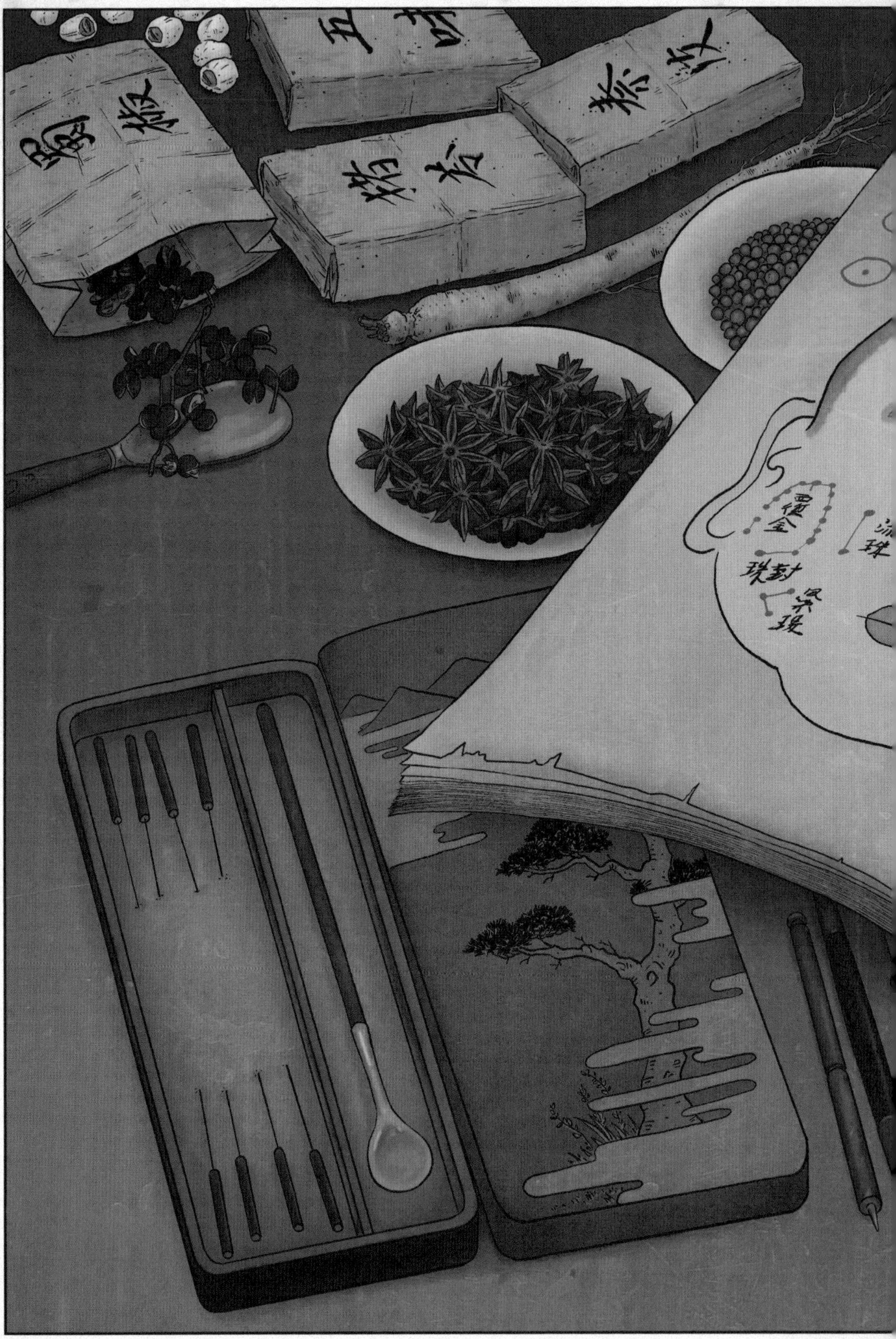

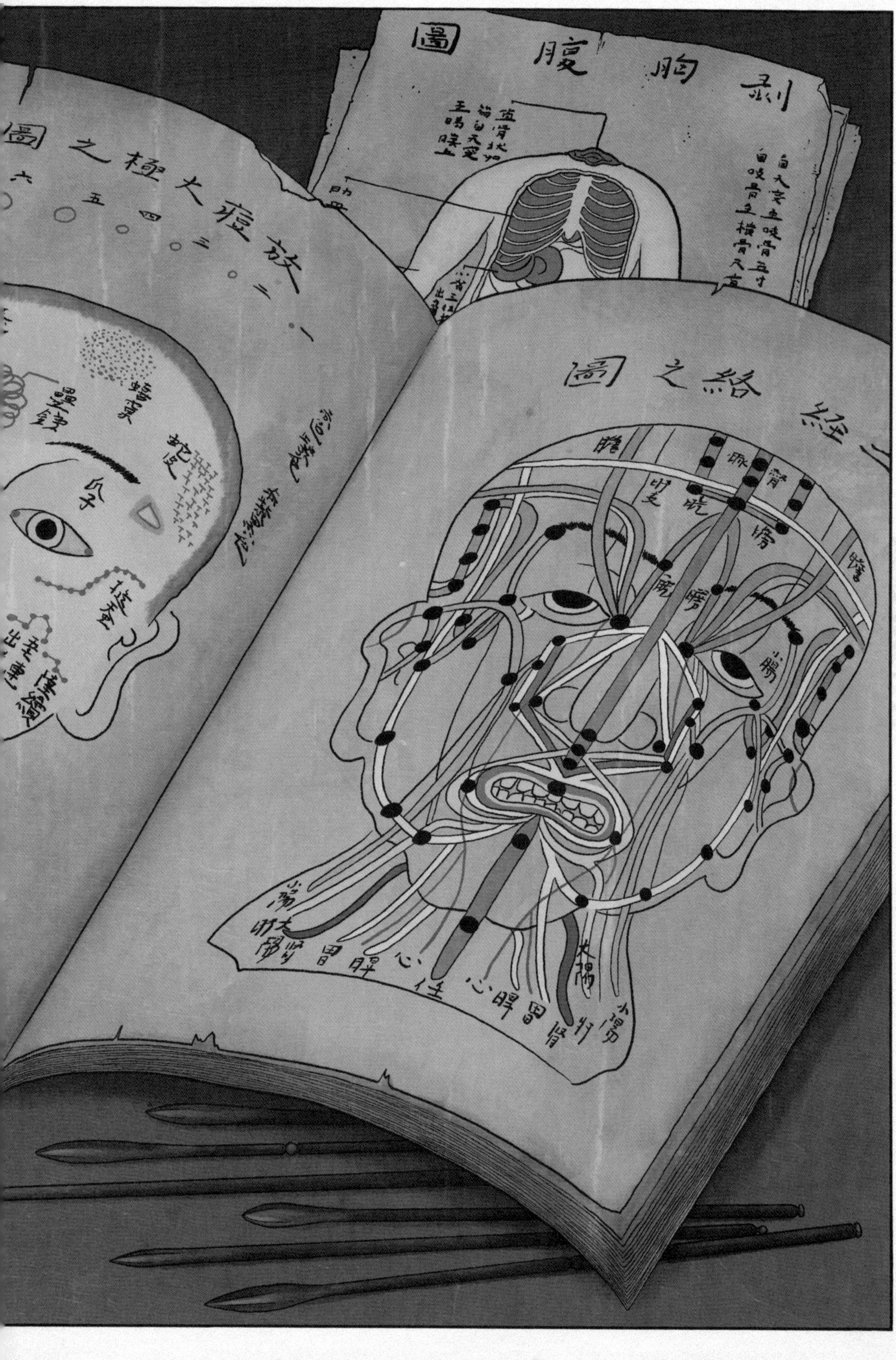
剖胸腹圖
放痘大極之圖
經絡之圖

KITSUNE TSUKI 狐憑き

TRANSLATION: fox possession

APPEARANCE: Until the advent of modern medicine, mental illness and insanity were thought to be caused by kitsune tsuki, possession by a fox spirit. Women were more susceptible to kitsune tsuki than men, as were the weak-minded.

INTERACTIONS: When a kitsune possessed an individual, it was often in retaliation—for something like killing one of its family members, for example. The kitsune caused its host to behave erratically and emotionally, making them prone to violent outbreaks and hysteria. They might run naked through the streets. They might foam at the mouth or yelp like a fox. Victims of kitsune tsuki were often able to speak and read languages that they previously had no knowledge of. Kitsune were able speak through their hosts mouths. They could control their hosts like puppets and cause them to do evil.

Some fox spirits served families, making them rich and fertile. These families were called *kitsune mochi* (fox owners). In addition to bringing their owners prosperity, kitsune would bring ruin upon the family's enemies. They placed curses, inflicted sickness, or possessed rival families. Kitsune mochi families kept their fox spirits for generations, handing down the secrets from parent to child. They honored and cared for their foxes; for the spirits could just as easily bring the same ruin upon the kitsune mochi family if angered. Families suspected of being kitsune mochi were mistrusted and feared by their neighbors. Even today in some parts of Japan, people belonging to kitsune mochi lineages occasionally have trouble finding marriage partners. Few parents would knowingly allow their son or daughter to join such a family.

Kitsune tsuki was also used in religious rituals. A willing person was used as a vessel to perform divinations. The kitsune entered the medium's body and spoke through their mouth, predicting the future or imparting secret knowledge. This was a dangerous practice. It relied on the willingness of the kitsune to leave the body after the possession was over.

A person possessed by a kitsune often developed telltale foxlike physical features, such as sharper teeth or a streamlined, pointy face. Recognizing kitsune tsuki in a person could be difficult if the victim did not display any obvious physical signs. However, there were a few clues that aided diagnosis. Despite being invisible, kitsune have certain traits which betray their presence. They love fried tofu and azuki beans. A possessed person craved these foods, often eating them in large amounts without feeling full. A possessed person also developed a fear of dogs. Finally, a small lump could often be found hidden somewhere on the victim's body. This is the place where the fox spirit resided. If pushed or pricked, the lump slipped away and moved to another part of the body. It could be caught or removed by any physical means.

Because of widespread belief in fox possession, several folk cures were invented over the centuries. Exorcism was usually performed at Inari shrines, as foxes are sacred to Inari. One fairly benign treatment included having the victim licked from head to toe by dogs. Foxes fear dogs, so this could drive the spirit away. A less benign treatment involved beating or burning the possessed in attempts to drive out the fox. Priests would also burn fresh pine leaves, suffocating the patient in thick, toxic smoke in an attempt to drive out the spirit. Unfortunately, this could kill the patient before driving out the kitsune.

Even if a person was cured of their possession, they and their families—as well as anyone accused of being behind the possession—often suffered ostracism and social isolation for the rest of their lives.

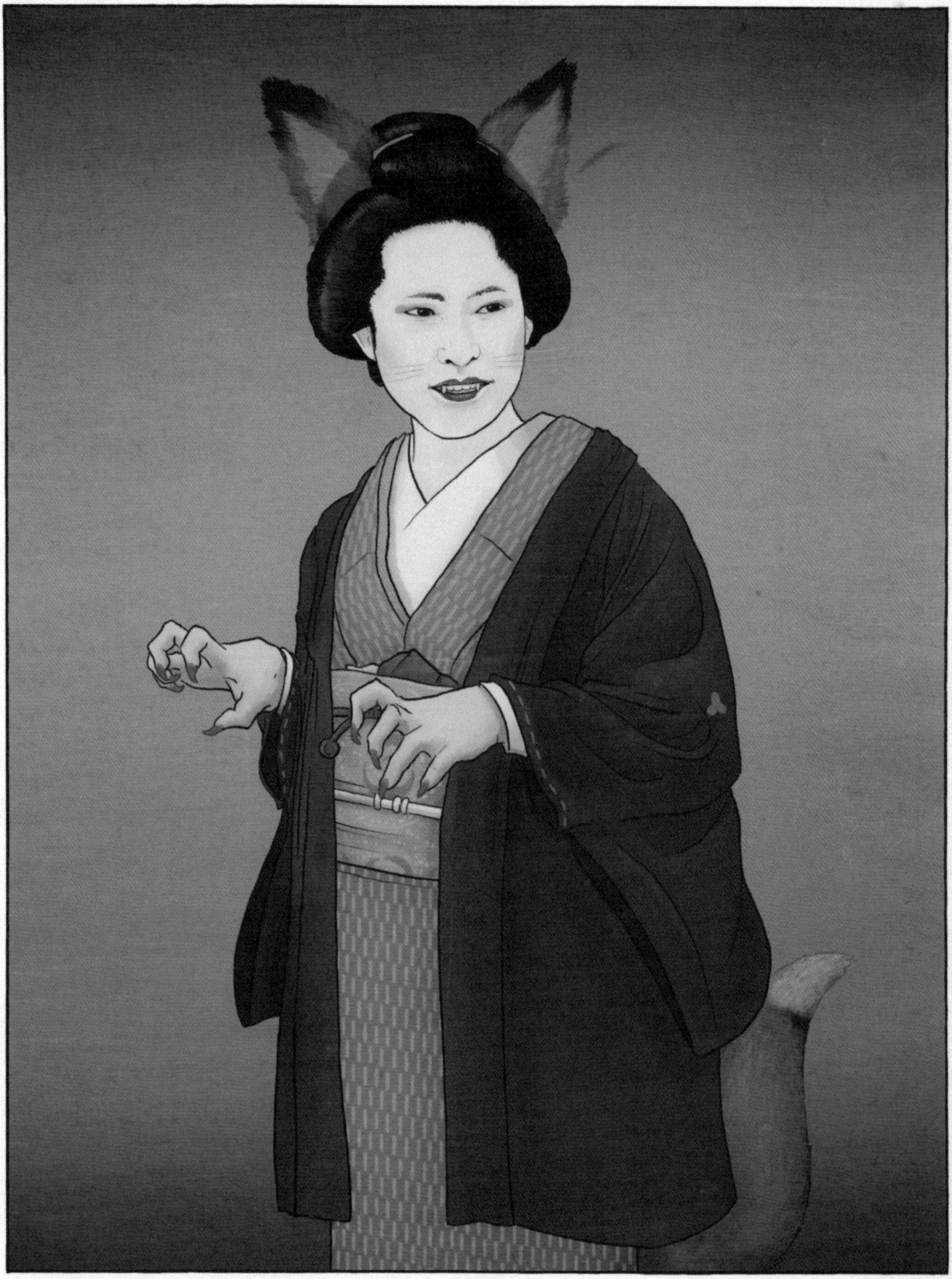

HAIMUSHI 肺虫

TRANSLATION: lung bug

APPEARANCE: Haimushi are tiny moth-like creatures with segmented bodies and four wings. They live in their host's lungs most of the time, but occasionally leave the body and fly through the air. They have red faces with triple-forked mouths, and white bodies like that of maggots. They have colorful, feathery wings. They feed mainly on cooked rice.

INTERACTIONS: Haimushi infect the lungs and cause various health problems. If a haimushi leaves its host and gets lost, the person will die. The haimushi will then turn into a fireball and burn up.

A haimushi infection can be treated with *byakujutsu*, a traditional remedy made from the powdered root of the herb *Atractylodes japonica*.

HAISHAKU 肺積

TRANSLATION: lung *shaku* (a type of infection)
ALTERNATE NAMES: sokuhon

APPEARANCE: Haishaku originate under the right armpit and gradually migrate into the lungs. They grow from smaller, larval forms into large, white, lumpy shapes that envelop the lungs and cause sickness. Their noses open directly into the lungs, so they are extremely sensitive to smells.

INTERACTIONS: People infected with haishaku develop smooth, white skin. They dislike strong smells, good or bad. Instead they prefer raw, fishy smells. They prefer spicy foods over bland ones. They also become pessimistic and depressed. Because haishaku are shaped like clouds, their hearts also become cloudy and subdued. When infected with haishaku, tears will flow like rain.

Haishaku infections can be treated with gentle and shallow acupuncture. Anything stronger than that will be too painful for the victim.

GYŪKAN 牛癇

TRANSLATION: cow *kan* (kind of infection)
ALTERNATE NAMES: kiukan, hainoju, haikan (lung kan)

APPEARANCE: Gyūkan are a type of *kan no mushi*—creatures which causes distemper and irritability in children. Kan no mushi can take many shapes and infect many parts of the body. A gyūkan is a kan no mushi which takes the shape of a cow and infects the lungs. They have long tongues and sharp hooves. The lower part of their body is red.

INTERACTIONS: Gyūkan tend to act up when their hosts eat and drink. From their position in the lungs, they can sense when food enters the throat. They become excited and cause their hosts to faint.

There are many of ways to treat them with acupuncture. However, as they grow older their horns become longer and sharper. Recovery becomes more difficult.

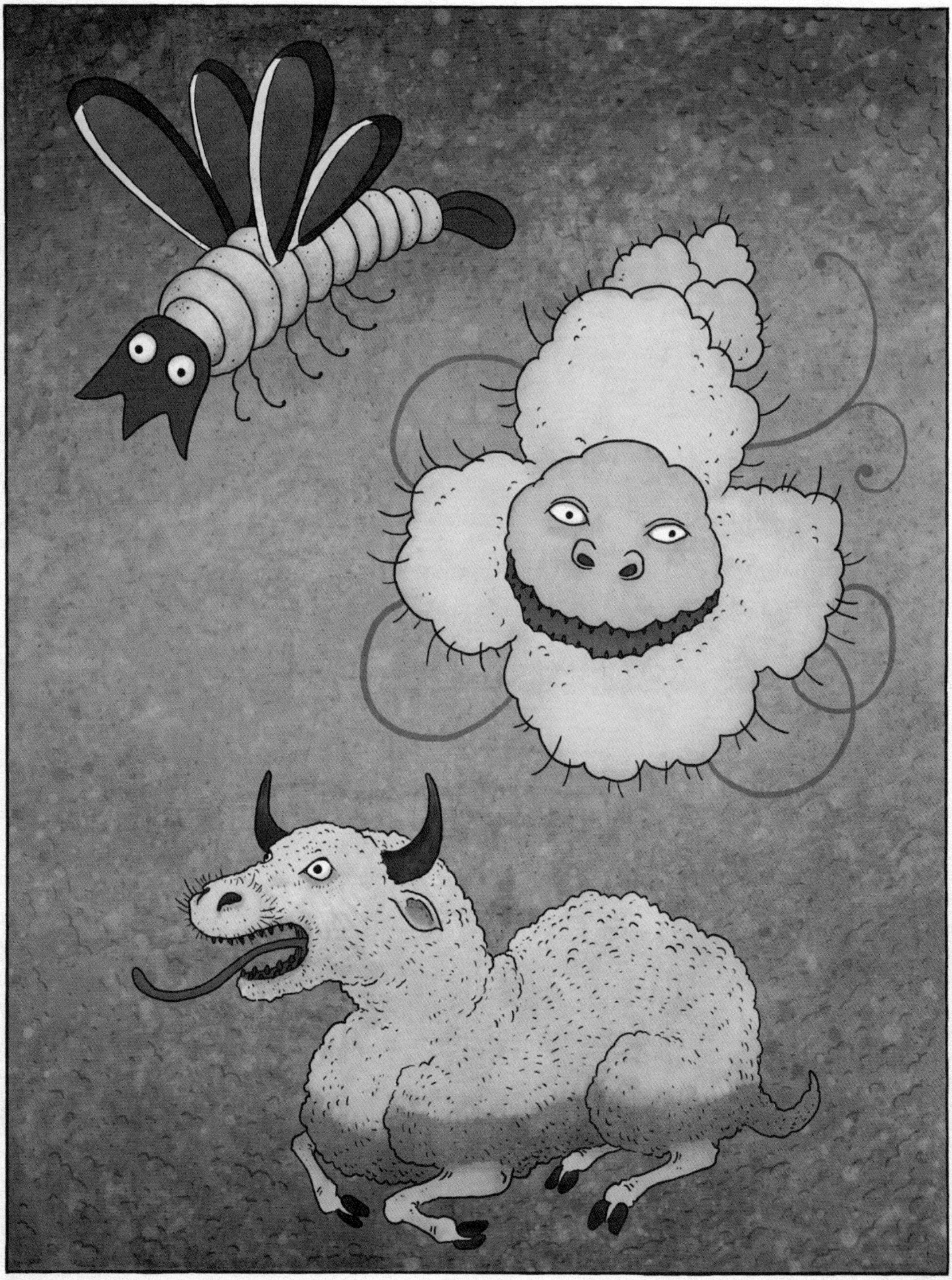

HISHAKU 脾積

TRANSLATION: spleen *shaku* (a type of infection)
ALTERNATE NAMES: hiki

APPEARANCE: Hishaku are microbes which live near the belly button and infect the spleen. They have fuzzy, yellowish, wolf-like bodies and long red tongues. They have no legs. A large red pentagon-like shape appears on a hishaku's side; this is a representation of the belly button.

INTERACTIONS: Hishaku mainly infect women. They cause an extreme fondness for sweets, as well as a yellow tinge to the face. Hishaku hosts tend to hum constantly. They can cause extremely heavy menstrual bleeding as well as irregular vaginal discharge. Women infected with hishaku suffer difficulty getting out of bed. Hishaku infections are most likely to occur during the changing of the seasons. This is because hishaku are related to the element of earth in Chinese element theory. Days when the seasons change are closely related to the element of earth.

Hishaku can be treated with acupuncture in an area about one centimeter around the belly button. The techniques for this treatment are only passed down orally.

HINOSHU 脾ノ聚

TRANSLATION: spleen *shu* (a type of infection)

APPEARANCE: Hinoshu are microbial yōkai with a lumpy, boulder-like appearance and extremely large mouths. They infect the spleen.

INTERACTIONS: Hinoshu attacks occur when the host is relaxing outside or when the host is among a crowd of people. They roll about inside the body, bruising every part and causing a lot of pain. The victim feels as if they have fallen from a height onto an enormous boulder. Viewing beautiful rocks, such as in a Zen garden, causes this infection to act up much more strongly, as the hinoshu becomes excited in the presence of beautiful rocks.

When an infection takes this form, it becomes difficult to recover. Traditionally, acupuncture is used to treat it, however the treatment is too complicated to learn in a book. It must be learned orally, from someone who has treated a hinoshu infection before.

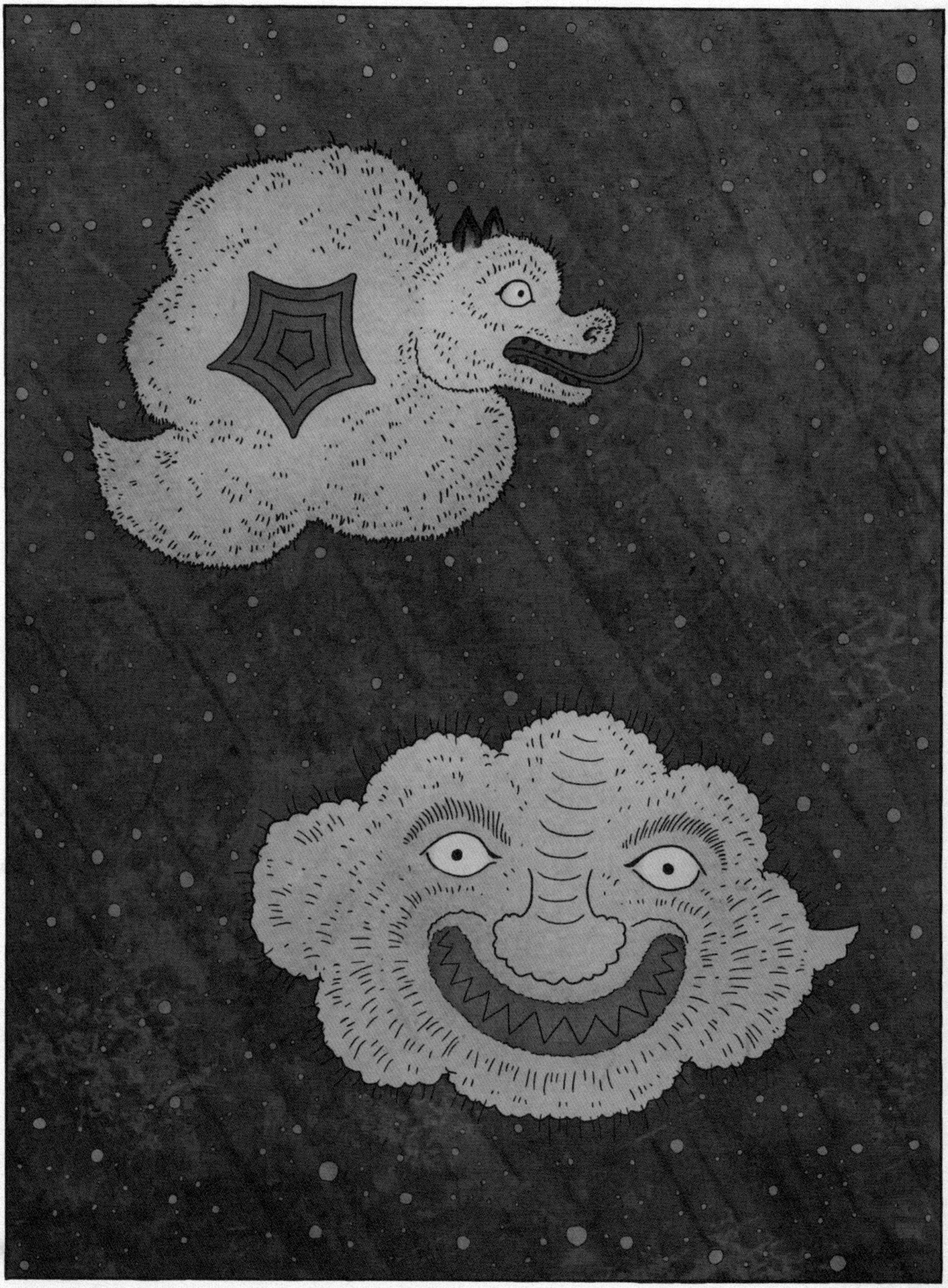

Hizō no mushi 脾臓の虫

TRANSLATION: spleen bug

APPEARANCE: Hizō no mushi live in the spleen and attack the liver and muscles. They have bright red bodies which are hot. Their limbs are tipped with sharp claws. They stagger throughout the body on their spindly legs.

INTERACTIONS: People infected with hizō no mushi take on some of their characteristics; most notably the staggering style of walking, with left and right arms spread wide. When hizō no mushi reach out from the spleen and grasp the liver in their talons, their victims develop hyperthermia. When hizō no mushi grasp the muscles in their talons, their victim's bodies become hot. They begin to feel dizzy as if hit on the head.

A hizō no mushi infection can be cured by taking Chinese medicine made from *mokkō* (a species of thistle) and *daiō* (a kind of rheum).

Akuchū 悪虫

TRANSLATION: evil bug

APPEARANCE: Akuchū are dangerous bugs which infect the spleen. They can easily move throughout their hosts with their flexible segmented bodies and broad tails. They have six sharp claws with which they strongly grasp the spleen.

INTERACTIONS: Akuchū cling to the spleen and with their hooked bills and steal the food that their hosts eat. No matter how much food is ingested, their hosts will gain no weight and receive no nourishment while infected.

Akuchū infections can be easily cured with *mokkō* (Chinese medicine made from a species of thistle).

Hizō no kasamushi 脾臓の笠虫

TRANSLATION: capped spleen bug

APPEARANCE: Hizō no kasamushi get their name from the bright red, cap-like feature on top of their heads. They have a long, worm-like body covered in short red hairs, which ends in a hairy forked tail.

INTERACTIONS: The hizō no kasamushi's cap interferes with the normal intake of food. People infected with this worm become pale and weak. They cause either rapid weight loss or extreme weight gain.

This bug is difficult to remove, but its symptoms can be somewhat relieved by taking Chinese medicine made from *agi* (dried gum from the roots of ferula plants) and *gajutsu* (made from the stems and roots of turmeric plants).

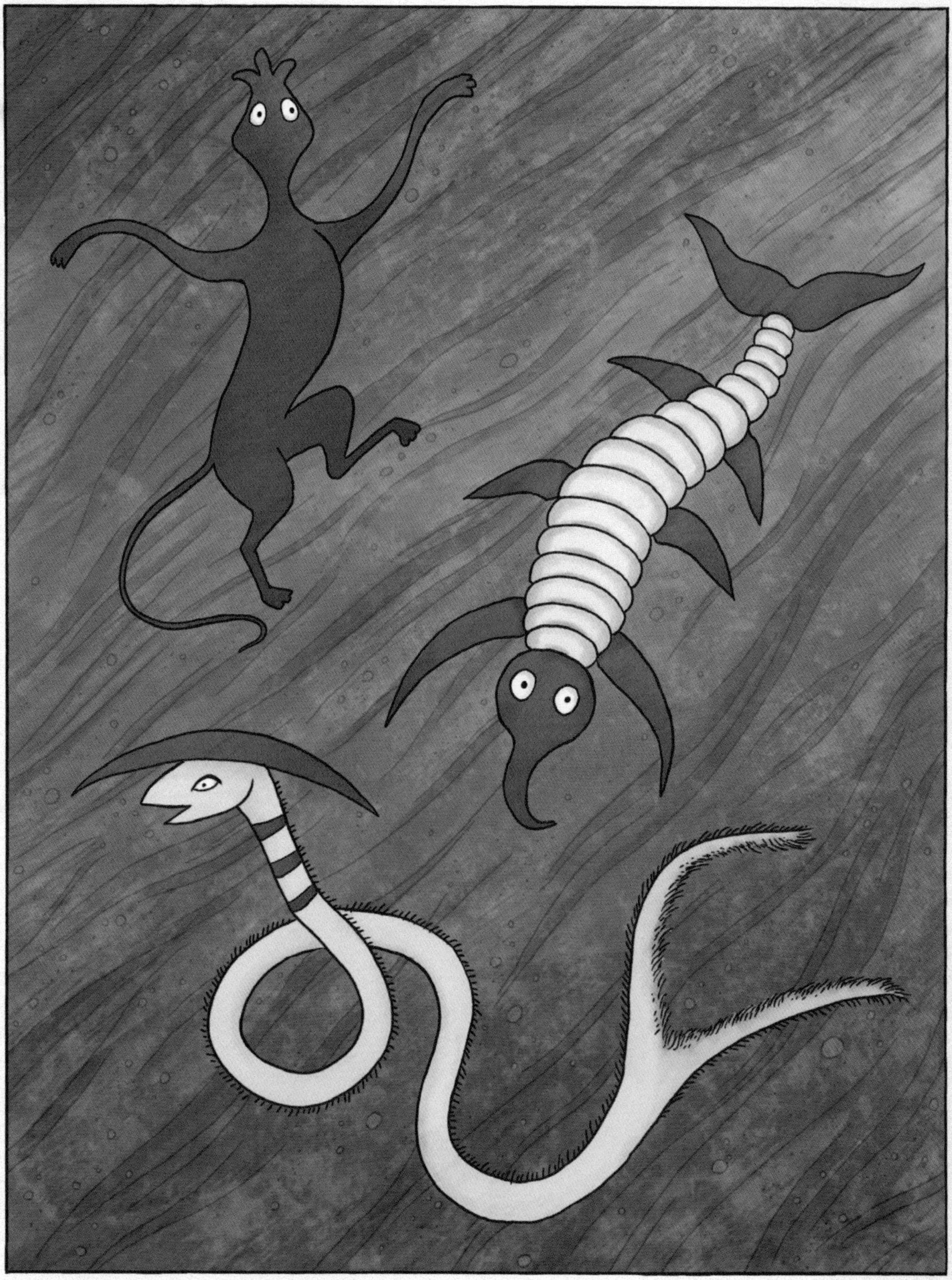

Koshō 小姓

TRANSLATION: page, apprentice
ALTERNATE NAMES: koseu

APPEARANCE: Koshō are parasitic yōkai with snakelike bodies and child-like faces. They have white, scruffy beards and umbrella-like protrusions on the top of their heads. They can speak, and constantly chatter like children. They love sweet sake. They live in between the heart and the diaphragm where neither medicine nor needles can reach.

INTERACTIONS: A koshō infection is a terminal illness. Not even the best doctors have ever come up with a way to treat it. The umbrella-like protrusion on their heads block medicine, and they hide too deep in the body for acupuncture to be effective.

Ōzake no mushi 大酒の虫

TRANSLATION: heavy drinking bug

APPEARANCE: Ōzake no mushi have bright red bodies with several worm-like appendages branching out. They are warm and become warmer when their hosts drink alcohol. They look like lumpy satchels tied up at the top.

INTERACTIONS: People infected with ōzake no mushi become heavy drinkers. If the satchel-like shell is broken, the ōzake no mushi erupts, spilling what looks like red sand throughout the body. In fact, these are countless other worms which live inside its red body. Even after its host dies, these parasites will survive inside of the abdomen.

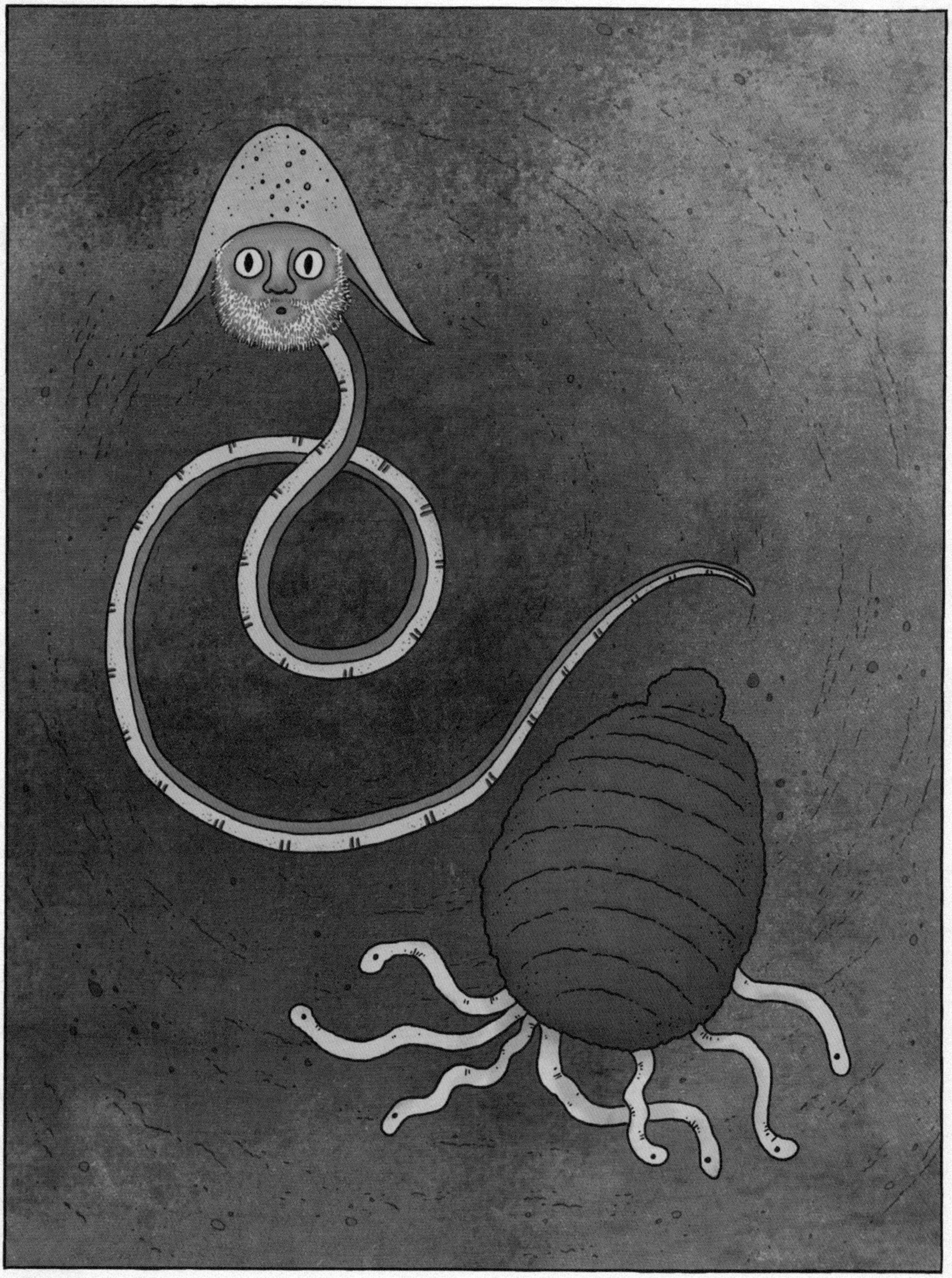

Taibyō no kesshaku 大病の血積

TRANSLATION: terrible disease blood *shaku* (a type of infection)
ALTERNATE NAMES: kesshaku, chishaku

APPEARANCE: This yōkai infects hosts after they have suffered from a terrible sickness. Their bodies are shaped like flexible bulbs. They have flippers and broad tails which help them swim about the stomach. Their heads are shaped like hammers, and they use them to smash through the stomach wall and enter the heart, where they feed off of their hosts' blood.

INTERACTIONS: A person infected with a taibyō no kesshaku becomes pale, with thin and emaciated cheeks. The victim's entire body becomes weak and worn out. This infection can be cured by vomiting up the taibyō no kesshaku and sprinkling it with *shukusha* (medicine made from black cardamom seed). When a taibyō no kesshaku is smashed, its body rips open and an enormous blood clot is released.

Kakuran no mushi 霍乱の虫

TRANSLATION: vomit and diarrhea bug

APPEARANCE: Kakuran no mushi are parasitic yōkai which live in the stomach. They have black heads and red bodies. Tiny legs are interspersed across their long bodies. Their facial expression resembles that of a person who is about to vomit: with open mouths and tiny pinpoints for eyes.

INTERACTIONS: People infected with kakuran no mushi suffer symptoms similar to food poisoning: frequent diarrhea and vomiting. This infection can be cured by taking *goshuyu*, a medicine made from a dried, unripe fruit (*Tetradium ruticarpum*).

In one record of a kakuran no mushi infection, this yōkai's head was briefly visible in its host's mouth during a particularly violent bout of vomiting. A friend of the victim grabbed the kakuran no mushi's head to try to pull it out, but the victim weakened and seemed as if he was about to lose consciousness. The friend let go of the head. The kakuran no mushi retreated into its host's body. Afterwards, the victim died. When an autopsy was performed, the doctor found the kakuran no mushi wrapped up around its host's liver so tightly that he couldn't remove it. The doctor ground up *shazenshi* (*Plantago asiatica*) and *mokkō* (*Saussurea costus*) and sprinkled it over the kakuran no mushi. The creature disappeared.

Kishaku 気積

TRANSLATION: mind/spirit/mood *shaku* (a type of infection)

APPEARANCE: Kishaku's most distinguishing feature are their mouths, which are split three ways. They have red, furry bodies with a white stripe and black tails. Kishaku love greasy, oily foods. They live in the stomach and feed off oily foods their hosts eat, such as fish and chicken. They completely ignore rice and other foods they don't like.

INTERACTIONS: People infected with kishaku experience an extreme increase in sexual desire. This sickness can be cured with medicine made from a tiger's intestines.

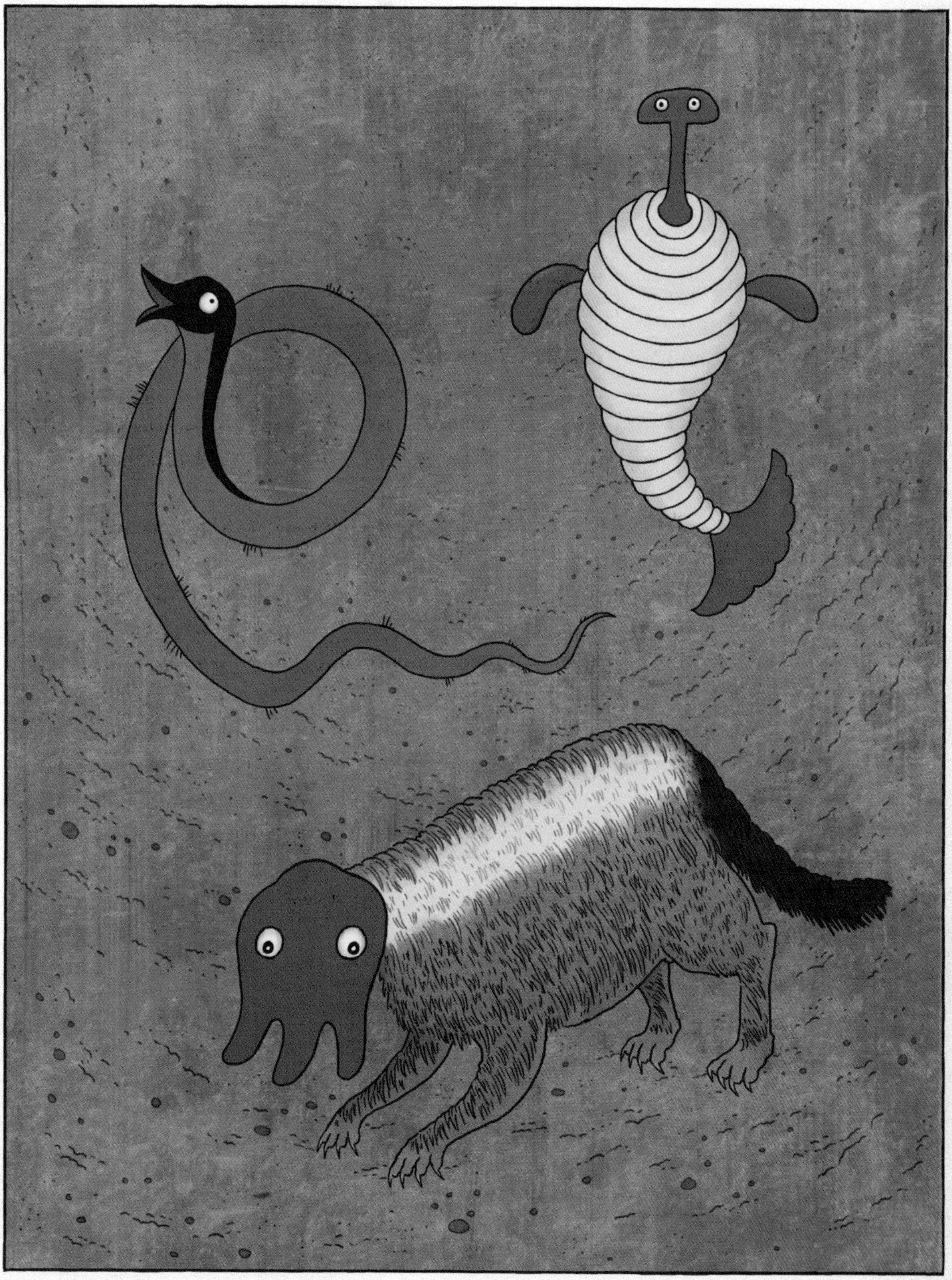

SORI NO KANMUSHI ソリの肝虫

TRANSLATION: back-bending liver bug

APPEARANCE: Sori no kanmushi are terrible parasitic bugs with wide bug eyes, blue backs, and white bellies. Their hands are like flippers and their tails are brush-like. They like spicy foods. They live in the liver, but the symptoms they cause affect the spine.

INTERACTIONS: Sori no kanmushi bite the backs of their hosts, causing great pain. Their victims develop a warped or curved spine, a condition which long ago was called sori (thus this creature's name). *Mokkō* (*Saussurea costus*) and *byakujutsu* (*Atractylodes japonica*) are effective medicines against this bug.

UMAKAN 馬癇

TRANSLATION: horse *kan* (kind of infection)
ALTERNATE NAMES: shinnoju

APPEARANCE: Umakan are infectious parasites with the appearance of splendid, fast horses. Their heads, necks, and backs are deep red. Their tail, belly, and legs are white. They act up in bright sunlight, or in the light from large fires.

INTERACTIONS: Umakan victims suffer from weak heart and fainting spells. Upon awakening from a faint, they seem perfectly fine with no other problems. To treat this sickness, the victim must continuously build up strength in their heart. There are a number of effective ways to treat it with acupuncture as well. These are passed down orally from teacher to student.

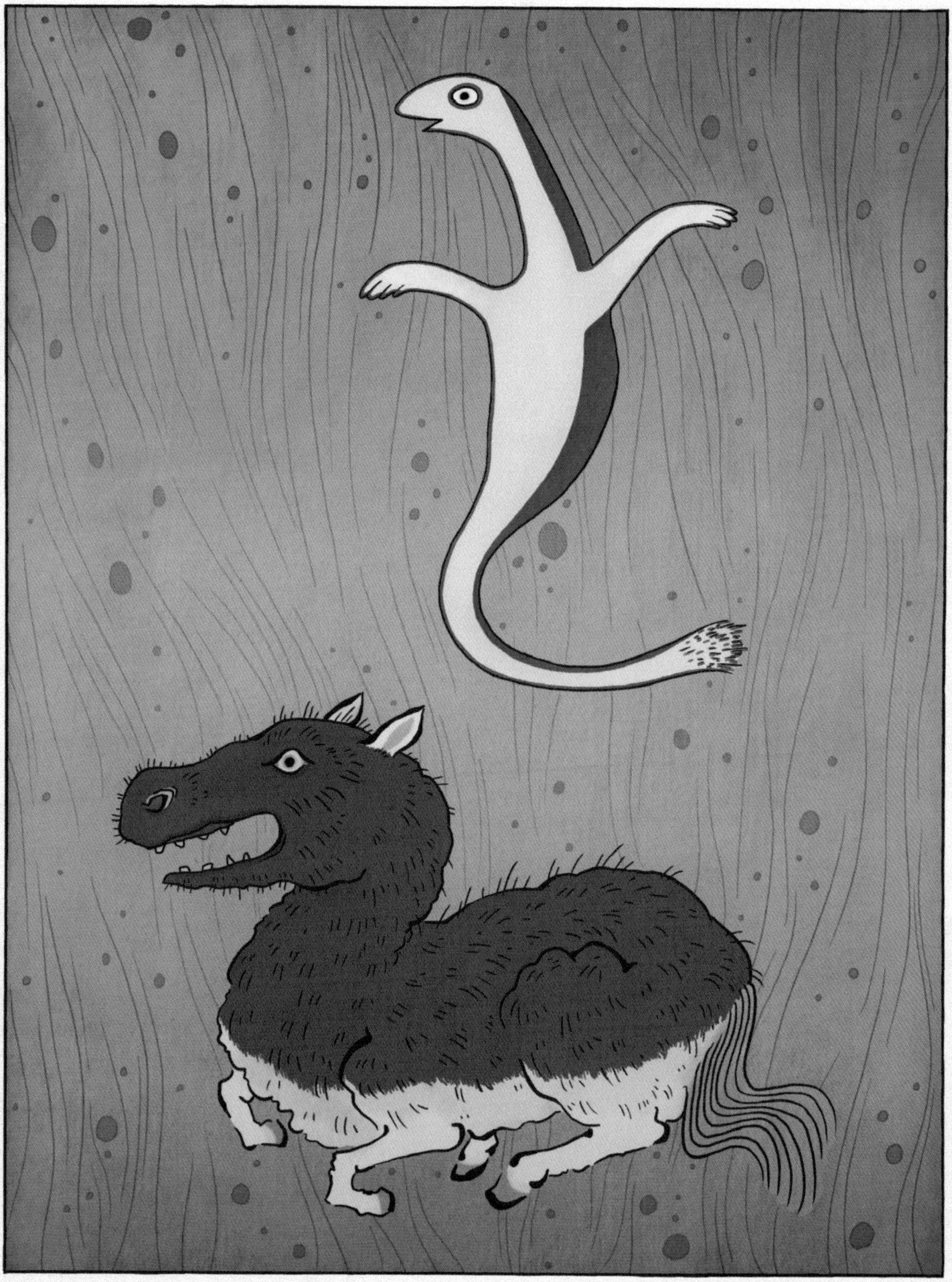

GYŌCHŪ 蟯虫

TRANSLATION: intestinal worm; pinworm

APPEARANCE: Gyōchū are infectious yōkai with six arms and long red tongues. They are extremely fond of chatting and gossiping. They live and reproduce in the sex organs, making them a sexually transmitted yōkai. Gyōchū reproduce in the sex organs on Kōshin night, a holy night which occurs every sixty days in the esoteric Kōshin religion. Gyōchū leave their hosts on these nights and visit Enma Daiō, the king of hell and judge of the damned. They tattle on their hosts, telling Enma about all their hosts' dreams, desires, and sins. Enma then inflicts his divine wrath on them accordingly.

INTERACTIONS: There is no treatment for a gyōchū infection. The only way to keep safe from this infection is to avoid any chance of contracting an infection by abstaining from sex on Kōshin night. Traditionally, Kōshin night is reserved for praying. Believers gather together and refrain from sleeping for the whole night, so faithful practitioners should have no problem avoiding contracting gyōchū. People who have sex on these holy nights are committing a grave sacrilege which the gyōchū will report to King Enma. During the feudal era, terrible diseases (leprosy, for example) were believed to be divine punishments for those who disrespect the gods.

Today, the name gyōchū refers to the pinworm.

KITAI 鬼胎

TRANSLATION: demon uterus

APPEARANCE: Kitai are grotesque, infectious yōkai which begin as blood clots the size of a large sake cup. Their life cycle begins in the left abdomen, and as they grow they migrate to the uterus. Gradually, they develop faces that look like a frightful cow: bright red with black horns. They grow long bodies which coil around like snakes. Kitai have short tempers. They move extremely slow, like slugs. Because of this they tend to feel a lot of stress which they pass on to their hosts.

INTERACTIONS: Once a kitai takes on its adult form it is difficult to recover from. When a kitai slithers about inside of its host, it causes bouts of hysteria. They are difficult to treat with acupuncture, because the needles often cause the kitai to become stressed, which worsens the condition. There are secret ways of treating slow moving bugs like the kitai, but they are passed on orally from master to student.

MIMIMUSHI 耳虫

TRANSLATION: ear bug

APPEARANCE: Mimimushi are infectious yōkai with long ears and spotted, snake-like bodies. They writhe and slither back and forth as they migrate between the ears and the heart, causing discomfort in their hosts.

INTERACTIONS: People infected with mimimushi crave cold foods and avoid hot food. Their stomachs appear swollen and bloated. Infections can be treated with remedies made from the herb *byakujutsu* (*Atractylodes japonica*) and the mushroom *bukuryō* (*Poria cocos*).

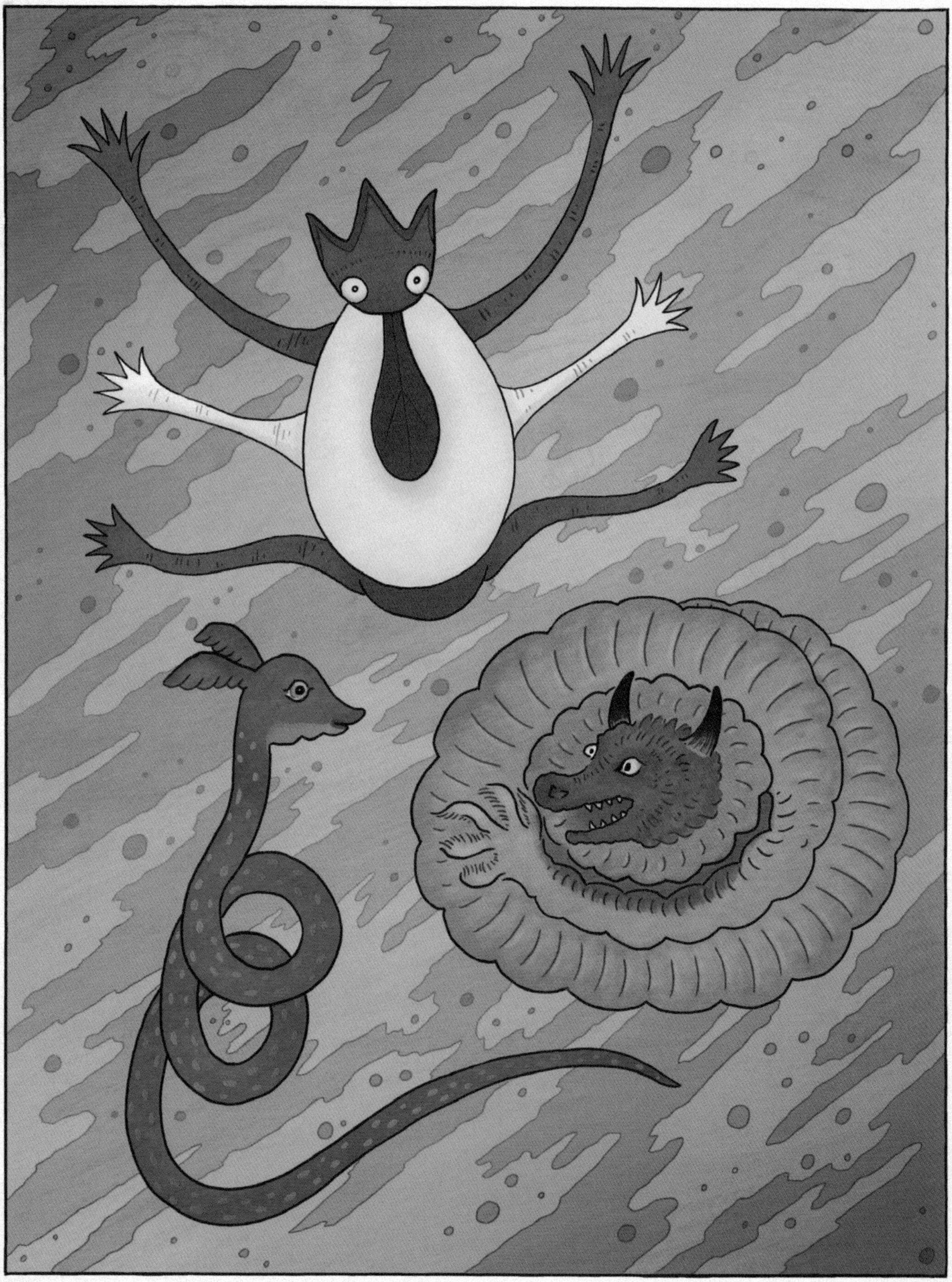

Acknowledgments

Like its predecessors (*The Night Parade of One Hundred Demons* and *The Hour of Meeting Evil Spirits*), this book owes its existence to the dedication of die-hard yōkai lovers. In the absence of a large publishing company providing the finances to cover research, translation, writing, and painting, the support of fans from all over the world has made it possible to sustain this project. I would like to give my sincerest thanks to everyone who supported this project and my work on Patreon and Kickstarter. Their patronage and communication throughout this long project has made them an important part of this book. In fact, many of the entries in this volume were requested by fans who wanted to know more about their favorite yōkai.

I owe a great deal of thanks to my wife. She has been by my side throughout all three volumes of my yōkai encyclopedia. When my eyes are blurry from staring at screens, and when my head hurts from trying to decipher old calligraphy, she is there to help me through it. When I can't find the source of a particular story, or when I need clarification of an obscure cultural reference, she helps me find them. She accompanies me to art exhibitions of original yōkai paintings by masters like Kawanabe Kyōsai—reminding me that I can't stay locked up in my studio painting all day.

Many of the yōkai found in these pages come from sources that are in the public domain and can easily be viewed online. Toriyama Sekien's encyclopedias and the work of other Edo period artists serve as the primary source for most of the paintings and the entries in this book. The International Research Center for Japanese Studies' online yōkai database has also been an invaluable source of both reference images and folk tales; as have the works of Japanese folklorists like Mizuki Shigeru, Kenji Murakami, and Komatsu Kazuhiko. I'm grateful for the hard work of the folklorists and historians who have endeavored to preserve yōkai and make them easily accessible.

When I first started painting yōkai ten years ago, I had no idea that it would grow into a three-volume encyclopedia with hundreds of illustrations. Back then the word yōkai would have elicited blank stares and confusion from most people. But today, yōkai are known by so many people all around the world; enough that the international appeal of yōkai has been covered on Japanese television shows. Today, when I visit conventions and festivals, I don't have to explain what yōkai are. People recognize them and come up to speak to me, because they have seen yōkai online or in recent books. This is thanks to a small community of dedicated folklorists who have helped introduce Japanese folklore to the West, following in the footsteps of Lafcadio Hearn more than a century ago. I am grateful to the authors and online communities which bring so many new fans into the world of yōkai.

I'm frequently asked, "How many yōkai are there?" or "How many books do you plan to write?" I always say that I will keep painting and writing about yōkai as long as people are willing to keep reading. I'm certain that I will never run out of yōkai. I only hope that I never run out of readers. So thank you—for reading this book and for giving me a reason to write another.

Yōkai References and Further Reading

Books

Davisson, Zack. *Yūrei: The Japanese Ghost*. Seattle: Chin Music Press Inc., 2015.

Mizuki Shigeru. *Ketteiban Nihon yōkai taizen: Yōkai, ano yo, kamisama*. Tōkyō: Kōdansha Ltd., 2014.

Murakami Kenji. *Yōkai jiten*. Tōkyō: Mainichi Newspaper Co. Ltd., 2000.

Nagano Hitoshi and Higashi Noboru. *Sengokujidai no haramushi: Harikikigaki no yukaina byōmatachi*. Tōkyō: Kokushokankōkai Inc., 2007.

Tada Katsumi. *Edo yōkai karuta*. Tōkyō: Kokusho Kankōkai, 1998.

Toriyama Sekien. *Toriyama Sekien gazu hyakki yagyō zen gashū*. Tōkyō: Kadokawa Shoten Publishing Co., 2005.

Yumoto Kōichi. *Nihon no genjū zufu: Ōedo fushigi seibutsu shutsugen roku*. Tōkyō: Tōkyō Bijutsu, 2016.

Yumoto Kōichi. *Yokai Wonderland: More from YUMOTO Koichi Collection: Supernatural Beings in Japanese Art*. Tōkyō: PIE Books, 2018.

Yoda, Hiroko and Matt Alt. *Japandemonium Illustrated: The Yokai Encyclopedias of Toriyama Sekien*. Mineola: Dover Publications, Inc., 2016.

Online

Database of Images of Strange Phenomena and Yōkai. International Research Center for Japanese Studies. <http://www.nichibun.ac.jp/YoukaiGazouMenu/>.

Folktale Data of Strange Phenomena and Yōkai. International Research Center for Japanese Studies. <http://www.nichibun.ac.jp/YoukaiDB/>.

Index of Yōkai

Printed in Great Britain
by Amazon